WHITE-COLLAR
CRIME
RECONSIDERED

WHITE-COLLAR CRIME RECONSIDERED

Edited by Kip Schlegel & David Weisburd

Northeastern University Press

BOSTON

Northeastern University Press

with support from
The National Science Foundation
The National Institute of Justice
Indiana University

Library of Congress Cataloging-in-Publication Data

White-collar crime reconsidered / edited by Kip Schlegel, David
Weisburd.
p.   cm.
Papers originally presented at a conference held at Indiana
University in May 1990.
Includes bibliographical references and index.
ISBN 1-55553-141-5 (cloth : alk. paper)
1. White collar crimes—United States—Congresses. I. Schlegel,
Kip. II. Weisburd, David.
HV6771.U6W47   1992
364.1′68′0973—dc20   92-15361

Designed by James F. Brisson

This book was composed in Century Expanded by
Coghill Composition Company in Richmond, Virginia.
It was printed and bound by The Maple Press Company in
York, Pennsylvania.
The paper is Sebago Antique, an acid-free sheet.

MANUFACTURED IN THE UNITED STATES OF AMERICA
96   95   94   93   92   5   4   3   2   1

These essays are in honor of

EDWIN H. SUTHERLAND

· CONTENTS ·

· A C K N O W L E D G M E N T S ·

Because this volume arose from a conference, it clearly could not exist without those who recognized the value of such a gathering. The individual most deserving of credit in this regard is Felice Levine, at that time the program director for the Law and Social Science Program of the National Science Foundation. It was her willingness to support this conference that paved the way for the meeting and for the additional support.

Our gratitude also goes to Chip Stewart and Lois Mock of the National Institute of Justice for their contribution in supporting the conference and in publishing this volume. We would also like to thank Deans Morton Lowengrub and George Walker, at Indiana University, for their contributions and support, and to Phil Parnell, chair of the Criminal Justice Department at Indiana University.

Special thanks are given to three scholars who took part in the Sutherland Conference and who have given much to the field: Karl Schuessler, emeritus professor of sociology at Indiana University; Marshall Clinard, emeritus professor of sociology at the University of Wisconsin; and Albert Cohen, emeritus professor of sociology at the University of Connecticut. Each of these individuals had connection to Edwin Sutherland as colleague or student and provided a valuable historical perspective to the conference. More importantly, each is a true scholar, offering us all very important role models.

Finally, thanks go to Deborah Kops at Northeastern University

Press, who was receptive to a lengthy and somewhat unmanageable manuscript, and to Judy Kelley and Gina Doglione at Indiana University for their expertise and patience in getting this volume together.

The essays that appear in this volume were delivered at a conference on white-collar crime held at Indiana University in May of 1990. Though the conference marked the five decades since Edwin Sutherland coined the term in 1939, the purpose was not to regurgitate the scholarship since Sutherland. Rather, the intent was to convene the leading scholars in the field to present new research and insights on white-collar crime, broadly defined.

Rather than ask these individuals to write on predetermined topics within some artificial parameters, we felt that the conference would produce the most interesting work if the contributors were left free to present their ideas and research on topics that were of the most interest to them. As such, the scope of the essays is quite broad, and consequently, difficult to structure or organize in an orderly way for presentation to the public. Nonetheless, for the sake of order we have tried to divide the essays into logical sections.

The first essay, by the editors, serves as an introduction, grounding the essays in the previous research conducted in the field. Unlike much of the recent literature that begins with the call to eliminate the term "white-collar crime" for its lack of definitional rigor, we argue that the value of the term lies precisely in the conceptual obscurity that surrounds it. From that obscurity comes variegated perspectives and insights, not only on white-collar crime, but more importantly, on crime generally.

This introduction is followed by five essays on theory and definition. The first two provide readers with a "progress report" of the evolution of the definition (Geis) and theory (Coleman) since Sutherland originated the term. At the same time, both these distinguished authors offer their own views on where we have gone and where we may want to head in the future. Having, we hope, brought the reader up to speed, the next three chapters (by John Braithwaite, Stanton Wheeler, and Diane Vaughan) provide new theoretical insights into white-collar crime. John Braithwaite and Stanton Wheeler direct their attention to individual motivation for white-collar crime, while Diane Vaughan's essay explores the important linkages between organizational forces and individual choices in organizational misconduct.

These chapters are followed by two essays on white-collar victimization. The essay by Paul Jesilow, Esther Klempner, and Victoria Chiao provides new research on the process of reporting consumer and major frauds. Michael Levi's essay gives an international flavor by presenting findings on the victimization of white-collar crimes in Great Britain.

We move from here to several essays that deal with enforcement issues. Pontell and Calavita's piece on crimes in the savings and loan industry and Ronald Kramer's essay on the space shuttle Challenger's explosion offer captivating case studies as well as insights on issues involving social control. Nancy Reichman's essay on the role of compliance in the regulation of securities activities provides an important glimpse at an area largely untraversed—self-regulation. The chapter by Benson, Cullen, and Maakestad takes a different perspective on enforcement by empirically testing the relationship between community factors and enforcement practices in white-collar crime.

From enforcement we move to sanctioning. Sally Simpson's essay provides an interesting account of how executives and managers view corporate-crime deterrence and corporate control policies. Exploring issues relating to the sentencing of organizations, Steven Walt and William Laufer present a model of corporate incapacitative sanctions, designed to reflect the punitive nature of incapacitative strategies provided to offenders in human form. Finally, as Sutherland himself observed, most white-collar offenders are handled not by criminal law, but by civil law, often through punitive damages awarded in tort. Kenneth Mann provides an interesting discussion of the punitive nature of the civil remedy and its applicability to white-collar crime. The book concludes with a final chapter by the editors, which offers some thoughts on the future direction of research in this area.

The essays presented here entail research and insights by individuals from around the world and from a variety of disciplines. The myriad perspectives contained in this volume epitomize the tremendous interest in white-collar crime and its control. More importantly, they demonstrate a body of knowledge with a depth increasingly commensurate to its breadth.

WHITE-COLLAR
CRIME
RECONSIDERED

White-Collar Crime

The Parallax View

KIP SCHLEGEL

DAVID WEISBURD

A little more than half a century ago, Edwin Sutherland stood before a gathering of the American Sociological Society to impress upon that group the need to expand the boundaries of the study of crime to include the criminal acts of respectable individuals in the course of their occupations. He labeled these crimes, for the apparent lack of a better name, "white-collar crimes," and thus was born a term soon to become an established part of the vernacular of criminology. Yet, as Geis notes (chapter 1) perhaps no other term has engendered as much debate and confusion. Since 1939 the scholarship on white-collar crime has largely reflected the parallactic nature of the subject. Perhaps out of dissatisfaction with the slow progress to date, much of the most recent scholarship has sounded the call to bring order and focus to the term. Those who focus on offender-based definitions stress the referents of social class, power, status, and respectability, while those who emphasize offense-based definitions tend to reject such concerns in favor of characteristics of the act (for example, the use of guile, concealment, fraud, trust, and the like). Others have focused their attention on organizational crime (usually corporate) as the subject most worthy of study. Such efforts have moved the study of white-collar crime in useful directions. However, the by-product of such attempts, perhaps by intent, is to fracture the original concept into fragments of ideas that become increasingly more difficult to put back together in any meaningful or coherent way.

We take a somewhat different perspective in this chapter, and indeed, in the arrangement of this book. First, we suggest (in what we believe to be the Sutherland tradition) that such efforts to bring order to the term "white-collar crime" are tantamount to reifying what is better left as an abstract idea. In arguing the case for abstraction, we believe that the most valuable approach to the study of white-collar crime is not to take the path of isolating unique factors that make up white-collar crime, but rather to search for the interactions along the different dimensions and between the multiple components that make up crime and societal reactions to crime. The intent of this chapter, then, is to link some of the scholarship on white-collar crime, including the research presented in this volume, as it relates to such dimensions of crime as criminal behavior (both individual and organizational); victimization; and guardianship, which includes both the legal structures and their enforcers. These dimensions of crime are obviously subjective and open to debate and are not the only ways we may conceptualize crime. What is important is that we view white-collar crime not from one single perspective (for example, the offense, offender, legal structure), but from a series of reference points, ideally as they work in interaction with one another.

Second, we hold the premise that the knowledge we search for is not merely the knowledge of white-collar crime, but of crime generally. In spite of the obvious relevance of this point, it seems that one result of the definitional and operational debate has been to turn the study of white-collar crime into an end in itself, this being achieved by turning white-collar crime into some "thing" in itself. We suggest here a different perspective—not because we believe that there is little of importance in white-collar crime, quite the opposite. Rather, we believe that attention to white-collar crime will best be served in the future by studying the similarities and differences between white-collar crimes and those referred to as "common crimes." Thus, where possible in this chapter, we try to link the research to our broader understanding of crime generally.

White-Collar Crime and Criminal Behavior

Individual Motivation

As Geis (and others) have noted, Sutherland himself was unclear about what he meant by white-collar crime. The ambiguity was enhanced by his own definition, which included terms such as "respectability," "high social status," and "occupation" (Sutherland, 1949, p. 9), and the subsequent focus of his research and writings, which centered on the legal violations by corporations, interspersed with occasional descriptions of rather mundane frauds by, sociologically speaking, uninteresting folks (Sutherland, 1983). It is clear, however, that for Sutherland the offender characteristics of respectability and high social status had little relevance as causal factors in explaining criminal behavior. The significance of an offender's respectability or high social status lies primarily in the refutation of existing theories that look to the causes of crime in poverty and social disorganization. For Sutherland, the fact that an offender is respectable, or of high social status, or employed is no more important in explaining crime than is poverty or unemployment in explaining the crimes of others.

This is not to suggest, however, that these factors have no relevance in understanding crime. One's respectability, occupational position, or access to wealth and power leads to and creates opportunity structures for crime that can be unique in and of themselves, or that may have corollaries to or spinoffs from what are often called common crimes.

In addition to the creation of unique opportunity structures for crime, one's social status or position also has relevance in understanding what Sutherland termed the "differential implementation" of the law. This will be discussed in greater detail later, but its importance to crime is certain. First, as Sutherland so clearly pointed out in his research, the avenues available to the white-collar offender through the civil and administrative remedies allow such offenders to escape the traditional stigma of the criminal sanction, even though the harm of their actions is often as great or greater than the offenses normally trapped by the machinations of the criminal law. Yet, the differential implementation of the law seems applicable to Sutherland's own general theory of crime as well, despite his claim that the "variations in administrative procedures are not significant from the point of view of causation of crime" (1983, p. 7). If the direction of one's motives, drives, rationalizations, and attitudes stem from the perception one has of the legal code as being favorable or unfavorable, then both the content and the process of that legal code would appear to have some bearing on what one learns about the opportunity structures for both law-breaking and law-abiding behavior. The research in white-collar crime appears to be heading, at least implicitly, in this direction. Of interest here is not only how the structure and process of the law pertaining to white-collar crimes affect or influence actions of white-collar offenders, but also how the differential application of the law affects the way others with less power and privilege construct their own attitudes, rationalizations, and so on, about their behavior.

Braithwaite's essay (chapter 3) is especially important in light of these concerns. First, he challenges Sutherland's proposition that social status plays no role in causative accounts of criminal behavior. He argues that inequality in wealth and power "is relevant to the explanation of both crime in the streets and crime in the suites." Drawing from opportunity theories of crime, Braithwaite contends that "inequality causes crimes of poverty motivated by need for goods for use" and at the same time produces "crimes of wealth motivated by greed enabled by goods for exchange." Furthermore, Braithwaite notes that factors such as economic inequality, inequality in political power, racism, ageism, and patriarchy produce inegalitarian societies that are structurally humiliating for citizens, particularly those without power. This structural humiliation in turn leads those in impoverished conditions to feel increasingly powerless and exploited, while lending to the wealthy a view that power and exploitation are legitimate. Both conditions engender crime.

The etiological literature to date suggests the complexity inherent in studying white-collar crime. Much of the literature refers to conditions of offenders in dichotomous terms. Offenders are either poor or wealthy, powerless or powerful, and so on. Crimes committed by the poor tend to be portrayed as simple, if not brutish; the crimes of the powerful are portrayed as intricate and exploitive. Yet, as we all know, there is a wide spectrum comprising both offenders and offenses. Surprisingly, the literature is just now beginning to explore the factors "white-collarness" is said to comprise. One recent contribution in this regard is the work of Weisburd, Wheeler, Waring, and Bode (1991). Their research suggests that many of the offenders whose actions fit the legal categories of white-collar crime can best be described as falling into the "broad middle of society." They add with regard to the offenses:

> Although they differ systematically from common-crime offenses, the white-collar crimes committed by those we

studied have a mundane, common, everyday character. Their basic ingredients are lying, cheating, and fraud, and for every truly complicated and rarefied offense there are many others that are simple and can be carried out by almost anyone who can read, write, and give an outward appearance of stability. (P. 171)

Surely one question of significance then is how we operationalize the vocabulary relating to white-collar crime. Indeed, many of the central terms are bantered about in the literature with a disturbing casualness. Terms such as "high social status," "power," "wealth," "inequity," and "trust" continue to be tossed about as if there is total agreement on their meaning. By "status" do we mean financial or social position? Or, should we be concerned with attachments to a particular class (and the benefits that accrue from those attachments)? Obviously, wealth is a relative notion, and the degree to which one possesses power depends on the answers to these questions: what kinds of power? and power in relation to what? One merely need cite the extensive literature on power in the field of political science to underscore the importance of specification (Bachrach and Baratz, 1970; Dahl, 1957; Frey, 1971; Gaventa, 1980; Lukes, 1974). Empirically speaking, then, the challenge for scholars in this area is to operationalize these important constructs so as to capture their spectrum and allow for attempts to disprove them through scientific method.

Stanton Wheeler's essay (chapter 4) provides a somewhat different account of offender motivation that enhances our understanding of the broad spectrum of white-collar offenders and offending. Borrowing from fields of microeconomics, social psychology, and risk management, he asserts that "principles of perception and utility" can inform us about offender choices to engage in white-collar criminality. Though not refuting Braithwaite's account of white-collar crime as greed for more, Wheeler adds that many white-collar offenders may be motivated less by the desire to attain more than from fear of falling from their current positions. Of course, how and under what conditions offenders differ in their perceptions of utility remain equally open to empirical scrutiny, and as Wheeler encourages, research into such questions should go directly to those involved in such choices.

Organizational Offenders and Criminal Motivation

As Reiss (1981) has noted, our construction of both crime and victimization tends to be person-centered, rather than organization-centered. Researchers are beginning to fill this lacuna by examining the offenses of organizations, whether the organization takes the form of a for-profit corporation, a not-for-profit organization, a governmental entity, or a pension fund. For the purposes of this discussion, the essence of organization lies in the formal and informal structure and operating rules that allow the organization to continue irrespective of the individuals who occupy those structural positions and engage in those operating tasks. In particular, researchers have taken aim at the organizational structure, its core technology, and its operating environment in an effort to distinguish organizational characteristics that account for organizational misconduct and crime. Ronald Kramer's essay (chapter 9) on the space shuttle *Challenger* explosion is a nice example of the efforts in this direction.

It is arguable whether Sutherland himself considered the idea of organizational offenders as actors in their own right, though clearly the roots of the idea trace back to his own study of the "life careers of 70 corporations" (1983). For Sutherland, however, the idea of a corporation acting *as a corporation*, received less attention than the actions of the individuals involved in these corporations. After all, Sutherland, in his research notes on the Ford Motor Company asks, "what is the problem of Henry Ford" not "what is the problem of the Ford Motor Company?" (Sutherland's papers and extensive research note on the corporations in his study can be found at the Lilly Library at Indiana University.) There are several possible explanations for his perspective. First, while Sutherland's own background in political economy and the sociology of labor organizations (Geis and Goff, 1983, p. xxv) made him well aware of organizational theory, there was little literature in the field that explored, in depth, the idea of organizational actions. Though Sutherland noted "the culture of the business world" and the organizational aspect of much of white-collar crime, he did not spend a great deal of time developing these ideas, perhaps because there was not much to go on.

More important perhaps was Sutherland's own familiarity with and reliance on the legal literature of corporate culpability (Canfield, 1941; Lee, 1928; Snyder, 1938, 1939). Sutherland's focus was on the executives and high officers (managers) of corporations (1949, p. 9), a perspective in keeping with the doctrine of vicarious liability transferred from the law of tort to the criminal law, and one that is still alive and kicking in the jurisprudence of corporate sanctioning. A corporation, from this perspective, is said to violate the law, and is thus criminally responsible when the individuals (generally upper-level) within the corporation commit an offense within their occupational roles.

Though the law moves in its own mysterious ways, the current organizational-theory literature supports a wider conception of corporate action, and much of the recent research in the field of white-collar crime has tapped that literature to explain the behavior of corporate offenders. Many of the focal concerns lie in examining the relationships among a corporation's environment (customers, competitors, suppliers, and regulations, to use Thompson's [1967] description), its structure, operating policies, goals and objectives, and so on, which are designed to minimize uncertainty. One factor to receive considerable attention is corporate profit status (Staw and Szwajkowski, 1975; Pfeffer and Salancik, 1978; Clinard and Yeager, 1980). There is some evidence to suggest that as a corporation's profit status declines, the risk of criminal conduct increases, at least in some industries or markets. However, such data must be interpreted cautiously, since the independent variable (profit status) may have more to say about the risks of being caught than about the causes of the behavior. Indeed, Jesilow, Klempner, and Chiao's research (chapter 6) on consumer-fraud complaints suggests that the likelihood of action taken against a business is at least partially determined by the "status" of the business, and profitability is certainly one measure of status in this regard.

James Coleman's essay (chapter 2) provides a nice summary of the theoretical trends in the scholarship on organizational criminality, particularly in light of Geis's preceding essay on the definitional evolution of white-collar crime. It makes sense that the concerns noted above in relation to individual white-collar offenders pertain to much of the organizational literature as well; mainly, there appears to be a pervasive view that organizations, by definition, possess the requisite characteristics of white-collar criminals in human form—power, respectability, status, trust, and the like. In other words, corporations commit crime and get away with it because they are corporations. However, the factors that are said to make up organizational power and status are not clearly elaborated, and it is surely the case that however they are defined, organizations vary in the degree to which they possess them. There is evidence that the organizational literature is moving in the direction of greater specification, and it is clear that research in this area will have much to offer, not simply in understanding the etiology of organizational crime, but in understanding victimization by organizations, and the role that such factors play in the ability to define and structure enforcement and regulation.

Linking Individuals and Organizations: The Macro-Micro Connection

The application of organizational theory to white-collar crime has sparked a debate regarding the degree to which organizational factors should enter into what many believe are essentially individual actions. Indeed, it was Sutherland's own protégé, Donald Cressey (1989), who cautioned criminologists not to be misled by philosophical discourse on the ontological status of corporations, since such "fiction" distracts our attention away from the individual behaviors that are of importance in understanding organizational crime (see Walt and Laufer, chapter 13).

Diane Vaughan's essay (chapter 5) seeks something of the middle ground in this debate. She terms this the "macro-micro connection," noting that "our ability to offer a full causal explanation rests upon exploring . . . (w)hat structural factors govern or influence patterns of individual choice, and how are those choices constructed." Only in this way can we begin to answer the question "Why do 'good' people do 'dirty' work?" Her model of theory elaboration is built on three major components: (1) the competitive environment that generates pressures upon organizations to violate the law; (2) the organizational characteristics, including the structure, processes, and transactions that shape organizational opportunities for deviance; and (3) the regulatory environment. Individuals make choices to engage in criminality (to varying degrees) when confronted with these organizational pressures depending on such things as their position within the organization and their interpretation or reaction to the systems of rewards and punishments from the organization and/or its regulatory environment.

The model offered by Vaughan suggests that what shapes individual differences in choices to offend has more to do with structural forces acting on individuals' pursuits of agreed-upon goals than with differences in the goals themselves. This is evident by the question posed: why do good people do dirty work? One need not shape the question in such a fashion, of course. The question may be reworded to "why do dishonest people do good work to criminal ends?" Or, more properly, "How do individuals who choose to commit crime take advantage of the opportunity structures offered by their legitimate work to achieve their illegitimate aims?" The latter would assume that there is no inherent proneness to law breaking by virtue of certain organizational pressures, but instead that certain structural and environmental conditions can be manipulated by individuals with differing goals and values, often to illegally gainful ends. This would seem to be the case when organizations are set up for the specific purpose of defrauding clientele, as in boiler-room scams in securities and futures trading, or in many of the instances of "collective embezzlement" in the savings and loan industry, as demonstrated by Pontell and Calavita (chapter 8).

The importance of Vaughan's line of reasoning, however, cannot be understated. In particular, her model of theory elaboration could account for the diversity across the spectrum of individuals involved in white-collar crime in keeping with the data. Her model also offers a way of examining deviance across a range of organizational units—from corporations to churches to university athletics to families.

Victimization

Much of what we know about crime comes from victims. They can tell us about the situational factors surrounding the event, including their own participation, the extent of their injury, their rationale for reporting or not reporting, and sometimes they can even provide information about the offender. Yet offenses that have typically been defined as white-collar crimes do not lend such information readily. Many white-collar crimes tend to be diffuse in their victimization—affecting a large number of victims with injuries ranging from trivial to great. Furthermore, the temporal feature of many white-collar crimes both masks and complicates the victimization. It masks the victimization because the injuries often occur much later than the actual act. It complicates victimizations because the crimes are often not singular or isolated acts, but part of a sequential chain of events leading to detectable injury. The recent litigation over Agent Orange and asbestos come to mind here. The likelihood of cancers from exposure to Agent Orange or to asbestos is strongly correlated with other factors that independently increase the risk of cancers. Piecing these components together to form a model of causality is difficult enough in a scientific setting, much less a legal one.

The nature of the injury often suffered in white-collar crimes also has important implications for how we think of the qualities of power, trust, and respect. As the research points out (Gottfredson, and Gottfredson, 1988), the decision to report victimization is directly related to the seriousness of the offense. Though "seriousness" involves other factors, two crucial components stand out: the injury suffered or risked by the act, and the intent on the part of the actor. Much of the "power" in white-collar crimes lies in the ability of the offender to shape perceptions about these important dimensions. Perhaps more so than with common offenses, the white-collar crime victim may often try to remedy the problem by speaking directly with the offender, or by communicating dissatisfaction to others outside the criminal justice system, where these perceptions of seriousness may be formed, clarified, or altered altogether. Clearly, such negotiations must be thought of in terms of power relationships, often of considerable inequality. The offender can attempt to convince the victim that no injury took place, or that other factors unrelated to the offender's actions, such as the victim himself or herself, was somehow accountable through neglect, oversight, or some other consideration, for the injurious event, and probably in the same way that they attempt to convince judges that his or her conduct was not blameworthy (Mann, 1985). Perhaps more typically, the offender can influence perceptions of intent by either offering to settle the dispute privately, or having it moved outside the scope of the criminal justice system. It also seems apparent that much of the ability to negotiate, or coerce, such settlements lies in the power derived from approximating legitimate business activity. Though it is an empirical question, it is likely that there is a strong inverse correlation between the likelihood to perceive the event as a crime and its proximity to legitimate business behavior. The research presented by Jesilow et al. and Levi in this volume suggests such a correlation.

Richard Sparks's (1982) research on victimization highlights the importance of the victim's own role in the offense. It may be argued that the relationship between offenders and victims plays an even larger role in white-collar offenses. While the white-collar crimes receiving the most publicity tend to be those where the victim is painted as completely powerless and/or ignorant of the offense or its risk, a certain amount of white-collar crime is put into play by virtue of the victim's interest in deriving some gain. Bogus investment firms that solicit participation by offering an unusually high return on investments require individuals who are at least willing to circle the bait. While many victims may not recognize the potential for injury, many others enter cognizant, albeit perhaps wary, of the questionability of the practice. To this extent, Vaughan's discussion of offending as a dimension of risk management applies equally well to victims. This general point holds true within organizational settings as well, whether the victimization takes place against other organizations, or within the organization by individuals. To the extent that such factors as management autonomy and/or decentralization are related to proneness to victimization, such proneness can readily be understood as a factor in risk management, to be weighed in relation to the benefits derived from such organizational structuring or operations. Again, the significance of these issues lies in understanding the relationships of power and trust that adhere to particular positions within organizations or between individuals in business activities. Finally, such an understanding requires the important temporal dimension as well. The study of white-collar crime thus lends itself to research on the victimization "career."

Reiss (1981) has pointed out the complexity of white-collar victimization as it relates to organizational actors. Understanding such victimization becomes complicated when it may involve organizations against individuals, organizations against other organizations, individuals outside the organization against the organization, or individuals within the organization against the organization. Furthermore, the variety of organizational forms involved in victimization (for-profit, nonprofit, governmental [see Kramer's discussion of "state-corporate crime" in this regard], trusts, pension funds, and so on) and the relational nature between victim and offender affect the quality of, and the organizational response to, the victimization.

Two essays in this volume deal directly with different forms of white-collar victimization. Jesilow, Klempner, and Chiao's essay (chapter 6) on consumer complaints of major frauds explores the public's knowledge of reporting procedures and the rationale behind the decision to pursue or disregard criminal remedies. Some findings parrot victim responses to common offenses: most do not file formal complaints, often on the grounds that the officials could do little to help them. Other findings seem unique to consumer frauds, in particular the fact that victims have difficulty locating the agency responsible for handling the matter. The cause of such difficulty lies in the lack of resources and media coverage provided to these offenses—factors influencing enforcement found in Benson, Cullen, and Maakestad's (chapter 11), and Pontell and Calavita's essays (chapter 8) as well.

Michael Levi's (chapter seven) essay examines victimization of a different sort. His study is of victimization against corporations and private individuals "by fraudsters outside of 'reputable' spheres of business." As with the findings by Jesilow et al., many parallel those typically associated with common offenses, in particular, offenders tend to victimize individuals similar to themselves: "the poor are defrauded by the relatively poor and the wealthy 'rip off' the wealthy." Similarly, the gap between fear of crime and actual risk of crime is quite large. There are, however, some important differences. To a large extent, neither private victims nor commercial victims were protected by insurance against loss, thus removing one important incentive for reporting found in common offenses for gain. Perhaps most significantly, Levi's data indicate that corporations do not maintain an advantage over private individuals in relation to the quality of policing services they receive. Corporate victims (like some individual victims) are constrained in reporting their loss, largely because of a combination of concerns about organizational prestige and the financial-opportunity costs of reporting.

Guardianship

Policing

Of all the areas of research in white-collar crime, we probably know the least about policing. This is so for several reasons. First, to the extent that we do know about policing, the scope of that knowledge (at least empirically) rests on the kinds of white-collar offenses that receive the attention of the traditional kinds of policing in the criminal justice system: employee thefts, con games, welfare scams, and the like (see chapter 7 in this volume, however, for important differences in the United Kingdom). That the police are called at all is in part a product of the nature of those particular victimizations. While these offenses can be complex in design and may continue over a period of time, their injuries tend to be direct and temporally succinct. Furthermore, the geographic boundaries of the victimization and the mobility of the offenders tend to be confined within jurisdictional boundaries of the policing agency. As those boundaries expand, resource and legal barriers act to restrict typical police involvement. Second, as Shapiro (1984) clearly demonstrates, the organizational structure of enforcement largely defines the kinds of offenses targeted and the kinds of offenders caught. As public policing is structured around and limited to certain kinds of fraud, it is not surprising that we find the limited kinds of white-collar crimes captured by the traditional enforcement mechanisms of the criminal justice system. Similarly, as Katz (1979) points out, because of the complexity of many kinds of white-collar crimes, enforcement dictates the combining of investigative and prosecution functions. Such a structure is not typically found in traditional police agencies, though this is changing to a degree with the development of such strategies as multijurisdictional task forces.

Recalling Sutherland once again, the apparatus of enforcement and remedy for many kinds of white-collar offenses extends beyond the traditional confines of the criminal justice system. In fact, many kinds of white-collar crime come primarily, or at least firstly, under the scrutiny of private policing, or some form of it, as represented by professional associations responsible for self-regulation. As with the research on private policing of common offenses, the world of private policing and white-collar crime is only now getting the systematic attention it deserves. While important strides have been made regarding regulatory enforcement models (Braithwaite et al., 1987; Hawkins and Thomas, 1989; Reiss, 1984; Scholz, 1984), the role of self-regulation of professional groups (Pontell et al., 1982) in addition to the self-regulation of market activities (Abolafia, 1981; Stenning and Shearing, 1987; Gunningham, 1988; Ewick, 1985; and Reichman [chapter 10]), there are significant obstacles in researching this area that account for our limited knowledge. Perhaps most significant is the difficulty in obtaining data from such regulatory groups. In part this difficulty arises from the nature of the relationship between enforcer and those enforced. Unlike the public police, those who enforce the rules and regulations of professional associations are generally professionals themselves. There is a clear concern that research directed at the misconduct of professionals will cast a negative light on the profession as a whole. Thus, as gatekeepers, they have a prohibitive, yet understandable, self-interest in ensuring that the actions of a few are not inferred to the population as a whole.

Second, the conduct that comes under the province of regulation covers the continuum of harms—from serious offenses to, more typically, violations of regulatory rules, procedures, and requirements. There is, we think, a general anathema on the part of the regulatory officials directed toward researchers who are bent on treating all illicit conduct the same. Many of the offenses noted in Pontell and Calavita's study (chapter 8) on savings and loan violations and Reichman's study of securities violations and compliance practices (chapter 10) reveal the gray areas of illicit conduct. Of course, the dilemmas raised here call back to the Sutherland (1945)/ Tappan (1947) debate about what sorts of conduct should properly be called crimes. Reducing criminal conduct to its lowest common denominator (generally, that it is a crime according to the statute) may be a useful way of "counting" acts, but offers considerably less insight into offending conduct. This debate is not restricted to the white-collar crime area (as Sutherland himself noted in drawing the parallel between sanctioning white-collar crime and juvenile delinquency), but has become an important part of the discussions regarding the "criminal career." If we want to understand crime, it is crucial to make distinctions between the kinds of conduct committed, by whom, and their frequency over time.

One last obstacle to obtaining information from regulatory agencies is the differing paradigms from which the conduct is viewed (Levi, 1987). Those interested in crime and social control are, virtually by definition, likely to view the conduct from a normative perspective entailing moral connotations of "wrongdoing." Yet many involved in the regulation of activity do not view the behavior in such a fashion, but instead view it, or at least much of it, in economic terms. Nowhere is this more evident than in the regulation of securities transactions, where deviant behavior is more likely to be thought of as a factor producing disequilibrium in the market and requiring adjustments to enhance efficiency (Fischel and Grossman, 1984).

Several essays in this volume offer insights on enforcement efforts in white-collar crime. Levi's essay is replete with data about victimization and enforcement too extensive to summarize here. However, among his findings he notes evidence of the general level of satisfaction by victims regarding enforcement efforts. Unlike enforcement in the United States, traditional police agencies in the United Kingdom play a primary role in the handling of complaints involving many white-collar offenses. Levi notes the curvilinear relationship in reporting of fraud—"companies made either extensive use, or almost no use of the police or other regulatory agencies."

The essay by Benson, Cullen, and Maakestad (chapter 11) affords a different and equally insightful perspective on the prosecution of white-collar offenses. The focus of their essay is on the community context in which enforcement takes place. As demonstrated in the research on common offense, styles of enforcement are shaped by the norms, concerns, and activities of local communities. Furthermore, the organizational structure and enforcement priorities vary significantly according to region. Developing on this general line of reasoning, Benson et al. argue that the economic conditions in communities or regions influence the nature and extent of enforcement actions against white-collar crime (see also Shover et al., 1986). Their national survey of prosecutors reveals that the economic health of a community may be associated with vigorous enforcement efforts to control corporate and business activity. While such efforts may indicate nothing more than the number of offenses prosecutable, the authors argue that both social organization and power must be considered: "Large, economically well-off communities may develop legal cultures less tolerant of corporate misconduct than economically depressed communities," and in response are less willing to tolerate such misconduct.

Reichman provides a different perspective on enforcement, as her essay (chapter 10) is directed toward the self-regulation of securities markets. Her interest is in exploring "how business discourse and practice actively participate in the construction of regulatory violations and pattern their distribution." While much of the earlier research concerns the role that business actors play in the formation of law, her attention is turned to "everyday business transactions," which ultimately come to define what regulatory law "is" as well as how it is violated and enforced. Her insights here provide a thoughtful perspective on a particular kind of power, what she terms "regulatory authority," in shaping both deviant conduct and the response to it.

Sanctioning

If we know little about the policing of white-collar crime, we know more about sanctioning, or at least this is the subject on which the greatest amount of ink has been spilled. Though the sentencing literature covers a wide range of topics, the two most important involve, first, the disparity in sentencing and, second, the sentencing of organizational actors. The former has been the subject of considerable empirical inquiry. The latter, until just recently, has largely been theoretical (jurisprudential) in scope.

Sentencing Disparity

Though much of Sutherland's work sought to illustrate the differential implementation of the law, he did not directly address the existence of sentence disparity in his own research. The corpus of knowledge on sentencing disparity grew primarily from research conducted by Hagan et al. (1980, 1982), Hagan and Parker (1985), Wheeler et al. (1982, 1988), Benson and Walker (1988), Daly (1989), and Weisburd et al. (1990). Geis (chapter 1) provides a summary of that research, which need not be repeated here. There are, however, two significant points we wish to make from those works. First, the research demonstrates (and has done so repeatedly) that there is a wide disparity between the public's perceptions about the kinds of crimes committed by white-collar offenders and the reality of white-collar offenses as they are disposed of in court. The fact remains that many white-collar offenses encountered in the federal courts involve relatively minor harms and that most are not committed by individuals with great wealth and power, but by individuals who fall in the middle classes (Weisburd et al., 1991).

The significance of these findings cannot be understated, however, at least in terms of their meaning for public policy. Katz (1980) has noted the importance of a social movement against white-collar crime in the development of legislative and jurisprudential change in response to white-collar crime. Yet, as Levi demonstrates (chapter 7), it appears likely that the social movement is generated in part by reactions to atypical white-collar crimes. Portrayals of insider trading are painted, and subsequently defined by, our knowledge of the Michael Milkens of white-collar crime. As an aside, this problem is not unique to white-collar crime, as demonstrated by Walker (1989) in his discussion of "celebrated cases." Yet the use of public opinion surveys about the harms of white-collar crimes for the purposes of developing policies, in particular sentencing policies, becomes especially problematic in this regard. First, the utility of harm in determining offense seriousness arises not from what it is perceived to be, but what it is. Second, for the purposes of sentencing policy, what in fact the harm is should be derived from typical cases rather than outliers.

The second point we wish to make is not to make too much out of the first point. Focusing solely on those cases that reach and are disposed of in the courts neglects many wrongs that have been central to the study of white-collar crime, at least as the term was (it seems) intended by Sutherland. As Reichman's essay attests, the power, status, and prestige of both individuals and organizations play important roles in both the construction of harms for legal purposes, and the differential application of the laws once they are constructed (see also Shapiro, 1985). Thus we must continually remind ourselves that what arise as typical cases may appear as such because the social organization of the system of enforcement structures (limits) itself to these cases (Shapiro, 1984). Kramer's study of the *Challenger* explosion (chapter 9) is a case in point.

Organizational Sanctions

The United States Sentencing Commission has recently released its final report on organizational sanctions (1990). The guidelines proposed in that report are a culmination of several years of construction, testing, and revision. If anything, the commission's report highlights the Sisyphean task of constructing sanctions that combine the myriad and often confused goals of punishment as spelled out in the congressional mandate: deterrence, rehabilitation, public protection, and "just punishment." Various drafts of the report have ranged from guidelines constructed almost entirely around economic principles (optimal penalty theories) to maximize deterrence to those giving greater significance to rehabilitation through corporate probation.

As the commission's efforts demonstrate, designing sentencing guidelines for organizational offenders involves several sticky problems. Two will be discussed here. First are the substantive issues of organizational accountability that serve, in part, as the foundation for sentencing options. The assumption underlying punishments directed at the organization, as opposed or in addition to responsible individuals, is not simply that one can exact more punishment if the organization is targeted, but that it is the organizational nature of the conduct that makes the corporate actor responsible, and thus blameworthy, for the offense. The commission largely circumvented these issues of corporate culpability by adopting with little discussion the legal doctrine of vicarious liability noted earlier. Clearly, however, the degree to which corporate sanctions either exact deterrence, allow for rehabilitation, or serve as expressions of condemnation and censure depends on demonstrating the role that organizational components play in causing, facilitating, or failing to prevent the criminal event. This topic has, of course, been the subject of considerable scholarly debate (Stone, 1975; Coffee, 1981; French, 1984; Schlegel, 1990). The debate, however, has been largely theoretical in scope, the validity of the arguments in some instances resting solely on the number of times they have been repeated.

Perhaps more notably, the commission's guidelines pertaining to individual sanctions for organizational illegality demonstrate the lack of empirical knowledge we have about the role that organizational forces (structure, environment, relationships, and so on) have on individual decision making. It is in this context that the macro-micro connection discussed by Vaughan becomes particularly useful. At present, we lack any systematic understanding of how the factors noted by Vaughan (external competitive pressures, position within an organization, reference group, hierarchy, past decision making, organizational culture, and the like) affect individual decision making and subsequently the likelihood, if any, that sanctions aimed at individuals within organizations will successfully address those concerns with any meaningful impact.

Simpson's essay (chapter 12) has important implications in this regard. Her survey of corporate executives and managers concerning unethical conduct points to a candid disregard for the legal consequences of such conduct. At the same time her data also demonstrate that corporate actions leading to unethical conduct seldom display the character of rationality assumed in many of the arguments favoring utilitarian punishment strategies. The focus of her queries involves unethical as opposed to criminal conduct, and her data do suggest differences in perceptions based on increasing degrees of wrongfulness in conduct. This being said, however, her research raises questions about the confidence often held regarding the deterrent effectiveness of the criminal sanction on individuals in organizational (particularly corporate) spheres.

The second problem facing the development of organizational sanctions goes again to the heart of Sutherland's point about the differential implementation of the law. How can organizational sanctions be created in a fashion that adequately distinguishes criminal punishments from civil remedies, and concomitantly, what type and form should those sanctions take to effect their desired aim? In theory at least, there are important differences between the criminal and civil sanctions. Oversimplifying to be sure, one important distinction is that civil remedies generally impose costs for engaging in harm-producing behavior. To the extent that one can cover such costs, the behavior is largely considered permissible, though obviously undesired.

The criminal sanction, on the other hand, is constructed around the unacceptability of the harm or risk of harm produced by given acts. The criminal law renders such acts unacceptable by secondarily imposing sanctions of a prohibitive nature (often found in civil sanctions as well) and primarily by stigmatizing both the act and the actor as (respectively) morally wrong and morally blameworthy.

The literature on organizational sanctions revolves largely around the type and amount of criminal sanctions that will produce the desired results. In fact, a good bit of it debates the utility or lack thereof of fines, since they constitute the bulk of sentences imposed (Coffee, 1980; Kennedy, 1985). Perhaps out of frustration with the endeavors, recent writings offer alternative organizational sanctions that properly encourage deterrence and at the same time reflect the principles of the criminal law. Two essays in this volume (chapters 13 and 14) contribute directly to this effort.

In an interesting twist on the ideas of disparity in sentencing, Walt and Laufer (chapter 13) address the disparity that arises in sanctions between offenders and corporations for similar kinds of white-collar crimes. Given the expressive function of the criminal sanction (Hart, 1958; Feinberg, 1970), they contend that the most severe of organizational sanctions typically imposed (cash fines) do not approximate the condemnatory features found in the incapacitative sentences given to individuals for serious wrongdoing and, as a result, the "truncated selection of sanctions for corporations fails to express the attitudes of indignation and condemnation necessary for criminal punishment" (chapter 13). In order to ensure that commensurate condemnation is provided to both individual and corporate offenders for similar conduct, they advocate the development of a corporate analog to individual imprisonment—corporate incapacitative sanctions. They outline six forms that such sanctions may take against corporations (imposed in the form of probation conditions), ranging from revoking or limiting corporate charters to requiring corporate divestiture of offending units or subsidiaries to placing the corporation in receivership.

The alternative model offered by Walt and Laufer is clearly grounded in the principles of criminal law. Yet criminal law is not the remedy most widely employed against corporate misconduct. Shapiro's study of the Securities and Exchange Commission found that only 10 percent of offenses were handled through the criminal sanction, while the remainder were disposed of through the civil or administrative remedy (1984). Given this reality, it is imperative that we understand the important dimension of corporate social control afforded by civil and administrative remedies. Kenneth Mann (chapter 14) offers a glimpse of this process in his essay on civil penalties for white-collar crime. It is particularly interesting to note the evolution of the civil sanction away from its remedial role. Many civil proceedings are now essentially punitive in nature. Perhaps the most obvious trend in this regard applies to civil forfeiture provisions, widely used in drug-enforcement efforts. Mann notes that one consequence of the hybrid development of the civil sanction is to turn the entire legal system in the direction of increasing punitiveness.

It is hard to say whether Sutherland would view this trend with approval. Sutherland's own disdain for the differential application of the law was the product of two concerns, albeit interrelated. The first involved the escape from the stigma attached to the criminal sanction. Without such stigma an essential ingredient to crime control went missing. It may well be that the punitive nature of modern civil sanctions (both in the ever-increasing harshness of sanctions and in the tonal quality reflecting greater condemnation and censure) would approximate the desired aim sought by Sutherland. But Sutherland was also concerned that the civil remedy was largely the instrument of the rich and powerful. Unlike the criminal sanction which, in theory at least, speaks in the name of the myriad interests of the state, the civil sanction has notoriously been a tool of the business class, most typically through the punitive damages awarded in tort. Mann's essay hints at some of these concerns when he speaks of the issues relating to the current (and growing) bifurcated process of punitive civil sanctions, one brought forth by the state, the other by private hands. We can only conclude that if nothing else, Sutherland would surely agree that it is an area deserving of future attention.

Conclusion

Our discussion in this introductory chapter only begins to scratch the surface of the scholarship directed toward white-collar crime in the past half century. Indeed, the summary here has provided firsthand evidence of the difficulty, and perhaps futility, that comes with charting the progress of work in this area. Yet our intent here is primarily to demonstrate the broad spectrum of interests that have been captured by Sutherland's net. Rather than to delineate what should or should not be included in the scope of white-collar crime, our aim is to show the wealth derived by Sutherland's own seeming ambivalence toward specifying the term. The result has led to a treasure trove of insights, brought forth by a freedom to explore the idea from myriad perspectives along different dimensions of crime and social control.

REFERENCES

Abolafia, M. Y. (1981). Taming the markets: Self-regulation in the commodity futures industry. Unpublished doctoral dissertation, State University of New York at Stony Brook.

Bachrach, P., and Baratz, M. S. (1970). *Power and poverty.* New York: Oxford University Press.

Benson, M. L., Cullen, F. T., and Maakestad, W. J. (1992). Community context and the prosecution of corporate crime. (This volume.)

Benson, M. L., and Walker, E. (1988). Sentencing the white-collar offender. *American Sociological Review, 53*, 294–302.

Braithwaite, J. (1992). Poverty, power, and white-collar crime: Sutherland and the paradoxes of criminological theory. (This volume.)

Braithwaite, J., Walker, J., and Grabosky, P. (1987). An enforcement taxonomy of regulatory agencies. *Law and Policy, 9*, 323.

Canfield, G. F. (1941). Corporate responsibility for crime. *Columbia Law Review, 14*, 469–481.

Clinard, M. B., and Yeager, P. C. (1980). *Corporate crime.* New York: Free Press.

Coffee, J. (1980). Making the punishment fit the corporation: The problem of finding the optimal corporate criminal sanction. *Northern Illinois University Law Review, 1*, 3–36.

———. (1981). Corporate crime and punishment: A non-Chicago view of the economics of criminal punishment. *American Criminal Law Review, 79*, 419.

Coleman, J. W. (1992). The theory of white-collar crime: From Sutherland to the 1990s. (This volume.)

Cressey, D. R. (1988). The poverty of theory in corporate crime research. In W. S. Laufer and F. Adler, eds. *Advances in criminological theory.* New Brunswick, N.J.: Transaction Books.

Dahl, R. A. (1957). The concept of power. *Behavioral Science, 2*, 201–205.

Daly, K. (1989). Gender and varieties of white-collar crime. *Criminology, 27*, 769–793.

Ewick, P. (1985). Redundant regulation: Sanctioning broker-dealers. *Law and Policy, 7*, 423.

Feinberg, J. (1970). *Doing and deserving: Essays in the theory of responsibility.* Princeton, N.J.: Princeton University Press.

Fischel, D. R. and Grossman, S. R. (1984). Customer protection in futures and securities markets. *Journal of Futures Markets, 4*, 273–295.

French, P. A. (1984). *Collective and corporate responsibility.* New York: Columbia University Press.

Frey, F. W. (1971). Comment: On issues and non-issues in the study of power. *American Political Science Review, 65*, 1081–1101.

Gaventa, J. (1980). *Power and powerlessness: Quiescence and rebellion in an Appalachian valley.* Urbana: University of Illinois Press.

Geis, G. (1992). White-collar crime: What Is It? (This volume.)

Geis, G., and Goff, C. (1983). Introduction. In E. H. Sutherland, *White collar crime: The uncut version.* New Haven: Yale University Press.

Gottfredson, M. R., and Gottfredson, D. M. (1988). *Decision making in criminal justice: Toward the rational exercise of discretion.* (2d. ed.). New York: Plenum Press.

Gunningham, N. (1988). Moving the goalposts: Financial market regulation in Hong Kong and the crash of October 1987. *Law and Social Inquiry*, *15*, 1–48.

Hagan, J. (1988). *Structural Criminology*. Oxford: Polity Press.

Hagan, J., Nagel-Bernstein, I. H., and Albonetti, C. (1980). The differential sentencing of white-collar offenders in ten federal district courts. *American Sociological Review*, *45*, 802–820.

Hagan, J., Nagel-Bernstein, I. H., and Albonetti, C. (1982). The social organization of white-collar sanctions: A study of prosecution and punishment in the federal courts. In P. Wickman and T. Dailey, eds. *White-collar and economic crime*, 259–275. Lexington, Mass.: Lexington Books.

Hagan, J., and Parker, P. (1985). White-collar crime and punishment: The class structure and legal sanctioning of securities violations. *American Sociological Review*, *50*, 302–316.

Hart, H. M., Jr. (1958). The Aims of the Criminal Law. *Law and Contemporary Problem*, *23*, 401–413.

Hawkins, K., and Thomas, J., eds., (1989). *Making regulatory policy*. Pittsburgh: University of Pittsburgh Press.

Jesilow, P., Klempner, E., and Chiao, V. (1992). Reporting consumer and major fraud: A survey of complainants. (This volume.)

Katz, J. (1979). Legality and equality: Plea bargaining in the prosecution of white-collar and common crimes. *Law and Society Review*, *13*, 431–459.

———. (1980). The social movement against white-collar crime. In E. Bittner and S. Messinger, eds. *Criminology Review Yearbook*. Vol. 2. Beverly Hills: Sage.

Kennedy, C. (1985). Criminal sentences for corporations: Alternative fining mechanisms. *California Law Review*, March, 443–482.

Lee, F. P. (1928). Corporate criminal liability. *Columbia Law Review*, *28*, 1–28.

Levi, M. (1987). Regulatory fraud: White-collar crime and the criminal process. London: Routledge & Kegan Paul.

Levi, M. (1992). White-collar crime victimization. (This volume.)

Lukes, S. (1974). *Power: A radical view*. London: Macmillan.

Mann, K. (1985). *Defending white-collar crime: A portrait of attorneys at work*. New Haven: Yale University Press.

———. (1992). Procedural rules and information control: Gaining Leverage in applying punitive civil sanctions to white-collar crime. (This volume.)

Pfeffer, J., and Salancik, G. R. (1978). *The external control of organizations: A resource dependence perspective*. New York: Harper & Row.

Pontell, H. N., Jesilow, P. D., and Geis, G. (1982). Policing physicians:

Practitioner fraud and abuse in a government benefit program. *Social Problems*, *30*, 117–125.

Reichman, N. (1992). Moving backstage: Uncovering the role of compliance practices in shaping regulatory policy. (This volume.)

Reiss, A. (1981). Organizations in violation and in victimization by crime. Paper presented on the occasion of the Edwin Sutherland Award, American Society of Criminology Meeting, November, Washington, D.C.

Reiss, A. J., Jr. (1984). Selecting strategies of social control over organizational life. In K. Hawkins and J. M. Thomas, eds. *Enforcing regulation*. Boston: Kluwer-Nijoff.

Schlegel, K. (1990). *Just desserts for corporate criminals*. Boston: Northeastern University Press.

Scholz, J. T. (1984). Cooperation, deterrence and the ecology of regulatory enforcement. *Law and Society Review*, *18*, 179.

Shapiro, S. P. (1984). *Wayward capitalists: Target of the Securities and Exchange Commission*. New Haven: Yale University Press.

———. (1985). The road not taken: The elusive path to criminal prosecution for white-collar offenders. *Law and Society Review*, *19*, 179–217.

Shover, N., Clelland, D. A., and Lynxwiler, J. P. (1986). *Enforcement or negotiation*. Albany: State University of New York Press.

Simpson, S. S. (1992). Corporate-crime deterrence and corporate-control policies: Views from the inside. (This volume.)

Snyder, O. C. (1938, 1939). Criminal breach of trust and corporate mismanagement. *Mississippi Law Journal*, *11*, 123–151, 262–289, 386–389.

Sparks, R. F. (1982). *Research on victims of crime*. Washington, D.C.: U.S. Government Printing Office.

Staw, B. M., and Szwajkowski, E. (1975). The scarcity munificence component of organizational environments and the commission of illegal acts. *Administrative Science Quarterly*, *20*, 345.

Stenning, P., and Shearing, C. (1987). Controlling organizational crime: Public and private options—Some reflections on the nature of regulation. Paper presented at thirty-ninth annual meeting of the American Society of Criminology, Montreal, Canada.

Stone, C. D. (1975). *Where the law ends: The social control of corporate behavior*. New York: Harper & Row.

Sutherland, E. H. (1940). White collar criminality. *American Sociological Review*, *5*, 1.

Sutherland, E. H. (1945). Is "white collar crime" crime? *American Sociological Review*, *10*, 132–139.

Sutherland, E. H. (1949). *White collar crime*. New York: Dryden Press.

Sutherland, E. H. (1983). *White collar crime: The uncut version*. New Haven: Yale University Press.

Tappan, P. W. (1947). Who is the criminal? *American Sociological Review*, *12*, 96–102.

Thompson, J. A. (1967). *Organizations in action*. New York: McGraw-Hill.

U.S. Sentencing Commission (1990). Draft guidelines for the sentencing of corporations. Chapter 8.

Vaughan, D. (1992). The macro-micro connection in white-collar crime theory. (This volume.)

Von Hirsch, A. (1976). *Doing justice: The choice of punishments*. New York: Hill and Wang.

Walker, S. (1989). *Sense and nonsense about crime*. Pacific Grove, Calif.: Brooks Cole.

Walt, S., and Laufer, W. (1992). Corporate criminal liability and the comparative mix of sanctions. (This volume.)

Weisburd, D., Waring, E., and Wheeler, S. (1990). Class, status, and the punishment of white-collar criminals. *Law and Social Inquiry, 15, 2,* 223–243.

Weisburd, D., Wheeler, S., Waring, E., and Bode, N. (1991). *Crimes of the middle classes: White-collar offenders in the federal courts*. New Haven: Yale University Press.

Wheeler, S., Weisburd, D., and Bode, N. (1982). Sentencing the white-collar offender: Rhetoric and reality. *American Sociological Review, 47,* 641–659.

Wheeler, S., Weisburd, D., Waring, E., and Bode, N. (1988). White collar crimes and criminals. *American Criminal Law Review, 25,* 331–35.

·I·

DEFINITION AND THEORY

· 1 ·

White-Collar Crime

What Is It?

GILBERT GEIS

Few, if any, legal or criminological terms are surrounded by as much dispute as white-collar crime. Sociologists, who dominate the field of academic criminology, are wont to insist that by "white-collar crime" they mean to pinpoint a coterie of offenses committed by persons of reasonably high standing in the course of their business, professional, or political work. Especially clear illustrations would be an antitrust conspiracy among vice presidents of several major corporations, the acceptance of a bribe by a member of the national cabinet, and Medicare fraud by a surgeon.

Persons with criminal law or regulatory law backgrounds, for their part, are likely to point out that no such designation as "white-collar crime" is to be found in the statute books and that the kinds of criminal offenses that sometimes are embraced within the term— such as insider trading, embezzlement, and a large variety of frauds—are committed by persons who might be located anywhere on a status hierarchy. While antitrust conspiracies are not likely to be carried out by lower-echelon employees (though they could in theory involve executives' secretaries), bribery transactions often include lower-level go-betweens, and fraud against medical insurance programs is perpetrated by pharmacy employees and ambulance drivers as well as medical doctors. Why, it is asked, should a distinction be drawn between persons who have committed the same type of offense merely because they hold different occupational positions? This is but one of the disputes about definition that both plague and invigorate research and writing on white-collar crime.

Cynics are apt to view jousting about the definition of white-collar crime the same way they regard disputes about the definition of pornography: We all can recognize it when we see it, so why bother overmuch with attempting to pinpoint precise parameters? Those rejecting this viewpoint maintain that it is vital to establish an exact meaning for a term so that everyone employing it is talking about the same thing, and so that scientific investigations can build one upon the other rather than going off in various directions because of incompatible definitions of their subject matter.

On the debit side in this long-standing debate is the fact that a great deal of energy and ingenuity has been dedicated to defending one or another of the supposed characteristics of the term "white-collar crime" that could have been employed to increase our understanding of the behaviors involved and to determine more satisfactory methods for dealing with them. The credit side lists improved insight and understanding that result when good minds ask hard questions regarding precisely what is meant by words and terms that appear to be employed imprecisely. In the remainder of this chapter, I want to indicate the course of the intellectual fray regarding the definition of white-collar crime, so that readers might be better able to decide for themselves what resolution satisfies them.

Sutherland and His Early Disciples

The term "white-collar crime" was introduced to the academic world by Edwin H. Sutherland in 1939 during his presidential address to the American Sociological Society in Philadelphia. Fifty-six years old at the time, Sutherland was at the peak of a distinguished career marked primarily by his authorship of a sophisticated textbook, *Criminology*, that had first been published in 1924. Though he had lapsed from the orthodox religious faith of his father, a Baptist minister and college president, Sutherland had intensely strong moral convictions about commercial, political, and professional wrongdoing. He also had been deeply influenced by the populist ideas that permeated the Nebraska of his youth (Cherney, 1981), ideas that depicted corrupt business practices as undermining the well-being of the hard-working, God-fearing frontier people among whom Sutherland had been brought up.[1]

In Sutherland's presidential address, he insisted that he had undertaken his work on "crime in the upper, white-collar class, which is composed of respectable, or at least respected, business and professional men" only "for the purpose of developing the theories of criminal behavior, not for the purpose of muckraking or of reforming anything except criminology" (Sutherland, 1940, p. 1). This patently disingenuous disclaimer was primarily a bow to the ethos of sociology at the time, an ethos that insisted on a "value-free" and "neutral" research stance. A proper definition of his subject matter did not occupy Sutherland's attention in this paper; rather, he used anecdotal stories of rapacious acts by America's notorious "robber barons" and their successors to flay then-popular explanations of criminal activity such as poverty, low intelligence, and offender psychopathy.

Ten years later, in *White Collar Crime*, Sutherland (1949) fleshed out his presidential address, but did little to pin down with any more precision the definition of his subject matter. That he buried part of his definition in a footnote attests to his indifference to the matter. In the text, Sutherland declared that a white-collar crime "may be defined approximately as a crime committed by a person of respectability and high social status in the course of his occupation" (p. 9). He then added that the definition consequently "excludes many crimes of the upper class, such as most of their cases of murder, adultery, and intoxication, since these are not customarily a part of their occupational procedures" (p. 9). The footnoted observation added that " 'white collar' is used here to refer principally to business managers and executives, in the sense that it was used by a president of General Motors who wrote *An Autobiography of a White Collar Worker*" (p. 9). However, within two pages of this pronouncement Sutherland illustrated white-collar crime with examples of thefts by employees in chain stores and overcharges by garage mechanics and watch repairers. It may have been a dearth of material at his disposal that led Sutherland to use these illustrations; more likely, it was the inconstancy of his definitional focus. Sutherland believed that all crime could be understood by a single interpretative scheme—his theory of differential association—and therefore, this being so, he saw no compelling reason to distinguish sharply between various forms of illegal activity.

Besides the ill-considered use of fudge words such as "approximately" and "principally" in his definition, Sutherland further muddied the semantic waters by planting here and there other equally amorphous clues to what he might have had in mind. The year before he published *White Collar Crime*, in a speech at DePauw University in Indiana, Sutherland had said:

> I have used the term white-collar criminal to refer to a person in the upper socioeconomic class who violates the laws designed to regulate his occupation. The term white-collar is used in the sense in which it was used by President Sloan of General Motors, who wrote a book titled *The Autobiography of a White Collar Worker*. The term is used more generally to refer to the wage-earning class which wears good clothes at work, such as clerks in stores. (Sutherland, 1956, p. 79)

The fact that Sutherland, usually a meticulous scholar in such matters, wrongly cites the Sloan book (it was *Adventures of a White Collar Man*) (Sloan and Sparkes, 1941) and that Sloan's book offers no further definitional enlightenment adds to the confusion. A strict constructionist might argue that the fact that Sutherland abandoned the final sentence in the foregoing quotation about the wage-earning class and its dress when he incorporated this material into his monograph the following year indicates that he had second thoughts, and that he intended to confine his focus to upper-class offenders.

The most straightforward definition that Sutherland offered has rarely been noted. It appeared in the *Encyclopedia of Criminology* (1949, p. 511) almost co-terminously with the publication of *White Collar Crime*. Here, Sutherland wrote that "the white collar criminal is defined as a person with high socioeconomic status who violates the laws designed to regulate his occupational activities." Such laws, Sutherland added, can be found in the penal code but also included federal and state trade regulations, as well as special war regulations and laws regarding advertising, patents, trademarks, and copyrights. Thereafter, he observed:

> The white collar criminal should be differentiated, on the one hand, from the person of lower socio-economic status who violates the regular penal code or the special trade

regulations which apply to him; and, on the other hand, from the person of high socio-economic status who violates the regular penal code in ways not connected with his occupation. (P. 511)

It has to be an uncertain exegetic exercise to comb these different proclamations in order to try to state what was "truly" meant as the definition of the phenomenon Sutherland had so effectively called to academic and public attention. Certainly, the definitions are uncrystallized and, at times, contradictory. For me, though, what stands out is a sense that Sutherland was most concerned with the illegal abuse of power by upper-echelon businessmen in the service of their corporations, by high-ranking politicians against their codes of conduct and their constituencies, and by professional persons against the government and against their clients and patients.

Particularly significant, I find, is Sutherland's specific exclusion in the last of the definitions quoted of a person from the lower socioeconomic class who violates "special trade regulations which apply to him." It must be granted, however, that this phrase too has its ambiguities. Did Sutherland mean to include lower socioeconomic class persons who violated regulations that applied *both* to them and to those above them in the power structure—such as the printer's devil and the corporate president who trade on insider information? Was it the law or the status of the perpetrator—or both linked together—that concerned him? It is said that Sutherland once was asked by Edwin Lemert, a noted criminologist, whether he meant by white-collar crime a type of crime committed by a special class of people, and he replied that "he was not sure" (Sparks, 1979, p. 17). Given its progenitor's alleged uncertainty, it is not surprising that those who try to perform as glossarists on the Sutherland definitional text often are befuddled. Besides, it should be stressed that Sutherland's definition, whatever its essence, has no necessary standing if more useful conceptualizations of the subject matter emerge.

In Sutherland's Wake

The focus of this chapter will almost exclusively be on definitional issues raised in the United States, primarily because most writers outside America have rather sanguinely ignored the question of the "proper" parameters for white-collar crime. In part, this is probably because it typically requires a large corps of communicants for some to devote their time to matters that have no immediate utilitarian result. Also, criminology outside the United States has only recently emerged as a social science enterprise distinctive from law and medical faculties, and the concept of white-collar crime is a characteristically social science formulation.

The term "white-collar crime" itself has been widely incorporated into popular and scholarly language throughout the world, though the designation "economic crime" tends to be preferred in socialist countries and is also widely used elsewhere. The United Nations, for its part, has adopted the phrase "abuse of power" for those behaviors that correspond to white-collar crimes. In addition, other designations, such as "upperworld crime," "crimes by the powerful," "crime in the suites," and "organizational crime" have their devotees.

Sutherland's position on white-collar crime elicited some early stinging but off-target critiques from two sociologists (Tappan, 1947; Caldwell, 1958), both of whom also held law degrees. Rather than focusing on Sutherland's definitional imprecision, both castigated him for what they saw as his anti business bias and his use of a conceptual brush to tar persons who had not been convicted by a criminal court. Sutherland got much the better of this debate by arguing that it was what the person actually had done in terms of the mandate of the criminal law, not how the criminal justice system responded to what they had done, that was essential to whether they should be regarded as criminal offenders (Sutherland, 1945, pp. 132–139).

The pioneering empirical studies that followed in the wake of Sutherland's enunciation of a new area of inquiry did little to clarify the definitional uncertainty. Marshall Clinard (1952), studying black-market offenses during the Second World War, devoted his attention to the issue of whether what he had investigated truly was a crime rather than whether it might mesh with the ingredients necessary to characterize the behaviors as white-collar crime. Clinard also argued that the personalities of the perpetrators—such as egocentricity, emotional insecurity, and feelings of personal inadequacy—were at least as significant as Sutherland's differential association theory in accounting for the black-market violations.

Donald Cressey's (1953) interviews with embezzlers in federal prisons led him to question whether these offenders met the criteria for categorization as white-collar offenders, since they typically cheated their employers, and "[w]hile, with a few exceptions, the persons interviewed were in no sense poverty stricken, neither can they be considered as persons of high social status in the sense that Sutherland uses the phrase."[2]

As had Clinard, Frank Hartung (1950), in the third early major study of white-collar crime, addressed almost all of his definitional remarks to the debate over whether what the violators of the wartime regulations in the meat industry had done could be considered criminal (he believed, with solid evidence, that it could), and not whether, if so, the perpetrators were white-collar criminals. What particularly marked Hartung's contribution, however, was the feisty response it drew from a preeminent sociologist, Ernest Burgess (1950). Burgess insisted that persons violating regulatory laws, such as black marketers, could not be regarded as criminals because they did not so view themselves and were not so viewed by the public. Besides, Burgess maintained, this would mean that half the country's population, given the widespread disregard of rationing during the war, were criminals, a conclusion he apparently found intellectually intolerable. Hartung tried to assuage Burgess, a power in the discipline, but had understandable difficulty with the idea that a person is not a criminal unless that person thinks of himself or herself as a criminal.

Summarizing these early days of white-collar crime scholarship, Donald Newman (1958) maintained that the chief criterion for a crime to be white-collar is that it occurs as a part of or as a deviation from the violator's occupational role. "Technically," Newman insisted, "this is more crucial than the type of law violated or the relative prestige of the violator, although these factors have necessarily come to be major issues in the white-collar crime controversy" (p. 737). This had happened, he argued, because most of the laws involved were not part of the traditional criminal codes, and because most of the violators were a cut above the ordinary criminal in social standing. Yet, in the same article, Newman notes that "[w]hether he likes it or not, the criminologist finds himself involved in an analysis of prestige, power, and differential privilege when he studies upperworld crime" (p. 746). Writing slightly later, Richard Quinney (1964) maintained that the concept of white-collar crime lacked conceptual clarity, and thought that it ought to embrace the derelictions of persons in all kinds of occupations. This, however, created another dilemma for Quinney—the question of what constitutes an occupational act. Is the filing of a tax return part of a retired person's occupation?[3] Is a welfare recipient who cheats the social services engaged in a white-collar crime because being on the dole is an occupational pursuit? Quinney, thus, added some more riddles, but, like those who had written before him, he was unable to put forward a definitional manifesto that could elicit widespread agreement.

The Middle Years

After the first burst of creative research on white-collar crime, the subject was virtually abandoned by scholars in the United States during the 1960s. Undoubtedly, this was in large part because of the reluctance to tackle iconoclastic ventures with the threat of McCarthyism hanging over the country (Schrenker, 1986). Ultimately, the surge for power by blacks, the challenge to the Vietnam conflict, Watergate, and similar events served to refocus attention on abuses of power. At the same time, as the study of crime in countries other than America moved away from being solely an enterprise conducted by black-letter lawyers and medical doctors, scholars throughout the world began to turn their attention to white-collar crime.[4]

On the definitional front, there was, first, an ineffectual and probably ill-conceived attempt in 1962 by the present author to restrict the term "white-collar crime" to the realm of corporate violations (Geis, 1962). Then, in 1970, Herbert Edelhertz, at the time the chief of the fraud section of the federal Department of Justice, offered a definition that drew exclusively upon legal understanding and, as he indicated, one that differed "markedly" from that advanced by Sutherland, which Edelhertz believed was "far too restrictive." "White collar crime is democratic," Edelhertz asserted, and "can be committed by a bank teller or the head of his institution" (pp. 3–4). Edelhertz proposed that a useful definition of white-collar crime would be "an illegal act or series of illegal acts committed by nonphysical means and by concealment or guile, to obtain money or property, to avoid the payment or loss of money or property, or to obtain business or personal advantage" (p. 3). He set out four subdivisions to embrace diverse forms of white-collar crime: (1) crimes by persons operating on an individual, ad hoc basis, for personal gain in a nonbusiness context; (2) crimes in the course of their occupations by those operating inside businesses, government, or other establishments, or in a professional capacity, in violation of their duty of loyalty and fidelity to employer or client; (3) crimes incidental to and in furtherance of business operations, but not the central purpose of such business operations; and (4) white-collar crime as a business, or as the central activity of the business. The last, Edelhertz indicated, referred to confidence games as forms of crime (pp. 19–20).

Criticism of the Edelhertz position predictably came from sociologists who regretted his slighting of the idea of abuse of power as the key aspect of white-collar offenses and his expansive extension of the term to such a variegated range of behaviors. They were puzzled by the excision of violence from the realm of white-collar crime, noting that crimes such as unnecessary surgical operations, the manufacture of unsafe automobiles, and the failure to label poisonous substances at the workplace could be regarded as white-collar crimes with a strong component of violence. Miriam Saxon (1980), for instance, in challenging Edelhertz's viewpoint, noted that the MER/29 case involved a pharmaceutical corporation that knowingly sold an anti-cholesterol drug that subjected at least five thousand persons to such serious side effects as cataracts and hair loss. Later, the American Bar Association would adopt the term "economic offense" for behaviors within the white-collar crime realm set forth by Edelhertz, and would modify the term "nonviolent" with the footnoted observation that this referred to "the means by which the crime is committed" even though "the harm to society can frequently be described as violent" (p. 5).

In 1973, Clinard and Quinney (p. 188) put forward what has become a widely accepted distinction in scholarship on white-collar crime, that between (1) occupational criminal behavior and (2) corporate criminal behavior. The former is meant to include persons at all levels of the social structure and was defined as the "violation of the criminal law in the course of activity of a legitimate occupation." The category included offenses of employees against their employers. Corporate crime for its part was to consist of offenses committed by corporate officials for their corporation and the offenses of the corporation itself[5] (p. 189).

Seven years later—in 1980—Albert Reiss and Albert Biderman, two particularly sophisticated scholars, suggested the following definition of white-collar crime in a monograph that sought, with a singular lack of success, to establish some basis for counting in a systematic manner the number of such offenses committed annually:

> White-collar violations are those violations of law to which penalties are attached that involve the use of a violator's position of significant power, influence, or trust in the legitimate economic or political institutional order for the purpose of illegal gain, or to commit an illegal act for personal or organizational gain. (P. 4)

What is notable about this stab at achieving definitional order is the return to what I see as Sutherland's clarion point, that the offense involve "the use of a violator's position of significant power, influence, or trust."

Another contribution of note was that by Richard Sparks (1979), who preferred to abandon the law as the essential ingredient of a white-collar offense and, instead, to incorporate both deviancy and illegality within its purview. By white-collar crime (or, as he preferred, "crime as business"), Sparks wrote that he meant acts possessing "all or most of the following features":

1. They are carried out primarily for economic gain, and involve some form of commerce, industry, or trade.
2. They necessarily involve some form of organization, in the sense of more or less formal relationships between the parties involved in committing the criminal acts. This organization is either based on, or adapted to, the commission of crimes.
3. They necessarily involve either the use or the misuse, or both, of legitimate forms and techniques of business, trade, or industry. What distinguishes such things as price-fixing conspiracies, invoice faking, and bankruptcy fraud from robbery, burglary, and shoplifting is that the former do, but the latter typically do not, involve methods and techniques that are also used for legitimate business purposes. (P. 172)

Perhaps the most interesting aspect of Sparks's definitional venture is his linkage of what has been called "organized crime" with white-collar crime. Dwight Smith (1981), in particular, has long insisted, though for the most part he has remained a lone voice, that conceptually there is little to distinguish the two forms of lawbreaking.

Current Controversies

Sentencing Studies

Science, both the social and natural varieties, progresses by testing ideas empirically, preferably by experimental means that utilize control or comparison groups. Some ideas—that there is resurrection after life, for instance—remain impervious to scientific scrutiny; others can be tested with greater or lesser difficulty. The field of white-collar crime, for its part, is notably resistant to experimental work. In some measure, this is because the standing of the perpetrators protects them from the kinds of manipulations that constitute so large a portion of experimental research.

A number of Sutherland's ideas concerning possible judicial favoritism towards white-collar offenders, however, have been converted into testable propositions in ways that have had an important impact on the manner in which white-collar crime is defined. In these instances, the nature of the available information dictated the definition employed.

One of the major studies, by John Hagan, Ilene Nagel, and Celesta Albonetti (1980), used college education and income as proxies for white-collar status in its review of the sentences handed out in ten American federal courts. The roster of white-collar offenses was initially derived intuitively from all acts in the statute books that plausibly might fit the category. Then it was refined by asking U.S. attorneys for their views. Ultimately, thirty-one offenses came to be regarded as white-collar offenses. The list included such arguable acts as failure to file a tax return, embezzlement or theft by bank employees, mail fraud swindles, and fraudulent acceptance of veterans' benefit payments. The research then was directed toward determining whether offenders convicted of committing such acts got tougher sentences than persons who had committed non-white-collar offenses—it was found that they did. In the other major sentencing study, Stanton Wheeler, David Weisburd, and Nancy Bode (1982) employed eight broad categories of federal offenses for their representation of white-collar crime: securities fraud, antitrust violations, bribery, tax offenses, bank embezzlement, postal and wire fraud, false claims and statements, and credit- and lending-institution fraud. They directed their inquiry toward discovering whether persons with higher social status were sentenced more leniently for such offenses than those with lower social status—it was found that they were not.[6]

The conclusions of the Wheeler study have been disputed on the ground, among others, that they fail to take into account the considerable screening that takes places in regard to white-collar offenses prior to the point where the remaining perpetrators go to court to plead or to be tried and, if found guilty, to be sentenced.[7] Perhaps a more basic issue is whether or not either team of researchers truly was studying persons who might reasonably be regarded as white-collar criminals. Kathleen Daly (1989), reanalyzing the data used in the Wheeler et al. investigation to determine the fate of women who committed white-collar crimes, came to the paradoxical conclusion that it was "occupational marginality" that best explained such offenses; virtually all of the bank embezzlers in her sample, for instance, were clerical workers, and as many as a third of the women in some offense categories were unemployed. For the men, Wheeler and his colleagues had reported that among the credit-fraud, false-claim, and mail-fraud offenders, fewer than half were steadily employed and a quarter were unemployed at the time of their offenses (Wheeler et al., 1988). At the end of her study, Daly, in an aside almost plaintive in nature, mused, "The women's socioeconomic profile, coupled with the nature of their crimes, makes one wonder if 'white-collar' aptly describes them or their illegalities."[8]

Responding in part to the criticism that he had corrupted the essential nature of white-collar crime in his sentencing study (Geis, 1984, p. 146), Hagan, in collaboration with Patricia Parker (1985), later refocused his attention on securities violations during a seventeen-year period in the province of Ontario in Canada. He now employed as the determinant of white-collar power what he called "relational indicators," such as ownership and authority, which located individuals in class positions directly relevant to the perpetration of their offenses. Hagan and Parker also looked at regulatory enforcement under the Securities Act, arguing that the majority of the offenses in which they were interested never came before the criminal courts. This research overturned the earlier counterintuitive conclusion that white-collar offenders are treated more leniently; instead, it was found that employers often escaped both criminal-court appearance and regulatory punishment for Securities Act violations and that managers bore the heaviest burden of the sanctioning process. Regarding the importance of their different definitional focus, Hagan and Parker noted: "Empirical results of our work suggest that the substitution of class for status measures [for example, education and income] is crucial."

Organizational Foci

Parallel to the contretemps regarding the definitional boundaries of white-collar crime elicited by the sentencing studies, there has been an increasing focus on offenses by organizations as part of the territory of white-collar crime. Sutherland himself had devoted a major portion of his monograph to a compilation of the official records of wrongdoing by the seventy largest American corporations (and, as a result, had labeled most of them "criminal recidivists"), and Clinard and Quinney had established corporate crime as a separable unit of white-collar crime analysis.

Chief among the proponents of an organizational focus are M. David Ermann and Richard Lundman (1978) who note in their definitional framework that, among other things, to be considered deviant an organizational act must be contrary to norms maintained outside the organization and must have support from the dominant administrative coalition of the organization. Laura Schrager and James F. Short, Jr., (1977) define organizational crime in the following manner:

> The illegal acts of omission or commission of an individual or a group of individuals in a formal organization in accordance with the operative goals of the organization, which have a serious physical or economic impact on employees, consumers, or the general public. (P. 408)

The inclusion of a measure of the consequence of the offense ("a serious . . . impact") as an aspect of its definition seems puzzling, since various forms of illegal economic activity, such as some kinds of antitrust activity (for example, pooling resources by different companies to finance research on serious diseases), are at best arguably detrimental to economic health and vitality, but have been outlawed as a consequence of the force of a particular marketplace philosophy (Kadish, 1963).

Attention to organizational activity in white-collar crime studies has drawn heavy criticism from Donald R. Cressey (1989), who argued that the idea that corporations commit crimes is merely a legal fiction. Cressey maintained that "so-called organizational crime (another name for corporate crime) is committed by corporation executives, not by organizations." Cressey's position, for its part, has been criticized by John Braithwaite and Brent Fisse (1990). They argued that "sound scientific theories can be based on a foundation of corporate action," and noted that "[b]ecause the makeup of a corporation is different from that of a human being, it can do things that are not humanly possible, such as growing from infant to adult in a year, securing immortality." The essence of Braithwaite and Fisse's position appears in the following paragraph:

> The notion that individuals are real, observable, flesh and blood, while corporations are legal fictions, is false. Plainly, many features of corporations are observable (their assets, factories, decision-making procedures), while many features of individuals are not (e.g., personality, intention, unconscious minds).[9] (P. 19)

Finally, Braithwaite and Fisse insist that "[t]he products of organizations are more than the sum of the products of individual actions" (p. 22). Albert K. Cohen (1990) recently has supported the Braithwaite and Fisse viewpoint, and offered some guidelines to white-collar crime students for a better understanding of the "organization as an actor."

General Theory and Abuse of Trust

Two major forays into the definitional realm regarding white-collar crime have emerged in the past few years. Both offer strong arguments for the idiosyncratic stances they adopt. Whether either will have more than a passing influence on the manner in which white-collar crime comes to be viewed seems uncertain.

Travis Hirschi and Michael Gottfredson (1987) maintain that white-collar crime is nothing more than another form of lawbreaking—like rape, vandalism, and simple assault—and readily can be incorporated into an explanatory framework that accounts for the causes of all criminal behavior. For them, there is no relevant distinction that would necessitate white-collar crime being regarded as a special category of offense. They argue that focusing on the class position of the offender precludes all theories except those based on psychological differences between lawbreakers as an explanation for what they have done. Hirschi and Gottfredson maintain that persons studying juvenile delinquency have found no utility in examining as separate entities vandalism, arson, rape, or burglary, and that, therefore, "there is little reason to think that the idea of specialization in white-collar offenses will bear fruit."[10] They also argue, apropos white-collar crime, that crimes have in common features that make those engaging in any one of them extremely likely to engage in others as well, a proposition that could be upheld in regard to white-collar offenders only if the category of behavior is defined extremely broadly, as it is by these authors. Critics of Hirschi and Gottfredson maintain that the pursuit of a single explanation that will permit understanding of all forms of criminal activity is a chimera, doomed to eternal failure.

The second call to reconceptualize white-collar crime—or, as she terms it, to "liberate" the term—is that offered by Susan Shapiro (1990), who insists that white-collar crime ought to refer specifically and only to the violation of trust by which persons are enabled "to rob without violence and burgle without trespass" (p. 346). Such persons manipulate norms of disclosure, disinterestedness, and role competence. Their behaviors involve lying, misrepresentation, stealing, misappropriation, self-dealing, corruption, and role conflict. As a whimsical example of misrepresentation, Shapiro tells the story of "Zoogate"—that the zoo in Houston advertised live cobras but actually displayed rubber replicas, since live cobras could not live under the lights in the area where they would have to be kept. Prosecution of crimes involving abuse of trust is handicapped, Shapiro points out, because of the ambiguity that renders victims unwitting and therefore unable to assist in prosecution, and the fact that the suspects tend to have custody of the crucial evidence against them. Shapiro grants that the Sutherland definitional heritage is not readily cast aside, because the concept of white-collar crime is "polemically powerful" and "palpably self-evident" (p. 357). She also grants that her redesign of the concept has its own problems—for instance, that it excludes antitrust crimes as well as corporate violence that grows out of deliberate decisions or negligence. Nonetheless, Shapiro concludes with a resounding indictment of the consequences of the usual way of looking at white-collar crime, which is said to have

> created an imprisoning framework for contemporary scholarship, impoverishing theory, distorting empirical inquiry, oversimplifying policy analysis, inflaming our muckraking instincts, and obscuring fascinating questions about the relationships between social organization and crime. (P. 362)

Conclusion

I proposed at the outset of the chapter to set forth a sample of the major contributions directed toward providing a satisfactory definition of white-collar crime so that readers might be helped to adjudicate the debate for themselves. Most certainly, I have intruded into the presentation of viewpoints a relatively strong indication of my personal preferences. In this final section, I want to formalize how I see some of the issues that have been considered in this chapter.

In writing for newspapers, reporters often strive to tie their stories into a more significant or at least more recognizable overarching framework. This search for a "news peg" has its analog in scientific work: all of us generally attend more readily to things that relate to matters about which we already are concerned rather than to unfamiliar issues. The extensive and excellent work of Wheeler and his colleagues at Yale University was funded by the U.S. Department of Justice as a response to concern with what was known as "white-collar crime." Therefore, it was incumbent upon the grant recipients to place their research under that heading and, when they gained access to federal court data, to insist that such data represented white-collar crime rather than to regard them as a collection of information about certain kinds of offenses against federal law.

Similarly, Shapiro's contribution most basically asks that a new line of inquiry, that focuses on abuse of trust, be pursued in scholarly work. There is no compelling reason that this call-to-arms be allied to the abandonment of traditional research on white-collar crime. Her blueprint may produce worthwhile scholarly and policy products. Shapiro's argument against the traditional study of white-collar crime, however, seems gratuitous, since it is not—and probably cannot be—accompanied by a demonstration of the truth of the assertion that intellectual, political, or social life would be better served by attending to abuses of trust rather than abuses of power.

My personal belief is that, whatever the loss incurred by the mounting of wayward inquiries, the preferred situation is that which encourages research and policy people to pursue those kinds of inquiries that strike them as offering the greatest personal, professional, and public reward. That position, of course, so stated, has elements both of the platitudinous and the pious, but I know of no other way to convey it. In regard to white-collar crime, I remain persuaded that Sutherland, however errantly, focused on a matter of singular practical and intellectual importance—the abuse of power by persons who are situated in high places where they are provided with the opportunity for such abuse. To my mind, the excellent study by Hagan and Parker of the punishment of securities fraud in Canada illustrates how adherence to the Sutherland tradition can produce valuable findings. In my more ardent, youthful days I predicted that unless the term "white-collar crime" was accorded a tighter definition it would remain "so broad and indefinite as to fall into inevitable desuetude" (Geis, 1962, p. 171). Instead, as this chapter indicates, in my more ancient state, almost thirty years down the line, the concept remains vital and compelling. I find myself today in agreement with John Braithwaite's (1985, p. 19) suggestion that "[p]robably the most sensible way to proceed . . . is to stick with Sutherland's definition." This, he points out, at least excludes welfare cheats and credit-card frauds from the territory. Thereafter, Braithwaite would "partition the domain into major types of white collar crime" in order to generate sound theory (p. 3). If his were a legislative motion, and I a member, I would second it. Then, during debate, I would be certain to read into the record Robert Nisbet's (1965) advice:

Beyond a certain point, it is but a waste of time to seek tidy semantic justifications for concepts used by creative minds. The important and all-too-neglected task in philosophy and social theory is that of observing the ways in which abstract concepts are converted by their creators into methodologies and perspectives which provide new illumination of the world. (P. 39)

REFERENCES

Bell, D. (1960). Crime as an American way of life. In *The end of ideology.* New York: Free Press.

Benson, M. L., and Walker, E. (1988). Sentencing the white-collar offender. *American Sociological Review, 53,* 294–302.

Braithwaite, J. (1985). White collar crime. In R. H. Turner and J. F. Short, eds. *Annual review of sociology,* 1–25. Vol. 11. Palo Alto, Calif.: Annual Reviews.

Braithwaite, J., and Fisse, B. (1985). Varieties of responsibility and organizational crime. *Law & Policy, 7,* 315–343.

Braithwaite, J., and Fisse, B. (1990). On the plausibility of corporate crime theory. In W. S. Laufer and F. Adler, eds. *Advances in criminological theory,* Vol. 2, 15–38. New Brunswick, N.J.: Transaction Books.

Burgess, E. W. (1950). Comment, and concluding comment. *American Journal of Sociology, 56,* 32–34.

Caldwell, R. G. (1958). A re-examination of the concept of white-collar crime. *Federal Probation, 22,* 30–36.

Chapman, J. R. (1980). *Economic realities and the female offender.* Lexington, Mass.: Lexington Books.

Cherney, R. W. (1981). *Populism, progressivism and the transformation of Nebraska politics, 1885–1915.* Lincoln: University of Nebraska Press.

Clinard, M. B. (1952). *The black market: A study of white collar crime.* New York: Rinehart.

Clinard, M. B., and Quinney, R. (1973). *Criminal behavior systems: A typology* (2d ed.). New York: Holt, Rinehart and Winston.

Cohen, A. K. (1990). Criminal actors: Natural persons and collectivities. In School of Justice Studies, Arizona State University, ed. *New direction in the study of justice, law, and social control,* 101–125. New York: Plenum.

Coleman, J. W. (1989). *The criminal elite: The sociology of white collar crime* (2d ed.). New York: St. Martin's Press.

Cressey, D. R. (1953). *Other people's money: A study in the social psychology of embezzlement.* Glencoe, Ill.: Free Press.

———. (1989). The poverty of theory in corporate crime research. In W. S. Laufer and F. Adler, eds. *Advances in criminological theory,* Vol. 1, 31–56. New Brunswick, N.J.: Transaction Books.

Daly, K. (1989). Gender and varieties of white-collar crime. *Criminology, 27,* 769–793.

Edelhertz, H. (1970). *The nature, impact and prosecution of white-collar crime.* Washington, D.C.: Law Enforcement Assistance Administration, U.S. Department of Justice.

Ermann, M. D., and Lundman, R. J. (1978). Deviant acts by complex organizations: Deviance and social control at the organizational level of analysis. *The Sociological Quarterly, 19,* 56–67.

Geis, G. (1962). Toward a delineation of white-collar offenses. *Sociological Inquiry, 32,* 160–171.

———. (1984). White-collar and corporate crime. In R. F. Meier, ed. *Major forms of crime,* 137–166. Beverly Hills: Sage.

Green, G. S. (1990). *Organizational crime.* Chicago: Nelson Hall.

Hagan, J., Nagel-Bernstein, I. H., and Albonetti, C. (1980). The differential sentencing of white-collar offenders in ten federal district courts. *American Sociological Review, 45,* 802–820.

Hagan, J., and Parker, P. (1985). White-collar crime and punishment: The class structure and legal sanctioning of securities violations. *American Sociological Review, 50,* 302–316.

Hartung, F. E. (1950). White-collar offenses in the wholesale meat industry in Detroit. *American Journal of Sociology, 56,* 25–34.

Hirschi, T., and Gottfredson, M. (1987). Causes of white-collar crime. *Criminology, 25,* 957.

Hopkins, A. (1978). *Crime, law and business: The sociological aspects of Australian monopoly law.* Canberra, Australia: Australian Institute of Criminology.

Kadish, S. H. (1963). Some observations on the use of criminal sanctions in enforcing economic regulations. *University of Chicago Law Review, 30,* 423–449.

Kellens, G. (1974). *Banqueroute et banqueroutiers.* Brussels: Dessart et Mardaga.

Levi, M. (1981). *The phantom capitalists: The organisation and control of long-firm fraud.* London: Heinemann.

Liebl, H., and Liebl, K. (1985). *Internationale bibliographie zur wirtschaftskriminalitat.* Pfaffenweiler, Germany: Centaurus-Verlagsgesellschaft.

Lin, Dong-Mao (1984). *The study of economic crime.* Taipei: Central Police College.

Mason, R., and Calvin, L. D. (1978). A study of admitted income tax evasion. *Law and Society Reveiw, 13,* 73–89.

Newman, D. J. (1958). White-collar crime: An overview and analysis. *Law and Contemporary Problems, 23,* 737.

Nisbet, R. A. (1965). *Makers of modern social science: Emile Durkheim.* Englewood Cliffs, N.J.: Prentice Hall.

Pepinsky, H. E. (1976). *Crime and conflict: A study of law and society.* New York: Academic Press.

Quinney, R. (1964). The study of white collar crime: Toward a reorientation in theory and research. *Journal of Criminology, Criminal Law, and Police Science, 55,* 208–214.

Reiss, A. J., Jr., and Biderman, A. D. (1980). *Data sources on white-collar lawbreaking.* Washington, D.C.: Government Printing Office.

Rheingold, P. D. (1968). The MER/29 story: An instance of successful mass disaster litigation. *California Law Review, 56,* 116–148.

Saxon, M. S. (1980). *White collar crime: The problem and the federal response.* Washington, D.C.: Congressional Research Service, Library of Congress.

Schrager, L. S., and Short, J. F., Jr. (1977). Toward a sociology of organizational crime. *Social Problems, 25,* 407–419.

Schrenker, E. W. (1986). *No ivory tower: McCarthyism and the universities.* New York: Oxford University Press.

Shapiro, S. P. (1985). The road not taken: The elusive path to criminal prosecution for white-collar offenders. *Law and Society Review, 19,* 179–217.

―――. (1990). Collaring the crime, not the criminal: Liberating the concept of white-collar crime. *American Sociological Review, 55,* 346.

Sloan, A. P., Jr., and Sparkes, B. (1941). *Adventures of a white collar man.* New York: Doubleday Doran.

Smith, D. C., Jr. (1981). White-collar crime, organized crime, and the business establishment: Resolving a crisis in criminological theory. In P. Wickman and T. Dailey, eds. *White-collar and economic crime: Multidisciplinary and cross-national perspectives,* 23–38. Lexington, Mass.: Lexington Books.

Sparks, R. F. (1979). "Crime as business" and the female offender. In F. Adler and R. J. Simon, eds. *The criminology of deviant women,* 171–179. Boston: Houghton Mifflin Company.

Steffensmeier, D. (1989). On the causes of "white-collar" crime. *Criminology, 27,* 345–358.

Sutherland, E. H. (1940). White collar criminality. *American Sociological Review, 5,* 1–12.

―――. (1945). Is "white collar crime" crime? *American Sociological Review, 10,* 132–139.

————. (1949). The white collar criminal. In V. C. Branham and S. B. Kutash, *Encyclopedia of Criminology*, 511–515. New York: Philosophical Library.

————. (1949). *White collar crime*. New York: Dryden Press.

————. (1956). Crime of corporations. In A. K. Cohen, A. Lindesmith, and K. Schuessler, eds. *The Sutherland Papers*, 78–96. Bloomington: Indiana University Press.

————. (1983). *White collar crime: The uncut version*. New Haven: Yale University Press.

Tappan, P. W. (1947). Who is the criminal? *American Sociological Review*, *12*, 96–102.

Wheeler, S., and Rothman, M. (1982). The organization as weapon in white-collar crime. *Michigan Law Review*, *80*, 1403–1426.

Wheeler, S., Weisburd, D., and Bode, N. (1982). Sentencing the white-collar offender: Rhetoric and reality. *American Sociological Review*, *47*, 641–659.

Wheeler, S., Weisburd, D., Waring, E., and Bode, N. (1988). White collar crimes and criminals. *American Criminal Law Review*, *25*, 346.

NOTES

1. For biographical details regarding Sutherland, see Gilbert Geis and Colin Goff, "Introduction," in Edwin H. Sutherland, *White Collar Crime: The Uncut Version* (New Haven: Yale University Press, 1983), ix–xxxiii.

2. Daniel Bell similarly excludes embezzlers from the white-collar territory because of their middle-class status: "Crime as an American Way of Life," in *The End of Ideology* (New York: Free Press, 1960), 382.

3. It has been argued that tax evasion ought to be regarded as a white-collar crime, and that all persons, regardless of their social positions, who evade taxes ought to be studied together. Robert Mason and Lyle D. Calvin, "A Study of Admitted Income Tax Evasion," *Law and Society Review*, *13* (1978), 73–89.

4. A brief sample of non-American writings includes Lin Dong-Mao, *The Study of Economic Crime* (Taipei: Central Police College, 1984); Andrew Hopkins, *Crime, Law and Business: The Sociological Aspects of Australian Monopoly Law* (Canberra, Australia: Australian Institute of Criminology, 1978); Georges Kellens, *Banqueroute et Banqueroutiers* (Brussels: Dessart et Mardaga, 1974); Michael Levi, *The Phantom Capitalists: The Organisation and Control of Long-Firm Fraud* (London: Heinemann, 1981). The most comprehensive white-collar crime bibliography has been produced in Germany: Hildegard Liebl and Karlhans Liebl, *Internationale Bibliographie zur Wirtshcaftskriminalitat* (Pfaffenweiler, Germany: Centaurus-Verlagsgesellschaft, 1985).

5. The two American textbooks on white-collar crime employ slight variants of the Clinard and Quinney position. James S. Coleman defines white-collar crime as a "violation of the law committed by a person or group of persons in the course of their otherwise respected and legitimate occupation or financial activity" (*The Criminal Elite*, 2d ed., New York: St. Martin's Press, 1989, 5). Gary S. Green entitled his text *Organizational Crime* (Chicago: Nelson Hall, 1990), and defined its subject as (1) acts punishable by law; and (2) those committed through opportunity created by an occupational role that is legal (p. 13).

6. A replication of the study using different courts has reached somewhat different conclusions: Michael Benson and Esteban Walker, "Sentencing the White-Collar Offender," *American Sociological Review*, 53 (1988), 294–302.

7. For a defense of the sample, see Stanton Wheeler and Mitchell Rothman, "The Organization as Weapon in White-Collar Crime," *Michigan Law Review*, *80* (1982), 1403–1426.

8. Another writer has more aptly described such offenders as "frayed-collar criminals." Jane Roberts Chapman, *Economic Realities and the Female Offender* (Lexington, Mass.: Lexington Books, 1980), 68.

9. See also John Braithwaite and Brent Fisse, "Varieties of Responsibility and Organizational Crime," *Law & Policy*, *7* (1985), 315–343.

10. A critique is found in Darrell Steffensmeier, "On the Causes of 'White-Collar' Crime," *Criminology*, *27* (1989), 345–358.

· 2 ·

The Theory of White-Collar Crime

From Sutherland to the 1990s

JAMES WILLIAM COLEMAN

Right from the beginning of his work on white-collar crime, Sutherland always gave central importance to the theoretical understanding of its causes. The first two sentences in *White-Collar Crime* state that "This book is a study in the theory of criminal behavior. It is an attempt to reform the theory of criminal behavior, not to reform anything else" (1949, p. v). Sutherland's emphasis on the importance of theory was not, however, shared by most of his successors. Many works on white-collar crime either display a kind of atheoretical empiricism (albeit based on a thick network of unexamined theoretical assumptions), or such a narrow area of theoretical concern that their conclusions float unattached to any general understanding of white-collar crime. But the literature also contains a body of perceptive theoretical work that has grown substantially over the years, and it is the objective of this essay to trace its central themes and the outlines of its development. Geis (1985) divides the general study of white-collar crime into three periods, and these categories also apply reasonably well to its theoretical development. The first of these periods began in 1939 with Sutherland's introduction of the term and continued on until the early 1960s when the interest he stimulated among students, colleagues, and critics finally began to die down. The second period, from around 1964 to 1975, was a time of relative quiescence. The current era began in the second half of the 1970s with a virtual explosion of interest in white-collar crime, which led to the sustained scholarly attention that continues to this day.

The First Wave: Sutherland and His Students

Sutherland's name has become almost synonymous with his famous theory of differential association that he believed was able to account for all types of crime including, of course, the white-collar crimes. Simply put, differential association holds that criminal behavior is learned like any other behavior, and that this process of learning takes place primarily in intimate, personal groups. The more one associates with those with favorable attitudes toward crime, the more likely one is to become a criminal. Applying these principles to white-collar crime, Sutherland vigorously rejected any notion that it was caused by the immorality, physical make-up, or psychological characteristics of the criminals. People become white-collar criminals because they learn to act that way, often from their associates on the job. In Sutherland's eyes at least, many types of business careers virtually require some criminal activities, as can be seen from his often-repeated characterization of the major corporations as habitual criminals.

Students of white-collar crime have too often seen Sutherland's theoretical contribution solely in terms of the differential association theory. But he was too sophisticated a sociologist to ignore the need to explain the origins of the attitudes that were learned through differential association. In the various editions of *Principles of Criminology* (1924, 1934, 1939, 1947), he gave considerable attention to this issue, which he explained through the use of the concept of social disorganization. (In its last edition, Sutherland said the term "differential social organization" was preferable to social disorganization, but the substantive content of his discussion was largely unchanged.) Sutherland, however, seems to have had second thoughts about the value of this approach by the time *White Collar Crime* was published in 1949, since he concluded that "social disorganization has not proved to be a very useful hypothesis up to the present time" (p. 256).

Whatever the causes of this change in attitude, it is clearly a mistake to view *White Collar Crime* as Sutherland's only, or even his most convincing, attempt to explain the causes of this phenomenon. Sutherland was deeply concerned with the crimes of the rich and powerful long before he ever used the term "white-collar crime" to describe them. For example, in the second edition of *Principles of Criminology*, published five years before he introduced the concept of white-collar crime in 1939, Sutherland wrote that many of the activities of the "well-to-do classes" are "properly regarded as crimes and are probably much more prevalent and much more injurious to society than the robberies, burglaries, kidnappings, and murders which are direct and personal" (1934, p. 63). In the second edition, Sutherland also introduced a historical analysis of the societal processes that produce crimes, which set the background for the differential association theory introduced in the 1939 edition.

Sutherland began his analysis by comparing contemporary society with preliterate and peasant societies, where "the influences surrounding a person were steady, uniform, harmonious and consistent" (1934, p. 63). An individual's main satisfactions, according to Sutherland, were derived from cooperation with his or her family, and the family in turn took care of the individual's social and economic needs. Thus, most people were presented with a consistent set of expectations that provided only a single pattern of behavior to follow, and as a result "almost no crimes were committed" (p. 64). In contrast, the members of contemporary Western society are faced with a confusing mishmash of conflicting attitudes, values, standards, and ideals. Thus, Western society is characterized by a high degree of social disorganization, and, as a result, a great deal of crime.

Sutherland saw several causes of this disorganization that all stemmed from industrialization and the growth of capitalism. The principal agencies of social control—the large family and homogeneous neighborhood—broke down as a result of the increase in mobility. The ideal of political and economic individualism that developed as part of the revolt against the feudal system was not a "positive principle of social organization" and encouraged an individual to "disregard social welfare in the interest of his selfish satisfactions" (p. 66). Sutherland argued that the identification of wealth with personal worth produced an intense materialism that encouraged criminal behavior. Although he did see some trend toward social "reorganization" in the growth of corporations and associations, he felt that they were still under the sway of this ideology of individualism and "have no more interest in social welfare than did the competing individuals who preceded them" (p. 69).

How well have Sutherland's theories withstood the test of time? Despite its important contribution, the differential association theory certainly does not live up to Sutherland's claims to be an all-encompassing theory of crime. In one sense, Sutherland's assumption that all crime is learned from criminally oriented groups denies the possibility of true deviance, since everyone is seen to be conforming to the expectations of one group or another. But even if we grant that the majority of white-collar crimes are learned from others, we must still explain the origins of the deviant attitudes, values, and definitions that are passed from person to person. However, if the differential association theory is placed in the context of his discussion of social disorganization, Sutherland's approach becomes a much more powerful one that effectively combines the social psychological and structural dimensions of criminal etiology. But Sutherland's structural theorizing has its problems as well: for one thing his rosy view of life in traditional agricultural societies is hardly tenable in light of contemporary scholarship. Another weakness is his sketchy and incomplete discussion of the causes of the changes that produced the criminogenic conditions of contemporary industrial capitalism. But these quibbles can hardly take away from the fact that Sutherland's work was an enormous breakthrough that profoundly influenced succeeding generations of criminologists.

Sutherland's harbinger call for criminologists to pay attention to the crimes of the rich and powerful created two responses. One was the long-running debate with his critics about whether white-collar crime was "really" crime, and the other was a new interest in empirical studies of various white-collar crimes. Of this first wave of new research, it was Donald R. Cressey's (1953) study of convicted embezzlers that proved to have the most lasting theoretical importance. After a series of intensive interviews with incarcerated embezzlers, Cressey concluded that three conditions were necessary for an embezzlement to occur: first, the potential embezzler must have a "non-sharable" financial problem; second, he or she must have the knowledge necessary to commit an embezzlement, and; third, embezzlers must use a suitable rationalization to "adjust" the contradiction between their actions and the normative standards of society. While the first proposition has not been supported by subsequent research (Nettler, 1974; Zietz, 1981) and the second is rather self-evident, Cressey's concern with the process of rationalization was to become one of the major themes for white-collar research in the years ahead.

In exploring the rationalizations embezzlers used to justify their crimes, Cressey was providing empirical support for the theory of differential association by showing the specific definitions that were learned by embezzlers. But Cressey also expanded Sutherland's original formulation by drawing more broadly from the symbolic interactionist theory of motivation, which had been part of the original inspiration for the theory of differential association. A key point Cressey stressed was that these rationalizations were not just ex post facto excuses cooked up to justify an action already taken, but were psychologically present before the crime was committed and were a major part of the original motivation for the act. Four years after the publication of *Other People's Money*, Sykes and Matza (1957) called such rationalizations "techniques of neutralization"—a term that is now common in the literature on white-collar crime. Almost four decades later, there is little doubt that the general process of rationalization Cressey outlined is of central importance in understanding the motivation of white-collar criminals.

The Period of Latency

The controversy that Sutherland stimulated eventually died away, but unfortunately so did the basic research. Although white-collar crime won acceptance as an important field of criminology, there was very little new research in the period that runs from roughly 1964 to 1975. The major exception was the work of Gilbert Geis. His 1967 study of the price-fixing scandal in the heavy electrical industry was particularly noteworthy. Although it didn't break new theoretical ground, it did find support for the differential association theory and for Cressey's ideas about the importance of rationalizations. In the following year, Geis (1968) published a reader on white-collar crime that played a major role in keeping this subject before the criminological community.

It is difficult to be certain about the reasons the study of white-collar crime fell into such a lethargy. But Geis's (1985) suggestion that it was a delayed effect of McCarthyism and the cold-war demand for ideological conformity seems to hit close to the mark. While we associate the 1960s with the turmoil of the civil rights and anti-war movements, much of its academic agenda was set in the previous decade as criminology students in graduate schools selected their fields of study. Another factor, which is still very much with us today, was the unwillingness of government agencies to fund research likely to produce conclusions that are threatening to powerful corporate interests.

The Resurgence of Interest

Beginning in the middle of the 1970s, there was a remarkable resurgence of academic interest in white-collar crime. Although the reasons for this change are not entirely clear, it seems that the critical spirit of the 1960s had finally worked its way through the graduate schools and into the academic journals. The Watergate scandal also played a major role in alerting the public and the criminological community to the importance of crime in high places, and a string of new scandals—from Koreagate to the collapse of the savings and loan industry—have continually renewed those concerns. Even the federal government finally began funding studies of white-collar crime during the 1970s.

The volume and breadth of interest of this new research makes it difficult to summarize neatly, but it is fair to say that the theoretical work that emerged during this period focused in three general areas. First, there was the social psychology of white-collar crime and the motivation of individual criminals. The second area of concern was the overarching societal structures that produce white-collar offenses. And finally, corporate crime generated renewed interest, which benefited from an infusion of new perspectives from organizational theory.

The Social Psychology of White-Collar Crime

The central question in the social psychology of white-collar crime has remained the same ever since Sutherland's time: Why do white-collar criminals do it? Or, a bit more precisely put: What are the origins of the motivation for white-collar crime? Sutherland's answer was, of course, that white-collar criminals learn their behavior from association with others, and Cressey added that they also learn rationalizations that help neutralize the normative standards that condemn such behavior. A great deal of subsequent research— including Geis (1967), Chibnall and Saunders (1977), Conklin (1977), Meier and Geis (1982), Benson (1985), Coleman (1987), and Daly (1989)—utilized this approach. There is, however, a wide variation in the theoretical sophistication among such studies. On the most simplistic level are the journalistically oriented works in which a group of white-collar offenders are interviewed about the reasons for their behavior, and their accounts are presented without theoretical background or interpretation. While such efforts can provide useful material for later analysis, they are of little direct theoretical importance. More typical among academic works are those that combine some description of the offenders' motivations and rationalizations with either differential association or rationalization theory.

At its most sophisticated, this work also embeds the insights of those theories in the broader interactionist theory of motivation. From this perspective, motivation is a symbolic construct and individual behavior is explained in terms of the way actors define themselves and the social situations they face. Although Sutherland felt that such definitions were learned almost entirely from others, Mead himself gave a much greater role to individual creativity in actively constructing social reality. Although Cressey also cast a disparaging eye toward anyone claiming that "free will" held a role in human behavior, his theory of rationalization actually works better when seen as an account of the way white-collar criminals actively reconstruct their symbolic understanding of the world so that they can pursue criminal activities while maintaining a positive self-concept.

Although interactionist theory is the dominant paradigm in the literature on the motivation of white-collar offenders, there is another common approach rooted in the widely held notion that white-collar criminals commit their offenses because they simply want to make a "fast buck," and their crimes are easy to get away with. Such assumptions stand behind a great deal of work on white-collar crime, but they are often so much a part of the researchers' taken-for-granted reality that they are given little direct analytic attention. One exception can be found in the deterrence theory used, for example, in the work of Hollinger and Clark (1983). But by itself, the failure of deterrence (the reasons for which will be touched upon in the next section of this essay) provides only half an answer to the problem of why people commit white-collar crime. A theory of deterrence must be combined with some notion of what motivates people to commit the crime in the first place, and in most cases classical theory is used to supply the answer.

This theory is based on the notion that people choose the course of action they believe will bring them the most pleasure and the least pain, and by this standard, white-collar crimes often look very attractive. As Hirschi and Gottfredson put it, "White-collar crimes . . . provide relatively quick, relatively certain benefit with minimum effort" (1987, p. 959). Hirschi and Gottfredson see the classical theory as a foundation for a general theory that accounts for all types of crime. They argue that it not only contradicts the differential association theory pioneered by Sutherland, but is clearly superior to it. Yet, ironically, they fell into the same trap as Sutherland by claiming their theory as a universally valid explanation of all crime.

There is, in fact, little to be gained from casting the classical and interactionist theories as mutually exclusive competitors or claiming superiority of one approach over the other, as Sutherland and Hirshi and Gottfredson all did. The soundest foundation for a theory of white-collar crime is laid by synthesizing the insights of these approaches. Classical theory provides a strong corrective to the interactionists' tendency to ignore the biological basis of behavior. Everything is not learned: humans are genetically programmed to seek pleasure and avoid pain. But the classical theorists are far too simplistic in their understanding of how that basic fact influences behavior. The unique human capacity for reflective self-consciousness means that unlike other animals, humans guide their behavior from a symbolic understanding of their environment. Humans do not simply seek pleasure and avoid pain. Biological pleasures and pains become associated with symbolic constructs in complex ways on both the conscious and unconscious levels. Individuals determine which courses of action are open to them, and the kinds of pleasures and pains each are likely to bring, by means of the symbolic processes analyzed by interactionist theory.

The Structural Dimension:
Law and Culture

Seen from a structural viewpoint, the causes of white-collar crime appear quite different from the social psychological explanations just discussed. But there is a strong link between the two—the cultural predispositions that are embedded in our social structure and shared by individual actors. Over the years, numerous criminologists have commented on the criminogenic values and attitudes that are characteristic of Western culture. Meier and Geis (1982, p. 98), for example, write that

> much criminal activity is responsive to the kinds of things for which we stand. Individualism, hedonism, material-ism—these are criminogenic values: they have utility for the production of many social and individual boons, they may be preferable on some grounds to different social emphases. But they have their price, and part of that price clearly appears to be the phenomenon of white-collar crime.

Unfortunately, only a few sociologists have followed up on such insights to create a complete theory of the nature and causes of these criminogenic values. Among the first of these was Sutherland himself, who saw the cultural roots of the crime problem in the social disorganization already discussed and what he called the "ideology of individualism" (1934, p. 69).

This system of beliefs, which might better be termed the "ideology of competitive individualism," holds that each person is an autonomous individual with the power of reason and free choice and is in large measure responsible for his or her own destiny. And this destiny is seen principally in terms of economic self-interest and the efforts to surpass one's fellows in the accumulation of wealth and status. I have argued elsewhere (Coleman 1987, 1988) that the origins of this new cultural orientation, which stands in sharp contrast to the equalitarian cooperative ethos characteristic of traditional hunting and gathering societies, can be traced to structural changes in the economic and ecological relationships that began with the agricultural revolution and were intensified by the process of industrialization. The growth of surplus wealth that created the

· 61

economic foundation for a structured system of social inequality and status competition was a key factor. The higher level of economic insecurity characteristic of more "advanced" systems of social organization, and the status insecurity that is particularly intense in industrial society, were also important elements.

Geis (1982), Braithwaite (1988), and others have argued that the existence of a substantial amount of white-collar crime in communist nations indicates that the capitalist economic system cannot be the cause of white-collar crime. There is considerable logic in this reasoning, and it is clear that the origins of these criminogenic tendencies are to be found in industrialism itself, whether in its capitalist or communist versions. But it is also important not to be led to false conclusions based on an unrealistic picture of the nature of those communist societies. Despite official ideology, these nations have always had a high level of inequality accompanied by considerable social mobility, and, therefore, status competition to win the higher positions of power and privilege is inevitable. Despite the official exhortations to work for the common good, the individualistic desire to win personal gain is still a strong motivator of criminal behavior in communist nations (Coleman, 1988).

Another important set of structural issues revolves around the law and its enforcement. The idea that white-collar offenders commit their crimes because they are unlikely to be punished has been repeated so often that it has become something of a sociological truism. But while there is no doubt that white-collar and especially corporate offenders are far less likely to be punished for their crimes than other criminals (for a review of some of the evidence on this point see Coleman, 1989, pp. 153–198), the question of why this is so has received surprisingly little theoretical attention. Although a few researchers have explored the specific techniques used to thwart the enforcement process (for example, Cressey, 1976; Conklin, 1977, pp. 109–129; Dowie, 1979; Clinard and Yeager, 1980; Coleman, 1985), most have simply chalked it up to the vast economic and political power of the corporations and left it at that.

This weakness of the enforcement effort was widely acknowledged from the beginning of the upsurge of interest in white-collar crime in the 1970s, but that fact soon posed to criminologists a puzzling question: If the corporations are so powerful that they are usually able to defeat the government's enforcement efforts with relative ease, how is it that they allowed these laws to be enacted in the first place? The pluralists' answer is simply that the corporations are really not that powerful and they were unable to prevent the criminalization of activities that were so damaging to other interest groups. Such a solution has, however, seldom been advanced by criminologists concerned with white-collar crime—at least in that form. One reason may be that it contradicts most of the contemporary sociological literature on the structure of power in industrial capitalism and ignores the evidence of great corporate power derived from so many studies of white-collar crime. A second problem is that the pluralist response still leaves us with another equally puzzling question. If the corporations are not powerful enough to shape the legislative process, why have they been so successful at defeating the enforcement effort?

In 1979, McCormick drew on the general literature regarding the sociology of law to argue that the Sherman Antitrust Act was "essentially an effort to protect and preserve the dominant economic structure by deflecting the potentially disruptive power of dissident groups" (p. 411). He did grant some power to dissident groups, holding that the act "fully represented the short-run interest of neither class involved." In the long run, however, "the power of the dominant economic elite was such that it was considerably more successful in having its interests and views expressed in the form and substance of the law" (p. 414). Thus, antitrust legislation is still seen as a result of pressure from below, but the actual goal is to placate this opposition without threatening elite interests, rather than to serve the greater good of society. The idea that a particular piece of legislation was intended for symbolic rather than instrumental purposes was subsequently applied to numerous other pieces of white-collar crime legislation as well (for example, Donnelly, 1982, and Stearns, 1979).

Around the same time, Harold Barnett (1979, 1981) drew on the critical theory of the state to broaden the theory of legal formation. In these articles, Barnett argued that the state must meet two contradictory demands in dealing with such problems. The state must promote the capital accumulation (profits) necessary for economic prosperity in a capitalist society, but it must also preserve its legitimacy of the eyes of the public by responding to its concerns about the harm caused by white-collar deviance. Obviously, this is a situation most easily resolved by the kind of symbolic gestures described above. Calavita (1983) added a key insight to our understanding of the dynamics of symbolic politics in her study of the Occupational Safety and Health Administration. She concluded that although OSHA was created merely as a symbolic gesture to win political support from concerned workers, those symbolic gains eventually helped to produce real substantive advantages for workers by legitimatizing their demands for occupational safety and providing encouragement and hope that their goals could actually be achieved. Laureen Snider (1987) expanded on this logic, arguing that most of the gains won against corporate offenders in recent years were not due to government enforcement efforts, but to ideological changes that "upped the ante" required for corporations to maintain public legitimacy.

The Theory of Organizational Crime

One of the most significant recent trends has been the growth of a new theory of organizational crime in the middle ground between the social psychological theories of individual motivation and the macro level structural theories. Drawing heavily from the general theories of organizational behavior, and, at its best, integrating social psychological and structural level variables, the theory of organizational crime has received more attention in the last two decades than any other area in the field of white-collar crime. This new concern first began in the middle 1970s when Stone (1975), Cohen (1977), Schrager and Short (1978), and Ermann and Lundman (1978), among others, began calling attention to the need to understand corporate and organizational crime in its own terms and not just as an adjunct to individualistically oriented explanations. But most of these early works did not attempt to advance a theoretical explanation for organizational crime. One of the first efforts to present a comprehensive theory was undertaken by Conklin (1977, pp. 34–71), and he was soon followed by many others including Sherman (1978), Gross (1978, 1980), Kramer (1982), Vaughan (1983), and Braithwaite (1989). Following Kramer (1982), we will organize their findings about the causes of organizational crime under three headings: organizational goals, organizational environment, and organizational structure.

Organizational Goals

One of the most obvious influences on organizational criminality is the goals an organization is trying to pursue. Many theorists of organizational crime employ some form of opportunity theory to argue that the greater the difficulty in obtaining organizational goals legitimately, the greater likelihood that some sort of illegal means will be used. Since most of the research has been on corporate crime, the goal of profitability has been the focus of the most interest. Over four decades of research on corporate crime has shown that firms with weak or declining profits are the most likely to break the law (Katona, 1946; Lane, 1954; Staw and Szwajkowski, 1975; Barnett, 1984). As Clinard and Yeager (1980) put it in summarizing the conclusions from their broadly based study of corporate crime, "Firms in depressed industries as well as relatively poorly performing firms in all industries tend to violate the law to a greater degree" (p. 129).

Profit is not, of course, the only goal that organizations pursue. Gross (1978) argues that there is nothing especially criminogenic about profit as an organizational goal. Rather, he sees the culprit as any demand for goal achievement. For example, the desire by a political party to eliminate its opposition or of a nationalized industry to meet its production goals may also stimulate organizational crime. Moreover, as Perrow (1972) and Kramer (1982) point out, general organizational goals must be translated into specific subgoals for different segments of an organization. A large corporation cannot simply tell its engineering department or its advertising agency to "make a profit." It must provide specific objectives for them to pursue, and it is those objectives that will most directly influence their criminal behavior. For example, Kramer's work on the Ford Pinto shows its poor safety to be the result of the subgoals its engineers were given (that is, that the car weigh less than 2,000 pounds and cost less than $2,000). Another common subgoal is to control the various resources necessary to achieve the primary organizational goals (see Vaughn, 1983, pp. 54–104). Yet with all this said, it would be a mistake to assume that all organizational goals are equally criminogenic. Although there is, to my knowledge, no quantitative work on this issue, the efforts of a religious organization to "save souls" or a welfare agency to help the poor seem far less likely to encourage crime than the demand that a private corporation turn a profit or cease to exist.

Organizational Environment

A second major influence on organizational criminality is the external environment of the organization (see Pfeffer and Salancik, 1978). At least for the corporate organizations that have received most of the scholarly attention, there seem to be two general sets of environmental conditions that are of key importance—the legal restraints and the economic structure of the industry. Concerning the former, it is clear that corporations whose activities are subject to tight legal restrictions that are weakly enforced are the most likely to violate the law. Although lawyers and legally oriented social scientists tend to take the definition of corporate criminality as a given, the corporations actually have a great deal of power to influence their legal environment both in terms of specific legislative acts and the way those acts are enforced. In addition to the general structural considerations discussed above, at least three sets of forces are critical in determining the legal environment of the corporations in different industries. One factor is the political power of the corporations subject to a particular type of regulation, which, in turn, is determined by such factors as their overall economic strength, their degree of political organization, and their centrality to networks of elite power. The second factor is the strength of the organized groups advocating legal restraints on corporate activities. The power of such groups is determined, at least in part, by their size, their economic resources, and their degree of external support, and all of those are strongly influenced by the visibility and the perceived harm caused by the corporate deviance at issue. A third factor is the overall climate of public opinion and the values and ideology it reflects (see Coleman, 1989, pp. 124–152).

The most salient economic factors in the corporate environment concern the market structure and economic organization of its industry. The most heavily researched question concerning market structure is the relationship between antitrust violations and economic concentration (Burton, 1966; Reidel, 1968; Pfeffer and Salancik, 1978; Hay and Kelly, 1974; Posner, 1970; Asch and Seneca, 1969; and Clinard et al., 1979). However, the findings of this research have been contradictory and no clear conclusions can be drawn from the current evidence. One of the principle problems, like so many other quantitative studies of white-collar crime, is the reliance on the reports of enforcement agencies as the sole indicator of the rate of criminal violations. There is, however, general agreement on one point, although it is based as much on theoretical as empirical grounds: The opportunities to engage in antitrust violations are less attractive to firms in industries with a very low concentration ratio, because such a conspiracy would require so many participants that it would be extremely difficult to conceal. But even this point is open to some question. Gross (1980) argues that "organizational sets"—groups of similar organizations whose actions are visible to each other—may facilitate antitrust conspiracies by reducing the number of players that must enter into a conspiracy. The key point about these sets is that they tend to have an internal system of stratification with dominant organizations, middle-level organizations, and marginal organizations. If there is a relatively small number of firms at the top of these stratified organizational sets, then the attractiveness of antitrust conspiracies will increase regardless of the total number of firms in the industry.

The relationship between manufacturers and the companies that handle their distribution and sales may also be conducive to white-collar crime. In the 1970s, Farberman (1975) and Leonard and Weber (1970) concluded that the economic organization of the automobile industry virtually forces individual dealers to engage in shady business practices, because intense sales pressures from the oligopolistic firms that control the supply of new automobiles force dealers to sell cars at an unprofitably low price in order to maximize their sales volume. Denzin (1977) found similar conditions in the liquor industry, where distillers impose such high sales quotas on their distributors that they feel compelled to give illegal, under-the-table incentives to retailers.

However, Needleman and Needleman (1979) criticized the assumption in such studies that the participants are forced into criminal activity. They argue that it is usually more accurate to talk about "crime-facilitative" rather than "crime-coercive" systems. Their study of the securities industry, for example, found many conditions that facilitate criminal activities—the legal doctrines limiting the financial risk in handling stolen securities, the strong financial incentives to keep up market flow, and the traditions of trust and professional solidarity in the banking industry—but those conditions did not actually force individuals to participate in criminal acts.

Another critical set of environmental factors comes from the business practices of a firm's competition within its industry. There is considerable evidence that illegal activities spread from one organization in an industry to another (Barnett, 1984; Sutherland, 1949, pp. 241–246; Clinard and Yeager, 1980, pp. 60–63; Cressey, 1976). The knowledge about possible illegal opportunities is inevitably shared among individuals who work for different firms in the same industry. Seeing a competitor increase its profits by illegal means is also likely to enhance the attractiveness of such behavior, while the failure of a competitor's illegal enterprise is likely to have the opposite effect. Moreover, the profits generated by illegal means may allow a firm to lower its prices or take other advantages over its competition, thus placing strong pressure on other firms to follow suit or face serious economic consequences.

Internal Culture and Structure

Sociologists have examined many different variables that operate within organizations to promote or retard criminal behavior, including organizational size, the structure of internal controls, and organizational subcultures. Many have claimed that there is a relationship between the size of a corporation and its involvement in crime. Most often, the impersonality of the large corporation is held to promote criminality, but a few have claimed that the large corporation's superior professional expertise better enables it to comply with complicated government regulations. However, empirical research has generally not found a strong relationship between these two variables. Lane (1954), for example, found firm size to have contradictory effects on criminality depending on the industry and the type of violation involved and concluded that there is "no clear relationship between size and violations" (p. 98). Clinard and Yeager (1980, p. 130) reached similar conclusions. Although size per se is not clearly linked to corporate criminality, many criminologists have argued that the diffusion of authority that may occur within a very large organization is highly criminogenic. Clinard and his associates (1979, p. 7) claim that the decentralization of decision making "is almost by definition, accompanied by the establishment of elaborate hierarchies, based on authority position and functional duties. This allows the abdication of personal responsibility for almost every type of decision. . . . Under these conditions almost any type of corporate criminality, from production of faulty or dangerous products to bribery, bid-rigging and even theft is possible." Taking a slightly different tack, Gross (1980) holds that the proliferation of semi-independent organizational structures within large corporations promotes illegal activities simply by creating so many more autonomous organizational actors.

Another variable in corporate structure concerns its institutionalized response to the demands of the law. Braithwaite (1984, 1989) holds that corporations that have formally institutionalized "compliance divisions" to ensure conformity to the law are less likely than others to engage in criminal activities. And this is especially true if the compliance division is given real power within the organization and a central location in its information flow.

But more important than the variations in the formal structure of the corporations are the subcultures they foster. Numerous social scientists have commented on the way large corporations encourage a narrow pragmatic approach to organizational responsibilities among their employees, which strongly discourages independent ethical judgments. Weber's (1964, pp. 329–341) early work on bureaucracy pointed out the importance of having employees' behavior determined by the formal requirement of the roles they occupy, and not individual characteristics such as personal, ethical codes. C. Wright Mills (1959, p. 343) saw this as part of the "structural immorality" of American society, and more recent students of organizational behavior have identified several processes that operate to dull individual moral sensibilities. One of the primary techniques of organizational control is the ability of an organization to shape the symbolic definition of the situations employees face on the job (see Perrow, 1972). The network of definitions in which employees participate may make unethical or illegal activities appear as just another routine aspect of the job and of no particular moral significance.

Another factor that facilitates this process of "ethical numbing" is the relative isolation of corporate managers from significant interactions with those outside their own social world. As Peter Drucker (1972, p. 88) put it, the executive's "contacts outside of business tend to be limited to people of the same set, if not to people working for the same organization" (also see Sutherland,

1949, pp. 247–253). A third factor in this process is the advantage those who are, as Edward Gross (1978) put it, "morally flexible" have when it comes to hiring and promoting. As a result of these forces, persons who rise to key decision-making positions are unlikely to have strong ethical convictions that might run counter to the financial interests of the corporation. And in addition to these social-psychological processes is the blunt fact that employees who refuse to go along with their firm's illegal schemes may face dismissal or loss of lucrative promotions.

All these pressures to conform to corporate expectations makes the norms and "ethical climate" to which employees adapt that much more important. One widely recognized influence on the ethical climate is the corporation's chief executive officer. Cressey's (1980) findings on this issue are fairly typical: "I interviewed about two dozen internal and external auditors. Every one of these financial executives said that the ethical behavior of company personnel is determined by the example set by top management." (For similar conclusions see Clinard and Yeager, 1980, p. 60; Clinard, 1982.) Of course, this influence is not a one-way street, and the attitudes of the chief executive officer are influenced and constrained by the corporate subculture, just like those of any other employee.

Braithwaite (1989) argues that corporations subject to government regulation tend to develop "culture of compliance" or a "culture of resistance" to the demands of the law. He holds that enforcement agencies and the larger community have an important influence in determining which kind of subculture develops. When enforcement agencies are perceived to be unreasonable and they treat corporations and their leadership as "irredeemably crooked," a culture of resistance is encouraged. On the other hand, the likelihood that a culture of compliance will develop is enhanced when enforcement is firm but flexible, and the enforcement agencies and the wider community help to shame those responsible for corporate illegalities.

Perhaps because it is the newest field of interest among students of white-collar crime, the research on the organizational level is the most scattered and lacking in coherent focus. Although it is fair to say that the research is coalescing around the exploration of the organizational cultures, the organizational structures, and the organizational environments that encourage illegal activities, there are an unusually large number of conflicting findings in this area.

One of the main problems is that so many researchers have been seduced into carrying on empirical research based on unreliable data. In my view, at least, the reports of official enforcement agencies are far too weak a measure of the actual rate of criminal behavior to serve as the basis for reliable statistical analysis. The best work done so far in this field is the case studies that carefully analyze the conditions in particular organizations or industries, and I would suggest that lacking the development of a significant new data base, this approach offers the brightest hope of future progress in the years ahead.

Putting It All Together

The explosion of interest in the theory of white-collar crime has produced something of an embarrassment of riches. As we have seen, the field now sports a bewildering variety of different theories and approaches. While this is certainly preferable to the sole reliance on Sutherland and his followers that characterized past eras, a salad bar of bits and pieces from which researchers build their own theories is likely to leave us without a clear, coherent focus. Yet despite all the contradictions and conflicts, an underlying theoretical framework for an understanding of white-collar crime on the individual, organizational, and societal levels is taking shape. All the researchers in these different areas certainly do not agree on a particular set of theoretical conclusions, or even a common approach, but as this review has shown there are enough convergences in their findings to prove that some very significant progress has been made. The next step, as Vaughan (chapter 5) suggests, is to show the interrelationships between different levels of analysis and link them together into an integrated theory of white-collar crime.

One striking fact that emerges from the effort to integrate and restate the research findings on these three levels is that each body of work points out a similar contradiction between the effort to achieve particularistic and universal goals. While this tension assumes a somewhat different form at each level, these contractions clearly reflect and reinforce each other.

On the individual level, this contradiction takes the form of the conflict between the desire for maximum individual reward and the desire to maintain a positive construction of ourselves and our behavior. The classical theory's contention that those rewards are essentially the maximization of pleasure and the minimization of pain certainly rings true, but we must also recognize the social dimension that reflexive human consciousness adds to the physiology of pleasure and pain. This same human capacity for self-consciousness also creates powerful restraints on the pursuit of those fundamental goals. Our ability to stand back and see our behavior from the eyes of others leads to the condemnation of many courses of action that would otherwise be highly rewarding. The research on white-collar crime shows that this tension is often resolved through the use of justifications which allow the offender to maintain a positive image of self while pursuing otherwise condemned behavior. But this struggle does not take place in isolation—organizational and societal pressures forcefully impinge on the individual to tilt the scales in one direction or the other. On the one hand, strongly held societal and subcultural norms reinforce the condemnation of predatory behavior, while stores of cultural knowledge provide rationalizations that help neutralize those norms. On the other hand, society and its organizational structures create opportunities for reward and threats of punishment that determine the original attractiveness of a particular white-collar crime.

This same contradiction is carried through to the organizational level, although in a somewhat different form. In one sense, organizations are merely trying to meet their participants' desires for reward on a group basis rather than an individual basis. But the matter is much more complex than that since organizations obviously do not give equal priority to rewarding all of their participants. At a minimum, complex organizations attempt to provide the greatest possible reward for their dominant coalitions and sufficient reinforcements to maintain the cooperation of their other participants. The normative restraints on complex organizations are particularly dependent on external pressures, such as the threat of government sanctions or loss of consumer confidence. But there are also significant internal pressures from the individual level via employees who want the organization to live up to their own ethical standards.

At the level of intersocietal competition, the state operates much like any other organization. But in its role as a mediator of conflict and regulator of internal social behavior, it functions on a different basis. The state is too far removed to be responsive to the desires of most single individuals (there are, of course, usually a few powerful individuals who are exceptions to this rule), but the state does respond to the demands of powerful groups that are, in turn, responding to the self-interests of their individual participants. In a capitalist society, that generally means the interest of business groups, while in other societies military or political bureaucracies may be the dominant influence. But in any case, the same kind of normative pressures that are brought to bear on individuals and private organizations also influence the state. Thus, the demand that the state satisfy universalistic expectations to promote social justice conflicts with the pressures from powerful groups for special consideration; just as the individual's desire for personal gratification often conflicts with his or her need to maintain a positive self-image. Rather than the process of rationalization, the principal mediating mechanism at the societal level is the "symbolic politics" previously discussed. Thus, the state makes symbolic concessions to the demand that it promote universalistic standards of justice and fair play, while attempting to avoid any actual threat to powerful special interests.

Conclusions

The first thing that stands out from this review is the enormous influence that the work of Edwin Sutherland continues to have over the study of white-collar crime. Although his theoretical contribution is often seen solely in terms of the differential association theory, his legacy also includes a sophisticated theory about the structural origins of white-collar crime. Sutherland encouraged a whole generation of students of white-collar crime—deeply influencing the kinds of things they studied and those they ignored.

In the last two decades we have, however, moved far beyond Sutherland's original contribution. Considerable new work has linked the theory of white-collar crime with more general social psychological paradigms, a broader understanding of the operation of contemporary political economy, and the growing field of organizational behavior. While the literature is replete with conflicting perspectives and conclusions, I argue that a general framework for understanding white collar-crime is beginning to emerge at the individual, organizational, and societal levels.

The next step is to integrate these emerging frameworks together into a coherent whole. This is obviously a major undertaking which will take considerable time to complete even if the interest in the theory of white-collar crime continues to grow in the coming decade. Fortunately, an examination of the literature shows strong parallels in the forces that promote white-collar crime on these three levels, which can serve as an important integrating principle. But much work remains to be done if we are to provide the kind of coherent understanding that can exercise a significant influence over social policy formation in this highly politicized arena.

REFERENCES

Asch, P., and Seneca, J. J. (1969). Is collusion profitable? *The Review of Economics and Statistics, 58*, 1–12.

Barnett, H. C. (1979). Wealth, crime and capital accumulation. *Contemporary Crises, 3*, 171–186.

———. (1981). Corporate capitalism, corporate crime. *Crime & Delinquency, 27*, 4–23.

Barnett, H. C. (1984). Branch culture and economic structure: Correlates of tax noncompliance in Sweden. Revised version of a paper presented to the American Society of Criminology, November, Cincinnati, Ohio.

Benson, M. L. (1985). Denying the guilty mind: Accounting for involvement in a white-collar crime. *Criminology, 23*, 583–607.

Braithwaite, J. (1984). *Corporate crime in the pharmaceutical industry.* London: Routledge & Kegan Paul.

———. (1988). White-collar crime, competition, and capitalism: Comment on Coleman. *American Journal of Sociology, 94*, 627–632.

———. (1989). Criminological theory and organizational crime. *Justice Quarterly, 6*, 333–358.

Burton, J. F. (1966). An economic analysis of Sherman Act criminal cases. In J. M. Clabault and J. F. Burton, eds. *Sherman Act indictments 1955-1965: A legal and economic analysis.* New York: Federal Legal Publications.

Calavita, K. (1983). The demise of the occupational safety and health administration: A case study in symbolic action. *Social Problems, 30*, 437–448.

Chibnall, S., and Saunders, P. (1977). Worlds apart: Notes on the social relativity of corruption. *British Journal of Sociology, 28*, 197.

Clinard, M. B. (1982). *Corporate ethics, illegal behavior and government regulation: Views of middle management.* Washington D.C.: National Institute of Mental Health.

Clinard, M. B., and Yeager, P. C. (1980). *Corporate crime.* New York: Free Press.

Clinard, M. B., Yeager, P. C., Brissette, D., Petrashek, Harries, E. (1979). *Illegal corporate behavior.* Washington, D.C.: U.S. Government Printing Office.

Cohen, A. (1977). The concept of criminal organization. *British Journal of Criminology, 17,* 97–111.

Cohen, A., Lindesmith, A., and Schuessler, K., eds. (1956). *The Sutherland Papers.* Bloomington: Indiana University Press.

Coleman, J. W. (1985). Law and power: The Sherman Antitrust Act and its enforcement in the petroleum industry. *Social Problems, 32,* 264–274.

———. (1987). Toward an integrated theory of white-collar crime. *American Journal of Sociology, 93,* 406–439.

———. (1988). Competition and the structure of industrial society: Reply to Braithwaite. *American Journal of Sociology, 94,* 632–636.

———. (1989). *The criminal elite: The sociology of white collar crime* (2d ed.). New York: St. Martin's Press.

Conklin, J. E. (1977). *Illegal but not criminal: Business crime in America.* Englewood Cliffs, N.J.: Prentice-Hall.

Cressey, D. R. (1953). *Other people's money: A study in the social psychology of embezzlement.* Belmont, Calif.: Wadsworth (Wadsworth edition published in 1971).

———. (1976). Restraints of trade, recidivism and delinquent neighborhoods. In J. Short, Jr., ed. *Delinquency, crime and society.* Chicago: University of Chicago Press.

———. (1980). Employee theft: The reasons why. *Security World,* October, 31–36.

Daly, K. (1989). Gender and varieties of white-collar crime. *Criminology, 27,* 769–794.

Denzin, N. (1977). Notes on the criminogenic hypothesis: A case study of the American liquor industry. *American Sociological Review, 42,* 905–920.

Donnelly, D. L. (1982). Origins of the occupational safety and health act of 1970. *Social Problems, 30,* 13–25.

Dowie, M. (1979). Pinto madness. In J. Skolnick and E. Currie, eds. *Crisis in American institutions* (4th ed.). Boston: Little, Brown and Company.

Drucker, P. F. (1972). *Concept of the Corporation* (rev. ed.). New York: John Day Company.

Ermann, M. D., and Lundman, R. J. (1978). Deviant acts by complex organizations: Deviance and social control at the organizational level of analysis. *The Sociological Quarterly, 19*, 55–67.

Farberman, H. A. (1975). A criminogenic market structure: The automobile industry. *The Sociological Quarterly, 16*, Autumn, 438–457.

Geis, G. (1967). The heavy electrical equipment antitrust cases of 1961. In M. B. Clinard and R. Quinney, eds. *Criminal behavior systems: A typology*, 139–150. New York: Holt, Rinehart and Winston.

———. (1968). *White-collar criminal: The offender in business and the professions.* New York: Atherton.

———. (1982). *On white-collar crime.* Lexington, Mass.: Lexington Books.

———. (1985). Criminological perspectives on corporate regulation: A review of research. In B. Fisse and P. A. French, eds. *Corrigible corporation and unruly law*, 63–84. San Antonio: Trinity University Press.

Gross, E. (1978). Organizational crime: A theoretical perspective. In N. K. Denzin, ed. *Studies in symbolic interaction*, 55–85. Greenwich, Conn.: JAI.

———. (1980). Organizational structure and organizational crime. In G. Geis and E. Stotland, eds. *White-collar crime: Theory and research*, 52–77. Beverly Hills: Sage.

Hay, G., and Kelly, D. (1974). An empirical survey of price-fixing conspiracies. *Journal of Law and Economics, 17*, 13–39.

Hirschi, T., and Gottfredson, M. (1987). Causes of white-collar crime. *Criminology, 25*, 949–974.

Hollinger, R. D., and Clark, J. P. (1983). Deviance in the workplace: Perceived certainty, perceived severity and employee theft. *Social Forces, 62*, 398–418.

Katona, G. (1946). *Price control and business.* Bloomington: Indiana University Press.

Kramer, R. C. (1982). Corporate crime: An organizational perspective. In P. Wickman and T. Dailey eds. *White-collar and economic crime*, 75–94. Lexington, Mass.: Lexington Books.

Lane, R. E. (1954). *The regulation of businessmen: Social conditions of government control.* New Haven: Yale University Press.

Leonard, W. N., and Weber, M. G. (1970). Automakers and dealers: A study of criminogenic market forces. *Law and Society Review, 4*, 407–424.

McCormick, A. E. (1977). Rule enforcement and moral indignation: Some observations on the effects of criminal anti-trust convictions upon societal reaction processes. *Social Problems, 25*, 30–39.

Meier, R. F., and Geis, G. (1982). The psychology of the white-collar offender. In G. Geis, ed. *On white-collar crime*, 85–102. Lexington, Mass.: Lexington Books.

Mills, C. W. (1959). *The power elite.* New York: Oxford University Press.

Needleman, M. L., and Needleman, C. (1979). Organizational crime: Two models of criminogenesis. *The Sociological Quarterly, 20*, 517–528.

Nettler, G. (1974). Embezzlement without problems. *British Journal of Criminology, 14*, 70–77.

Perrow, C. (1972). *Complex organizations: A critical essay.* Glenview, Ill.: Scott Foresman.

Pfeffer, J., and Salancik, G. R. (1978). *The external control of organizations: A resource dependence perspective.* New York: Harper & Row.

Posner, R. (1970). A statistical study of antitrust enforcement. *Journal of Law and Economics, 13*, 365–420.

Schrager, L. S., and Short, J. F., Jr. (1977). Toward a sociology of organizational crime. *Social Problems, 25*, 407–419.

Sherman, L. W. (1978). *Scandal and reform: Controlling police corruption.* Berkeley: University of California Press.

Snider, L. (1987). Towards a political economy of reform, regulation, and corporate crime. *Law & Policy, 9*, 37–68.

Staw, B. M., and Szwajkowski, E. (1975). The scarcity-munificence component of organizational environments and the commission of illegal acts. *Administrative Science Quarterly, 20*, 345–354.

Stearns, L. (1979). Fact and fiction of a model enforcement bureaucracy: The labor inspectorate of Sweden. *British Journal of Law and Society, 6*, 1–23.

Stone, C. D. (1975). Where the law ends: The social control of corporate behavior. New York: Harper & Row.

Sutherland, E. H. (1924). *Criminology.* Chicago: J. B. Lippincott.

———. (1934, 1939, 1947). *Principles of criminology.* Chicago: J. B. Lippincott.

———. (1949). *White collar crime.* New York: Dryden Press.

Sykes, G. K., and Matza, D. (1957). Techniques of neutralization: A theory of delinquency. *American Sociological Review, 22*, 667–670.

Weber, M. (1964). *The theory of social and economic organization.* A. M. Henderson and T. Parsons, trans. New York: Free Press.

Vaughan, D. (1983). *Controlling unlawful organizational behavior: Social structure and corporate misconduct.* Chicago: University of Chicago Press.

———. (1992). The macro-micro connection in "white-collar crime" theory. (This volume.)

Zietz, D. (1981). *Women who embezzle or defraud: A study of convicted felons.* New York: Praeger.

· 3 ·

Poverty, Power, and White-Collar Crime

Sutherland and the Paradoxes of Criminological Theory

JOHN BRAITHWAITE

Unlike many contemporary criminologists, I continue to be motivated by the goal that Sutherland set for us of developing criminological theory of maximum possible generality. Like most contemporary criminologists, I accept that Sutherland's revelation of the nature and extent of white collar crime creates some acute problems for traditional criminological theories. And as Sutherland so convincingly argued, the dominant tradition of criminological theory that excises white-collar crime from its explanatory scope lays the foundations for a class-biased criminology and criminal justice policy.

Having accepted all this, I now want to reject Sutherland's view that the widespread reality of white-collar crime means that poverty and inequality cannot be important variables in a general theory of crime. Sutherland is provocative on this point: "If it can be shown that white collar crimes are frequent, a general theory that crime is due to poverty and its related pathologies is shown to be invalid" (Sutherland, 1983, p. 7). Sutherland did show that white-collar crime is frequent when white-collar crime is defined as "a crime committed by a person of respectability and high social status in the course of his occupation" (Sutherland, 1983, p. 7). Indeed, work since Sutherland leaves little doubt that more of the most serious crimes that cause the greatest property loss and the greatest physical injury are perpetrated by the rich than by the poor (see Cullen, Maakestaad, and Cavender, 1987; Clinard and Yeager, 1980; Pepinsky and Jesilow, 1984; Geis, 1973; Pearce, 1976).

My contention is that inequality is relevant to the explanation of both crime in the streets and crime in the suites. I will argue that this is true of various forms of inequality—based on class, race, age, and gender. This essay is an attempt to move a step forward with the theoretical program of building a republican criminology, which I share with Philip Pettit. The small contribution I make in this paper is to show how issues of inequality of wealth and power connect with my explanatory theory of crime in *Crime, Shame and Reintegration* (1989). In a sense, what I do here is couple the work in that book with my 1979 book, *Inequality, Crime and Public Policy*. This first attempt to make sense of the connection between the analysis of inequality and crime, and the analysis of shaming and crime has become possible thanks to a number of recent and exciting contributions by American criminologists. These are Jack Katz's (1988) *Seductions of Crime*, the work of Scheff (1988) and Benson (1990) on humiliation and rage, and another contribution from Indiana University, Cohen and Machalek's (1988) "General Theory of Expropriative Crime."

In this paper I will not summarize the evidence for the inequality–crime association compiled in *Inequality, Crime and Public Policy*, nor the evidence accumulated since (for more recent reviews, see Belknap, 1989; Box, 1987). My purpose here is simply to advance a theoretical solution to a problem left by Sutherland. It is to show that the claim that poverty is causally implicated in crime can, in fact, be reconciled with the widespread reality of white-collar crime documented by Sutherland. While the reconciliation is theoretically interesting, whether it is empirically correct is something that I simply leave on criminology's research agenda. Even if it is correct, inequality is advanced only as a partial explanation of crime of modest explanatory power. More impressive explanatory capacity is only likely when inequality is integrated with other explanatory variables, perhaps in the ways suggested by Coleman (1992) in the preceding chapter, or perhaps in the way I suggested in *Crime, Shame and Reintegration*.

I regard the theoretical work in this paper as relevant to explaining crime conceived in either of two ways. First, as in *Crime, Shame and Reintegration*, it can be read as an attempt to explain what Glaser (1978, 31–32) conceived as "predatory crime" (crime where an offender preys on others). What I advance does not seem to me a very good theory of nonpredatory crimes such as drug use.

Alternatively, this essay can be read as theory concerning the domain of crimes that republicans ought to regard as crimes. Republican normative theory contends that acts ought to be criminalized only when they threaten the dominion of citizens, and when there is no less intrusive way of protecting that dominion than criminalization (Braithwaite and Pettit, 1990). Dominion is a republican conception of liberty or freedom. It includes the sphere of control citizens properly enjoy over their persons, their property, and their province. To enjoy dominion, a citizen must live in a social world where other citizens respect his or her liberty and where this mutual respect is socially assured and generally recognized. One attraction of the republican definition for our present purposes is that it connects with a key empirical claim I will advance: When inequality of wealth and power is structurally humiliating, this undermines respect for the dominion of others. And a society where respect for dominion is lost will be a society riddled with crime.

Republican normative commitments direct us to take seriously both political and economic inequality (Montesquieu, 1977, chapters 3–4; Pettit, 1989) and community disapproval (Pocock, 1977; Braithwaite and Pettit, 1990) as issues. Sunstein (1988) advances four characteristics of republicanism: (1) deliberation in government that shapes as well as balances interests (as opposed to deals between prepolitical interests); (2) political equality; (3) universality, or debate to reconcile competing views, as a regulative ideal; and (4) citizenship—community participation in public life.

The purpose of this paper is, therefore, to show that Sutherland's aspiration for a general theory of both white-collar and common crime can be pursued by focusing on inequality as an explanatory variable. Powerlessness and poverty increase the chances that needs are so little satisfied that crime is an irresistible temptation to actors alienated from the social order. Powerlessness and poverty increase the chances that punishment is noncredible to actors who have nothing to lose. I will argue that it may be theoretically fruitful to move away from a positivist conception of "need" to needs that are socially constructed as wants that can be satisfied (contrasted with greed—socially constructed as insatiable wants). When needs are satisfied, further power and wealth enables crime motivated by greed. New types of criminal opportunities and new paths to immunity from accountability are constituted by concentrations of wealth and power. The conclusion of the first half of the paper is, therefore, that inequality worsens both crimes of poverty motivated by *need* for goods for *use* and crimes of wealth motivated by *greed* enabled by goods for *exchange*.

In the second half of the paper, I argue that much crime, particularly violent crime, is motivated by the humiliation of the offender and the offender's perceived right to humiliate the victim. Inegalitarian societies, it is argued, are more structurally humiliating. Dimensions of inequality that will be advanced as relevant to the explanation of both white-collar and common crime are economic inequality, inequality in political power (slavery, totalitarianism), racism, ageism, and patriarchy. None of these lines of explanation is advanced as the whole story on crimes of the powerless or crimes of the powerful; but they may be a theoretically interesting and politically important part of the whole story.

Opportunity Theory

In this section, I argue the following: (1) that crime is motivated in part by needs; (2) that needs are more likely to be satisfied as we move up the class structure; and (3) that redistributive policies will do more to increase the need satisfaction of the poor than to decrease the need satisfaction of the rich.

Notwithstanding these three hypotheses, greed motivates crime even after need is satisfied. More importantly, wealthy actors who have their needs satisfied will want to accumulate goods for exchange rather than use. Accumulations of goods for exchange enable the constitution of illegitimate opportunities for the rich that cannot be constituted for the poor. Hence, I will argue that inequality increases crime by (1) decreasing the goods available for *use* by the poor to satisfy needs; and (2) increasing the goods available to rich people (and organizations) who have needs satisfied, but whose accumulation of goods for exchange constitutes criminal opportunities to indulge greed. Inequality, at the same time, causes

crimes of *poverty* motivated by *need* for goods for *use*	crimes of *wealth* motivated by *greed* enabled by goods for *exchange* (that are surplus to those required for use).

Inequality, Crime and Public Policy began to explore the theory and empirical evidence in support of the proposition that societies with more unequal distributions of wealth and power will have deeper crime problems. An account was advanced as to why inequality will often worsen both crime in the streets and crime in the suites. Through building on Cohen and Machalek (1988), I believe we can more clearly theorize the dynamics of this proposition than I was able to manage in *Inequality, Crime and Public Policy*.

The traditional account of opportunity theory as an explanation for crimes of the powerless continues to hold great attraction. This starts with Merton's (1957) observation that in any society there are a number of widely shared goals that provide an aspirational frame of reference. The most important of these in America is material success. In addition to cultural goals held up as worth striving for, there are defined legitimate, institutionalized means for achieving the cultural goals. When these are blocked, crime is more likely to occur. Elaborating on Merton, Cloward and Ohlin (1960) maintained that if delinquency is to result from blockage of legitimate means to achieving a cultural goal, then there is a second requirement: illegitimate means for achieving the goal must be open. The problem is reconciling white-collar crime within this framework. White collar crime highlights the fact that illegitimate opportunities are grasped not only to satisfy need but also to gratify greed. In a sense, what I will set up here is explication of a transition as we move up the class structure from crime motivated by beliefs about the importance of satisfying needs to crime motivated by greed—even by the belief, in the immortal words of Michael Douglas from the movie *Wall Street*, that "greed is good."

But first things first—crime motivated by beliefs about needs. I am not interested in a positivist definition of need. I am interested in the phenomenon of need being socially constructed in culturally contingent ways that motivate crime. So we have criminals who act on a subsistence model of need, as in the classic case of English slum dwellers transported to Australia for stealing loaves of bread to feed their families. There are criminals who act on models of need represented at every point of Maslow's (1954) hierarchy of needs. There are criminals motivated by the need for a decent standard of living, where "decent" can mean what they perceive most people in their community to enjoy, what whites but not blacks enjoy, what they used to enjoy before they lost their jobs, or what they were led to expect to enjoy by the advertising and dramatization of bourgeois lifestyles on television. In short, the social construction of needs that motivate crime is culturally relative.

However relative they are, I advance one claim about them of general import: As we become wealthier, it becomes more likely that any and all conceptions of need will be satisfied. If my income doubles—irrespective of whether my needs are framed in terms of subsistence, the average standard of living, or unrealistic expectations or aspirations—it is likely that I will view those needs as better met than they were before. The general claim is that as we move up the class structure, people are more likely to view their needs as satisfied. This, of course, is an empirically rebuttable claim.

Substituting the term "needs" in Cloward and Ohlin's (1960) formulation, the theory becomes that when legitimate means for satisfying needs are blocked and illegitimate means are open, crime is more likely. Let us then compare two societies with the same GNP, one with an equal distribution of wealth and one with an unequal distribution. It follows that because the poor will be poorer in the unequal case, those toward the bottom of the class structure will be less likely to perceive their needs as met (whether those needs are of a subsistence, absolute, or relative sort). Because they view so few of their needs as met, the poor are also more likely to take the view that they have little to lose through a criminal conviction. Put more polemically, the more unequal the class structure, the more scarce national wealth is devoted to gratifying greed among people whose needs are satisfied, the less is devoted to satisfying unmet needs.

Consider a socially defined need for housing. The more unequal the class structure, the greater the proportion of housing expenditure that will be devoted to building bigger and bigger mansions for the rich, the greater the number of homeless, and the more the poor will turn to crime in preference to being put out on the street. A more equal class structure may reduce the incidence of crimes of the poor connected to the need for housing.

Because wealthier people are more likely to be in positions where most of their needs are met, they are less likely to steal for this reason. As in standard welfare economics, let us assume that as we get richer we progressively work down our needs, starting with those that are most important to us (see also Wheeler, chapter 4). The wealthier we are, the lower are the marginal returns to need satisfaction from acquiring a dollar of extra wealth through crime. Our first dollar is worth more to us than our ten-millionth dollar. Hence, the crime-preventive effects of redistributing wealth from rich to poor to satisfy the needs of the poor will not be fully counterbalanced by crime-instigating effects on wealthy people who suffer reduced satisfaction of their needs.

Yet we know that even when wealthy people have all of their self-defined personal needs fully met, the extra dollar is not valueless to them. Even though a dollar has less value to a person whose needs are mostly satisfied than to one whose needs are not, the dollar will continue to have some value to people with satisfied needs. Such people can continue to be motivated to pursue wealth for many other reasons—to signify their worth by conspicuous consumption, to prove success to themselves, to build an empire, to leave an inheritance.

For this reason, it is sensible to also apply a Mertonian framework to the economic aspirations of the upper class. We can readily conceive of the blocked aspirations of the already wealthy man to become a millionaire. We might understand his behavior in paying a bribe in these terms: legitimate means for securing a contract are blocked at the time and an illegitimate opportunity to do so corruptly is open. Vaughan (1983, p. 59) suggests that a cultural emphasis on economic success motivates the setting of a new goal whenever the old one is attained. While needs are socially constructed as wants that can be satisfied, greed is distinguished as a want that can never be satisfied: Success is ever-receding; having more leads to wanting more again.

> While it is meaningless to accumulate certain sensual use-values indefinitely, since their worth is limited by their usefulness, the accretion of exchange-value, being merely quantitative, suffers no such constraints. (Haug, 1986, p. 18)

Wheeler's essay (chapter 4) directs us to the motivational importance of fear of falling as well as greed for gain in white-collar crime. There is no problem in accommodating this within the theoretical framework of the present chapter. Crime can be motivated by (a) a desire for goods for use; (b) a fear of losing goods for use; (c) a desire for goods for exchange; or (d) a fear of losing goods for exchange. My proposition is that (a) and (b) are more relevant to motivating the crimes of poor people; (c) and (d) are more relevant to motivating the crimes of wealthy people and organizations. These distributional tendencies can hold even though (a) through (d) might all be involved in the mixed motives driving, say, a single corporate crime. Some individuals who play a part in the crime may be motivated by (a), others by (b), others by (c), and others by (d). Indeed, some individuals may have mixed motives that range across the four categories. This does not change the distributional hypothesis that use-motivations will more often be involved in the criminal choices of the poor, and exchange-motivations more often involved in the criminal choices of the rich.

I will now argue that just as the poverty of the poor in unequal societies contributes to crime, so does the wealth of the wealthy. We have established that the latter cannot be true because of a purely Mertonian analysis of legitimate opportunities to satisfy needs because the rich have more of their needs satisfied by ready access to legitimate means of need satisfaction.

One line of argument here is that conspicuous concentrations of wealth increase the illegitimate opportunities available to the poor (and indeed the nonpoor). Being a car thief is more remunerative when there are many $50,000 cars available to be stolen than when $20,000 cars are the best one can find. Evidence that wealthy neighborhoods located near slums are especially likely to be victimized by property offenders supports this line of analysis (Boggs, 1965). But it is not a theoretical path I wish to pursue here. The theoretically important criminogenic effect of increasing concentrations of wealth is in enabling the constitution of new forms of illegitimate opportunity that are not available to the poor or the average-income earner, opportunities that can be extremely lucrative. It is important to understand here that increasing wealth for the poor or the average-income earner does not constitute new illegitimate opportunities in the way I will discuss.

Marx's distinction of value for use and value for exchange is helpful here. In his *Economic and Philosophical Manuscripts of 1844*, use is associated with need: "Every real and possible need is a weakness which will tempt the fly to the gluepot" (p. 148). Also every product that can be used "is a bait with which to seduce away the other's very being, his money." Up to the point where legitimate work generates for the worker only value for use (in meeting needs), she has no surplus. Up to this point, extra income is used instead of invested in the constitution of illegitimate opportunities. But when surplus is acquired (value for exchange rather than for use), it can be invested in the constitution of illegitimate opportunities.

A limitation of Cloward and Ohlin's (1960) analysis is that it tends to view illegitimate opportunities as a fact of society independent of the agency of the criminal actor—ready and waiting for the criminal actor to seize. This conception forgets the point that, if they are powerful enough, criminals can actively constitute illegitimate opportunities. This power is not totally explained by control of surplus value—the working-class juvenile can form a gang as a vehicle for collective criminal enterprises that would be beyond her grasp as an individual. But surplus value can be used to constitute criminal opportunities that are not available to the poor. As Weisburd et al. (1991) found in their systematic study of white-collar criminals in New York, "The most consequential white-collar crimes—in terms of their scope, impact and cost in dollars—appear to require for their commission, that their perpetrators operate in an environment that provides access to both money and the organization through which money moves."

Persons with some spare capital can start up a company. The company can be used as a vehicle to defraud consumers or investors. The principals can siphon off funds into a personal account, bankrupting the company and leaving creditors stranded. They can set up a Swiss bank account and a shell company in a tax haven. But to launder dirty money and employ the lawyers and accountants to evade taxes, they must have some surplus to start with. And the more they have, the more grand the illegitimate opportunities they can constitute. When they become big enough, shares in their company can be traded publicly. They can then indulge in some very lucrative forms of insider trading and market rigging. If they become billionaires like Nelson Bunker Hunt and W. Herbert Hunt, they can even try to manipulate the entire market for a commodity like silver (Abolafia, 1985). If they become oligopolists in a market, they can work with the other oligopolists to fix prices and breach other antitrust laws. If they become monopolists, a further array of illegal predatory practices becomes available. The proposition is that capital can be used to constitute illegitimate opportunities, and the more capital, the bigger the opportunities. Obversely to our analysis of need, an egalitarian redistribution of wealth away from surplus for the rich in favor of increased wealth for the poor will not correspondingly expand illegitimate opportunities for the poor. This is because in the hands of the poor, income is for use; it is not available as surplus for constituting illegitimate opportunities.

Other things being equal, the rich will prefer to stay out of trouble by investing in legitimate rather than illegitimate opportunities. But when goals are set with the expectation that they will be secured legitimately, environmental contingencies frequently intervene to block legitimate goal attainment. Powerful actors regularly have the opportunity in these circumstances to achieve the goal illegitimately. The production target cannot be achieved because the effluent treatment plant has broken down. So it is achieved by allowing untreated effluent to flow into the river late at night. Most capital investment simultaneously constitutes a range of both legitimate and illegitimate means of further increasing the wealth of the capitalist. The wealth that creates legal opportunities at the same time creates illegal opportunities for achieving the same result. In this additional sense, investment creates criminal opportunities in a way that use does not. It is just that there is a difference in the way we evaluate illegitimate opportunities that are inherent in any legitimate investment compared with illegitimate opportunities that are created intentionally. The former are unfortunate side effects of mostly desirable processes of creating wealth. The latter are the main and intended effects of a mostly undesirable process of criminal exploitation. Whatever the mix of desirable and undesirable effects of shifting wealth from the poor to the rich, the only effect we are theoretically interested in here is the creation of more illegitimate opportunities for the rich. My main point is that surplus can be used intentionally to constitute illegitimate opportunities— whether by setting up an illegal traffic in arms or drugs, or by setting up a tax-evasion scheme—in a way that income for use cannot.

Here, it is useful to think of the implications of Cohen and Machalek's (1988) evolutionary ecological approach to expropriative crime. The first point in this analysis is that the returns to an expropriative strategy vary inversely with the number of others who are engaging in the same strategy. In nature, a behavioral strategy of predation is more likely to persist if it is different from that used by other predators. There is no "best" strategy that will be adopted by every predator because it is the best; for a predator to opt for a strategy, it must be one that is not crowded out by others using a similar strategy. Minority strategies can flourish.

Extreme wealth fosters extraordinarily lucrative minority strategies. The wealthy can pursue illegitimate strategies that are novel and that excel because they cannot be contemplated by those who are not wealthy. Where there is no limit on what can be spent on an expropriative strategy, it can be designed to beat all alternative, less adequately funded strategies against which it must compete. This is why the most damaging and most lucrative expropriative strategies are white-collar crimes. Those who have no inhibitions against duck shooting out of season, who need spare no expense on their artillery, for whom no strategy is too novel (even shooting other hunters), are likely to get the best haul of ducks.

Much of the empirical material in this volume illustrates the point. Anyone can stage a bank robbery. But bank robbery is not a particularly cost-effective form of illegitimate work. Very few people can buy a bank. Yet as Pontell and Calavita (chapter 8) state in their paper on savings and loan fraud, "The best way to rob a bank is to own one."

Cohen and Machalek (1988) suggest that the "resource holding potential (RHP)" of the poor means they will commit crimes that amount to "making the best of a bad job." The RHP of the rich, in contrast, allows them to "take advantage of a good job." The rich will rarely resort to the illegitimate means that are criminal staples among the poor because they can secure much higher returns by pursuing either legitimate or illegitimate means to which the poor have no access. There will be little direct competition between the powerful and the powerless criminal. Instead, they will develop different minority strategies that reflect their different RHPs. Where there is direct competition, it is fragile. The small drug dealer can be crushed by the powerful, organized criminal unless the drug dealer finds a way of complementing the powerful criminal, picking up his crumbs, or operating outside his area instead of competing with him.

The other peculiar advantage that powerful criminals have is in the domain that evolutionary ecologists call counterstrategy dynamics. Fast predators activate a selective force that favors faster prey and vice versa (Cohen and Machalek, 1988). The expropriative strategy of conning consumers into buying dangerous or ineffective patent medicines was countered by the strategy of regulatory agencies seizing drugs that had not been through a premarketing clearance process. The most ruthless participants in the industry used their considerable resources to short-circuit such counter-strategies, however. They bribed those responsible for premarketing clearance decisions; they paid unethical researchers to produce fraudulent evidence that their products were safe and efficacious (Braithwaite, 1984). To indulge this kind of thwarting of the counterstrategy process requires abundant resources of a sort unavailable to indigent criminals. Box (1983, p. 59) has written at length on how the greatest comparative advantage of corporate criminals "lies in their ability to prevent their actions from becoming subject to criminal sanctions in the first place." Again, Pontell and Calavita's case study (chapter 8) of the savings and loan crisis illustrates that the counterstrategy relevant there was the deregulatory reforms that the financial sector extracted from the Congress and the executive in the early 1980s, thus rendering their power less accountable. In *Inequality, Crime and Public Policy*, I developed in some detail the proposition that it is the unaccountable power that accrues to the most wealthy that explains why they can get away with crimes of extreme seriousness. It was argued there that power corrupts and unaccountable power corrupts with impunity.[1] The upper class use their resources to ensure that their power is unaccountable; they benefit from a hegemony that renders their power corrupting. At its most basic level, only people in positions of power have opportunity to commit crimes that involve the abuse of power, and the more power they have, the more abusive those crimes can be. As Taylor, Walton, and Young (1973) put it:

> . . . radical deviancy theory has the task of demonstrating analytically that such rule breaking is institutionalized, regular and widespread among the powerful, that it is a given result of the structural position enjoyed by powerful men—whether they be cabinet ministers, judges, captains of industry or policemen. (P. 30)

In this analysis, power as well as money is conceived as something that can be exchanged—invested to generate more power. Hence, the crimes of a J. Edgar Hoover can be interpreted as motivated by an insatiable desire to accumulate more power for exchange. The extreme manifestation of this problem is seen in a Marcos or a Ceausescu, whose power is inestimable, whose immunity from accountability is total, and whose capacity for crime knows no bounds. In contrast to the insatiable demands of a totalitarian ruler to control more totally more and more people, the criminogenic powerlessness of the poor is bounded. It is bounded by the need to assert control over the life of just one person—their own persons.

Inequality, Crime and Public Policy argues that if crime in the suites arises from the fact that certain people have great wealth and power, and if crime in the streets arises from the fact that certain other people have very little wealth or power, then policies to redistribute wealth and power may simultaneously relieve both types of crime problems.

I have been led to the same conclusion by the considerations in this paper. If it is wealth and power that enable a range of extremely harmful expropriative strategies that are distinctive to those at the top of the class structure, then redistribution of wealth and power in favor of the upper class will increase that which enables their crimes. Redistribution of wealth and power away from the poor will worsen the "bad lot" of which the best they can make is crime. It will further exacerbate the blockage of legitimate means, thereby increasing the attraction of illegitimate means for satisfying needs. And it will increase the alienation, the hopelessness, the live-for-the-moment desperation of those who feel that they do not have power over their own future.

Moreover, it may be that extremes of wealth and power mean that the rich justify their exploitative class position with exploitive and criminogenic ideologies not so unlike the caricature, "Greed is good." It may be that just as the criminality of the rich is accounted for in terms of the fact that they exploit, the criminality of the poor is accounted for by the fact that they are exploited. While the forms of crime that predominate at the two ends of the class spectrum are sharply distinguishable minority strategies, they may be different sides of the same coin—both products of the same inequality, of the exploitation perceived by those who are exploited, and of the exploiting legitimated for those who exploit.

At both ends, criminal subcultures develop to communicate symbolic reassurance to those who decide to prey on others, to sustain techniques for neutralizing the evil of crime (Sykes and Matza,

1957), and to communicate knowledge about how to do it. Black criminal subcultures collect, dramatize, and transmit the injustices of a society dominated by whites and ruled by an oppressive Anglo-Saxon criminal justice system. The subcultures of Wall Street rationalize exploitative behavior as that which made America great. Business subcultures of tax evasion are memory files that collect the injustices of the Internal Revenue Service (see Matza, 1964, p. 102) and communicate resentment over the disproportionate tax burden shouldered by the rich. An oligopolistic, price-fixing subculture under the auspices of an industry association communicates the social benefits of "orderly marketing"; it constitutes and reproduces an illegitimate opportunity structure.

The focus of the discussion so far has been excessively on property crime. But it need not have been. A business subculture of resistance to the Occupational Safety and Health Administration can foster methods of legal defiance, circumvention, and counterattack that kill. The unaccountable power of a Marcos or a Ceausescu can be used to kill. A wealthy person can use her capital to establish a toxic-waste disposal company that directs the violence of cancer against an unsuspecting community by illegal dumping of toxins. The resentment of a black person who feels powerless and exploited because of his race can be manifested by violent as well as acquisitive crime. There are, however, some arguments about inequality that may have some special force in the domain of violent crime. To these I now turn. I will argue in the next section that humiliation is important to the explanation of crime and then that inequality is important to the patterning of humiliation.

The Social Structure of Humiliation

A stunning recent contribution to criminology is Jack Katz's *Seductions of Crime* (1988). On the central issue of this paper, Katz stands with Sutherland: "Because of its insistence on attributing causation to material conditions in personal and social backgrounds, modern social thought has been unable either to acknowledge the embrace of evil by common or street criminals, or, and for the same reason, develop empirical bite and intellectual depth in the study of criminality by the wealthy and powerful" (Katz, 1988, p. 10).

The importance of Katz's work resides in his analysis of violence or rage as "livid with the awareness of humiliation" (Katz, 1988, p. 23). Rage both recalls and transforms the experience of humiliation. The experience of a sense of righteousness is the stepping-stone from humiliation to rage; the embrace of righteous violence resolves humiliation "through the overwhelming sensuality of rage" (Katz, 1988, p. 24; see also Marangiu and Newman, 1987). For Katz, it is not coincidental that spouse assault is often associated with taunting about sexual performance or innuendo of sexual infidelity. Domestic homicide transforms such sexual degradation "in a last violent stand in defense of his basic worth" (p. 26). Rage transcends the offender's humiliation by giving him or her dominance over the situation.

Katz's analysis of righteous slaughter is a useful complement to the rather instrumental analysis of opportunity and strategy in the first part of this paper precisely because it is such a noninstrumental analysis. It is not that Katz tells the story of what most violence is like, but he tells a neglected story of what some violence is like. Katz notes the frequency with which murderers cease an attack long before death and indeed in the midst of evidence of persistent life such as screams and pleas for mercy (p. 32). The inference that rage is not instrumentally concerned with causing death is also warranted in cases where death is not a sufficient concern:

> In a "stomping," the attacker may announce to his victim the objective of "kicking your eyes out of your head." The specific practical objective—to remove precisely the condition of the attacker's humiliation, the victim's offending gaze—is more imaginatively related to the project of transcending humiliation than would be the victim's death. (P. 33)

Violence transcends humiliation by casting the person who degraded the offender into an ontologically lower status. Mounted in a flurry of curses, the attack "will be against some morally lower, polluted, corrupted, profanized form of life, and hence in honor of a morally higher, more sacred, and—this bears special emphasis—an eternally respectable realm of being" (p. 36). The claim that rage is about asserting respect, I will argue, is fundamental to distinguishing forms of shaming that provoke crime and forms that prevent it. Shame and respect are the key concepts for understanding crime. Far from being a self-interested, instrumental evildoer, the attacker is immersed in a frenzy of upholding the decent and respectable. Just as humiliation of the offender is implicated in the onset of his rage, so the need to humiliate the victim enables her victimization.

Katz reached these conclusions from an analysis of several hundred criminal acts quite independently of similar conclusions reached by psychiatric scholars. Kohut (1972), a psychoanalyst, identified "narcissistic rage" as a compound of shame and rage. Lewis's (1971) cases led her to conclude that unacknowledged shame and anger cause a feeling trap—alternation between shame and anger that can produce explosive violence she calls humiliated fury. The work of Lansky (1984, 1987) and Scheff et al. (1989) similarly emphasizes the importance of humiliation that is unacknowledged. Innuendo, underhanded disrespect more than overt insult, opens up a cycle of humiliation, revenge, counterrevenge, and ultimately violence. Scheff (1988) identified two ways of reacting to scorn—shame or anger. But sometimes humiliated actors alternate between the two in what Scheff calls a shame-rage spiral.

Katz denies that material circumstances have anything to do with his conclusions about humiliation and rage. Here, I believe he is wrong. Some societies and institutions are structurally more humiliating than others. For a black, living in South Africa is structurally more humiliating than living in Tanzania. Living in a prison is structurally more humiliating than living in a nursing home, and the latter is more humiliating than dwelling in a luxury apartment. Slavery is structurally more humiliating than freedom.

School systems such as I experienced as a child, where children are linearly ordered in their classroom according to their rank ("dunces" sitting at the front) are structurally humiliating for those who fail. These are school systems where dunces are regularly afflicted with degradation ceremonies. And there are alternative structures that are less humiliating, less the mouse race that caricatures the rat race for which children are prepared. An example is Knight's (1985) conception of redemptive schooling:

> A redemptive schooling practice would aim to integrate students into all aspects of school learning and not build fences around students through bureaucratic rituals or prior assumptions concerning student ability. A clear expectation from teachers must be that all students can be taught, and in turn an expectation on the part of students

that they can learn. A school succeeds democratically when everyone's competence is valued and is put to use in a variety of socially desirable projects. Indeed, the same may be said to hold for a good society. (P. 266)

More generally, *inegalitarian societies are structurally humiliating*. When parents cannot supply the most basic needs of their children, while at the same time they are assailed by the ostentatious consumption of the affluent, this is structurally humiliating for the poor. Where inequality is great, the rich humiliate the poor through conspicuous consumption and the poor are humiliated as failures for being poor. Both sides of this equation are important. The propensity to feel powerless and exploited among the poor and the propensity of the rich to see exploiting as legitimate both, as we have seen, enable crime.

Racist societies are structurally humiliating. These are societies where the despised racial group is viewed as unworthy of respect, where the superordinate group humiliates the subordinate group, and where the subordinate group feels daily humiliation. Such racist oppression can be criminogenic.

Patriarchy is structurally humiliating. Patriarchy is a condition where women enjoy limited dominion, where men do not respect the dominion of women, and where women are humiliated by men. However, it is common in patriarchal societies for women not to feel humiliated. Similarly, it is not uncommon for oppressed racial minorities and for the poor *not* to feel humiliated in racist and inegalitarian societies. Here, the Gramscian (1971) concept of hegemony is useful. It often happens that part of the success of the domination by the superordinate group is in persuading the subordinate group that they should accept the ideology of superordination; they identify their own interests with those of their rulers.[2] Their subordination is regarded as something natural rather than something to resent (see also Scheff, 1990).

But hegemony never works perfectly. A substantial fraction of the oppressed group is always humiliated by their oppression. It is just that historically, hegemony has tended to work better with the oppression of women than it has with the oppression of racial minorities. In the United States or Australia, for example, even though there are many more women than blacks, there are more cases of blacks than of women who feel humiliated to the point of daily, seething rage that explodes into violence.

To understand why women commit less crime than men, in spite of their oppression, we need to understand why it is that women, instead of feeling humiliation and rage, feel shame and guilt. I have begun to address this in *Crime, Shame and Reintegration* and will return to the issue later in this paper. For the moment, I note only how I would propose to deal with the critical issue of the operationalization problem with the infamously vague concept of hegemony. It is through measuring the things to which the theory proposes hegemony leads—shame and guilt when hegemony is present, humiliation and anger when it is not (see further Scheff, 1990).

The fact that patriarchy does not engender feelings of humiliation and rage among most women does not absolve patriarchy of criminogenesis. Remember, there are two sides to our story. The hypothesis is that humiliation both motivates violence among those humiliated and enables violence among those who humiliate. Hence, the degradation of women countenanced by men who do not grant women dominion enables rape and violence against women on a massive scale in patriarchal societies, not to mention commercial exploitation of the bodies of women by actors who might ambiguously be labeled white-collar criminals. Empirical work on homicides by men against women confirms that homicide can be viewed as an attempt by the male to assert "their power and control over their wives" (Wallace, 1986, p. 126; Daly and Wilson, 1988; Polk and Ranson, 1991). In passing, it is important to note that the willingness to humiliate women should, according to the theory, be more profound among men who see themselves as having been humiliated—as a black humiliated by whites, or as an American soldier in Vietnam humiliated by protesters back home, by "Gooks" who defeat him militarily, and by an authoritarian military.

Ageist societies are structurally humiliating. Where the very young or the very old are not worthy of respect, where they do not enjoy the dominion accorded human beings at the peak of their powers, the young and the old will be abused, including physically abused—both in the home and in institutions specializing in their care (schools and nursing homes). While the very old rarely have the physical power to transcend their humiliation with violent rage, the young do, especially as they become older, stronger, young males. The physical powerlessness of the very old makes their abuse the most invisible and insidious in complex societies. As Joel Handler (1989, p. 5) points out, even prisoners can riot, but the frail aged have neither muscle nor voice. The very young, and particularly the very old (Fattah and Sacco, 1989, p. 174–177), are also vulnerable and attractive targets for consumer fraud.

Ageist and gendered exploitation interact in important ways. Contemporarily, we see this in many studies of elder abuse that report over 70 percent, and sometimes over 80 percent, of victims of elderly abuse to be female (Hudson, 1986; Wolf and Pillemer, 1989, p. 33).[3] Historically, we see it in the victimization of older women labeled as witches in the sixteenth and seventeenth centuries in many parts of the Western world (Stearns, 1986, p. 7).

Totalitarian societies are structurally humiliating. Totalitarian societies are, by definition, disrespectful of the dominion of ordinary citizens. Totalitarianism means an unequal distribution of freedom or dominion. They are societies that trample on the dominion of individual citizens to serve the interests of the ruling party. Atrocities by the state are enabled by disrespect for its citizens—the disrespect that degraded citizens, in turn, accord to the laws of the totalitarian state is also criminogenic.

Retributive societies are structurally humiliating.[4] These are societies where evildoers are viewed as unworthy of respect, as enjoying no right to have their dominion protected, as worthy of humiliation. The degraded status of prisoners in retributive societies frees those responsible for their daily degradation from restraints to respect the dominion of prisoners. The result can be the systematic violence directed against prisoners that we saw documented in the Royal Commission into New South Wales Prisons (Jewson, 1978) and that was a central cultural fact of the first hundred years of my country's colonial history. We can see this in Stotland's interpretation of the slaughter of prisoners at Attica: "For both troopers and guards, sense of competence, violence and self-esteem . . . are linked" (Stotland, 1976, p. 88). "[A] person's self-esteem can be threatened by failure [and] insults" (p. 86). (See also Scheff et al., 1989, p. 187; McKay Commission, 1972.) In another study of the 1970 killings by National Guardsmen at Kent State University, Stotland and Martinez (1976) reached the same conclusion:

> The events . . . leading up to the killings were a series of
> inept, ineffectual, almost humiliating moves by the Guards-

men against the "enemy." . . . The answer to these threats
to their self-esteem, to their sense of competence, was
violence. . . . Another aspect . . . which added to the threat
to the self-esteem of the Guardsmen [was that] during their
presence on . . . campus . . . the students insulted Guardsmen . . . [and the Guardsmen] were not in a position to
answer back. Their relative silence was another humiliation
for them. (P. 12)

Scheff et al. (1989) have discussed both of these cases of collective
violence. They focused on the "brutality and humiliation of the
inmates" (such as forcing prisoners to crawl through mud) documented in the McKay Commission (1972) report. But the prison
officers were also humiliated by the assertion of inmate power, the
mistreatment of hostages, the recognition their superiors in the
prison administration gave to prisoner demands (treating them "as
if they were equals"), and their denunciation by the prisoners on
television. Scheff et al. (1989) interpreted this as a triple shame/
rage spiral:

The guards were shamed by the behavior of the administration and the inmates, were powerless to confront the administration, and became hostile toward the inmates, who in
turn were shamed by the guards' lack of respect and reacted
with an angry lack of respect toward the guards. (P. 193)

When two parties stigmatize each other, the stigmatization enables
one's violence and provokes the violence of the other.

In *Crime, Shame and Reintegration*, I have developed in more
detail the criminogenic consequences of stigmatization. Because I
mainly talk of stigmatization there rather than humiliation, it is
important to clarify the difference between the two terms. Humiliation means disrespectful disapproval. Stigmatization is humiliation
that is sustained over an indefinitely long period. In *Crime, Shame
and Reintegration*, I partitioned shaming into reintegrative shaming (which prevents crime) and stigmatization (which encourages
it).[5] Reintegrative shaming is disapproval extended while a relationship of respect is sustained with the offender. Stigmatization is
disrespectful, humiliating shaming where degradation ceremonies
are never terminated by gestures of reacceptance of the offender.

The offender is branded an evil person and cast out in a permanent, open-ended way. Reintegrative shaming, in contrast, might vigorously shame an evil deed, but the offender is cast as a respected person rather than an evil person. Even the shaming of the deed is finite in duration, terminated by ceremonies of forgiveness-apology-repentance. The preventive effect of reintegratively shaming criminals occurs when the offender recognizes the wrongdoing and shames himself. This distinction also appears in the work of Katz (1988, pp. 26–27): "Thus I may become ashamed of myself, but I do not become humiliated of myself."

The case is made in *Crime, Shame and Reintegration* that stigmatization fosters crime by increasing the attraction of criminal subcultures to the stigmatized; we have also seen in this paper that humiliation directly provokes violence. Here we have sought to suggest that stigmatization not only encourages crime *by* those stigmatized, but it also enables crime to be targeted *against* those stigmatized. For example, carers for the aged who have stigmatized images of the elderly are more likely to be found among those who abuse their old folk (Phillips, 1983).

The empirical claims derived from the theory in this chapter can be simply summarized. Nations will have more crime the more they have an unequal distribution of wealth and power, the more they are racist, patriarchal, ageist, totalitarian, and retributive. To the extent that hegemony works to convince the subordinate fractions of the population that their oppression is natural rather than humiliating, these effects will be attenuated—we will see evidence of feeling ashamed rather than feeling humiliated, perhaps of more inwardly-directed rather than other-directed violence. The prediction of the theory, nevertheless, is that even where hegemony is strong, inequality will still have some effect on the crime rate because (a) hegemony will never be total, and (b) hegemony undermines feelings of being exploited without undermining the ideology of exploitation that enables the victimization of the exploited. These hypotheses are not banal; they cut against the grain of some popular alternative accounts of crime—for example, the account of Sutherland, Katz, and others that materialist explanation does not work, the account that a high crime rate is a price we pay for freedom, the account that retributive crime-control policies will have crime-reducing deterrent effects. In the years ahead, I will be doing my best to apply some international comparative data to crude preliminary tests of these propositions.

It may be that when humiliation is deeply structured into a social system, it is not only the subordinate who suffer frequent humiliation. In a class system where the motivation to conspicuously flaunt superior wealth is profound, in a school system motivated by ranking in the class, dropping from number one to number two can be humiliating. Merton saw this point, quoting a well-to-do Hollywood resident of the 1930s: "In this town, I'm snubbed socially because I only get a thousand a week. That hurts" (Merton, 1968, p. 190). We also saw this in the case of the Attica riot: In a social system where the prisoners were totally subordinated, the very willingness of the administration to negotiate with the prisoners was humiliating to the prison officers.

This two-way street is perhaps most vivid in the domain of gender and sexuality. Patriarchy is often manifested as measuring the worth of women against a yardstick of youthful, physical beauty, while machismo is about male domination of women by sexual virility—the revered male is he who conquers the largest number of beautiful women. Needless to say, societies where success is so measured are structurally humiliating for women who inevitably lose their youth and resent being used as a score. But when resentment and humiliation is structured into sexuality, the male is also at risk. Katz's (1988) work shows how women taunt men for their poor sexual performance and how violence can be unleashed when they do so.

The key to a feminist criminology of some explanatory power, I submit, is to understand the relationship between gender and my two types of shaming. The sexually stratified structure of shame is why women kill less than men (Braithwaite, 1989). The sexually stratified structure of humiliation is why when women do kill, it is rarely other women (Zahn, 1980 p. 125; Katz, 1988; Polk and Ranson, 1991).

Just as in the first half of this paper the disproportionate emphasis was on property offenses, in the second half we have been developing an approach that seems most powerful in the domain of traditional violent offenses. However, the analysis is by no means without relevance to the explanation of property and white-collar offenses as well.

Katz (1988) makes much of the "badass" who takes pride in having a defiant reputation:

> The badass, with searing purposiveness, tries to scare humiliation off; as one ex-punk explained to me, after years of adolescent anxiety about the ugliness of his complexion and the stupidity of his every word, he found a wonderful calm in making "them" anxious about his perceptions and understandings. (Pp. 312–313)

The point here is that pride in a badness that transcends humiliation might just as well be the badness of vandalism or theft as the badness of violence. And this has been a repeated theme in street-corner criminological research. It is most strongly expressed in Albert Cohen's (1955) notion of reaction formation. Humiliation at school brings about a status problem for the children who fail in a competitive school system. This status problem is solved collectively with other students who have been similarly humiliated by the school—contempt for property and authority instead of respect for property and authority, immediate impulse gratification instead of impulse control, toughness instead of control of aggression. This inverted status system is one in which the delinquent is guaranteed some success. It is clear that many nonviolent forms of delinquency will do for dealing with humiliation by rejecting one's rejectors.

Benson (1990) has shown the importance of humiliation and rage among thirty convicted white-collar property offenders. Adjudication of their cases engendered anger and rage as well as shame and embarrassment. The way humiliation unfolded meant that anger usually won out over shame as a way of dealing with the situation. The likely result of feeling unfairly stigmatized, according to Benson, is reduced commitment to the legitimacy of the law. In this sense, Benson argues, a criminal justice system based on reintegrative shaming is less likely to be counterproductive than one based on stigmatization.

It would be perverse indeed to interpret the second half of this paper as only a story about the explanation of common violence in the streets. In the same year that Edwin Sutherland introduced white-collar crime into our lexicon, the greatest white-collar criminal of our century set the world alight. His name was Adolf Hitler.[6] Thomas Scheff points out that "every page of Hitler's *Mein Kampf* bristles with shame and rage" (Scheff, 1990, p. 147). Indeed, Hitler's appeal was the appeal of humiliated fury, an appeal which struck a responsive chord with many German people who felt they had been tricked and humiliated at Versailles,[7] defeated by traitors, Communists and Jews. War crimes are partly about blocked legitimate opportunities to achieve national economic objectives. But they are also about being humiliated, wanting to humiliate, and fear of being humiliated on both sides of a conflict.[8]

Criminology as a Model of How to Do Social Theory?

In this paper I have attempted to elaborate a theory of how inequality of wealth and power simultaneously worsens crimes of the powerless and crimes of the powerful. This was done in two ways: first, by focusing on the social structuring of feelings of need and greed; second, by focusing on the social structuring of the emotion of humiliation. I have argued that we can specify the mechanisms through which inequality exacerbates the feelings of need, greed, and humiliation that motivate crime.

With the recent developments in criminological theory I have discussed, it seems to me that we can do more than satisfy Sutherland's ideal of criminological theory that incorporates white-collar crime, which is maximally general in its scope. We can bring class back in (in a way that Sutherland would not approve of), and gender, race, age, and politics as well. We can call on normative theory, which is articulated to explanatory theory, to define objects of explanation that are not trivial to the human condition. Philip Pettit and my republican theory (Braithwaite and Pettit, 1990) is, we hope, the most comprehensively developed such normative theory of criminal justice. But there are Marxist, socialist realist, liberal, and retributivist models available that are also specified with increasing coherence.

Nevertheless, the most important accomplishment that might be within our grasp is at a more metatheoretical level. This involves integrating theoretically the following four ideas:

1. The reasoning individual (the strategist) and the reasoning collectivity (the corporate strategist)

2. The somatic, the body, emotions (humiliation, rage, shame, forgiveness, love, respect)
3. The micro-interaction (the degradation ceremony, the assault, the proffering of forgiveness, apology, the ceremony to decertify deviance)
4. The macro, the structural (relations of production, patriarchy, communitarianism, age structure, urbanization).

Each of these four levels can be shown to be actively shaping, enabling, and constraining the others. In *Crime, Shame and Reintegration*, I made much of the reasoning individual acting in ways enabled and constrained by structural factors, but exercising agency in microencounters that both reproduce and transform those very structures (for a sophisticated and complementary treatment of this issue, see Diane Vaughan's chapter 5).

Where I did not go far enough was in playing up a similar recursiveness among the somatic, the micro, and the macro. Yet we should be emboldened by the work of Scheff and Katz to take this extra step. We have Foucault more than anyone to thank for bringing the body back into social theory. But, as Barbalet and Lyon (forthcoming) have pointed out, for Foucault the body is little more than a text on which is inscribed disciplinary practices, relations of power: agency is rarely conceded to the somatic. Yet the nontrivial role of Hitler's humiliation and sustained rage in events that transformed the world shows that social theory that writes out somatic agency will have truncated explanatory power.

Katz failed to go beyond the interface between the compelling force of emotions and individual reasoning in the microencounter. It is the failure for which an earlier generation of microsociologists were so eloquently condemned by Taylor, Walton, and Young (1973). Why can we not put all of these newer elements together with the legacy of Sutherland to make criminology one of the best exemplars we have in the social sciences of how to do social theory and praxis? It is within our grasp to constructively bring together normative and explanatory theory. And explanatory theory is possible that illuminates the mutual shaping that occurs among reason, emotion, microprocess, and macrostructure.

REFERENCES

Abolafia, M. Y. (1985). Self-regulation as market maintenance: An organization perspective. In R. G. Noll, ed. *Regulatory policy and the social sciences*. Berkeley: University of California Press.

Barbalet, J., and Lyon, M. (forthcoming). Society's body: Emotion and the "somatization" of social theory. In T. J. Cordas, ed. *The body in culture, history and society* (working title). Albany: State University of New York Press.

Belknap, J. (1989). The economics-crime link. *Criminal Justice Abstracts*, March, 140–157.

Benson, M. (1990). Emotions and adjudication: A study of status degradation among white-collar criminals. Unpublished paper, Department of Sociology, University of Tennessee.

Boggs, S. L. (1965). Urban crime patterns. *American Sociological Review*, *30*, 899–908.

Box, S. (1983). *Power, crime and mystification*. London: Tavistock.

———. *Recession, crime and punishment*. London: Macmillan.

Braithwaite, J. (1979). *Inequality, crime and public policy*. London: Routledge & Kegan Paul.

———. (1982). Challenging just deserts: Punishing white-collar criminals. *Journal of Criminal Law and Criminology, 73*, 723–760.

———. (1984). *Corporate crime in the pharmaceutical industry*. London: Routledge & Kegan Paul.

———. (1989). *Crime, shame and reintegration*. Melbourne, Australia: Cambridge University Press.

Braithwaite, J., and Pettit, P. (1990). *Not just deserts: A republican theory of criminal justice*. Oxford: Oxford University Press.

Clinard, M. B., and Yeager, P. C. (1980). *Corporate crime*. New York: Free Press.

Cloward, R. A., and Ohlin, L. E. (1960). *Delinquency and opportunity: A theory of delinquent gangs*. Glencoe, Ill.: Free Press.

Cohen, A. K. (1955). *Delinquent boys: The culture of the gang*. Glencoe, Ill.: Free Press.

Cohen, L. E., and Machalek, R. B. (1988). A general theory of expropriative crime: An evolutionary ecological approach. *American Journal of Sociology, 93*, 465–501.

Coleman, J. (1992). The theory of white-collar crime: From Sutherland to the 1990s. (This volume.)

Cullen, F. T., Maakestaad, W. J., and Cavender, G. (1987). *Corporate crime under attack: The Ford Pinto case and beyond*. Cincinnati: Anderson Publishing.

Daly, M., and Wilson, M. (1988). *Homicide*. New York: Aldine de Gruyter.

De Bono, E. (1985). *Conflicts: A better way to resolve them*. London: Harrap.

Fattah, E. A., and Sacco, V. F. (1989). *Crime and victimization of the elderly*. New York: Springer-Verlag.

Geis, G. (1973). Victimization patterns in white-collar crime. In I. Drapkin and E. Viano, eds. *Victimology: A new focus.* Vol. 5. Lexington, Mass.: Lexington Books.

Glaser, D. (1978). *Crime in our changing society.* New York: Holt, Rinehart and Winston.

Gramsci, A. (1971). *Selections from the prison notebooks of A. Gramsci.* A. Hoare and G. Nowell-Smith, eds. and trans. London: Lawrence and Wishart.

Handler, J. F. (1989). Community care for the frail elderly: A theory of empowerment. Unpublished paper.

Haug, W. F. (1986). *Critique of commodity aesthetics: Appearance, sexuality and advertising in capitalist society.* R. Bock, trans. Cambridge, England: Polity Press.

Hudson, M. (1986). Elder mistreatment: Current research. In K. A. Pillemer and R. S. Wolf, eds. *Elder abuse: Conflict in the family.* Dover, Mass.: Auburn House.

Jewson, B. (1978). The prisoners' action group's summary of the Royal Commission into NSW prisons following the hearing of evidence. In P. R. Wilson and J. Braithwaite, eds. *Two faces of deviance: Crimes of the powerless and powerful.* Brisbane, Australia: University of Queensland Press.

Katz, J. (1988). *Seductions of crime: Moral and sensual attractions of doing evil.* New York: Basic Books.

Knight, T. (1985). Schools and delinquency. In A. Borowski and J. M. Murray, eds. *Juvenile delinquency in Australia.* Melbourne, Australia: Methuen.

Kohut, H. (1972). Thoughts on narcissism and narcissistic rage. *The Psychoanalytic Study of the Child, 27,* 360–400.

Lansky, M. (1984). Violence, shame and the family. *International Journal of Family Psychiatry, 5,* 21–40.

———. (1987). Shame and domestic violence. In D. Nathanson, ed. *The many faces of shame.* New York: Guildford.

Lewis, H. (1971). *Shame and guilt in neurosis.* New York: International Universities Press.

McKay Commission (New York State Special Commission on Attica) (1972). *Attica: A report.* New York: Praeger.

Marangiu, P., and Newman, G. (1987). *Vengeance: The fight against injustice.* Totowa, N.J.: Rowan and Littlefield.

Marx, K. (1973). *Economic and philosophic manuscripts of 1844.* M. Milligan, trans. London: Lawrence and Wishart.

Maslow, A. H. (1954). *Motivation and personality.* New York: Harper and Row.

Matza, D. (1964). *Delinquency and drift.* New York: Wiley.

Merton, R. K. (1968). *Social theory and social structure*. Glencoe, Ill.: Free Press.

Montesquieu, Baron de (1977). *The spirit of laws*. D. W. Carrithers, trans. Berkeley: University of California Press.

Pearce, F. (1976). *Crimes of the powerful: Marxism, crime and deviance*. London: Pluto Press.

Pepinsky, H. E., and Jesilow, P. (1984). *Myths that cause crime*. Washington D.C.: Seven Locks Press.

Pettit, P. (1989). Liberty in the republic. John Curtin Memorial Lecture, Research School of Social Sciences, Australian National University.

Phillips, L. R. (1983). Abuse and neglect of the frail elderly at home: An exploration of theoretical relationships. *Journal of Advanced Nursing*, *8*, 379–392.

Pillemer, K., and Finkelhor, D. (1988). The prevalence of elder abuse: A random sample survey. *The Gerontologist, 28*, pp. 51–57.

Pocock, J. G. A., ed. (1977). *The political works of James Harrington*. New York: Cambridge University Press.

Polk, K., and Ranson, D. L. (1991). Homicide in Victoria. In D. Chappell, P. Grabosky, and H. Strang, eds. *Australian violence: Contemporary perspectives*. Canberra, Australia: Australian Institute of Criminology.

Pontell, H., and Calavita, K. (1992). Bilking bankers and bad debts: White-collar crime and the savings and loan crisis. (This volume.)

Scheff, T. J. (1988). Shame and conformity: The deference-emotion system. *American Sociological Review, 53*, 395–406.

———. (1990). *Microsociology*. Chicago: University of Chicago Press.

Scheff, T. J., Retzinger, S. M., and Ryan, M. T. (1989). Crime, violence and self-esteem: Review and proposals. In A. Mecca, N. Smelser, and J. Vasconcellos, eds. *The social importance of self-esteem*. Berkeley: University of California Press.

Sorokin, P. A., and Lunden, W. A. (1959). *Power and morality*. Boston: Porter Sargent.

Stearns, P. N. (1986). Old age family conflict: The perspective of the past. In K. A. Pillemer and R. S. Wolf, eds. *Elder abuse: Conflict in the family*. Dover, Mass.: Auburn House.

Stotland, E. (1976). Self-esteem and violence by guards and troopers in Attica. *Criminal Justice and Behavior, 3*, 85–96.

Stotland, E., and Martinez, J. (1976). Self-esteem and mass violence at Kent State. *International Journal of Group Tensions, 6*, 885–896.

Sunstein, C. (1988). Beyond the republican revival. *Yale Law Journal, 97*, 1539–1590.

Sutherland, E. H. (1983). *White collar crime: The uncut version*. New Haven: Yale University Press.

Sykes, G. K., and Matza, D. (1957). Techniques of neutralization: A theory of delinquency. *American Sociological Review, 22,* 664–670.

Taylor, I., Walton, P., and Young, J. (1973). *The new criminology: For a social theory of deviance.* London: Routledge & Kegan Paul.

Vaughan, D. (1983). *Controlling unlawful organizational behavior: Social structure and corporate misconduct.* Chicago: University of Chicago Press.

Wallace, A. (1986). *Homicide: The social reality.* Sydney, Australia: New South Wales Bureau of Crime Statistics and Research.

Weisburd, D., Wheeler, S., Waring, E., and Bode, N. (1991). *Crimes of the middle classes.* New Haven: Yale University Press.

Wolf, R. S., and Pillemer, K. A. (1989). *Helping elderly victims: The reality of elder abuse.* New York: Columbia University Press.

Zahn, M. A. (1980). Homicide in the twentieth-century United States. In J. A. Inciardi and C. E. Faupel, eds. *History and crime.* Beverly Hills: Sage.

NOTES

1. Sorokin and Lunden (1959, p. 37) make essentially the same point: "The greater, more absolute, and coercive the power of rulers, political leaders, and big executives of business, labor and other organizations, and the less freely this power is approved by the rules population, the more corrupt and criminal such ruling groups and executives tend to be. . . . With a progressive limitation of their power, criminality of rulers and executives tends to decrease qualitatively (by becoming less grave and murderous) and quantitatively (by decreasing the rate of criminal action)."

2. Merton was not unaware of this issue. He conceded that where the poor do not aspire to the same material success goals held out as important for the upper classes, where there are "differential class symbols of success," they will not suffer the same frustration from blocked legitimate opportunities (Merton, 1968, p. 201).

3. The exception to this finding is the victim survey of Pillemer and Finkelhor (1988). In this study, elderly males were significantly more likely to be abused than elderly females, though the female victims suffered more severe victimizations than the males.

4. Retributiveness may not seem to be a dimension of inequality. But I have argued elsewhere (Braithwaite, 1982; Braithwaite and Pettit, 1990) that under retributive policies "just desserts" tends to be imposed successfully on the poor and unsuccessfully on the poor and rich. Retributivism exacerbates important inequalities under any feasible program of implementation. This, we argue, is true even with positive retributive policies motivated by theories that give a central place to

respect for offenders. More foundationally, retributivism is inequality of "hard treatment" between the "guilty" and the "innocent."

5. Stigmatization at least encourages crime among those who are stigmatized, though it will discourage crime among others who witness the stigmatization (see Braithwaite, 1989, chapter 5).

6. I trust that it is obvious that Hitler's genocide was a crime and fits Sutherland's definition of white-collar crime.

7. Certainly the emotions attributed to the Germans at the time were in the vocabulary of humiliation. The Australian press observer at Versailles described the arrival of the German foreign minister thus: "Count von Brockdorff-Rantzau appeared to feel the humiliation of his position, and stood bareheaded" (*Sydney Morning Herald*, 3 May, 1919).

8. There is fear of defeat and fear of humiliation. There is the great fear of being seen to be a loser. It could be argued that the reason the British war fleet was sent to the Falklands was really the fear of humiliation. The preservation of a self-image on a personal or national level is extremely important and fear of losing that image is a strong motivator. Indeed, Enoch Powell goaded Mrs. Thatcher in the House of Commons with exactly this approach: how could she, of all people, stand for this Argentine insult? (De Bono, 1985). When Saddam Hussein broadcast his appeal of August 10, 1990, to all Arabs, humiliation was a key repetitive element of his text: "Rise up, so that the voice of right can be heard in the Arab nation. Rebel against all attempts to humiliate Mecca. Make it clear to your rulers, the emirs of oil, as they serve the foreigner, tell them the traitors there is no place for them on Arab soil after they have humiliated Arab honor and dignity" (*The Times*, August 1990, p. 1). In turn, the slaughter of the withdrawing Iraqi troops by the Allies after Saddam Hussein had announced that he would comply with Allied demands by withdrawing was explicitly justified by the U.S. government in terms of the need to humiliate Mr. Saddam. "Humiliation is the name of the game," said one U.S. official on 24 February, 1991. "Or, to put it more positively, we want to make sure that Saddam cannot emerge as a mystical or heroic creature in the Arab world" (*The Canberra Times*, 25 February 1991, p. 14). The warmongers on both sides of this conflict were motivated by past humiliation.

· 4 ·

The Problem of White-Collar Crime Motivation

STANTON WHEELER

Introduction

For six years in the late 1970s and early 1980s, it was my good fortune to direct a program of research on white-collar crime at Yale University. With generous support from the National Institute of Justice, we launched a program that has culminated in a series of books (seven), monographs (five), and articles (over twenty). Several of the books have been published by the Yale University Press under a series titled Yale Studies in White-Collar Crime.

The main substantive thrust of the white-collar crime research program was directed to the criminal justice system response to white-collar crime. Accordingly, we studied such topics as how the SEC receives and processes its cases (Shapiro, 1984), how defense counsel represent white-collar defendants (Mann, 1985), and how federal judges sentence white-collar offenders (Wheeler, Mann, and Sarat, 1988). Only in our most recent volume did we examine the nature of the offenders themselves and their offending behavior (Weisburd, Wheeler, Waring, and Bode, 1991). Even here, we were able to devote little attention to the motivations white-collar offenders bring to their offenses. However, over the course of our research the problem of white-collar crime motivation arose often, and I would like to devote this essay to the topic.

The "why" question has always intrigued criminologists, along with journalists and others, but it seems to have special appeal in white-collar crime cases. This is, in part, because white-collar crime seems counterintuitive. We can understand intuitively why those who are down-and-out may commit economic crimes, or why those under extreme pressure as a result of gambling debts or an expensive addiction may feel that they have "Nothing to Lose" (to quote the title of a dissertation on bank robbery) by risking criminal activity (Camp, 1967). But these forms of reasoning apply less easily to persons well placed in the society, who have more in the way of material goods to begin with and who have much to lose if caught in the commission of crimes.

Sutherland applied his own theory of differential association to white-collar and common criminals alike. People will commit crimes the greater the frequency, duration, and intensity of their contacts with others who condone or participate in criminal activity. The culture of capitalism in the age of the robber barons surely encouraged rapacious, greedy conduct on the part of many industrial leaders. In more recent memory, at least until passage of the Foreign Corrupt Practices Act, the culture of the corporate world seemed to encourage bribery of foreign officials. Even more recently, the culture of Wall Street, or at least one of Wall Street's many subcultures, seemed to encourage insider trading, though we really don't know how extensive the illegalities were. So Sutherland's theory has at least some plausible explanatory power.

However, it seems only a partial explanation at best, and not successful in explaining one particular facet of white-collar crime that became clear in our studies: Many white-collar offenders have led lives not only unmarked by prior trouble with the law, but characterized by positive contributions to family and community life. Perhaps a fast-moving, highly mobile society that values entrepreneurship will find it hard to draw a sharp, clean line between legitimate and illegitimate activity, and these people will stretch the line and in some cases stray over it. That can happen in a world of multiple moralities and normative conflict. But a number of those we studied didn't just stray over. They made a conscious though difficult decision to engage in illegality when they apparently hadn't done so before. It is not easy, then, to explain their conduct solely by appeal to differential association with others in a culture of illegality. So how then can we explain it?

Since Sutherland's day there have been dozens of efforts to

explain white-collar crime as well as other forms of illegality—so many that to cite some would be to slight others. But in what follows I would like to combine what was learned in our studies with one narrow subject of recent scholarship and with one older sociological tradition. The recent scholarship has emerged primarily in microeconomics, social psychology, and risk management, and gives us fresh ways of looking at criminal motivation.[1] I confess to becoming familiar with these developments only recently, but they seem to me compatible, surprisingly so, with what we have learned about the motivation of white-collar criminals in our studies.

The older tradition harkens back to the social psychology of George Herbert Mead and symbolic interaction, to the importance of verbalizations and accounts in explaining one's conduct, and is probably best represented by the work of Sutherland's student, research assistant, and collaborator, the late Donald R. Cressey, whose *Other People's Money* (1953), despite its encasement in the method of analytic induction, remains a sociological gem of its time. This tradition asks how offenders defined their world *before* the commission of the acts in question. How did they conceive of or fall into the offense, and how did they justify it to themselves and others?

To begin with the tradition growing out of microeconomics, and oversimplifying to be sure, one of the principles of conventional microeconomics is the "law of diminishing marginal utility." That law, as expressed in figure 1, asserts that the utility of any given unit of consumption (read "happiness, pleasure, reward," if you like) rises with each additional quantity of consumption, but that it rises at a diminishing rate. As the curve in figure 1 illustrates, the gain in utility as one goes up from 1,000 to 2,000 units of consumption (read "dollars," if you like) is much steeper than the gain in utility as one moves from 3,000 to 4,000 units of consumption. As expressed in one of the standard economics texts a few years ago:

> The assertion that people are characterized by diminishing Marginal Utility as consumption income rises is an empirical one. This assertion was and is widely believed, despite the absence of a generally accepted measuring rod for utilities. It corresponds to our common sense notion that more income makes us happier, but that our first

FIGURE 1 ·

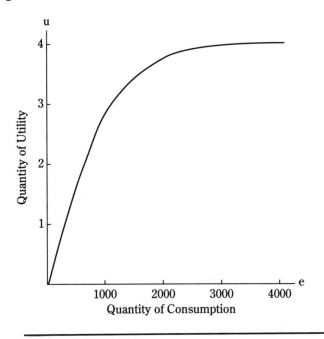

million gives us more of a kick than our tenth. (Hirshleifer, 1976, p. 61)

Now it is just this principle that might lead us to think of economic crimes committed by those who already have a fair amount of money as being counterintuitive. If one were inclined to risk taking at all, one would be more inclined to risk a theft that would boost income from $10,000 to $20,000 than one that would boost it from $100,000 to $110,000. That is what the law of diminishing marginal utility would tell us.

So how, then, do we explain people who seem willing to risk a lot when they already have a lot? It has become part of the conventional wisdom of microeconomics to imagine that, while risk aversion as in the law of diminishing returns may be the most common phenomenon, there will be some who are risk neutral, and still others who may be risk seekers—the mirror opposite of the risk-averse folks described in figure 1. Such people would be graphed as in figure 2,

FIGURE 2 ·

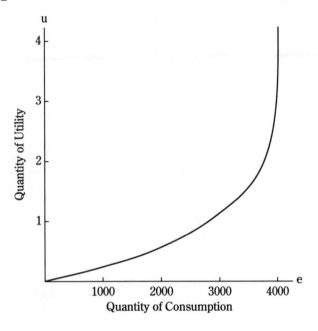

where each increase in income or consumption unit provides not a diminished increase in utility, but an accelerated one. These are persons for whom to move from the tenth to the eleventh million provides even greater psychological satisfaction than the move from the first to the second. They might be thought of as just what we mean by the concept of greed as a personality trait: people who want even more, the more they already have.[2]

Are there such people? If we had fuller motivational accounts it would be easier to know, but we do have the fictionalized account by Gordon Gekko, the antihero financier in the movie *Wall Street*, whose "Greed is Good" speech stunned many listeners. And we have a real-life history that might be called "Leona's Lament." Leona Helmsley, wife and partner to one of the largest and wealthiest real estate entrepreneurs in America, has enormous wealth, but it did not preclude her filing fraudulent income tax returns.[3]

If the pattern of greed described by Leona's Lament should be established and verified for some people, it would lead to further questions. Is the pattern reversible? What kind of socialization produces it? Is greed seeking just another form of risk taking, or are those who are risk seekers with regard to money and the criminal justice system actually risk averse in other spheres, such as their own health or physical safety? Perhaps most crucially, how are we to distinguish the presumably desirable forms of risk seeking engaged in by achievement-oriented entrepreneurs from the antisocial forms of greed seeking that lead to crimes?

And perhaps this pattern of greed is itself not a unitary phenomenon. For some it may take the form of a true pathology of personality—a person oblivious of the pattern though engaged in it, and thoroughly stunned and unprepared to be caught and "treated like a criminal." Others, more rationally motivated but still in a risk-taking mode, may have neutralized norms against fraud and self-dealing, and see themselves, in a kind of sporting theory of justice, as pitting *their* wits against those of the system in some very high-stakes games.[4]

Obtaining direct accounts of the defendant's thoughts and experiences will be necessary if we are to explore these possibilities in more detail, and thus learn more about the "lived experience" of offenders, to use Katz's phrase (1988). It is just such accounts that one would gather in interviews with convicted offenders.

In the meantime, we should learn what we can from available materials. In one of our studies, Rothman and Gandossy (1982) undertook to examine offenders' accounts of their offenses and to see if different accounts of their conduct would yield different outcomes.[5] Their sources of information were offender accounts in the presentence information reports (PSIs) prepared by the federal probation department. Although those accounts often capture the defendant's expressed attitude *after* the offense, few really give an extended picture of the offender's feelings, even as reconstructed later, just before and during the offense. But one of the "sad tales" they quoted gives an important motivational hint and suggests a pattern very different from the "risk seeking" just described:

> For me—just me—it would have been the best thing, but I was trapped between two families. My brothers on the one side, my wife and children on the other. I can't explain my feelings when I was told. I was shocked, hurt, confused, angry and damned everyone for putting me into this awful

position. The anguish I went through before and after my decision and living with it every day, built up to a point where I lost my health, and almost died from it. I realised I was wrong for not taking more interest in the financial end of the business. I have always done physical work and was not very bookish. I always thought they were smarter than I was. So besides finding out about the bank, I also found out the extent of what we owed the creditors. So when my brothers told me that the scheme was necessary to save the business, I agreed to the plan even though I knew it was wrong.

They were my flesh and blood and were so positive of the deals going through, I had to give them that chance. At home there was my wife and children. In the early years of our marriage, my wife had enough faith and trust in me to invest her own money in property to help me get started. She never got more than a salary and sometimes nothing when there was no work. I was a workaholic and left her to raise the children and solve the problems. If I let everything collapse I knew she would be hounded by bill collectors, dragged into the courts, her property and our home threatened. I was 53 years old with no skills, there was no pension, no Social Security for at least 10 years, a boy 16 and a 10-year-old girl still to raise. If my brothers were so close to closing those deals, that would save everyone. I had to give them a chance. To take a chance for them and their families and I for my own family. I am sorry I broke the law, sorry for all my mistakes, sorry so many innocent people got hurt. (Pp. 454–455)

In our recent book on white-collar offenders, my colleagues and I drew on accounts of this kind in a number of PSIs, which led us to speculate as follows about one type of white-collar offender

. . . who would be reasonably happy with the place they have achieved through conventional means if only they could keep that place. But the fate of organizational success and failure, or the changing nature of the economy in their line of work, may put them at least temporarily under great financial pressure, where they risk losing the lifestyle that they have achieved. They may perceive this situation as a short-term threat that can be met through short-term fraud—a temporary taking to be restored as soon as business fortunes turn around. The motivation for their crime is not selfish ego gratification, but rather the *fear of falling*—of losing what they have worked so hard to gain. (Weisburd, Wheeler, Waring, and Bode, 1991, p. 224)

This kind of story is surely inconsistent with a greedy, risk-seeking, the-more-you-have the-more-you-want account. The stress here is not on getting ahead, but on avoiding falling back. Yet it seems too strong and urgent in tone to be just another story of a risk-averse person for whom losses will always loom at least a little larger than gains, and so might encourage a little risk taking.

Enter Kahneman and Tversky. In a seminal paper in an economics journal some years ago, Kahneman and Tversky (1979) presented what they called "prospect theory," part of which provides a different understanding of the way utility works.[6] Drawing on some earlier work by Markowitz (1952), they assert that utility is judged on the basis of gains and losses rather than on final asset positions. They note that this assumption is compatible with basic principles of perception and judgment, which are "attuned to the evaluation of changes or differences rather than to the evaluation of absolute magnitudes."[7] The typical reference point, for example, would be one's current level of wealth, from which any prospective gain or loss would be judged.

Further, they argue that in judging the magnitude of a change in value, either of losses or of gains, the marginal value decreases with its magnitude. This will produce an S-shaped value function, concave above the reference point and convex below it. Finally, they argue that a salient characteristic of attitudes to changes in welfare is that *losses loom larger than gains*.[8] "The aggravation that one experiences in losing a sum of money appears to be greater than the pleasure associated with gaining the same amount." The value function will thus be steeper for losses than for gains.

The result is like that diagrammed in figure 3, and in marked contrast to the principle of diminishing marginal utility. Indeed, the Kahneman-Tversky loss function can be seen as a combination of the concave shape of risk aversion for prospective gains and the convex function of risk seeking for prospective losses, with the

FIGURE 3 ·

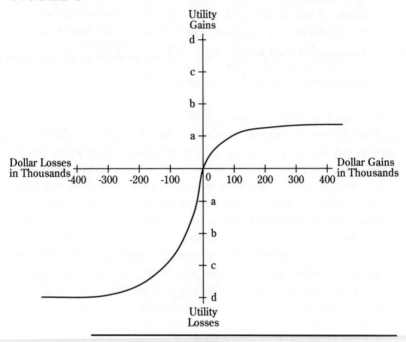

added wrinkle that the convex curve for losses is steeper (judged from the reference point) than the concave curve for gains.

Now let's go back to the fellow in Rothman and Gandossy's sad tale. Suppose the small company is now worth a million dollars and that the teller of the tale is at the intersection of figure 3. He has reason to believe that impending losses will take him to point c on the utility curve. A loss of roughly 15 percent of the company's worth sends his subjective utility plummeting to roughly half its former value. He listens to his brothers, who tell him the loss can be avoided by a few very short-term illegal deals, after which the company will be not only at the intersection but possibly above it.

In this narrative account, Sutherland's differential association is present in the very direct sense that his brothers are encouraging the commission of a crime. But if we are to believe his story, that would not have been enough in itself. It was the fear of serious financial loss, and what it would mean to him and his family, that led him to do something he knew was wrong.

Thus figure 3 seems to capture in a literally graphic way our general point about "fear of falling." The logic applies as well to the loss of status and prestige as to the loss of money. It might explain why someone like former president Nixon would engage in a massive cover-up and obstruction of justice rather than suffer the drop in prestige that would have occurred had he acknowledged that someone in the Republican party's Committee to Reelect the President had committed a third-rate burglary.[9] The equivalent for many white-collar offenders in the private sector might be the loss from a mortgage foreclosure, or having to shift the kids from a private to a public school.

This effect enables us to add one bit of specification to more general discussions about the "culture of competition." Coleman (1987) has noted, for example, that both the desire to achieve and the fear of failure may serve as factors conducive to white-collar crime.[10] If we are correct, in a world with roughly the same number of *prospective* gains and losses, it is among the latter that we should find the preponderance of white-collar offenders. Whatever the distribution, it should be among those in fear of falling, rather than those holding steady or on the rise, where a higher proportion of white-collar offenders may be found. Also, if Kahneman and Tversky are right, it is *falling* rather than *failing* that is crucial, in that the drop in utility is greatest just below the person's current position.

Kahneman and Tversky's basic "framing" effect with respect to losses and gains has been replicated in a variety of different designs, both in experiments and in the field (Shur, 1987; Feigenbaum and Thomas, 1988), and it does seem to make sense to apply risk analysis to the motivation of prospective white-collar offenders.[11] They are surely behaving under conditions of uncertainty, both with respect to income and prestige on the one hand, and the vagaries of who gets detected and prosecuted in the criminal justice system on the other.[12] And it raises one question of possible prevention: Would it help if lawyers, friends, and others with whom persons in these risky situations might find themselves *knew* of the Kahneman-Tversky principle and communicated it openly, so that it could be discussed? Perhaps one could convince at least some prospective offenders that there are alternatives—like bankruptcy, or simply living at a diminished level—that would make the risk of a presumably greater loss that comes from being labeled and treated as a criminal to be not worth it.[13]

One difficulty with this prospective solution is that it takes time, and as recent events have suggested, when the fall begins, the trip down can be very fast indeed. The recent failure of two law firms is instructive. The firm of Finley, Kumble, Wagner, Underberg, Manley, Myerson & Casey, one of the largest in the nation at the time, was probably at its height in May of 1987. It shut its doors January 4, 1988 (Jensen, 1988). The firm of Myerson and Kuhn was apparently making money at the end of December 1988. Things started awry in March of 1989, and the firm folded by December (Jensen, 1990). In the latter case, which could be a classic "fear of falling" tale, former baseball commissioner Bowie Kuhn personally guaranteed a multi-million dollar bank loan as late as June 1989. By the following winter, he had sold his home in New Jersey and moved to Florida, where houses cannot be taken in bankruptcy proceedings, thereby placing himself in possible jeopardy of federal bankruptcy fraud charges.

The frequency of "fear of falling" stories, relative to other motivational accounts, is of course a subject for further inquiry. In our research, we have many accounts of need-based offenses that are not easily subsumed under either "greed" or "fear of falling" scenarios. Other types that appear occasionally in our research, though usually at only modest levels of offending, are tax protesters whose crimes are ideological in nature, and occasional cases of revenge seekers, who are unhappy with the way they have been treated by their companies and who justify stealing from them. Some offenders may, of course, combine two or more of these sources of motivation for their offenses. One of the purposes of a much more detailed analysis of offenders and their accounts would be to document more clearly these various patterns. Understanding the situations of offenders as they experience them just *might* give us some thoughts about how to change the patterns in question.

These thoughts have been couched in individualistic, psychological terms, but it is surely worth asking if there are organizational and cultural parallels. For example, a traditional view would probably have it that small, new brokerage firms might be forced to take risks,[14] but that as they grow in size and prosperity they will follow the law of diminishing marginal utility and become more risk averse, and that a *climate* of risk aversion would become established in the firm. But what if the firm then hired a few greed seekers like those portrayed in figure 2? Might they not shift the climate in the firm from one of risk aversion to risk seeking?

That such a shift might occur is suggested in a recent report of changes in the Wall Street investment firm of Goldman, Sachs & Company. One long-term partner was quoted as saying that in the old days, he would have trusted any partner with his wallet, but not today. Another partner said, "The greediness of people is the one thing I dislike most of what I see" (*New York Times*, 1990). In any event, another benefit of interviewing offenders is that those who have been in the organizations that populate the financial world might be able to tell us *how they experienced* the corporate culture, and whether and how it encouraged or discouraged risk taking and illegality.

Finally, what relation do these models have to organizational misconduct itself? Will organizations respond to fear of falling in the same manner as individuals? Will the individual agent who is working for the organization rather than for himself respond along a different utility function? The growing literature on organizational deviance and on individual misconduct in organizations provides suggestive leads.[15]

I hope this shows that in our efforts to understand the motives of white-collar offenders we have much to gain by combining some of the newer developments in microeconomics, psychology, and risk analysis with a tradition that draws on narrative accounts provided by defendants. The models based on basic principles of perception and utility allow a cleaner, neater analytic framework, but at the possible cost of empirical validity. Whether the persons whose decisions we are trying to understand really behave like the models is an empirical question. My guess is that when we have a fuller and richer set of accounts of the white-collar defendant's "definition of the situation" to use W. I. Thomas's apt old phrase, we will find that even the sophisticated understanding yielded by models like the Kahneman-Tversky loss function will need to be elaborated. One form of elaboration might be to include critical judgments of timing: How long might we have to turn this situation around? Another might concern the trade-off between potential financial losses and moral-reputational losses. We will learn more about which elaborations are necessary, not by doing more experiments asking college students to respond to hypotheticals, but by getting closer to the real-life worlds of those in positions of trust or affluence who are facing an uncertain future.

REFERENCES

Camp, G. (1967). Nothing to lose: A study of bank robbery in America. Unpublished doctoral dissertation, Yale University.

Coleman, J. W. (1987). Toward an integrated theory of white-collar crime. *American Journal of Sociology, 93*, 406–439.

Cornish, D. B., and Clarke, R. V. (1986). *The reasoning criminal: Rational choice perspectives on offending.* New York: Springer-Verlag.

Cressey, D. R. (1953). *Other people's money: A study in the social psychology of embezzlement.* Glencoe, Ill.: Free Press.

Ellickson, R. (1989). Bringing culture and human frailty to rational actors: A critique of classical law and economics. *Chicago-Kent Law Review, 65*, no. 1, 23–65.

Feigenbaum, A., and Thomas, H. (1988). Attitudes toward risk and the risk-return paradox: Prospect theory explanations. *Academy of Management Journal, 31*, 85–106.

Heimer, K. (1988). Social structure, psychology and the estimation of risk. *Annual Review of Sociology, 14.* 491–519.

Hirshleifer, J. (1976). *Price theory and application.* Englewood Cliffs, N.J.. Prentice-Hall.

Jensen, R. H. (1988). *National Law Journal,* Feb. 8, 1, 44.

———. (1990). *National Law Journal,* Feb. 26, 2.

Johnson, E., and Payne, J. (1986). The decision to commit a crime: An information-processing analysis. In D. B. Cornish, and R. V. Clarke, *The reasoning criminal,* 170–185. New York: Springer-Verlag.

Kahneman, D., and Tversky, A. (1979). Prospect theory: An analysis of decision under risk. *Econometrica, 47*, (2), 263–291.

Katz, J. (1988). *Seductions of crime: Moral and sensual attractions of doing evil.* New York: Basic Books.

Lattimore, P., and Witte, A. (1986). Models of decision-making under uncertainty. In D. B. Cornish, and R. V. Clarke, *The reasoning criminal,* 129–155. New York: Springer-Verlag.

Machina, M. (1987). Choice under uncertainty: Problems solved and unsolved. *Economic Perspectives, 1*, (1), 121–154.

Mann, K. (1985). *Defending white-collar crime: A portrait of attorneys at work.* New Haven: Yale University Press.

Markowitz, H. (1952). The utility of wealth. *Journal of Political Economy, 60*, 151–158.

New York Times (1990). Jan. 25, D1, 3.

Rothman, M. L. and Gandossy, R. P. (1982). Sad tales: The accounts of white-collar defendants and the decision to sanction. *Pacific Sociological Review, 25*, 449–474.

Sanders, J. (1989). Firm risk management in the face of product liability rules. *Law & Policy, 11*, (3), 253–280.

Schur, P. H. (1987). Effects of gain and loss decision frames on risky purchase negotiations. *Journal of Applied Psychology, 72*, 351–358.

Shapiro, S. P. (1984). *Wayward capitalists: Target of the Securities and Exchange Commission*. New Haven: Yale University Press.

Short, J., ed. (1989). Social and legal aspects of risk and risk related behavior. *Law & Policy, 11*, (3).

Slovic, P., Fischoff, B., and Fichtenstein, S. (1985). Regulation of risk: A psychological perspective. In R. G. Noll, ed. *Regulatory policy and the social sciences*, 241. Berkeley: University of California Press.

Vaughan, D. (1983). *Controlling unlawful organizational behavior: Social structure and corporate misconduct*. Chicago: University of Chicago Press.

Weisburd, D., Wheeler, S., Waring E., and Bode, N. (1991). *Crimes of the middle classes: White-collar offenders in the federal courts*. New Haven: Yale University Press.

Wheeler, S., Mann, K., and Sarat, A. (1988). *Sitting in judgment: The sentencing of white-collar criminals*. New Haven: Yale University Press.

NOTES

1. The most central article is Daniel Kahneman and Amos Tversky, "Prospect Theory: An Analysis of Decision Under Risk," *Econometrica*, vol. 47, no. 2 (March 1979), 263–291. See also Tversky and Kahneman, "The Framing of Decisions and the Psychology of Choice," *Science, 211* (1981), 453–458. For a more recent review see Mark J. Machina, "Choice Under Uncertainty: Problems Solved and Unsolved," *Economic Perspectives*, vol. 1, no. 1, (summer 1987), 121–154.

   Although economists are primarily concerned with the relation of these new models to expected utility theory, the models are having an impact far beyond the traditional soil. See, for example, their use in a number of articles in a special issue of *Law & Policy* devoted to "Social and Legal Aspects of Risk and Risk Related Behavior," James F. Short, ed., vol. 11, no. 3, (July 1989), especially in Joseph Sanders, "Firm Risk Management in the Face of Product Liability Rules," 253–280. See also Robert C. Ellickson, "Bringing Culture and Human Frailty to Rational Actors: A Critique of Classical Law and Economics," *Chicago-Kent Law Review*, vol. 65, no. 1 (1989), 23–55; Carol A. Heimer, "Social

Structure, Psychology, and the Estimation of Risk," *Annual Review of Sociology*, vol. 14 (1988), 491–519.

2. All persons who are risk seeking become increasingly greedy as they get richer in the sense that the amount of utility they gain from a given increase in income increases as their income increases. But my economist colleagues Henry Hansmann and Avery Katz tell me this does not necessarily mean that they will become increasingly risk seeking in the sense that "bad bets" they would spurn when poor, they would accept when rich. Only utility functions that exhibit extreme degrees of risk seeking will have the latter property.

3. Or so said the district court. Her case is on appeal.

4. In thinking about what other phenomena might function in this way so that we could perhaps see this behavior as not unique to white-collar crime but more generalizable, two other thoughts occurred. One pertains to collectors. Those who want to collect every baseball card or every Chinese teacup presumably get increasing pleasure as they near the end of the completion of the set. If the total set has, say, one hundred objects, they get more pleasure out of the move from the ninetieth to the ninety-first object than in the move from the tenth to the eleventh. Similarly with records in sports—Joe DiMaggio's hit in the fiftieth consecutive game must have meant an even greater gain in satisfaction over the forty-ninth than did the move from ninth to the tenth. These may follow the same general curve, but may still be rather different in that at least with the collectors there is a *finite number* of objects and, therefore, a chance to complete the set, whereas Leona's Lament is precisely that—although each increment in dollars makes her happier, she can't corner it all. These thoughts owe to discussion with Zeb Landsman, a student in a white-collar crime seminar.

5. They did: Offenders with more successful accounts—those who emphasize need, accept responsibility, and express remorse—get better overall evaluations in the probation officer's report, and also get lighter sentences. Mitchell Lewis Rothman and Robert P. Gandossy, "Sad Tales: The Accounts of White-Collar Defendants and the Decision to Sanction," *Pacific Sociological Review*, vol. 25, no. 4 (October 1982), 449–474.

6. See Kahneman and Tversky, esp. pp. 277–280. My attention was drawn to this work through a paper presented by Roger Noll at a Law, Economics, and Organization workshop at Yale Law School: "Some Implications of Cognitive Psychology for Risk Regulation," October 1989. (The paper, co-authored by James Krier, is forthcoming in an issue of the *Journal of Legal Studies*.) I have benefited from critical readings by some of my L.E.O. workshop colleagues: Bob Ellickson, Henry Hansmann, Roberta Romano, and Susan Rose-Ackerman.

7. Kahneman and Tversky, p. 276. This has obvious parallels in the sociological tradition's concepts of relative deprivation and reference groups.

8. Kahneman and Tversky, p. 279. The statement that losses loom larger than gains is also true for the curve of diminishing returns. The basic "framing" point is that unlike the law of diminishing returns, the steepest part of the curve is that part just below where you are, whether that is at, say, $10,000.00 or $100,000.00, or $1,000,000.00.

9. This example was suggested by Roger Noll.

10. James William Coleman, "Toward an Integrated Theory of White-Collar Crime," *American Journal of Sociology*, vol, 32, no. 2 (September 1987), 406–439. See also Diane Vaughan, *Controlling Unlawful Organizational Behavior* (Chicago: University of Chicago Press, 1983), especially 39–68.

11. The general application to the prospective criminal's choice has been laid out in two chapters in Derek B. Cornish and Ronald V. Clarke, *The Reasoning Criminal* (New York: Springer-Verlag, 1986). See, in that volume, Pamela Lattimore and Anne Witte, "Models of Decision-Making Under Uncertainty," 129–155; also in that volume Eric Johnson and John Payne, "The Decision to Commit A Crime: An Information-Processing Analysis," 170–185. The latter has one specific application to tax cheating on p. 175.

12. Another one of the heuristics people seem to use—the "availability" heuristic—suggests that people underestimate the likelihood of events that have not occurred to them or that they haven't heard about recently. For potential white-collar offenders whose worlds are not populated with arrested offenders—presumably a common condition—the availability heuristic could lead to an underestimation of the probability of getting caught, which, coupled with fear of falling, could produce a powerful incentive for white-collar crime. On the availability heuristic, see Paul Slovic, Baruch Fischoff, and Sarah Fichtenstein, "Regulation of Risk: A Psychological Perspective," in Roger G. Noll, ed., *Regulatory Policy and the Social Sciences* (Berkeley: University of California Press, 1985), 241.

13. Cressey noted the possible effect of company policies designed to increase communication so as to reduce the number of "nonshareable problems" experienced by potential trust violators. See Cressey, p. 153.

14. In Shapiro's study of the SEC, roughly 50 percent of the organizations under investigation were less than three years old, and only 18 percent were ten years old or older. See Susan Shapiro, *Wayward Capitalists: Target of the Securities and Exchange Commission* (New Haven: Yale University Press, 1984), 41.

15. Again, there is a literature too large for individual citation, but see especially Diane Vaughan, *Controlling Unlawful Organizational Behavior* (Chicago: University of Chicago Press, 1983), and the arguments and works cited in Coleman, op. cit.

· 5 ·

The Macro-Micro Connection
in White-Collar Crime Theory

DIANE VAUGHAN

One of the enduring puzzles in our search for the causes of "white-collar crime"[1] is (to borrow from Everett C. Hughes, 1962) why "good" people do "dirty" work: Why is it that people who often appear to be pillars of the community (educated, employed, Scout leaders, churchgoers) engage in illegality and misconduct? We do not have very complete answers to this question. We know that typically these actions are engaged in by people in their organizational roles. But theoretical explanations of what variously has been called "white-collar crime," "economic crime," "occupational crime," "organizational deviance," and "organizational misconduct" have differed in the relative importance given to the organization as actor and the individual as actor. Furthermore, this macro-micro bifurcation is accompanied by two disagreements. First, can organizations be considered as actors when it is individuals within them who act on behalf of the organization? Second, can individuals be isolated for study without taking into account the organizational determinants of individual behavior? Yet the phenomenon occurs within a matrix of social organization, and general agreement exists that both individuals and social organization are involved (usually formal or complex organization).

Reiss was the first to argue for studying "the organizational matrix that encompasses the deviant behavior of persons and the deviant behavior of organizations" (1966, p. 12). Individual action

· 124

occurs within a world that is socially organized, and individual decisions are influenced, to varying degrees, by their context. Consequently, in order to answer the question of "good" people and "dirty" work, we must conceptualize individual action within its layered context—Persons as actors, the organization as a system of action, and the environment as the system of action within which the organization acts (Hechter, 1983; Thompson, 1967). Our ability to offer a full causal explanation rests upon exploring the macro-micro connection: What structural factors govern or influence patterns of individual choice, and how are those choices constructed?

To date, we have not traced the empirical connection between structural factors, individual decision making, and actions in "white-collar crime" theories. Our causal theories have been able to suggest the structural factors believed to impinge on individual choice, but without the benefit of micro-level data on those decisions we may be misled about structural effects. Further, by posing our questions in terms of "good" people and "dirty" work (or thinking in these terms, whether we officially pose the question or not), we often inappropriately tend to restrict our causal inquiry to the white-collar strata, and usually to the upper echelon of that strata, no less. We justifiably celebrate how Sutherland's work shifted our attention away from the traditional crimes of the working class to the violative behavior of the elite, reversing our neglect of the crimes and abuses of the powerful. Now, however, we must broaden our inquiry into the causes of "white-collar crime" to include the evidence that the social class of individual offenders can vary: Middle-class and working-class people also commit "white-collar crime" (Vaughan and Carlo, 1975; Hagan, Nagel, and Albonetti, 1980; Vaughan, 1983, pp. 84–87; Shapiro, 1990; Weisburd, Wheeler, Waring, and Bode, 1991). The question of "good" people and "dirty" work must be revised to include possible social class variation. At the simplest level, we might restate the causal puzzle more neutrally: Why do people in their organizational roles engage in illegality and misconduct?

A full answer to this question (and thus to the puzzle of "good" people and "dirty" work) must merge macro- and microanalysis. In this paper, I suggest a method of theory elaboration intended to fill this gap. Theory elaboration requires comparing case studies of misconduct in organizational forms of differing size, complexity, and function, and improving/altering theory by alternating between units of analysis. The advantage of proceeding in this manner is that the cases produce different sorts of data and, thus, potentially different theoretical insights. The possible results are (1) the elaboration of a broad-based, more generally applicable theory of organizational misconduct, (2) the elaboration of a more complete theory of corporate crime as a subtype of organizational misconduct, and (3) in both instances, theory that more fully merges macro- and microunderstandings. In this chapter, I describe the evolution of this method, its potential as a corrective to the business firm bias and the ambiguous macro-micro connection in "white-collar crime" theories, and how I am using it to guide my analysis of three examples of organizational misconduct: NASA and the Space Shuttle *Challenger* accident, police misconduct, and family violence. Finally, I suggest the potential for theoretical integration possible through acknowledging that all deviance takes place in settings that are socially organized.

Elaborating a Theory of Organizational Misconduct

By integrating Medicaid fraud case study data with existing theory and research on complex organizations and on deviance and social control, I developed a theory of organizational misconduct (Vaughan, 1983, pp. 54–104). While organizational misconduct can include both violations by individuals in their organizational roles acting in their own interest, as well as those by individuals acting in the interest of the organization or some subunit of it, the focus is primarily the latter. The major elements of this theory are:

1. The *competitive environment*, which generates pressures upon organizations to violate the law in order to attain goals (1983, pp. 54–66)
2. *Organizational characteristics* (structure, processes, and transactions), which provide opportunities to violate (1983, pp. 67–87)
3. The *regulatory environment*, which is affected by the relationship between regulators and those they regulate, frequently minimizing the capacity to control and deter violations, consequently contributing to their occurrence (1983, pp. 88–104).

Many other theories, models, and concepts developed by scholars in the five decades since Sutherland's 1939 address are included in this theory. It differs from, and hence adds to, the extant literature by (1) emphasizing these three elements as the major macrolevel theoretical building blocks, and (2) posing a linkage between them. Although each of these three building blocks is related to violative behavior, they are interrelated in that misconduct results from the three in combination: the competitive environment provides the structural impetus for misconduct; organizational characteristics provide opportunities; and the regulatory environment, systematically failing because of structurally engendered constraints, encourages individuals to respond to competitive pressures by taking advantage of the socially organized opportunities for deviance that are available in organizations. All three structural factors are necessary to a causal explanation because they combine to affect microlevel action: decision making in organizations.

I began elaborating this theory by applying Merton's (1968) social structure and anomie theory (SSAT) to organizations as the units of analysis. This resulted in a reconceptualization of Merton's theory (Vaughan, 1983, pp. 54–66; 86–87). Because Cloward and Ohlin's (1960) research is so often joined with SSAT, this reconceptualization quite naturally led me to analyze the applicability of their ideas about opportunity structures to legitimate organizations (Vaughan, 1983, pp. 67–87). With these two reconceptualized theories joined and applied to organizations, the role of the regulatory environment in shaping patterns of individual choice became clear and thus became the final structural element in the theory.[2]

Necessarily, the connection between these structural factors and decision making by individuals in organizations had to be traced: the old question of "why some do and why some don't" had to be addressed. Because empirical evidence concerning decisions to violate was unavailable, I resolved this question theoretically, focusing on the position of an individual in an organization (Vaughan, 1983, pp. 71–73; 83–87). Variation in subunit membership, position in the opportunity structure (affecting responsibility, skills, access to information), and rewards and punishments (from the organization in question and from other organizations in the environment) all play an important role in whether a person in a particular position will respond to competitive pressures with violative behavior in the organization's behalf. As the significance of rewards and punishments vary, so the patterns of individual choice will vary.

Developing a theory that elaborated the linkage between these three theoretical building blocks led to what was perhaps the most significant theoretical and methodological consequence of this first attempt at theory elaboration. Identifying the importance of position in an organization contradicted the social class implications of SSAT and Cloward and Ohlin, resulting in new insights about the social class of individuals who offend while in their organizational roles. Because organizations have internal hierarchies, all social classes potentially could be represented. Given a situation of economic strain, that strain may be differentially linked to subunit and also to position. Consequently, organizational misconduct may reflect diversity of social class among individual violators (1983, pp. 84–87).

The Business Firm Bias and the Ambiguous Macro-Micro Connection

At the time this theory was published, I was concerned about two limitations. First, I posed a general theoretical explanation intended to encompass the violative behavior of diverse types of organizations, but most of the data, concepts, and theories on which it was based came from research on corporate offenders. Because any broadly based theory of organizations must include corporate profit seekers, this literature was essential. But the business firm foundation undoubtedly made the scheme more appropriate for analyzing corporate crime than the violative behavior of other types of organizations. This bias was reduced by my inclusion of organization theories and concepts appropriate for all organizations (for example, socialization, information flows, organization culture, resource dependence theory). But what would research on misconduct in nonprofit organizations, worker-managed firms, small organizations, or nonhierarchical organizations reveal?

Sociological analysis of misconduct by organizations other than large, hierarchical corporations is scant. Despite news headlines that routinely announce misconduct in and by churches, collegiate and professional sports programs, the professions, educational institutions, the military, sororities and fraternities, and governments and government agencies, our research and theorizing have focused almost exclusively on the violative behavior and social control of corporate profit seekers. The important exceptions are an extensive literature on police deviance and a less extensive but developing literature on misconduct by government. More recently, researchers have begun to explore misconduct in financial markets (for example, Shapiro, 1987; Reichman, 1989b). Despite these promising developments, we have not explored the similarities and differences between misconduct in these various organizational settings. Consequently, we have not advanced toward a general explanation of organizational misconduct. I thought that exploring alternative organizational forms would not only produce a better foundation for a general theory of organizational misconduct, but also provide new insights about corporate crime.

My second concern about the (1983) theory was the macro-micro connection. Because data were not available to connect the structural building blocks of the scheme with the actions of individuals in organizations, I made the macro-micro connection theoretically: The empirical connection between structural determinants and individual behavior had not been traced. This failure was not peculiar to this theory but is common to all theories of "white-collar crime." Sociologists tend to explain individual choice (or rather, the lack of it) in two ways: normative and structural explanations (Hechter, 1983). In normative explanations, values shape individual action by eliminating some choices and predisposing others.[3] These values are acquired through our socialization as members of a variety of organizations: family, school, community, work and leisure organizations, and society. Although such normative constraints do influence individual choice, the fact that they exist does not lead to the invariable conclusion that people will abide by them. Moreover, by virtue of membership in numerous organizations (community, workplace, family, society), individuals are likely to be subject to conflicting norms, thus an individual who is deviant in one organizational setting may be conforming to the norms of another.

In structural explanations, the individual is subject to particular sets of social relations that narrow the individual's choice possibilities. Rather than normative constraints, it is the patterns of social relations that are viewed as causal factors. In this paradigm, social relations either constrain the individual's choice possibilities to one or reduce them so that the individual has only trivial decisions to make (Hechter, 1983, p. 5). The strength of structural explanations is that they point to why certain groups come to share certain life circumstances and hold certain interests in common, but (like normative explanations) they serve less well in indicating variable patterns in response to those circumstances or interests. In both normative and structural explanations, group- or societal-level parameters constrain or determine individual action. Consequently, we infer individual action from the relevant structural and/or normative factors. But our predictions are not always borne out, for despite normative and structural constraints, individuals exercise some discretion in decision making in the groups to which they belong.

Beginning with the classic period of inquiry, the search for the causes of "white-collar crime" has incorporated both normative and structural explanations (Vaughan, 1981). In investigating and theorizing about violations both in and by business firms, research has associated (for example) characteristics of the economic structure, industry structure and norms, occupational norms, organization structure, differential group association, organization culture, and normative conflict with corporate crime. Despite the advances made in understanding these correlates of misconduct, the dependent variable in these inquiries was violative behavior, *not the decision to violate itself*. Consequently, the answer to the question of "good" people and "dirty" work has remained elusive.

Kagan and Scholz (1984) pose three possible answers to this question. In the first, the business firm is portrayed as an amoral, profit-seeking organization whose actions are motivated by rational calculation of costs and opportunities (1984, pp. 69–72). In this model, managers are "amoral calculators." Driven by market pressures, they will violate the law unless the anticipated legal penalties (the expected costs weighed against the probability of delaying or avoiding them) exceed additional profits the firm could make by violation. The second model pictures the business firm as a political citizen, normally inclined to comply with the law, partly because of belief in the rule of law, partly as a matter of long-term self-interest. Business managers, however, have their own strongly held views regarding public policy and business conduct. Sometimes they violate rules and regulations from principled disagreement because they find them arbitrary and/or unreasonable (1984, pp. 74–79). The third model is of a business organization disposed to be law-abiding, but violating because of managerial incompetence.

Many violations result from neither principled disagreement nor amoral calculation, but from management failures to oversee subordinates properly, to calculate risks carefully, or to pay proper attention to regulatory demands (1984, pp. 80–84).

Of these three—the amoral calculator model, the principled-disagreement model, the organizational failure model—the model most frequently supported in the literature as an explanation of individual action in "white-collar crime" is the amoral calculator model. The support for this model comes from extensive empirical substantiation of the relationship between economic strain and corporate misconduct (for example, Staw and Szwajkowski, 1975; Perez, 1978; Clinard and Yeager, 1980; Barnett, 1981; Simpson, 1986). Yet, too infrequently have we empirically validated the effect of economic strain on a particular organization by examining individual decisions. Even in the few case studies where we do have evidence of the relationship between economic strain and choice in organizations (see, for example, Geis, 1967; Cullen et al., 1987), we seldom have information about the dynamics of decision making within the organization. Was the illegality a result of rational calculation of costs and benefits of some harmful act? Grabosky, in his (1989) research on illegality in the public sector, only found evidence of careful assessment and weighing of risks and benefits in possibly two of seventeen cases.

But Kagan and Scholz propose three models. Not only are there two possibilities in addition to the amoral calculator model, but they may occur in conjunction rather than separately, further muddying the conceptual waters. An organization may experience economic strain, misconduct may occur, but managers were not amoral calculators. The misconduct may result from managerial incompetence or principled disagreement, economic strain notwithstanding. Or, two of the models may combine to explain what happens. For example, a relationship may exist between managerial incompetence and economic strain: Inadequate resources result in decreased staffing, less attention to training, existing staff carrying extra responsibilities, or decreased allocations to meet regulatory demands. The result of these changes is a decrease in managerial effectiveness. Hence, a violation might occur under circumstances of economic strain, but the violation was the result of managerial incompetence, not amoral calculation.

The amoral calculator model, the principled disagreement model, and the organizational failure model all are unexplored hypotheses. All three focus on individual decision making: The amoral calculator model rests upon a pleasure-pain calculus; the principled disagreement model upon management choosing a stance after consideration of a particular public policy; the organizational failure model upon decisions about allocation of resources and planning. Yet individuals do not make decisions in a vacuum. In the nexus between structure and patterns of individual choice lies the answer to why "good" people do "dirty" work. Until we have data that allow us to theorize about individuals within their social milieu, like the work Katz (1988) has begun with traditional crime, we will not completely understand the relationship between "good" people and "dirty" work.

In large part, our inability to make the macro-micro connection in "white-collar crime" theory has been the logical consequence of limited access to data about the internal dynamics of organizational life. Documentation of misconduct within an organization prior to an enforcement action or public investigation is and always has been difficult for researchers to obtain. After a violation has become public knowledge, an offending organization is understandably reluctant to have a sociologist loosed in its midst, and evidence documenting internal activities that is obtained by social control agents is not always admissible in judicial proceedings, let alone open to perusal by social scientists. Moreover, the information that does become available is, at best, a partial record. Like historians, we are constrained by missing data: critical conversations never recorded; records undiscovered, distorted, destroyed. Research into the causes of "white-collar crime" has gone forward, nonetheless. Precluded from studying the actions of individuals, scholars made the most of the information that was available to them.

By default, quantitative research drew upon agency enforcement actions. Quantitative research was perfectly poised to identify structural factors correlated with misconduct and did so. Once a violator was identified, data lending themselves to structural analysis were plentiful and available to the diligent from sources that routinely collected them (Clinard and Yeager, 1978; Reiss and Biderman, 1980). Relying upon these sources, researchers have conducted explorations of economic trends, industry characteristics, or organization characteristics (such as size, complexity, productivity, or profit) and their association with misconduct (see, for example, Staw and Szwajkowski, 1975; Perez, 1978; Clinard and Yeager, 1980; Simpson, 1986). Qualitative research, in the form of case studies, sometimes yielded information about internal organizational activities, the characteristics of the individuals and their positions, and how the violative acts were carried out. Nonetheless, it, too, has had its limitations. Because researchers most often learn of an instance of misconduct only after it has become subject to public scrutiny, most analysis is retrospective. Dependent upon the accounts of whistle-blowers, those still committed to the organization, social control personnel, and journalists, researchers have not had access to the decision-making process itself or internal activities prior to the incident under investigation. Thus, lack of access and limited information about decision making have bracketed what could be known and inferred about the connection between structural factors and individual choice.

These limitations of qualitative and quantitative research have not inhibited scholars from wondering about the macro-micro connection, however. For example, Sutherland (1949), Cressey (1953), Quinney (1963), Geis (1967), Clinard (1983), and Cullen et al. (1987) have probed into particular parts of the macro-micro puzzle. But many questions remain. What exactly is the role of external competitive pressures, position in an organization, reference group, hierarchy, past decision making, organization culture, financial dependence, intra-organizational competitive pressures, multiple organization membership, and rewards and punishments (including those from regulators) on individual decisions? To what extent can we trust our structural and normative explanations without tracing the empirical connection between macrolevel factors and behavior at the microlevel? Many have used organization theory to fill gaps created in the absence of empirical evidence (see, for example, Gross, 1980; Finney and Lesieur, 1982; Kramer, 1982). Even so, scholarly theorizing often resulted in interpretations that required a leap of faith. Explanations incorporating the influence of the competitive environment, for example, tend to express that influence using concepts like "pressure," "stress," or "strain" upon the organization without linking it to the actions of individual organization members. As Donald Cressey wrote in response to the leaps of faith in my own (1983) research, "As long as we glibly attribute behavior to 'pressures' and 'strains,' we will continue to be ignorant about what is going on" (personal communication, 13 October 1986;

· 133

see also Cressey, 1988). The link between individual choice and the structural determinants of those choices is paramount to understanding misconduct both in and by organizations.

Theory Elaboration

Theory elaboration is a methodological strategy designed to correct the business firm bias and the ambiguous macro-micro connection that characterize "white-collar crime" theory. By elaboration, I mean the process of refining a theory, model, or concept through qualitative data that may lead to confirmation, fuller specification, contradiction, or rejection. The goal is not to test (in the positivistic, deductive tradition) the theoretical notion or notions of interest. Rather, it is to specify more carefully the circumstances in which the theory, model, or concept under consideration does or does not offer potential for explanation. Although this methodological strategy can be used to elaborate other theories about organizations, here we are concerned only with organizational misconduct.

Theory elaboration requires comparing case studies of misconduct in organizational forms of differing size, complexity, and function. We use a theory, concept, or model in a very loose fashion to guide the research. As the analysis proceeds, the guiding theoretical notion or notions is/are assessed in light of the findings. The elaborated theory then guides the next case analysis. This definition guides the selection of cases: *Violation of laws, administrative regulations, or internal or external rules by an act of omission or commission by an individual or group of individuals in their organizational roles acting on behalf of the organization or some subunit of it.* This definition, a variant of Shrager and Short's (1978), serves merely as a guide for case selection and is subject to alteration or rejection as the findings dictate. By including violations of internal and external rules to our traditional focus on violations of laws and administrative regulations, we can begin both neutrally and broadly enough to maximize discovery.

Whether a particular case is "illegality," "deviance," "crime," or "unethical behavior" cannot be decided until the analysis is complete. Moreover, analysis is necessary before we know whether a given case is misconduct in the interest of the organization or some subunit (thus conforming to the definition), or whether it is misconduct in an organization carried out by individuals acting solely in their own self-interest. If a given case turns out to be the latter, then we may decide to develop a parallel theory to explain this particular case and other similar examples. We must be open to the possibility that our analysis will show that the case is not an example of misconduct at all, but is simply "conduct." The first task of the sociologist is to determine empirically what a given case is a case *of*, and then present that information as a result of the analysis (Walton, 1992). Our evidence must convince our readers that the category to which we assign the case ("illegality," "deviance," "unethical behavior," and the like) is, to the best we can ascertain, correct.

Comparing case studies of organizational forms of differing size, complexity, and function is especially important for theories of organizational misconduct. Studying different kinds of organizations may create access to data previously unavailable because of the size, complexity, power, or norms of privacy of the organization being studied. By investigating other types of organizations in addition to large corporations, we may circumvent traditional research barriers, learning more about misconduct both in and by a variety of organizations. Equally significant, varying the organizational form (groups, simple formal organizations, complex organizations, subunits within them, networks) may permit varying the level of analysis, allowing us to get a better glimpse of internal organizational processes. Because of the different sorts of data available from macro- and microlevel analysis, choosing cases that vary both the unit of analysis and the level of analysis, when possible, may permit us to explore more fully the connection between the behavior of organizations and the behavior of individual organization members. Seldom, it seems, do we simultaneously have access to information about individual action and the structural determinants of those actions in our research. Or, perhaps we have access to both micro- and macrolevel data, but are prevented from working at both levels simultaneously because doing so is difficult, or because of paradigm preferences that cause us to ignore one or the other. Yet individual choice and structure are inextricably related: Choice creates structure, which then feeds back, constraining choice. Choosing and analyzing cases that vary both the unit of analysis and the level of analysis is one way of closing this gap.

To illustrate this methodological strategy and its potential, I will draw briefly from my current work. I am using the (1983) theory of organizational misconduct to analyze three case studies: NASA and the Space Shuttle *Challenger* accident, police misconduct, and family violence. These three cases provide desirable variation in organization size, complexity, and function, with potential for fleshing out the macro-micro connection. I will use only the NASA case as an example here. In the televised hearings of the presidential commission's investigation of the 1986 *Challenger* tragedy, the testimony indicated that factors having known association with corporate illegality existed at the National Aeronautics and Space Administration (NASA): competitive pressures, resource scarcity, a success-oriented organization culture, production pressures emphasized over safety standards, and regulatory failure. Moreover, my preliminary analysis, which was based upon published accounts and the first volume of the commission's (1986) report, indicated that internal rules and industry standards were violated in the events preceding the accident.

The NASA case appeared to be an example of organizational misconduct that would be fruitful to explore. First, it involved the combined activities of NASA, a government agency, and several corporations under contract to provide components for the Space Shuttle Program (for example, Morton Thiokol, Inc., the manufacturer of the flawed Solid Rocket Booster, and Rockwell International, responsible for the Main Engine). This combination of public and private complex organizations was sufficiently different from police misconduct and family violence to provide exactly the variation that I was seeking. Second, the tragedy generated enormous amounts of information from diverse sources: The official reports of the presidential commission (1986) and the House Committee on Science and Technology (1986), journalists, employees of NASA and Morton Thiokol, scientific experts, and space historians. Although analyzing this sensational case automatically invokes possible distortions for theorizing (Shapiro, 1983), the public pronouncements attending the accident allow me to analyze a complex, technical case perhaps not possible otherwise. The accident not only generated vast amounts of archival information (now stored at the National Archives, Washington, D.C.), but also public discourse by people more technically competent than I, leading me to sources and questions that otherwise might not have occurred to me. Most significant, a lot of information was available about decision making at NASA, not only for the *Challenger* launch, but for previous launches. This information created the possibility of exploring the macro-micro connection in a single case study.

I am using the (1983) theory heuristically to guide the case analyses. To organize the data, I reduced the theory to skeletal form, reconstituting it as an analytic framework. The three building blocks and their most definitive concepts constitute the analytic framework: environment (competition, scarce resources, norms); organization characteristics (structure, processes, transactions); regulatory environment (autonomy, interdependence). By using only the building blocks and a few key concepts as an analytic framework, we begin with conceptual categories sufficiently broad to maximize discovery. As the *linkage* between the three building blocks is the key to the macro-micro connection, this linkage is of central empirical and theoretical interest.

All of what we now know (or suspect) is of potential interest, however, and in a given case study, we may find data that leads to elaboration of many, few, or none of the many concepts that are part of our theoretical and empirical heritage. Not all concepts can be assessed by every case study. Depending upon the data available, we may learn about either the competitive environment, or organizational characteristics, or the regulatory environment rather than all three—or perhaps the research will let us consider only a single concept, model, or theory (for example, differential association) within one of these building blocks. The point is to proceed in a way that minimizes the possibility that our heritage blinds us to insights that might lead to innovative theorizing. Once a case analysis is complete, the findings are used to elaborate the theory's three major building blocks, the linkage between them, and the other theories, models, and concepts incorporated in it. Then the theory, in its elaborated form, guides the next case study.

The findings from the NASA case confirm the potential of theory elaboration to generate new insights. My analysis of the regulatory environment is complete (see Vaughan, 1990). The concepts of autonomy and interdependence previously have been used only to analyze regulatory effectiveness when legal agents of social control regulate business firms. The NASA case not only allows us to see that autonomy and interdependence undermined safety regulation of a government agency, but also demonstrates *how* they eroded social control capabilities. The analysis produced an additional insight. NASA was regulated by both internal and external regulatory organizations, so the case produced rare data on self-regulation. The analysis reveals the effects of autonomy and interdependence intraorganizationally as well as interorganizationally. These two concepts have primarily been used in the interpretation of interorganizational control relations, but their applicability can be broadened to intraorganizational control relations (i.e., self-regulation) as a result of this inquiry.

The analysis of the launch decision itself is still in progress. The data provide the material necessary for setting the decision within its structural and historic context as well as making available the details necessary to incorporate both macro- and microlevel factors in an explanation of the tragedy. While the details of my analysis are beyond the scope of this paper, I can report that the case gives us new insight into the relationship between "good" people and "dirty" work. The data allow us to see how the competitive environment, organization characteristics, and the regulatory environment combined to affect the launch decision, verifying the linkage between these major theoretical building blocks posited in the explanatory scheme (see Vaughan, 1989). Equally significant, the findings do not conform to the amoral calculator hypothesis as scholars of white-collar crime have traditionally viewed it. Instead, the explanation of the launch decision rests upon the social construction of risk and the multiple and diverse constructions held about the Solid Rocket Booster joints by the people at NASA and Morton Thiokol prior to the *Challenger* launch.

While the social construction of risk as the theme of this book-in-progress appears to privilege technological issues over misconduct, this is not the case. Risk is crucial to both. In considering individual criminality and deviance, we frequently have been preoccupied with deterrence and how the individual's calculation and weighing of rewards and punishments figure into it (Williams and Hawkins, 1986). Incorporated into this calculus is the probability of getting caught. Consequently, the social construction of risk looms as a crucial but often unarticulated factor in deterrence theory and research. In deterrence research, however, as in research on misconduct in and by organizations, the social construction of risk—individual perceptions of costs and benefits and the probability that they will be incurred—has seldom been unraveled (Pfohl, 1985, pp. 73–74; Wheeler, this volume). The NASA case study allows us a first look at how structural factors affect the individual perceptions that are the linchpin of deterrence theory.

The Potential of Theory Elaboration

I have suggested how to proceed toward a general theory by studying misconduct in and by organizational forms of different size, complexity, and function. Because each case gives us new information, this strategy allows us to elaborate the theories, models, or concepts that guide the analyses. The methodological issue that this method raises is the problem of "forcing fit."[4] Does approaching a case with specific theories, models, or concepts in mind inhibit the discovery so essential to this method and its foundation in qualitative work? Doesn't our conceptual heritage, begun with Sutherland's 1939 address, shape our decisions about both where to look and what we find? The answer to these questions is, of course, yes, as indicated by our historic blindness to misconduct in and by other than profit-seeking organizations and to the possible diversity of social class of individual "white-collar" offenders.

One method of simultaneously maximizing discovery and controlling the problem of "forcing fit" is secondary analysis of research on misconduct in and by a variety of organizations, conducted by scholars whose background and interest is *not* "white-collar crime." These case studies are free of the conceptual apparatus that guides studies of "white-collar crime." Consequently, they can be a fruitful source of data on misconduct. Dalton's (1964) revelations about deviance and cliques in manufacturing firms, for example, educate us to the major role of informal organization and intraorganizational competition and conflict in crafting decisions and, hence, organizational outcomes. His research suggests competitive pressures generated from the external environment may not be the only competitive pressures related to misconduct, but that internal competition may also be important. Also, his emphasis on cliques in the manufacturing firms he studied challenges commonly held assumptions that direct (and restrict) inquiry to actors acting on behalf of the organization or some formal subunit (see, for example, Shrager and Short, 1978, and the working definition I pose in the previous section.) Reading his work, we see that people in organizations may

· 139

also act on behalf of cliques. These actions may or may not be consistent with the goals of an organization or some subunit. By using Dalton's study as a subject of secondary analysis, we learn something new about organizational dynamics.

Similar benefits come from secondary analysis of deviance in other types of organizations. For example, Whyte (1955) gives us some stunning insights into political parties, and we learn about the processes that led Whyte himself to engage in misconduct in behalf of his local party as he conformed to party norms by becoming a ballot-box stuffer on election day. Further, his book shows that the competitive environment, organizational characteristics, and regulatory failure played the same role in the misconduct of the political parties he studied that they do in corporate crime (for other excellent examples, see Chambliss, 1989; Harriger, 1989; Reichman, 1989a; and Williams and Hawkins, 1989). Although Dalton and Whyte's research demonstrates the potential for bias reduction by elaborating theory through secondary analysis, secondary analysis has limitations of its own. When we don't control the design and execution of the research, we may not be able to consider some questions. But the same can be true when we initiate our own case studies. Even when we have abundant information, we never have all the information.

Bias can be controlled, but not eliminated. The different data produced by varying the organizational form can force us to acknowledge and alter our hidden assumptions, however. Moreover, examining misconduct in a variety of organizational forms has a major advantage: We can better explore the nexus between environment, organization, and individual acts. While this strategy allows us to consider the formal and complex organizations that are the traditional subjects of research in "white-collar crime" theory, it also allows us to explore misconduct in networks of organizations, cliques (informal organization within an organization, perhaps crosscutting formal structure), or a subunit of an organization. Also, we justifiably can elaborate theory from studying the misconduct of communities, classrooms, corporations, professions, hospitals, political parties, government agencies, research institutions, industries, social movement organizations, families, nation states, or an alliance of nation states.

By emphasizing the importance of organizational forms as a locus for misconduct and hence, research, I do not mean to contribute to the polarization that can result from disagreements about whether organizations can be considered as actors when it is individuals within them who act, or about whether individuals can be isolated for study without taking into account the organizational determinants of individual behavior. Nor do I mean to contribute to the schism between scholars who prioritize the organizational influences on "white-collar crime" and those who downplay or ignore them. To the contrary, my emphasis on the importance of organizational forms as a locus for action creates the possibility of joining these divergent interests and, perhaps ultimately, theoretical integration.

Social organization can be conceptualized as existing on a continuum according to increasing structural complexity: patterned interactions, crescive organizations (groups), simple formal organizations, and complex organizations[5] (Vaughan, 1992). Patterned interactions are the basis for all group life. Groups, simple formal organizations, and complex organizations are characterized by patterned interactions, common values and norms, and consciousness of kind. Although they vary in structural complexity, they also are characterized by division of labor and hierarchy. The structural similarities grounded in the hierarchical nature of organizational forms create alternative settings for research problems. These organizational forms also exhibit certain common processes: for example, conflict, competition, socialization, and change. Clearly, differences also exist both within and between these organizational forms. Regardless of the differences, the similarities are significant enough to create the potential for theoretical insight, allowing us not only to clarify the similarities, but also the differences.

Whenever we attempt structural or normative explanations in "white-collar crime" theorizing, we selectively study some aspect or aspects of social organization as it relates to violative behavior. Thus our research can always be thought of as organizational, although the form of social organization, the aspects of it selected for investigation, the unit of analysis, and the researcher's acknowledgment of the importance of the organizational context vary. Social organization is a general phenomenon, which, in its particularity, provides a context for all individual deviance. Consequently, building general theories of crime and deviance requires empirical comparison of deviance nested in patterned interaction, crescive organization, simple formal organization, and complex organization. By varying the organizational unit of analysis and making systematic comparisons, we can begin to identify and specifically articulate the similarities and differences of structural influences on individual choice across the continuum of social organization. Because hierarchy is present to varying degrees in all organizational forms, we can begin to focus on position in multiple organizational contexts, elaborating what we know about position, social class, and deviance.

REFERENCES

Barnett, H. C. (1981). Corporate capitalism, corporate crime. *Crime and Delinquency, 27*, 4.

Braithwaite, J. (1982). Challenging just desserts: Punishing white-collar criminals. *Journal of Criminal Law and Criminology, 73*, 723.

Chambliss, D. F. (1989). Slow codes and ambiguous euthanasia. Paper presented at the Law and Society Association Annual Meeting, June, Madison, Wisconsin.

Clinard, M. B. (1983). *Corporate ethics and crime: The role of middle management.* Beverly Hills: Sage.

Clinard, M. B., and Yeager, P. C. (1978). Corporate crime: Issues in research. *Criminology, 16*, 255.

———. (1980). *Corporate crime.* New York: Free Press.

Cloward, R. A., and Ohlin, L. E. (1960). *Delinquency and opportunity. A theory of delinquent gangs.* Glencoe, Ill.: Free Press.

Coleman, J. W. (1987). Toward an integrated theory of white-collar crime. *American Journal of Sociology, 93*, 406.

Cressey, D. R. (1953). *Other people's money: A study in the social psychology of embezzlement.* Glencoe, Ill.: Free Press.

———. (1988). The poverty of theory in corporate crime research. In William S. Laufer and Freda Adler, eds. *Advances in Criminological Theory, 1*, 31–55. New Brunswick, N.J.: Transaction Books.

Cullen, F. T., Maakestad, W. J., and Cavender, G. (1987). *Corporate crime under attack: The Ford Pinto case and beyond.* Cincinnati: Anderson Publishing.

Dalton, M. (1964). *Men who manage.* New York: Wiley.

Finney. H. C., and Lesieur, H. R. (1982). A contingency theory of organizational crime. In S. B. Bacharach, ed. *Research in the sociology of organizations*, 255–299. Greenwich, Conn.: JAI Press.

Geis, G. (1967). The heavy electrical equipment antitrust cases of 1961. In M. B. Clinard and R. Quinney, eds. *Criminal behavior systems: A typology*, 139–151. New York: Holt, Rinehart and Winston.

Grabosky, P. N. (1989). *Wayward governance: Illegality and its control in the public sector.* Woden, Australia: Australian Institute of Criminology.

Gross, E. (1980). Organizational structure, and organizational crime. In G. Geis and E. Stotland, eds. *White-collar crime: Theory and research.* Beverly Hills: Sage.

Hagan, J., Nagel-Bernstein, I. H., and Albonetti, C. (1980). The differential sentencing of white-collar offenders in ten federal district courts. *American Sociological Review, 45,* 802.

Harriger, K. (1989). Lessons from the Ethics Act prosecutions: Barriers to the effective investigation and prosecution of federal public officials. Paper presented at the Law and Society Association Annual Meeting, June, Madison Wisconsin.

Hechter, M., ed. (1983). *The microfoundations of macrosociology.* Philadelphia: Temple University Press.

Hirschi, T. (1969). *Causes of delinquency.* Berkeley: University of California Press.

Hughes, E. C. (1962). Good people and dirty work. *Social Problems, 10,* 3.

Kagan, R. A., and Scholz, J. T. (1984). The criminology of the corporation and regulatory enforcement strategies. In K. Hawkins and J. M. Thomas, eds. *Enforcing regulation,* 67–96. Boston: Kluwer-Nijhoff.

Katz, J. (1988). *Seductions of crime: Moral and sensual attractions of doing evil.* New York: Basic Books.

Kramer, R. C. (1982). Corporate crime: An organizational perspective. In P. Wickman and T. Daily, eds. *White-collar and economic crime,* 75–94. Lexington, Mass.: Lexington Books.

Merton, R. K. (1968). *Social theory and social structure.* Glencoe, Ill.: Free Press.

Perez, J. (1978). *Corporate criminality: A study of the one thousand largest industrial corporations in the U.S.A.* Doctoral dissertation, University of Pennsylvania.

Pfeffer, J., and Salancik, G. R. (1978). *The external control of organizations: A resource dependence perspective.* New York: Harper and Row.

Pfohl, S. J. (1985). *Images of deviance and social control.* New York: McGraw-Hill.

Quinney, E. R. (1963). Occupational structure and criminal behavior: Prescription violation by retail pharmacists. *Social Problems, 11,* 179.

Reichman, N. (1989a). Controlling scientific fraud and misconduct in the University: Some preliminary thoughts. Paper presented at the Law and Society Annual Meeting, June, Madison, Wisconsin.

———. (1989b). Breaking confidences: Organizational influences on insider trading. *The Sociological Quarterly, 30,* 185.

Reiss, A. J., Jr. (1966). Where the action is. *The Ohio Valley Sociologist, 32,* 1.

Reiss, A. J., Jr., and Biderman, A. D. (1980). *Data sources on white-collar lawbreaking*. Washington, D.C.: Government Printing Office.

Schrager, L. S., and Short, J. F., Jr. (1977). Toward a sociology of organizational crime. *Social Problems, 25*, 407.

Shapiro, S. P. (1983). The new moral entrepreneurs: Corporate crime crusaders. *Contemporary Sociology, 12*, 304.

———. (1984). *Wayward capitalists: Targets of the Securities and Exchange Commission*. New Haven: Yale University Press.

———. (1987). The social control of impersonal trust. *American Journal of Sociology, 93*, 623.

———. (1990). Collaring the crime, not the criminal: Liberating the concept of white-collar crime. *American Sociological Review, 55*, 346.

Sherman, L. W. (1978). *Scandal and reform: Controlling police corruption*. Berkeley: University of California Press.

Simpson, S. S. (1986). The decomposition of antitrust: Testing a multi-level longitudinal model of profit-squeeze. *American Sociological Review, 51*, 859.

Staw, B. M., and Szwajkowski, E. (1975). The scarcity-munificence component of organizational environments and the commission of illegal acts. *Administrative Science Quarterly, 20*, 345.

Stone, C. D. (1975). *Where the law ends: The social control of corporate behavior*. New York: Harper & Row.

Sutherland, E. H. (1940). White-collar criminality. *American Sociological Review, 5*, 1.

———. (1949). *White collar crime*. New York: Dryden Press.

Thompson, J. A. (1967). *Organizations in action*. New York: McGraw-Hill.

Vaughan, D. (1981). Developments in "white-collar crime" theory and research. In C. R. Huff and I. Barak, eds. *The mad, the bad, and the different*, 135–148. Lexington, Mass.: Lexington Books.

———. (1983). *Controlling unlawful organizational behavior: Social structure and corporate misconduct*. Chicago: University of Chicago Press.

———. (1989). Regulating risk: Implications of the *Challenger* accident. *Law and Policy, 11*, 333.

———. (1990). Autonomy, interdependence, and social control: NASA and the space shuttle *Challenger*. *Administrative Science Quarterly, 35*, 225.

———. (1992). Theory elaboration: The heuristics of case analysis. In C. Ragin and H. S. Becker, eds. *What is a case? Issues in the logic of social inquiry*. Cambridge and New York: Cambridge University Press.

Vaughan, D., and Carlo, G. (1975). The appliance repairman: A study of victim-responsiveness and fraud. *Journal of Research in Crime and Delinquency, 12,* 153.

Walton, J. (1992). Making the theoretical case. In C. Ragin and H. S. Becker, eds. *What is a case? Issues in the logic of social inquiry.* Cambridge and New York: Cambridge University Press.

Weisburd, D., Wheeler, S., Waring, E., and Bode, N. (1991). *Crimes of the middle classes: White-collar offenders in the federal courts.* New Haven: Yale University Press.

Wheeler, S. (1992). The problem of white-collar crime motivation. (This volume.)

Whyte, W. F. (1955). *Street corner society.* Chicago: University of Chicago Press.

Williams, K. R., and Hawkins, R. (1986). Perceptual research on general deterrence: A critical review. *Law and Society Review, 20,* 545.

―――. (1989). Controlling male aggression in intimate relationships. *Law and Society Review, 23,* 591.

NOTES

1. I use quotes around Sutherland's concept to indicate that in this chapter I am not using it as the conceptual definition he created. Rather, I use it to indicate the general field of study that includes a number of conceptual definitions: organizational crime, organizational misconduct, organizational deviance, occupational crime, elite deviance, white-collar crime, and so forth.

2. For analysis of this reconceptualization, see Vaughan, 1992.

3. While in these paragraphs I distinguish between normative and structural explanations, in the rest of the paper I use the term "structural" to encompass both.

4. For a full discussion of the problems of "forcing fit" and additional bias-reducing strategies, see Vaughan, 1992.

5. A network may develop from linkages within or between the several organizational forms on this imaginary continuum. They also are appropriate for study, but do not exist independently of these other forms, so are not included as a primary form on the continuum. A complex organization, for example, may be conceived of as a network of its subunits, as well as a participant in many interorganizational networks.

·II·

VICTIMIZATION

· 6 ·

Reporting Consumer and Major Fraud

A Survey of Complainants

PAUL JESILOW

ESTHER KLEMPNER

VICTORIA CHIAO

Most white-collar offenses do not come to the attention of authorities, and this hinders enforcement since the number of complaints against a business is a major factor in prosecutors' determinations to bring charges. One or two complaints do not make a case. Prosecutors must show consistent patterns of fraud in order to establish criminal intent on the part of the accused. Failures by victims to officially complain allow offenders to escape punishments.

The number and characteristics of individuals who are victimized by white-collar criminals, the magnitude of their losses, and the nature of the offenses against them are all matters of conjecture. Several factors limit our knowledge of these items, including the hidden nature of white-collar crime (Sutherland, 1945, p. 138; Geis, 1975), the public's lack of awareness regarding where to report such crimes (Pontell, Rosoff, and Goode, 1990), and the fact that victims feel that little can be accomplished for them even if they do report the offenses (Ennis, 1967). Reported crime, in general, is not merely a reflection of the extent of crime, but also is an indicator of the public's willingness to define behaviors as matters calling for police attention (Pepinsky, 1980). Loud neighbors, for example, may be defined as needing police control or one may try to quiet them personally. Similarly, not all incidents that result in consumer grievances are viewed by victims as necessitating police and prosecutorial interventions.

In this paper, we explore the public's knowledge of reporting procedures for white-collar crime as well as notions about why individuals do or do not pursue the possibility of criminal remedies. We examined characteristics of victims and their complaints to learn which items might be related to the filing of official actions with the district attorney. We also wished to determine the process by which victims report white-collar transgressions and to gather information on the percentage of people who complete the complaint process and reasons why they seek official action. The research utilized government records, interviews, and a survey of individuals who complained to a major metropolitan California county fraud unit, the Consumer Protection and Major Fraud Unit (CPMFU) of the Orange County District Attorney's office.

The White-Collar Crime Funnel

Our sample of victims and the crimes committed against them are the result of a selective funneling process common to many offenses, but most pronounced with white-collar crimes. Initially, the hidden nature of many white-collar misdeeds prevents victims from uncovering the offenses and entering the complaint process. Average consumers, for example, are not likely to know when a car repair garage is charging for parts that are not replaced. They may, at best, only have uneasy feelings that they have been swindled. By the same token, government agencies have not known that they were paying more for heavy electrical equipment because corporations were fixing prices (Geis, 1967). Edwin Sutherland noted, "These crimes are not as obvious as assault and battery, and can be appreciated readily only by persons who are expert in the occupations in which they occur" (1945, p. 138). The exact percentage of white-collar crimes that remain hidden must represent a very substantial portion of the total offenses.

An additional factor that hinders white-collar reporting is noted by Henry Pontell, Steve Rosoff, and Eric Goode (1990), who suggest that confused consumers may not know to whom they should report their victimizations. A call to the police is sufficient for most street crimes, but an array of agencies exist to handle the offenses of businessmen. The majority of individuals probably are not cognizant of such bodies, and if they are they possess at best only sketchy knowledge of the agencies' duties. In an earlier study of auto owners, for example, we found that only 28 percent of a sample of owners knew of the existence and function of a state agency that polices auto-repair outlets. This is true, despite the fact that large signs declaring the agency's existence and its toll-free telephone number hang on the walls of service outlets. Other white-collar crime control activities do not get such widespread publicity.

Finally, consumers who believe they have been victimized may assume that if they report their suspicions, the authorities may not, or cannot, respond to their complaints. The 1966 national victimization survey (Ennis, 1967), for example, noted that consumer fraud was the crime least reported to the police. Only 10 percent of the victims indicated that they had taken such actions. Individuals failed to report consumer fraud primarily because they believed that the matter was not of interest to the police and that the police would not be effective.

Research on White-Collar Victimization

The factors that limit the number of known victims make it difficult to conduct conclusive work in white-collar victimization. In this regard, Gilbert Geis (1975) noted that patterns of victimization with respect to white-collar offenses might suggest remedial social action, but that few studies have been accomplished. Similarly, Diane Vaughan and Giovanna Carlo (1976, p. 403) noted that white-collar "victimization is admittedly pervasive, yet infrequently researched due to difficulties both in proving the occurrence of a crime and in identification of the victims."

There have been several studies of consumer complaints but these, for the most part, deal with many issues other than crime (Nader, 1980; Best, 1981; Miller and Sarat, 1981; Merry and Silbey, 1984). Illustrative of this, Arthur Best and Alan Andreasen (1977) surveyed in excess of 2,400 households to determine consumers' satisfaction with their purchases. Only an unknown portion of the customers' dissatisfaction, however, was due to crime.

The few studies that do deal with complaints to crime control authorities have provided some food for thought. Vaughan and Carlo (1975, 1976) built on Geis's suggestion (as do we) that extensive studies of white-collar crime victims might reveal sociodemographic and personality characteristics related to victimization and reporting. The subjects of their study—victims of a crooked Ohio appliance repairman—make it difficult to generalize from their results, but their findings do provide information that may be affirmed or negated by other research. They found, for example, as did Ennis (1967), that victims were unlikely to call the police. Some of their findings, however, are idiosyncratic to appliance repair. Most of the victims, for example, were women, the plurality identifying themselves as housewives who may more likely be at home when the repairman arrives (1976). But, many of their findings may be applicable elsewhere. For example, they found that the majority of individuals complained to agencies by phone, while only about 25 percent made a written complaint (1975). Agency requirements for written complaints may greatly diminish offense reports.

This research is built upon these previous works. We wished to learn white-collar crime victims' knowledge of reporting procedures and to ascertain conditions under which they were more likely to officially complain to agencies with criminal prosecutorial power, specifically, in this case, Orange County, California's Consumer Protection and Major Fraud Unit.

Consumer Protection and Major Fraud Unit

The CPMFU was formed in 1970 partly as a response to the apparent need for a specialized unit to deal with numerous and complex fraud cases, but also because it was a period of reform when such units were developing nationally. The CPMFU is composed of three sections: the Major Fraud Unit, the Consumer Protection Unit, and the Environmental Protection/Toxic Waste Unit.

The Major Fraud section typically handles cases such as real-estate investment scams, telemarketing frauds, corporations and securities violations, and mail frauds. These cases must involve at least twelve victims and an aggregate loss of $100,000 before the Major Fraud Unit will take action. The Major Fraud branch, at the time of this research, was staffed by a supervisor, seven deputy district attorneys, seven investigators, as well as clerical personnel.

The Consumer Protection section of the CPMFU was formed in

1975. The primary function of the unit is to protect consumers from fraudulent business practices such as false and misleading advertising, bait-and-switch tactics, boiler-room schemes, as well as to protect law-abiding businesses from entrepreneurs who do not abide by the legal codes. The Consumer Protection Unit was staffed by a supervisor, two and a half deputy district attorneys, three investigators, and clerical personnel.

The Environmental Protection/Toxic Waste branch is the newest section of the CPMFU and is also the smallest, consisting of only one attorney.

The CPMFU learns of alleged violations of the law via three sources: consumers; government agencies (such as the California Labor Board, the Department of Motor Vehicles, and district attorneys from other jurisdictions); and, occasionally, from the personal experiences of the unit's staff. (One investigator, for example, told us that he spotted a fraud while he and his wife were shopping.) The unit, however, receives the vast majority of its information from consumers who report about people and businesses they feel have treated them unfairly.

If individuals telephone the CPMFU, they are sent complaint forms on which to file formal actions, though not all callers will be sent forms. Occasionally, the unit's receptionists will realize that the situations do not fall within the jurisdiction of the CPMFU and they will, if possible, refer the callers to more appropriate agencies. Returned complaint forms are put on file in the unit for use in possible prosecutions. The unit is now in the process of computerizing its filing system. At the time of this study, the file was an index noting the complaint, date of occurrence, name of the business or individual complained against, type of complaint, and a brief statement outlining the allegations. This index procedure is used as a follow-up tool for tracking businesses and individuals against whom a number of complaints have been logged. Persons who do file formal complaints receive a standard letter from the unit advising them of the status of their complaints and/or suggesting the proper agencies for referral. Formal complaints are the basis for a large percentage of the CPMFU cases.

Methodology

This study provides information on the process individuals follow to file complaints and the factors that affect the likelihood of their completing the process. The research for this study was both qualitative and quantitative. First, interviews were conducted with key members of the CPMFU in order to understand its operation and to highlight areas of possible research. Based on these interviews, it was determined that a survey of individuals who telephoned the unit for assistance would be most appropriate. Such a survey of the callers might reveal reasons why people do or do not formally report white-collar transgressions. In addition, the survey might shed light on the process the victims followed to report the offenses.

The subjects consisted of 302 men and women who telephoned the CPMFU with a complaint over a period of 114 days. The five receptionists who took telephone calls were instructed to record in a log book the name and address of each of the complainants.

A survey was developed based upon pilot interviews with complainants and the interviews of CPMFU personnel. The survey consisted of twenty-four items: the first six asked for demographic questions regarding (1) age, (2) sex, (3) country of birth, (4) English competency, (5) level of education, and (6) residence. We hypothesized that such information would be associated with whether a person filed a formal action—that is, returned the complaint form.

The next six survey items dealt with the situations that caused the subjects to contact the CPMFU. These items gained information about (1) the problem, (2) whether the complaint was against an individual or an organization, (3) if against an organization, how many employees the organization had, (4) whether the complainant was aware of others with similar complaints, (5) the amount of money in dispute, and (6) the location of the perpetrator. We believed these characteristics might be associated with whether a person filed a formal action.

The remaining twelve survey items dealt with the processes involved in contacting the CPMFU. These asked (1) if the subject attempted to settle the matter with the perpetrator before contacting any agencies, (2) whether the complainant first contacted any agencies other than the CPMFU, (3) if he or she had contacted other agencies, to list them, (4) how the subject learned of the CPMFU, (5) what the victim thought the unit would do for him or her before contacting it, (6) what he or she thought the unit would do for him or her after contacting it, (7) what instructions the victim received from the receptionist at the CPMFU, (8) whether or not he or she sent the complaint form back to the unit, (9) why the victim did or did not send the complaint form back, (10) whether or not the CPMFU had contacted him or her, (11) whether or not the victim planned to continue actions against the perpetrator, and (12) what those actions might be. These questions were designed to gather information regarding the process of reporting consumer complaints and how individuals' experiences might affect their reporting of white-collar crimes.

Fifty days after the last subject for our study was recorded in the log book and the subsequent complaint form sent out, surveys were mailed to the 302 subjects. The surveys were accompanied by self-addressed, stamped, business-reply envelopes. Also included with the survey was a cover letter from the supervising deputy district attorney at the CPMFU, which stated that the survey was voluntary, optional, completely confidential, and that participation would not affect their complaints.

Our research method has some weaknesses. We cannot be sure that the receptionists recorded every telephone complaint the unit received. Our 30 percent response rate is also problematic; a higher rate would have given us greater confidence in our findings. In addition, the four months chosen for the study may not be representative of year-round consumer complaints. Furthermore, Orange County, California is unlike other areas due to its affluence and racial mixture. These items limit our ability to generalize. This research, however, joins a handful of systematic studies of white-collar crime victims and provides more extensive information about the consumer complaint process.

Results

Reviews of the unit's records revealed that 108 of the 302 subjects (35.7 percent) eventually filed official actions by returning completed complaint forms. We were able to obtain information for 59 of the official complaints. Losses ranged from $20 to $25,000 (although a few survey respondents reported larger losses). People complained about a variety of transactions, including products not delivered, bounced checks, fraudulent sales, auto fraud, and mail fraud.

The present statistics provide a profile of those people (and their cases) who telephoned the CPMFU with a complaint and completed our survey. Ninety-two of the 302 subjects responded to our survey. Twelve surveys were returned by the post office as undeliverable. All of our respondents resided within the United States, approximately 81 percent from within California.

A handful of those who answered our questions mistook us for the CPMFU, even though half-inch letters, the seal of the University of California, the cover letter, and our address all proclaimed our affiliation. Such individuals provided us with many details of their victimizations including the phone numbers and addresses of their assailants, perhaps hoping that we would help them. Many of the respondents added comments to their surveys in seeming attempts "to get things off their chests." A woman, who, with her husband, had lost $6,000, lamented, "I know the complaint form will not get us anywhere. But I'm sure you or your secretary or someone will read this, which is good to know." Other victims used the occasion to vent their hostilities: "If I could find this bastard, I'd kick him in the balls and take his wallet," a swindled woman wrote us.

Thirty-seven percent of the survey respondents reported that they had not returned the complaint forms to the CPMFU, while almost 59 percent said they had. About 2 percent said they had never received a form, and the same number did not answer the question. It makes sense that those who returned their complaint forms to the unit would be more likely to return our survey. About half of the subjects who filed official complaints also answered our questions, while less than 20 percent of those who failed to officially complain returned their surveys to us.

Victim Characteristics and Complaint Filing

All who answered our survey said that they read and write English, and almost all (90.6 percent) were born in the United States. These statistics may indicate that those who are victimized but who were not born in the United States and do not read and/or write English may be less likely to report their victimizations. This possibility could prove a significant hindrance in the reporting of consumer crimes in areas such as Orange County, California, where much of the population is not English speaking.

Of our demographic questions, only education was associated with filing a formal complaint. Those survey respondents with at least a college degree were *less* likely to officially complain. Slightly more than 71 percent of those without a college degree took official action compared to only about 47 percent of those with at least a four-year degree (p<.05). Table 1 displays these results.

A disproportionate 42 percent of our respondents had at least a college education, which suggests that college-educated individuals were more likely to respond to our survey, or that those with less education are unlikely to telephone the CPMFU after they have been victimized, or some combination of the two. A third possibility, that the educated are more likely to be victimized, has some credence. The educated usually have larger incomes, which perhaps makes them more vulnerable. The suggestion is that illegal entrepreneurs are more likely to steal from those that have the wherewithal to make it worthwhile. But it seems more likely that the educated recognize their victimizations more readily and know to whom to report.

The fact that our study suggests that the highly educated are less likely to follow through with the complaint process, however, is counterintuitive. We thought that this finding might be an artifact of the data. Perhaps education was associated with another variable that might explain the finding. For example, it might be that the

TABLE 1 · **Respondents' education by whether they officially complained**

EDUCATION	OFFICIALLY COMPLAINED		
	NO	YES	TOTAL
NO 4-YEAR DEGREE	15	37	52
	28.8%	71.2%	59.1%
AT LEAST A 4-YEAR DEGREE	19	17	36
	52.8%	47.2%	40.1%
	34	54	
	38.6%	61.4%	

CHI SQUARE	5.138
SIGNIFICANCE	.023
PHI	.241

educated (those with at least a four-year degree) were more likely to continue actions in civil courts and therefore felt it unnecessary to return the complaint form. However, we found no such association. In fact, every attempt we made to try and explain the finding with our data proved unsuccessful. A likely explanation is that those without a college degree have a tendency to define more behaviors as criminal and worthy of reporting.

Offense Characteristics and Complaint Filing

The second category of survey items dealt with the situations that caused the subjects to complain to the CPMFU. The manner by which one learns of a product or service may be associated with the likelihood of filing formal complaints. Persons, for example, who are the victims of mail-order scams may feel that they are less able to recover their monies due to the typical remoteness of the perpetrators. This did not prove the case for our data, as we failed to find an association between the variables.

Subjects were asked, as a measure of social distance, whether their complaints were against individuals or organizations. We believed victims would be more likely to complain against an individual. Of the 91 respondents to this item, the overwhelming majority of complaints were against organizations rather than individuals. Table 2 displays the estimates of the size of offending organizations (measured by number of employees) provided us by victims. Complainants were no more likely to take formal action against individuals than against organizations, and the size of an organization also did not make a difference.

Subjects were asked if they knew of other people with similar

---

TABLE 2 · Size of offending organization

Single individual	21%
Four or less employees	18%
5 to 50 employees	45%
51 to 1,000 employees	9%
More than 1,000 employees	6%

---

problems. We wanted to determine if individuals would be more likely to complain if they thought they were not the only victims of the same or similar crimes. Approximately 41 percent of the 91 individuals who responded to this item said they did know of other people with a similar problem. Of the respondents who knew of individuals with similar problems, most knew of at least two others. Knowledge of other victims, however, did not affect official reporting.

When asked whether or not money was in dispute, approximately 96 percent of the 86 respondents to this item said that it was (see table 3). Vaughan and Carlo (1975) had found no particular association between the amount of one's loss and reporting, and our research duplicated this finding. Loss, of course, is a relative consideration. Perhaps we would have obtained a statistical association between loss and reporting if we had asked our subjects their perceptions of their losses. But, for many of our respondents, principle may have been more important than the money involved. A Rumanian immigrant, for example, noted that he had recouped his $40 loss in small-claims court. It seems unlikely that he would have expended the money and time necessary for court if financial loss was his primary consideration.

We also wanted to determine whether the locations of the perpetrators relative to the locations of their victims is associated with formal complaints. If offenders are located in other states (thus, relatively far from their victims), are victims less likely to take actions against them? One deputy district attorney within the unit, for example, commented:

> Most of the time, you don't have situations where the victims are out of state. However, defendants may want

TABLE 3 · Amount of loss

$100 or less	19%
$101 to $500	25%
$501 to $1,000	15%
$1,001 to $5,000	22%
$5,001 to $25,000	11%
More than $25,000	8%

their victims to be out of state, knowing that this is a problem [both for the reporting and prosecuting of white-collar crimes]. For example, they will take out an advertisement on the East Coast with a post-office box here. (Personal interview)

The attorney believes that many of those who victimize consumers know that creating reporting difficulties will minimize their chances of detection, prosecution, and punishment. Almost all of our respondents reported that the perpetrators were located in California. Our data do not reveal an association between out-of-state victims and nonfiling.

The Path to the Unit

We were interested in the paths victims follow to contact the CPMFU. Subjects were first asked whether they had attempted to settle the matter on their own before contacting any agencies. Approximately 89 percent of the 91 respondents to this item had made some effort to solve their difficulties with the businesses. This statistic is indicative of the fact that the subjects are a motivated group. Individuals who do not try to settle their grievances with the businesses may be unlikely to contact the CPMFU. They may be unmotivated or simply feel helpless.

We also asked subjects if they tried to complain to any agencies other than the CPMFU. Approximately 77 percent of the 91 respondents to this item said that they had contacted other agencies. The high percentage of individuals who carried their grievances beyond the contacting of one agency is, once again, indicative of high motivation. Of those individuals who contacted other agencies, the plurality first telephoned the Better Business Bureau (31 percent), while 20 percent initially contacted the police. Individuals who contact the Better Business Bureau may be unlikely to view their situations as ones involving crime, while the opposite may be true for those victims who call the police. In all but a handful of instances both these agencies failed to direct consumers to the CPMFU.

We also wanted to determine the process by which complainants learn of the CPMFU. Table 4 displays some of this information. The manner by which our subjects learned of the CPMFU was associated with whether they returned their complaint forms. Those who

TABLE 4 · How respondents learned of the CPMFU

Referred from another agency	33%
From a friend, family member, or acquaintance	30%
Common knowledge	15%
Printed matter	14%
In-house D.A. referral	6%
Other	2%

were informed about the agency when they contacted other officials (such as the Federal Trade Commission, Department of Motor Vehicles, police, Better Business Bureau, and numerous others) were much more likely to return their complaint forms than those who gained their knowledge of the unit from a friend, family member, acquaintance, or printed material ($p<.02$). Table 5 displays these results.

People who learn of the unit from official agents may be more likely to continue the complaint process for a number of reasons. In addition to individual motivation, they may feel that it is personally necessary for them to complete the process once they have started it. Those who learn of the unit from magazines, newspapers, and acquaintances may only be beginning the complaint process when they telephone the CPMFU and may feel less of a stake in the completion of their actions.

We asked the subjects what they thought the CPMFU would do for them before they contacted it and after they had contacted it. Between these two questions, they were asked what instructions the receptionists gave them during their first telephone call to the unit. Responses to the question of what the complainants thought the unit would do for them before they contacted it fell into three categories. Approximately 12 percent of the 90 respondents to this item felt "minimal action" would be taken, such as putting the complaint on file or providing advice. Eighty-four percent of the respondents felt that "significant action" would be taken, such as recovering money, punishing the perpetrator, investigating, or settling the matter. Approximately 4 percent of respondents failed to specify or were unsure what the unit would do.

TABLE 5 · How respondents learned of the unit by whether they officially complained

LEARNED OF THE UNIT	OFFICIALLY COMPLAINED		
	NO	YES	TOTAL
PRINTED MATERIAL	7	4	11
	63.6%	36.4%	13.3%
FRIEND, FAMILY	14	12	26
	53.8%	46.2%	31.3%
COMMON KNOWLEDGE	5	8	13
	38.5%	61.5%	15.7%
OTHER AGENCY	6	27	33
	18.2%	81.8%	39.8%
	32	51	
	38.6%	61.4%	

CHI SQUARE	11.269
SIGNIFICANCE	.01
MIN E.F.	4.241
GAMMA	.546

When subjects were asked what they thought the CPMFU would do for them after they contacted it, approximately 52 percent of the respondents to this item answered in the "minimal action" category, believing that the unit would file their complaints or do nothing. Approximately 41 percent answered in the "significant action" category, and 7 percent answered in the "other/unsure" category. The statistically significant change in the victims' attitudes ($p<.02$) must be attributed to the content of their conversations with the receptionists. Table 6 displays these results.

What subjects thought the CPMFU would do for them after they contacted it was associated with whether or not they filed official complaints. Slightly more than 45 percent of those who believed the unit would take only minimal action bothered to file official complaints, while 80 percent of those who felt the CPMFU would take significant action sent in their forms ($p<.01$). Table 7 presents these results.

TABLE 6 · **What respondents believed before and after they contacted the CPMFU**

BEFORE CONTACTING UNIT	AFTER CONTACTING UNIT		
	MINIMAL ACTION	SIGNIFICANT ACTION	TOTAL
MINIMAL ACTION	10 90.9%	1 9.1%	11 14.7%
SIGNIFICANT ACTION	30 46.9%	34 53.1%	64 85.3%
	40 53.3%	35 46.7%	

CHI SQ (AFTER YATES CORRECTION)	5.65
SIGNIFICANCE	.017
MIN E.F.	5.13
PHI	.312

TABLE 7 · **What respondents thought the unit would do by whether they officially complained**

EXPECTED UNIT ACTION	OFFICIALLY COMPLAINED		
	NO	YES	TOTAL
MINIMAL	24 54.5%	20 45.5%	44 55.7%
SIGNIFICANT	7 20%	28 80%	35 44.3%
	31 39.2%	48 60.8%	

CHI SQUARE	4.362
SIGNIFICANCE	.003
PHI	.351

A member of the CPMFU suggested that how people learn of the unit is associated with what they think the unit will do for them. Complainants who first contact other agencies may be told by the organizations that the CPMFU can help them. This information may override anything the unit's receptionists say. Indeed, how people learn of the unit is associated with what action they believe the unit will take (p<.01). Table 8 displays these results.

Table 9 displays the distribution of the receptionists' instructions to our respondents. Too small cell sizes prevented us from employing a statistical analysis with this variable.

Subjects were asked why they did or did not return the complaint form. Those who returned the form believed the CPMFU might

TABLE 8 · **What respondents thought the unit would do by how they learned about the unit**

EXPECTED UNIT ACTION	OTHER	OFFICIALS	TOTAL
MINIMAL	31	11	42
	73.8%	26.2%	55.3%
SIGNIFICANT	15	19	34
	44.1%	55.9%	44.7%
	46	30	
	60.5%	39.5%	

CHI SQUARE	6.933
SIGNIFICANCE	.009
PHI	.302

TABLE 9 · **Receptionists' instructions**

No instructions	48%
Complete and return form	19%
Referred to another agency	10%
Forward important documents	6%
Other	17%

stop the perpetrators (28 percent), investigate the offenses (28 percent), punish the perpetrators (16 percent), get their money back (8 percent), or help create large files against the perpetrators (16 percent), and one individual returned the form believing that to do otherwise would be illegal.

Reasons for not returning the form were as follows: it probably will not result in recovery of my money (20 percent); I expect no action to be taken by the unit (40 percent); I felt my case was hopeless (3 percent); my case was already settled (30 percent); and, I did not receive a form (6 percent). These findings are similar to Vaughan and Carlo's (1975).

These results suggest that individuals who view the CPMFU as possessing a police function are more likely to return their complaint forms. That is, items noted by respondents (such as stopping, investigating, and punishing perpetrators) are police activities. Only 8 percent of those who returned their forms saw the unit involved in civil activities—getting their money back. On the other hand, people who did not return their forms saw the unit as unable to perform police activities or civil functions.

Finally, subjects were asked if they planned to continue actions against perpetrators. Approximately 31 percent of the 88 people who responded to this item said they would not, while about 64 percent said they would, and approximately five percent were unsure of their future actions.

Conclusions

Respondents reported a painstaking process in obtaining access to the CPMFU. Over one-third were referred by other officials with some individuals contacting three or more agencies before finally speaking with the unit's receptionists. It must have been particularly frustrating for these individuals to learn that little could be done by the district attorney's office to help them.

The fact that, prior to their complaints, more than one-third of the complainants may have been ignorant of the existence of the CPMFU is also of interest. Unlike the police, the CPMFU is relatively unknown. One deputy district attorney in the unit made clear its inability to gain publicity is due, in part, to a lack of financial resources and a lack of media coverage because of the "unglamorous" nature of its work.

The results of the survey revealed numerous reasons why individuals fail, in such large numbers, to file formal complaints. The respondents indicated that it was their opinion that the unit would be able to do little to help them. Numerous individuals complained on the surveys about a perceived "do-nothing" attitude on the part of the CPMFU. A woman captured the feelings of many when she wrote, "in so many words we were told that they have many complaints and would add ours to their files. That was all we have heard from them." For other victims, the fact that the unit could not recover their money was reason enough not to bother filling out the forms.

The victims' comments of frustration should not be taken as indictments of the CPMFU. Most subjects recognized the matters were beyond the control of the organization. "You provide a good service just by being there," noted an elderly woman. A few subjects, however, wrote that their experiences had embittered them towards the criminal justice system. The words of one of our victims echo those of many who have seen the system up close and found it wanting: "My opinion is that the courts should be there to protect the innocent. I have come to the conclusion that our system is set up specifically to protect the criminal."

The fact that only 30 percent of those who originally complained eventually filed a formal action has an impact on the CPMFU prosecutions. Without numerous complaints against a particular individual or business, the unit, in most instances, will not take any action. One attorney explained that the CPMFU must produce several similar complaints against an establishment to indicate an illegal pattern. A single instance of fraud will not suffice.

Numerous complaints are also necessary to convince judges that the situation is worthy of the court's attention. They are also important for upholding the credibility of the unit. One attorney commented, "It's not appropriate to throw the power of the district attorney behind a few complaints."

We were also told by unit staff members that the requirement of numerous complaints angered victims who felt that the practice meant it was all right to steal as long as one only stole a few times. Our respondents added that the need for multiple victims also allowed offenders time to escape.

It may be that some business people realize that without formal complaints, the district attorney's office is unlikely to prosecute.

Such individuals may be quite willing to settle a dispute so as to prevent further action. For example, 40 percent of those who provided us reasons for not officially complaining stated that it was because their cases were already settled. Most enlightening was the tale of an elderly couple. They went to a seminar on lawsuits and were referred to an attorney who charged them $1,800 but then did nothing—failing even to admit that he had received the funds. Their attempts to recover the money were going nowhere "until," the wife writes, "I mentioned the District Attorney's office, [then] I received his attention. . . . [H]e told me that he would return the money if I would agree not to pursue this." The implication was not wasted on her. "I would imagine that they give these seminars nationwide and there may be similar complaints."

The receptionists may have much to do with whether or not a person files a formal complaint against a business. Due to its limited resources, the CPMFU is unable to do much about the majority of complaints it receives. For this reason, the receptionists may tend to discourage as many formal complaints as possible by referring individuals to other agencies or by letting the callers know that the unit must receive many complaints about the same perpetrator before it will proceed.

An increase in the number of formal complaints to the unit would appear to be highly desirable. The unit's members, however, are aware that additional complaints may overburden an already fully taxed office. The CPMFU's supervisor, when he took office, aptly illustrated the depth of his problem when he attached to his budget request a picture of himself measuring the office's "mountain" of overdue work. Additional formal actions may only produce frustrations for unit staff.

Most previous research on consumer complaints have focused on civil matters—items that are localized between the offender and complainant. Successful resolutions of such complaints have limited societal impact. Rather, the benefits of victory are enjoyed almost exclusively by victims. Our survey has concentrated on complaints to a prosecutor's office. Victims who officially filed complaints appeared to do so, in large part, because they believed that the police powers of the prosecutor would be used against offenders to protect consumers. This suggests a significant difference between complainants to a criminal prosecutor's office and individuals who seek civil or administrative solutions. Victims who officially complain to prosecutors may be seeking societal protection, while civil complainants may be more interested in personal compensations. If true, units such as the CPMFU provide a service beyond that which is available from civil courts and mediation efforts.

REFERENCES

Best, A. (1981). *When consumers complain*. New York: Columbia University Press.

Best, A., and Andreasen, A. (1977). Consumer response to unsatisfactory purchases: A survey of perceiving defects, voicing complaints, and obtaining redress. *Law & Society Review, 11*, 701.

Ennis, P. H. (1967). *Criminal victimization in the United States: A report of a national survey*. Washington, D.C.: Government Printing Office.

Geis, G. (1967). The heavy electrical equipment antitrust cases of 1961. In M. Clinard and R. Quinney, eds. *Criminal behavior systems*. New York: Holt, Rinehart and Winston, 139–150.

———. Victimization patterns in white-collar crime. In I. Drapkin and E. Viano, eds. *Victimology: A new focus. Exploiter and Exploited*. (Vol. 5). Lexington, Mass.: D.C. Heath.

Merry, S. E., and Silbey, S. (1984). What do plaintiffs want? Reexamining the concept of dispute. *The Justice System Journal, 9*, 151–178.

Miller, R. E., and Sarat, A. (1001). Grievances, claims, and disputes: Accessing the adversary culture. *Law and Society Review, 15*, 525–566.

Nader, L., ed. (1980). *No access to law: Alternatives to the American judicial system*. New York: Academic Press.

Pepinsky, H. E. (1980). *Crime control strategies*. N.Y.: Oxford University Press.

Pontell, H., Rosoff, S., and Goode, E. (1990). White-collar crime. In E. Goode, ed. *Deviant behavior*. Englewood Cliffs, N.J.: Prentice Hall.

Sutherland, E. H. (1945). Is "white collar crime" crime? *American Sociological Review, 10*, 260–271.

Vaughan, D., and Carlo, G. (1975). The appliance repairman: A study of victim-responsiveness and fraud. *Journal of Research in Crime and Delinquency 12*, 153–161.

———. (1976). Victims of fraud: Victim responsiveness, incidence and reporting. In Emilio C. Viano, ed. *Victims and society*, 403–412. Washington, D.C.: Visage Press.

· 7 ·

White-Collar Crime Victimization

MICHAEL LEVI

Introduction

Crime victimization surveys and the standard debates concerning "what should be done about the victims" almost invariably exclude discussion of corporate and white-collar crime. In this sense victim movements, like victim surveys, reinforce traditional ideologies of what crime is and who offenders are. While accepting that corporate health and safety and environmental violations are more serious in their social impact than financial white-collar crime and are perceived seriously by the general public, this article aims to redress that victimization research imbalance slightly by discussing some recent modest (and very modestly funded) attempts to examine the extent of fraud against business and business attitudes toward fraud in Britain. It is not claimed that these attempts are methodologically advanced, and conclusions can be no less erroneous because they are described as tentative. But although there are serious limits to the extent to which white-collar victimization studies can sidestep fundamental problems about definitional criteria for the label "crime," which bedevilled the Sutherland/Tappan debate (or, perhaps more accurately, *dialogue des sourds*), my aim is to illuminate some features of victimization against corporations and private individuals by fraudsters outside "reputable" spheres of business. Along with Jesilow et al. and this volume on consumer fraud (which often is committed by "reputable" corporations), I hope to supplement the comparatively undeveloped analysis of white-collar victimization found in Sutherland's work.

Images of offenders and victims are important in the anathematization process. As Fattah (1986) observes, the relative invisibility of white-collar crime victims within the "victim movement" is more than just a question of the time taken to show damage and the obviousness of impact. There are important notions of victim culpability that enter into the equation. One example is in the film *The Sting*, where harm is diminished by the context in which an ugly, dishonest, nasty racketeer is ripped off by charming and attractive con men who get him to bet on fixed races. So it makes a great deal of difference what sort of fraud we have in mind when we answer questions about its harmfulness and seriousness: seriousness surveys deracinated from their social context may mislead us (see the reviews in Levi, 1987, chapter 3, and Grabosky et al., 1987).

Popular images of what a given type of crime is like may often be mistaken. Burglary is a good illustration, where, in the U.K., expectations of vandalism, mess, and even rape abound, despite their observed rarity (Maguire, 1982; Hough and Mayhew, 1983, 1985; Mayhew et al., 1989). Despite the best efforts of moral entrepreneurs, and the misleading homogeneity of the label "white-collar crime," white-collar victimization carries little of this emotive baggage. Even where the crime is taken seriously, one of the central things that defendants do in white-collar crime cases is to try to convince the investigators, judge, and jury that their personal role was not blameworthy (Mann, 1985; Wheeler et al., 1988; and my own observations in British courts). Such attempts are often successful in reducing sentence or even avoiding conviction, particularly in the case of senior personnel in organizational crime who can distance themselves from culpability.

By contrast with the consumer frauds discussed by Jesilow, the frauds in this chapter occupy a complex moral arena in which wealthy corporations and individuals and—less rewardingly because they have less to steal—the poor are defrauded by the relatively poor, and by the wealthy criminal professionals and professional criminals. My analysis will draw primarily upon a recent study carried out for the Economic and Social Research Council (Levi and Pithouse, forthcoming); on two modest, exploratory, corporate-fraud victimization surveys conducted in 1985 and 1989 in collaboration with the accounting firm Ernst & Young (Levi, 1987; Levi and Sherwin, 1989); and on a study of check and credit-card fraud for the Home Office (Levi et al., 1991).

Methodology and Sources of Evidence

The regulation of fraud is a messy activity. Governmental and quasi-governmental agencies that are engaged in investigating it include the police—both fraud squads and divisional criminal investigation departments—the Post Office, Department of Trade and Industry, H.M. Customs and Excise, the Inland Revenue, the Serious Fraud Office, the Office of Fair Trading, the Bank of England, Lloyd's of London, the Securities and Investments Board, and self-regulatory organizations such as the Securities and Futures Association and the Financial Intermediaries, Managers, and Brokers Regulatory Association. In addition, there is a vast array of commercial bodies—from Visa International and Dun & Bradstreet to gumshoes in pokey offices—whose investigation and recovery services are purchased by victims. Officials from all of these types of agencies were interviewed.

Also interviewed were a sample of victims of fraud drawn from court records at the London Central Criminal Court (1984–1985) and Cardiff Crown Court (1983–1984) and a more ad hoc set of victims known to my private-sector "police" contacts. The former were selected so as to represent both "repeat players"—larger commercial organizations such as insurance companies, who were generally multiple victims—and "one-shot players," generally private individuals such as investor fraud victims. We (Levi and Pithouse, forthcoming) were able to discuss fraud with representatives of prominent companies in banking, credit finance, insurance, and building-society sectors. Victims in our court sample who were not interviewed were given postal questionnaires regarding the impact of fraud and their experience with the criminal justice system. The years were selected as the most recent two-year periods for which full records were available: examining the records was a very time-consuming process.

The corporate-victimization survey conducted by Levi and Sherwin (1989) involved (1) an anonymous survey sent to the chairpersons of 200 corporations representative of all large-quoted companies, of which 67 (drawn from all sectors asked) returned questionnaires, and over 20 others replied stating basically that since they had experienced no fraud, they saw little point in completing the questionnaire; and (2) a telephone survey of 144 companies, stratified to include a disproportionate number of financial-services firms, which was devised and conducted by a market research company. However, cold calling even senior executives with complex questions about levels of fraud experienced in their organizations and about their responses to it seems to be of very limited value. My detailed discussions indicate that few such executives know all the details of corporate victimization due to the segmentation of such knowledge because of diffuse responsibilities and intraorganizational cover-ups of fraud. Moreover, informal feedback suggests that telephone personnel were sometimes given data of doubtful validity simply to terminate the interviews. Consequently, I shall refer to the telephone survey findings only where I judge the results to be reasonably valid and will refer explicitly to the origins of the data.

Finally, the check and credit card fraud study by Levi et al. (1991) involved extensive interviews with all major financial institutions and security printers in the U.K., as well as an analysis of their officially reported and unreported fraud data. I also interviewed three professional fraudsters in the course of this latter study, to supplement the dozens of fraudsters I have interviewed since 1973.

Research Findings

Although the term "white-collar crime" is usually treated—at least by noncriminologists—as a synonym for fraud, most frauds taken to court would be depicted more accurately as "blue-collar crime," being committed by people of modest social origin (see Weisburd et al., 1991, for U.S. data drawn from federal cases that comes to similar conclusions). On the other hand, looked at in terms of average sums involved and total costs, the major fraud victims were financial services firms and the major offenders were white-collar males.

Most victims whose cases were prosecuted were organizations: only 15 percent were private individuals. The smaller frauds are typically what might be described as "hit-and-run" thefts against banks and credit card companies by "blue-collar" males. The larger ones typically involve more social and commercial interaction between victims and offenders, and are carried out by white-collar males using business organizations who defraud, on average, twice as many victims as do the others.

The Victims

The victims at both Cardiff Crown Court and the London Central Criminal Court (Old Bailey) were typically businesses providing financial services. Private citizen victims were a distinct minority in both places: they comprised just 36 out of 291 at Cardiff, and among this group those that lost most did so at the hands of family and friends (or former friends!). Frauds by kith and kin constituted just 3 of the 36 cases, and averaged £4,500 compared with £300 for the average individual victims defrauded by outsiders. At the Old Bailey, there were only 10 private citizens among 116 victims: 4 were relieved of an average of £11,500 by "close friends"; 2 lost (but later recovered) their family home from relatives who forged documents to remortgage their property without their knowledge; and the remainder lost an average of £1,000 in various business encounters. In short, friends and family seem to be in a better position than strangers to defraud large sums from private citizens. As one fraudster interviewed in an earlier study expressed it, "Do your friends first; they're easier" (Levi, 1981). It appears also that friends are more profitable!

In both courts, the majority of victims were commercial organizations. Those who lost most were (in descending order): banks, customers or clients in an assumed fiduciary relationship with the fraudster, employers, suppliers of goods and services, insurance companies, finance companies, building societies, and retail services. Since then, there has been a spate of revelations regarding rings of mortgage frauds, with multiple mortgages on the same— or even a nonexistent—property. So building societies (savings and loans in the U.S.) will have increased their market share as fraud victims, even prior to their wider involvement in the supply of financial services as part of the deregulation process. Likewise, there have been several large pension fund frauds, such as those concerned with the late Robert Maxwell. The retail sector suffered less because unless negligence or conspiracy is shown, many frauds in this sector impact not on them but on the credit card and hire-purchase companies whose credit facilities are misused. (Though the artificially low ceiling on check guarantee cards set by the banks means that many losses on larger checks are borne not by the bankers, but by the sellers of the goods and services, or by international organizations such as Transax, which use their data-bases to guarantee—or refuse to guarantee—checks in exchange for a fee proportionate to the transaction.) Banks lost a total of £3.2 million: £170,000 of this was stolen by 13 blue-collar fraudsters, the remainder by 23 white-collar ones. Eleven white-collar fraudsters relieved their trusting clients or customers of £1.8 million. Employers lost £1.7 million, mainly to 28 white-collar employees. Suppliers of goods and services lost £1.1 million to 10 white-collar, and £10,000 to 3 blue-collar defendants. Insurance companies lost £230,000 to 9 white-collar fraudsters, and £60,000 to 16 blue-collar ones.

To place these cost data in context, in 1986, excluding attempts and cases where nothing was taken, the average losses of nonfraud property crime were £644 for burglary dwelling; £578 for burglary other than in a dwelling; £1,191 for robbery; and £150 for thefts, excluding auto theft. The median figures are much lower than this. These findings on the sectoral distribution of fraud victimization correspond reasonably well with the survey by Levi (1988) of cases handled by fraud squads nationally in 1985 (though these exclude the normally smaller cases handled by the Criminal Investigation Department officers on division, as well as frauds dealt with by other public sector agencies).

However, there is one sense in which looking at costs in absolute terms is misleading: the impact of fraud (and other crimes) should properly be seen in terms of the victim's means, net of insurance costs and benefits. In other words, a fraud of £100 upon a poor person may be more damaging than a fraud of £10 million upon an asset-rich insurance company, though the latter appears to be more serious and, unlike the £100 fraud, is likely to receive the attention of the Serious Fraud Office launched in April 1988 under the Criminal Justice Act of 1987, which normally will not handle a fraud unless at least £2 million has been lost. (And properly so, since small frauds do not need the attention of specialist accountants and lawyers. On the other hand, in practice, the allocation of regulatory resources is a zero-sum game, and more go into cases with a high media and/or political profile than into those with "needy" but unsensational victims.) An alternative method of judging seriousness is to look at how seriously the victims regard their loss. In our survey, 37 percent of all victims thought that their frauds were serious or very serious losses to themselves or to their organizations; the remainder thought the loss was either moderate or not significant at all (Levi and Pithouse, forthcoming).

The 1989 Corporate Victimization Findings on the Amount of Fraud against Large Companies

In the past five years, a third of large U.K. companies in our sample reported to the authorities at least one fraud involving over £50,000; 6 percent reported more than two such frauds (Levi and Sherwin, 1989). Since 1986, 7 percent of the companies surveyed reported a fraud involving more than £500,000. The reporting of fraud tended towards extremes: companies made either extensive use, or almost no use, of the police and other regulatory agencies.

In order not to have findings distorted by small frauds, we asked companies to give us some details about the worst fraud cases that they had reported since January 1986, the date of the previous fraud survey (see Levi, 1987). In these cases, the average amount actually obtained was £215,180, and the average amount attempted was £232,487. The average losses to financial services companies were substantially greater. Of the companies reporting fraud, the median sum of money obtained in the worst fraud was £40,000, thus emphasizing the importance of examining medians in modest samples, for a small number of million-pound frauds can distort the mean. (In 1985, Levi had asked a slightly different question about the most recent fraud they had reported, which screened in small check and credit card frauds. There, the mean was £89,537 and the median £15,000; see Levi, 1987.)

How did these worst frauds come to light? Only one came to light during an external audit (and the telephone survey found only four frauds of whatever seriousness that came to light during external audits). This confirms other studies of auditor nondetection in the U.K. and the U.S.: The poor record of the auditors of savings and loan corporations in detecting and/or reporting frauds that caused their downfall was the rationale for the decision in 1990 not to permit five out of the six largest audit firms to carry out work on the rescue of savings and loans. Levi and Sherwin (1989) found that by far the most common source of detection was internal checks and internal audit—occasionally on the systems advice of external auditors—followed by information from junior employees and information from customers. Less orthodox sources of enlightenment came when (1) a bribe was (unsuccessfully) offered to a new employee to keep quiet, (2) when research was carried out to decide whether or not to close down a subsidiary, and (3) when the offender was away on holiday! Disgruntled lovers—a phenomenon observed in our 1985 survey as a salient source of reports—did not feature in the 1989 survey. Perhaps this is a reflection of the heavier executive workload in the late 1980s, unless executives learned from our previous survey that they should retain them or "cool them out" more subtly!

Clearly, these studies of fraud victims are predicated upon the selection processes used to sample them. The corporate and individual victim sample in Levi and Sherwin (1989) did go beyond the court-derived one of Levi and Pithouse (forthcoming), and, to the extent that changes in the policing and prosecution process—described by Levi (1987) and Wood (1989)—broaden the base of prosecutions, one might anticipate changes in victim acts in the future, particularly in the corporate manipulation case where there are fewer clear-cut victims. At all stages, however, we are propelled to utilize some implicit or explicit concept of "white-collar crime" when deciding who is and is not a legitimate sample member. (See, further, Shapiro, 1980; Levi, 1989; Weisburd et al., 1991.) In 1989, arrests were made following a vast fraud upon mainly elderly investors who were induced to believe that they were investing in government securities when, in reality, it appears that they were investing in speedboats and speculative corporate ventures (Le Quesne, 1988). On some occasions, this would merely have led to a decision that no crime had occurred, or that there was insufficient evidence to yield more than than a 50 percent probability of conviction (however such a judgment is made), or that prosecution was not "in the public interest" (whatever that is!). However, public and political pressure assisted in the prioritization of this case, making it into a crime. (In February 1992, the principal was jailed for ten years, though two codefendants were acquitted. Had they all been acquitted, should this have been classified as a crime?) After an enormous amount of lobbying and massive media support, and a critical report by the parliamentary commissioner, the losers were mainly repaid by the Department of Trade and Industry, which had continued to license the British part of the investment firm when it (or, more precisely, some officials within it) had received strong representations that the firm was misleading investors. However, even though repaid, the victims still suffered emotional and physical hardship in a way not entirely related to the materiality of their financial losses as a proportion of their liquid and illiquid assets (Levi and Pithouse, forthcoming). The measurement of this damage, except in terms of general-health questionnaires and sad tales, is, however, extremely difficult to ascertain. This issue of measuring victim impact raises problems for retributivists that lie outside the scope of this article.

Investigation and Prosecution: The Victim Experience

The questionnaire data from Levi and Pithouse (forthcoming) yielded some recurrent views among certain victim types in respect to police and court management of their cases. To begin with, just under half of the private citizens and commercial organizations discovered the fraud through their own investigations. The remainder did so through information received from banks, trading standards officials, commercial contacts, and—in the case of private victims—through neighbors or their banks. No private victims and only 13 percent of commercial victims were protected by insurance against loss; an important factor in reporting behavior for "normal" crime for gain. This dimension is significant in explaining differential reporting rates between crimes against corporations, at least in the U.K. where fidelity insurance is relatively undeveloped. Once the fraud was discovered, the majority of all victims who reported (88 percent) notified the police themselves. In doing so, almost half discovered that the police were already involved by dint of other offenses committed by the fraudsters. The idea that fraud can be prevented by victims spreading the word to others at risk was not shared widely among our victim set. Just under half of all victims informed other organizations, trade associations, commercial contacts, friends, or neighbors about the frauds.

Only a minority (12 percent) of private victims had reported a fraud previously, compared with nearly half of the commercial victims. The majority considered the police to have responded appropriately to their complaints. None of the private citizens thought that the interest of the police flagged when dealing with their complaint, whereas some 17 percent of commercial victims thought this. A third of all victims stated that the police had suggested that they—the victims—investigate further the alleged frauds that they had reported. Half of all victims stated that the police gave them advice on how their cases would be dealt with, and the majority of these victims (83 percent) were satisfied with the advice they received.

For most victims the main source of information and advice about their cases came from the police. Only a minority (10 percent) mentioned lawyers, colleagues, or friends in this respect. Over a third actually appeared in court as witnesses. Their experiences in court differed because private citizens were mainly first-timers, whereas 59 percent of the commercial victims had appeared before. Overall, 80 percent of victims indicated that they suffered moderate to minimal inconvenience due to the court appearance.

Much of the literature focuses on the courtroom as an alienating experience in which offenders and victims alike are passive tools of the prosecution process: victims are, in a sense, stripped by police and lawyers of control over their experiences. This is often linked to class and status differences between legal professionals and court users. Are white-collar victims (and, though not considered here, offenders) different? Half of both private and commercial victims stated that court appearance was a difficult and uncomfortable event, but 83 percent stated that they were not reluctant to appear. Commercial victims were more likely than private ones to be cross-examined: 82 percent compared with half. Three-quarters of the victims were able to follow the procedures and formalities of court. Eighty-eight percent of commercial but only 57 percent of private victims considered that the jury had understood their cases. The longer the case took to come to trial, the more stressful the appearance in court due to recall difficulties.

What Did Victims Feel about the Way "Their" Offenders Were Dealt With?

On average, white-collar fraudsters received prison sentences of 25 months at the Old Bailey and 15 months at Cardiff Crown Court, compared with 13 months and 11 months respectively for blue-collar fraudsters. Some 56 percent of white-collar defendants were imprisoned, compared with 75 percent of the blue-collar ones. Prison or suspended prison sentences were the typical sentences for all fraudsters. Seventy-seven percent of victims knew the verdicts in their cases and also stated that it was important for them to know the outcomes. Around half of all victims thought the sentences were lenient or very lenient; the remainder considered them to be adequate. None thought the sentences too severe. Only 40 percent of commercial and 56 percent of private victims applied for compensation, and of those who did apply, only 11 percent of commercial and 20 percent of private victims were actually awarded compensation. Forty percent of all victims believed that their rights had not been fully enforced, particularly in respect to compensation. But 70 percent thought that their involvement in the case had led to others being better protected and that the law also had been upheld. Most victims believed that the necessity for honesty in commercial dealings had been strengthened by their participation in the case. Some 30 percent of victims thought that there were no benefits at all from their involvement in the case, and of this group the private victims were twice as likely as commercial ones to perceive that there were few if any benefits from going to court.

Interviews with fraud managers from major companies in the financial services sector revealed views that matched those contained in the questionnaire survey. While most interviewees stated that they were satisfied with the service they received from the police, there were divisions over their experiences with the prosecution process. These reactions were partly the product of initial expectations. Commercial victims were more likely than private ones to believe ex post facto that there were benefits resulting from taking fraud to court and appeared to have better court experiences. This could be explained by their being "repeat players" and having often had prior police experience. Our data support what has become conventional criminological wisdom regarding the critical role played by victims in managing their victimization and in activating the criminal justice system. Reporting was a conscious decision made after some deliberation. Neither retribution nor compensation figured significantly as motives for pursuing fraudsters. Rather, ritualistic citing of company policy and "general deterrence" were the central rationales. General deterrence was asserted as an article of faith rather than something empirically demonstrated; however, commercial victims are not alone in this respect! What was proven in their minds was that the cost and effort of participating in the formal legal system was not usually borne out in just deserts for themselves or for the fraudsters. Like many police, "repeat complainants" saw themselves as an underappreciated group desperately trying to hold the thin blue line (or perhaps black line) against "the criminal," without real support from the archaic courts.

The 1989 Survey of Corporate Experiences of Policing and Criminal Justice

The more general survey of corporations—whether or not they appeared in a court sample—suggested that in the case of the worst frauds reported, there was general satisfaction with policing. Three-quarters of the reporters were satisfied or very satisfied by the way their case had been handled; while 15 percent were dissatisfied or very dissatisfied. Financial services victims were significantly more likely than others to be dissatisfied or very dissatisfied. (Unfortunately, one consequence of genuinely anonymous surveys is that panel data are not feasible. Given that over half the cases had not yet come to trial, this is a significant disadvantage.)

Credit card frauds also were the subject of dissatisfaction about existing levels of policing, particularly among financial services and retailing firms. This has been reinforced subsequently by a study which indicates that because of police unwillingness to handle credit card frauds, less than 20 percent of such frauds are reported to the police by the credit card issuers in the U.K. (Levi et al., 1991). Plainly, white-collar victims could readily generate an artificial crime rate increase by a change in their reporting policy, but to do so would alienate the police on whom they depend for those prosecutions that do occur. Cases that are reported are those that are estimated as having a reasonably high prospect of conviction without a great deal further investigative work by the police.

As in our previous 1985 survey, "City fraud" was seen to consist of very different levels of serious crime: investment fraud is seen as worse than insider dealing, which in turn is seen as substantially worse than the dishonest making of multiple share applications. (Internal fraud, which was rated very low on the list of things that should receive more police attention, was so viewed because this was primarily a matter for companies themselves to refer on to the police, or not. Also interesting was the fact that both corporate sectors viewed tax fraud as a higher priority than social security fraud by the poor.)

Business Motives for Reporting Fraud and Confidence in the Authorities

When asked what their motives had been for reporting frauds, the order of priorities given was as follows: (1) to get the money back; (2) to deter others from committing fraud against one's company in the future; (3) to stop the offenders from doing it again to others; and (4) out of social obligation. Other reasons given included to publicize details of those involved and to punish the offender. Almost a third of financial services and two-thirds of other companies stated that they would be more likely to report fraud in the future if there was a greater likelihood of obtaining compensation—one objective of the 1988 Criminal Justice Act (though not one that has helped fraud victims much in reality).

The 1980s witnessed substantial media and political criticism of the policing of serious fraud. With regard to confidence that if their companies reported a suspected fraud, it would be dealt with by the agency to whom it was reported in a satisfactory manner:

1. No financial services company and under one-third of other companies expressed confidence that the police would deal satisfactorily with a £10,000 fraud committed against their companies. Almost half of the financial services and a quarter of other companies expressed little confidence in the police. Nonfinancial services companies had a less unfavorable impression than did financial services organizations of police action over small frauds.
2. Two-thirds of financial services and four-fifths of other companies had confidence in police handling of a fraud against their companies involving £1 million: almost a quarter of the nonfinancial services companies (but none of the financial services organizations) expressed a "great deal" rather than just "a lot" of confidence here.
3. No financial services company and only one in eight of other

companies expressed any confidence in police handling of a computer fraud, and over half of both sectors expressed little or very little confidence. No one who knowingly had experienced broadly defined computer-related fraud—whether reported or not—had any positive confidence in the police. The majority of nonvictims expressed little or very little confidence. It is clear that there is a credibility gap over the investigation of computer crime for the police to bridge.

4. Less than a quarter of financial services companies had any confidence that if they reported to a self-regulatory organization (such as the stock exchange's regulator) a fraud involving £10,000, it would be dealt with satisfactorily; over half had little confidence. When the size of the fraud rose to £1 million, however, over half of financial services companies had a lot of confidence, and only one in seven of them expressed little confidence.

5. The Department of Trade and Industry—which has overall responsibility for investigating misconduct involving the management of companies and for insolvency fraud—had the most negative image of all: three-quarters of financial services companies and three out of five other companies had little or very little confidence that the DTI would deal satisfactorily with a £10,000 fraud.

6. Confidence in the DTI's handling of a £1 million fraud was greater, with over a third expressing a lot of confidence. But a quarter of the respondents expressed little confidence.

Looking at all three fraud vignettes involving £1 million, the greatest confidence was expressed in the police, followed by the self-regulatory organization, and finally the Department of Trade and Industry.

What about reasons for not reporting frauds of which one believes oneself the victim? Overall, the most common reason cited for not reporting frauds was that too much management time was tied up in reporting one. Embarrassment at the revelation of the fraud was far more significant to financial services companies than to others, while the additional burden of reporting upon expensive management time was more salient to companies outside the financial sector than to those inside it. The supposed softness of the courts played almost no role in decisions not to report, though in 1992, my interviews support that this is beginning to affect prosecution decisions.

Reporting Fraud and Confidence in Policing

Much of the debate in attitude research questions the value of opinions ungrounded in experience. This is too serious an issue to be examined here, but beliefs about the consequences of reporting have effects on businesses and individuals, though such views may be mediated by (paid) investigative agencies and lawyers who act as surrogate "repeat players" under the instructions of victims. Nevertheless, it is useful to examine separately the relationship between actual reporting of fraud and confidence in the authorities:

1. Those who had reported a fraud to the police had slightly more confidence or slightly less confidence in the competence of the police than did nonreporters: they were firmer in their judgments. On balance, reporters were slightly more positive than others about the police, whether over reporting large or small frauds.
2. Those few who had reported a fraud to the Department of Trade and Industry had much less confidence in the DTI's ability than those who had not.
3. Those few who had reported a fraud to a self-regulatory organization had much less confidence than those who had not that the SRO would deal efficiently with fraud, though the difference diminished (and the confidence of reporters increased) when the size of the fraud was £1 million rather than £10,000.
4. Those few who had reported to the Serious Fraud Office had substantially more confidence than those who had not that frauds were dealt with better since the SFO and the Securities and Investments Board were established. (Though this was mainly because four out of five nonreporters were neither more nor less confident that policing had improved.)

Company Policies on Fraud Reporting and Prosecution

The ideological interpretation of company policies on the reporting and prevention of company fraud presents some intriguing possibilities. On the one hand, it seems plain that control over the investigation process and decision to prosecute is important to corporate justice and is a major influence on the rapid development of private investigative agencies in this arena. Since frauds involving senior executives (or the sexual partners of senior executives) have the greatest potential for corporate embarrassment, this is likely to advantage senior figures. Furthermore, at an evidentiary level, it is harder to pin fraud on a senior official in cases where others lower down the line are involved, a point made also by Hagan (1988) in the context of securities violations.

An equal number of companies—both financial services and others—had as did not have a company policy on the reporting of fraud. However, about two-thirds of companies had a policy on fraud prevention. There was a great deal of variation in the extent to which either policy was promulgated within or outside the company. Nonfinancial services companies tended not to communicate their policies to suppliers or customers. However, the existence of policies does not guarantee adherence to them, and I have been given many examples where, because of fear of their exposure of director misconduct, junior and middle-management employees have been excused prosecution. Furthermore, many staff at all levels escape prosecution because senior staff consider that it is not worth the effort: there is no particular class or status bias here.

One reason cited by many companies for not reporting was the harmful publicity they expected to accrue. Our 1989 survey (Levi and Sherwin, 1989) examined the extent to which corporate fraud victims received media coverage and what effects it had upon the companies. This is an important question because bad experiences may lead companies not to report frauds in the future, and the prospect of bad publicity is used by some companies as a reason or excuse for not reporting frauds. A third of the companies stated that there had been some media coverage. Of these, two-thirds stated that it was fair and one-third that it was mixed. (No one said it was unfair.) They all stated that on balance, the publicity made no difference to the company—neither adverse nor beneficial.

Companies were also asked about other fraud cases they had reported. Only one in nine stated that the media had been unfair then—and this had not deterred them from reporting the next time despite the adverse effect on the firm—and a quarter said that the publicity had actually benefited the company. (However, as with heroin users who had previously used marijuana, one cannot infer from this sample of repeat complainants who had not been deterred from reporting future frauds that some corporations are not deterred from reporting by their actual or expected negative media experiences. Informally, bankers acknowledge that negative media publicity on their role in fraud prevention or merely advertising the fact that they could not protect themselves reduced their reporting.)

A Social Movement against White-Collar Crime?

In an oft-cited article, Katz (1980) asserts that there exists a social movement against white-collar crime. Yet as Jesilow et al. observe in this volume, this does not seem to be reflected in widespread consumer awareness. One of the problems in applying this social movement concept to business crime is deciding what the boundaries of analysis are: if we have concern about insider dealing but not about monopolies and price fixing or about violations of minimum-wage laws, can we say that there is a social movement against white-collar crime? It is arguable that inasmuch as there is a social movement at all, it may be a social movement against prestigious criminals who commit some subset of white-collar and/ or non-white-collar crimes, rather than against white-collar crime in the general sense. To the extent that there is a populist concern about the powerful "getting away with it" that is more than tautology—that is, where membership of "the powerful" does not entail remaining unconvicted or unimprisoned for "long" periods—the difficulties of making adequate empirical comparisons multiply. For example, the distinction often made between "white-collar crime" (or high-level fraud) and "corporate crime" (or regulatory offenses by corporations) becomes less valuable, unless we wish to examine empirically the nature of the "it" with which "the public" is concerned that "the powerful" are getting away. (Here, we cannot properly use seriousness surveys as a proxy for public views on police priorities, though without care we also cannot assume that public responses to questions about the priorities of the police are the same as their views on priorities of policing: it may be that the public wants more done about white-collar and/or corporate offenses, and that they do not want this done by the police, but rather by some more specialized body.) In short, even where people such as U.S. attorneys or media producers see themselves as conducting a campaign against white-collar crime, we need to disaggregate somewhat the notion of a social movement against white-collar crime and look more concretely at what sorts of persons and activities upset different audiences—businesspeople, consumers, unemployed persons, investors—and why these movements develop over time.

In terms of media and political interest, there is a certain irony in the fact that most of the boom in attention that falsifies early (and still repeated) statements about the lack of media attention given to white-collar crime has been in the field of insider trading, which arguably is the area of white-collar crime that has least direct harmful implications for victims. Some may be tempted to fit this into an analytic perspective in which it serves capitalist interests to refocus attention away from harm to individuals. However, this is implausible since it may be closer to representing a populist resentment/distorted envy against "Lifestyles of the Rich and (in)Famous" and undeserved wealth: in Britain, the immense publicity given to allegations by the stock exchange insider-dealing unit that groups of/rings of elite insider dealers are "escaping justice" reinforces this point. (Such claims—which many criminologists would discredit if made by police about political crime, street crime, or organized crime—seldom receive the critical attention they may merit.) The alliance between bureaucratic interests seeking to expand their powers and staffing, and media obsession with secret conspiracies is well known in the study of "moral panics" regarding narcotics and organized crime.

But there are other areas of investor fraud where successful campaigns have been mounted in the British media, which have led to the compensation of defrauded individuals by governmental regulators who were alleged to have been negligent in their licensing of firms to trade in securities (Le Quesne, 1988). The media portrayal of the investors as elderly people who were not particularly greedy but were lured by brokers targeting the retired and retiring into "investing in safety" in government securities—albeit at a rate slightly higher than other safe investments but not so high as to signal that it was an obviously predictable scam—was very sympathetic. The media also played on the poor reputation of the Department of Trade and Industry (known also as the "Department of Temerity and Inactivity") for regulatory response, transforming it as well as the alleged fraudsters into "folk devils." Fortunately for the government, the new regulatory system introduced by the 1986 Financial Services Act enabled it to claim that these failures were simply historical relics of the ancient regulatory régime, and that all was now in order. However, in the light of successive scandals, such claims have become implausible, and the fraud-preventative benefits have been looked at with increasing scepticism when juxtaposed with the real costs of the regulatory structure.

Although corporations have been quite modest in their demands upon the formal criminal justice system, some corporations seek to mobilize latent or even nonexistent concern by stressing the harmfulness of some forms of fraud or the interaction between, say, credit card fraud and the financing of retail or even wholesale narcotics purchases. Since the experience of fraud of any one businessperson is limited, executives' construction of crime prevalence and risk has great potential to be affected by media treatment, where believed, or reference group members. Whereas in both the questionnaire and the telephone surveys executives expressed considerable concern about computer fraud and hacking, responses revealed that if we exclude simple forgery of input or output documents—which can be effected quite adequately without a computer—only one of the "worst frauds" reported since 1986 was a real computer fraud. Even in a later section of the questionnaire that dealt with unreported as well as reported fraud, there were no computer frauds by outsiders, and no computer fraud by users and systems people exceeded £1 million in any case in our sample. Although more than two-thirds of the companies stated that computer viruses and hacking were fairly or very serious, only 11 percent had experienced either of these and 5 percent both of them. Consequently, as other research on the fear of crime indicates, there is a considerable gap between fear and risk of crime.

However, whereas normally there is some positive relationship between the fear of crime and the risk of crime in different areas—even if most people, particularly inhabitants of low crime areas, overestimate the risks—this appears not to be true for computer fraud. Thus, even incorporating information from informal sources about unreported computer fraud, it seems that in this case the "moral panic" over computer fraud is misplaced. The media and business concern over it may be attributable to the moral and financial entrepreneurial activities of computer security salespeople, but the evidence suggests that computer espionage and damage are more serious risks than computer fraud (whatever that label means in practice, since mostly it is just electronic funds transfer that could have been effected—more slowly perhaps—manually). Even here, the moral panic has enjoyed only modest success in driving legislation in the U.K., since influential bodies such as the Law Commission opposed granting major police powers or imposing heavy sentences to deal with mere hacking: they drew analogies with the noncriminality of trespass without dishonesty or violence. Consequently, the Computer Misuse Act 1990 makes it an offense punishable by a fine of no more than six months' imprisonment to secure unauthorized access to a computer intentionally (s 1), though unauthorized access to facilitate other offenses and unauthorized modification of computer material can lead to sentences of up to five years. One might even argue that the obsession with technological subversion provides a paradoxical reassurance that "the enemy" is without rather than within, and, intentionally or not, diverts attention from the misconduct by senior staff that has been implicated in most serious financial fraud in the U.K. and the U.S.

White-Collar Advantage: Justice for All?

The victim movement has focused some limited attention on the social-distributional aspects of police resource allocation. What kinds of victims enjoy the advantage of having their complaints taken seriously and pursued to conviction? Do corporate victims enjoy an unfair advantage over other sorts of victims, as some radical critics (Pearce, 1976; Reiman, 1984) suggest? Hagan (1988, chapter 2) looked primarily at the victims of recorded burglary and theft and found that more victims were corporate than were individual entities, and that significantly more corporate than individual victims saw their accused convicted. Corporate victims are more likely than individual victims to believe that they could have prevented the offense and less likely to believe that crime prevention is the job of the police. (The latter view was shared by U.K. business victims of fraud, Levi, 1988; Levi and Sherwin, 1989.) On the other hand, one corollary of this, which was unexamined by Hagan, is that corporate victims of fraud may be seen as more blameworthy (or victim-precipitating) than other victims of property crime, a possibility that is enhanced by the fact that—except in the rare case of computer hacking—they parted with the money or goods voluntarily, albeit under false assumptions. If we include nonreporting corporate victims, we can see that, unlike other property crime victims who have not themselves been involved in illegal or stigmatized activities, they often feel constrained, for reasons of organizational or personal prestige, not to take criminal action against major victimizations. Banks, for example, may be worried about the disastrous loss of public confidence in their integrity or capital adequacy. (Less nobly, they may keep silent because their senior management may themselves—though hardly ever in the U.K.—be using the corporation as a personal source of loans for themselves and friends—a practice prevalent in the U.S. and the Far East and a principal cause of the collapse of the Bank of Credit and Commerce International.) Of course, such stigma in being a victim does exist for individual victims, particularly for victims of heterosexual and homosexual assaults. But the inclusion of fraud (and nonreporters of fraud) does not indicate any clear corporate advantage. There are no systematic studies of the nonreporting of frauds against individual fraud victims, but although repeat players who can organize their complaints better with more resources prior to reporting can expect a better service from policing agencies— largely because there is a better chance of a result (that is, a conviction) from a well-prepared case—the corporate advantage in reporting fraud is unlikely to be very great. Here, the greater resources of the corporation in assembling a good prima facie case for victimization are counterbalanced by the greater "populist" appeal of individual victims and by the financial opportunity costs to the organization of the time spent on reporting fraud rather than "putting it down to experience."

Additionally, in credit card fraud cases, the U.K. police justify their inaction because the credit card companies (1) have deep pockets; (2) take insufficient prevention measures (as the police deem them), such as fail to put photographs on cards; and (3) make conviction more difficult by—unlike the rest of the world—allowing the customer to take away the top copy from the credit card voucher, which contains both a good signature and fingerprints.

This leaves poor forensic evidence for the police (see Levi et al., 1991). My methodology does not enable me to make inferences regarding corporate victims of theft and burglary—more likely to be the model business crimes written about in Hagan's chapter—but the financial effects of fraud were probably greater than the sum of the much more frequently occurring nonfraud crimes against corporations (Levi, 1988). If there is less attention given to corporate victims in Britain than in Canada or the U.S., this may be due to greater police autonomy in the U.K., ironic though this may be in the light of the enthusiasm for increased police accountability among the political left. In short, my data do not support Hagan's interpretation that corporations enjoy an advantage over private indivduals in terms of the standard of policing services they receive. Rather, frauds against "widows and orphans" receive more political and media pressure, and more police attention, than frauds against corporations that fall short of causing economic ruin. Of course, it can be argued that such priorities have broader "system maintaining" functions, but this "critique" descends into a functionalist tautology.

This brief review of British and North American victimization literature applied to the area of white-collar crime illustrates not only some of the progress made since Sutherland, but also some of the major gaps in knowledge still to be filled and the more intractable conceptual and methodological difficulties that are inherent to this area of criminological research. I close by drawing attention to a paradox. Most moral panics about crime develop through exploiting an image of hurt victims who can readily be drawn from cultural definitions of "the vulnerable," combined with either explicit or implicit conceptions of the psychopathic, heartless offender. Yet in much financial white-collar crime—as opposed to safety violations in the workplace or environment—images of evil are hard to generate and we are left with a frisson of envy and resentment that requires, for its emotional "kick," the fall from grace of those who are caught by shifts in regulatory attitude and competence and who, bemused, find themselves before the criminal courts for actions that they may have known to be illegal, but over which they never expected to face criminal charges. This is particularly true in the U.K., where the prosecution of securities violations is much newer than it is in the U.S. Given the ill-developed empathy that exists towards the victims, a shift in the attitudes of the general public, media, or influential public figures could easily leave us blaming not the offender, but rather both prosecutors (for "hounding businesspeople who are the foundation of our enterprise system") and victims (for lack of Victorian prudence in failing to invest more cautiously). The white-collar victimization of my title would then refer to the persecution of white-collar defendants by the overzealous, publicity-hungry prosecutors so eloquently satirized in Tom Wolfe's *Bonfire of the Vanities*. This wave of sympathy for defendants has happened already in the U.S. and—in February 1992—in the U.K., over the prosecution of bankers and professional advisers involved in manipulating the U.K. stock flotation needed to finance the U.S. takeover of Manpower by Blue Arrow in 1987. The judge—who acquitted the two corporate and two individual defendants during the trial—and most of the press castigated the prosecution, and the four defendants convicted after a year-long jury trial were given suspended prison sentences and were neither fined nor disqualified from future business activity. "Equal oppression for all" is a difficult line to defend ethically or politically once the mood of the public shifts from stressing the benefits to stressing the costs of white-collar crime control.

REFERENCES

Fattah, E., ed. (1986). *From crime policy to victim policy*. London: Macmillan.

Frantz, D. (1989). *Mr. Diamond*. London: Pan.

Grabosky, P., Braithwaite, J., and Wilson, P. (1987). The myth of community tolerance toward white-collar crime. *Australian and New Zealand Journal of Criminology*, *20*, 33–44.

Hagan, J. (1988). *Structural Criminology*. Oxford: Polity Press.

Hough, M., and Mayhew, P. (1983). *The British crime survey*. London: Her Majesty's Stationery Office.

———. (1985). *Taking account of crime: Key findings from the British crime survey*. London: Her Majesty's Stationery Office.

Katz, J. (1980). The social movement against white-collar crime. In E. Bittner and S. Messenger, eds. *Criminology Review Yearbook*. vol. 2. Beverly Hills: Sage.

Law Commission (1989). *Jurisdiction over offences of fraud and dishonesty with a foreign element*. London: Her Majesty's Stationery Office.

Levi, M. (1981). *The phantom capitalists: The organisation and control of long-firm fraud*. Aldeshot, England: Gower.

————. (1987). *Regulating fraud: White-collar crime and the criminal process*. London: Routledge.

————. (1988). The prevention of fraud. Home office Prevention Unit Paper 17. London: Home Office.

————. (1989). Recent texts on white-collar crime: An overview. *British Journal of Criminology, 29* (4), 412–415.

————. (1991). *Customer confidentiality, money-laundering, and police-bank relationships*. London: Police Foundation.

Levi, M., and Sherwin, D. (1989). *Fraud '89: The extent of fraud against large companies and executive views on what should be done about it*. London: Ernst & Young (accountants).

Levi, M., Bissell, P., and Richardson, T. (1991). The prevention of cheque and credit card fraud. Home Office Crime Prevention Unit Paper. London: Home Office.

Levi, M., and Pithouse, A. (forthcoming). *The victims of fraud*. Milton Keynes, England: Open University Press.

Le Quesne, G. (1988). *Barlow Clowes: Report of Sir Godfrey Le Quesne QC to the secretary of state for trade and industry*. London: Her Majesty's Stationery Office.

Maguire, M. (1982). *Burglary in a dwelling*. Aldershot, England: Gower.

Mann, K. (1985). *Defending white-collar crime: A portrait of attorneys at work*. New Haven: Yale University Press.

Mayhew, P., Elliott, D., and Dowds, L. (1989). *The 1988 British crime survey*. London: Her Majesty's Stationery Office.

Pearce, F. (1976). *Crimes of the powerful: Marxism, crime and deviance*. London: Pluto Press.

Reiman, J. (1984). *The rich get richer and the poor get prison*. New York: Wiley.

Shapiro, S. (1980). *Thinking about white-collar crime: Matters of conceptualization and research*. Washington, D.C.: Department of Justice, National Institute of Justice.

Sutherland, E. H. (1983). *White collar crime: The uncut version*. New Haven: Yale University Press.

Weisburd, D., Wheeler, S., Waring, E., and Bode, N. (1991). *Crimes of the middle classes: White-collar offenders in the federal courts*. New Haven: Yale University Press.

Wheeler, S., Mann, K., and Sarat, A. (1988). *Sitting in judgment: The sentencing of white-collar criminals*. New Haven: Yale University Press.

Wood, J. (1989). The serious fraud office. *Criminal Law Review*, March, 175–184.

·III·

ENFORCEMENT

· 8 ·

Bilking Bankers and Bad Debts

White-Collar Crime and the Savings and Loan Crisis

HENRY N. PONTELL

KITTY CALAVITA

Introduction

Fraud in savings and loan institutions could very well constitute the most costly single set of white-collar crimes in history. The savings and loan crisis goes far beyond the usual parameters of ordinary thrift and bank failures. In 1989, official estimates of the bailout costs for insolvent thrifts were placed at $200 billion over the next decade, with a range from $300 billion to $473 billion by the year 2021 (U.S. Congress, House Committee on Ways and Means, 1989, p. 20; U.S. Congress, Senate Committee on Banking, Housing, and Urban Affairs, 1989, p. 9). The Government Accounting Office, in April 1990, revised its estimate and claimed that it "will now cost at least $325 billion and could cost as much as $500 billion over the next 30 to 40 years" (Johnston, 1990). The same report projected an increase of $68 billion over the official estimate of the previous summer, and was "subject to significant change" depending on the general economic health of the country. Others, including Edwin Gray, former chairman of the Federal Home Loan Bank Board, have estimated the eventual cost of the debacle will exceed one trillion dollars (personal interview). Since its inception in August 1989, the Resolution Trust Corporation (RTC), which was formed by federal legislation to dispose of seized S&L assets, had "resolved" (sold or merged with another institution) 361 of 543 thrifts through January 14, 1991 (RTC, 1990). During the same time period it had already managed over $138 billion in thrift assets (RTC, 1991).

At the same time, there is growing evidence of massive amounts of white-collar crime involved in the insolvencies that constitute "the crisis." Government reports strongly suggest that criminal activity in the form of fraud was a central factor in 70 to 80 percent of these failures (General Accounting Office, 1989b; U.S. Congress, House Committee on Government Operations, 1988, p. 51). Government hearings attest to the backlog of extremely complex criminal cases and the potential inability of federal enforcement agencies to respond effectively. In April 1990, there were 1,298 "inactive cases," each involving over $100,000, which under current official definitions, designates them as "significant," but there were not enough FBI agents or U.S. attorneys to investigate or prosecute them (Rosenblatt, 1990a). Since that time, Congress has given additional resources to the Department of Justice to process S&L fraud cases. The Secret Service has also recently become involved in investigating S&L crime.

Additional information on the potential extent of S&L crimes is brought to light in a summary report by the Resolution Trust Corporation, which claims that about 51 percent of RTC-controlled thrifts (insolvent institutions) have had suspected criminal misconduct referred to the FBI, and that insider fraud and crime were significant factors in the insolvencies of approximately 41 percent of RTC thrifts (RTC, 1990, p. 9).

There remains little doubt that white-collar crime is an integral part of the S&L crisis, and helps account for the staggering losses that will accrue and be left to generations of taxpayers. Equally important is the response of regulators and law enforcement officials, not only in the conviction and punishment of wrongdoers, but, perhaps more importantly, in their capacity to detect, investigate, and indeed to label such acts as "crime" in the first place. Unlike most common crimes that are recognizable as such, and in which extensive investigations are not necessary before criminal cases can be brought, white-collar crimes are less obvious and many times well hidden by intricate "paper trails" that require thorough documentation and substantial evidence before the case can even be brought to a prosecutor. As Katz (1979) has noted in this regard, the investigative and prosecutorial functions in white-collar crimes are often one and the same. Thus, one important determinant of the "extent of white-collar crime" is the capacity and willingness of enforcers to define it as such.

Given the widespread nature of the S&L crisis, the complex and time-consuming nature of fraud cases, the alternative administrative and civil routes for dealing with them, and the high degree of interagency dependence necessary for successful prosecution, ferreting out and defining white-collar crime in savings and loan institutions represents one of the most difficult and challenging tasks in the history of law enforcement. In fact, it could be argued that given this scenario, not all crimes will be discovered, and many that are will not be prosecuted, or if prosecuted, will not result in full sanctioning on the original charges. Highly publicized cases regarding the largest and most egregious frauds present a distorted picture of government enforcement efforts. These "media cases" may not represent in either scale or nature the thousands of others that have not had comparable amounts of media attention or enforcement resources invested in them.

Even an enormous investment of resources, however, provides no guarantee of success, as suggested by the failure in the prosecution of "S&L kingpin" Don Dixon of Vernon Savings and Loan in Texas, who received a five-year sentence after being convicted of leading his institution to insolvency through fraud. Described by the attorney general of the United States as "the highest of the high fliers among the savings and loan crooks" and "the most visible of the Texas savings and loan renegades convicted of looting the industry in the 1980s," Dixon was convicted of twenty-three counts of fraud and could have received a maximum sentence of 120 years in prison and a $5.75 million fine (Bates, 1991). The taxpayer cost of Vernon's fraud-induced failure is about $1.3 billion. The outcome of this case does not bode well for the government in the multitude of others that will be brought in coming years.

This paper will examine both the forms and potential extent of S&L crime. In so doing, it draws from the criminological literature regarding white-collar and corporate crime, focusing on the similarities and differences between crime in the savings and loan industry and other types of white-collar crime. It uses government reports, hearings, personal interviews, and media accounts as its primary sources of information.

Defining S&L Fraud

The Federal Home Loan Bank Board, in a report to Congress in 1988 (quoted in General Accounting Office [GAO], 1989b, p. 22) defined fraud as it relates to the savings and loan industry:

> Individuals in a position of trust in the institution or closely affiliated with it have, in general terms, breached their fiduciary duties; traded on inside information; usurped opportunities or profits; engaged in self-dealing; or otherwise used the institution for personal advantage. Specific examples of insider abuse include loans to insiders in excess of that allowed by regulation; high risk speculative ventures; payment of exorbitant dividends at times when the institution is at or near insolvency; payment from institution funds for personal vacations, automobiles, clothing, and art; payment of unwarranted commissions and fees to companies owned by the shareholder; payment of "consulting fees" to insiders or their companies; use of insiders' companies for association business; and putting friends and relatives on the payroll of the institutions

Using this broad definition, the GAO found that each and every one of the 26 failed thrifts in its sample was a victim of fraud and abuse in some form. Earlier testimony by the Bank Board indicated that fraud was by no means confined to the 26 thrifts selected. In fact, the Bank Board had referred over 6,000 cases for prosecution in 1987, and another 5,000 were referred during 1988, up significantly from 1985 and 1986—434 and 1,979, respectively (General Accounting Office, 1989a, p. 11). Some of the more common weaknesses at the failed thrifts included the following: (1) inadequate board supervision and dominance by one or more individuals (73 percent of failed thrifts); (2) transactions not made in thrift's interest; (3) inadequate underwriting of loan administration; (4) appraisal deficiencies; (5) noncompliance with loan terms; (6) excessive compensation and expenditures; (7) high-risk acquisition, development and construction (ADC) loans; (8) loans to borrowers exceeding legal limits; (9) inadequate record keeping; and (10) transactions recorded in a deceptive manner.

The GAO (1989a) cites one thrift that paid a chairman of its board a $500,000 bonus the same year that the thrift lost almost $23 million. After regulators told another thrift that a bonus of over $800,000 (one-third of the thrift's earnings) paid to one officer was a waste of assets, the management paid the individual in question $350,000 to relinquish his right to future bonuses, and increased his salary from $100,000 to $250,000. It was also reported that extravagant expenditures were made by officers and their families for private planes, homes, and expensive parties. In one thrift, a majority stockholder used $2 million of thrift funds to buy a beach house and spent another $500,000 for related expenses, all of which were nonbusiness related.

The Committee on Banking, Housing, and Urban Affairs of the U.S. Senate suggested that such criminal activity was a major factor in the S&L crisis:

> Little doubt exists that fraud and insider abuse contributed substantially to the current crisis. According to the United States Department of Justice, the most prevalent forms of fraud and insider abuse included nominee loans, double pledging of collateral, reciprocal loan arrangements, land flips, embezzlement, and check kiting. In addition, witnesses have told the Committee of extravagant parties, exorbitant spending on frivolous corporate aircraft, lavish office suites, and numerous other squanderings of federally insured deposit monies. "At the very least," related David W. Gleeson, President of Lincoln Asset Management Company, "there was an enormous failure of individuals to exercise their fiduciary responsibilities as managers, directors, auditors, appraisers, and lawyers. . . . The extent of irresponsible and questionable transactions was so pervasive, and reckless lending policies, wildly aggressive appraisals, and ludicrous deals were so widespread that each new round of transactions enticed the perpetrators on to larger, more complex, and more [creative] deals with an ever-increasing disregard for sound economics and market demand." (1989, p. 9)

It may take years before the true extent of fraud in failed thrifts is known. Early estimates of fraud do not take into account the additional wrongdoings discovered after an institution comes under government control and is examined thoroughly. RTC investigators have uncovered elaborate schemes in their review of seized thrift documents that were designed to keep examiners in the dark, misrepresent the financial health of the organization, and hide fraudulent transactions. The latter were kept invisible to the examiner's eye through the use of cover-ups. One thrift operator went so far as to keep two sets of books—one for internal use and one for the regulators (personal interview).

The hidden and complex nature of "bank fraud" is described in detail by Alt and Siglin (1990), who use the term broadly to include frauds against "all depository institutions, including banks, thrifts and credit unions" (1990, p. 1). The term can refer to:

> . . . at least three different things: (1) an arrangement or transaction that [violates] the technical, legal standards established by statute or criminal law; (2) a deliberate or willful violation of certain prudential regulations, like loan-to-one borrower provisions, or requirements for obtaining an appraisal before making a real estate loan; and (3) certain kinds of complex financial transactions or arrangements that are not illegal in and of themselves but typically depend on one or more prohibited acts. (1990, pp. 1–2)

Usually, conduct that comprises criminal bank fraud may also provide the grounds for a civil bank fraud suit by victims (shareholders or the government). The first standard cited by Alt and Siglin refers to behavior that is in violation of the criminal statute; the second includes acts that are in violation of regulatory standards or civil law; the third category is not a distinct class of fraud, but rather contains behavior that may be *useful* to the perpetration of criminal or regulatory violations. Most importantly, complex financial transactions may be vehicles by which laws are broken and money stolen while simultaneously providing a cover-up. Land flips, nominee loans, reciprocal lending arrangements, and linked financing present the regulator with the formidable task of untangling these deals, and it is often precisely the purpose of these complex transactions to disguise the fraudulent intent behind them.

Forms of White-Collar Crime in the Savings and Loan Industry

While the list of fraudulent activity perpetrated by thrift operators and connected outsiders is a long one, their deviance can generally be classified into three analytically distinct categories of white-collar crime. These are unlawful risk taking, collective embezzlement, and covering-up (Calavita and Pontell, 1990). The categories sometimes overlap in actual cases of thrift fraud, both because the same thrift operators may commit several types of fraud and because the same business transaction may involve more than one type.

Unlawful Risk-Taking

The General Accounting Office, in its study of 26 insolvent savings and loans, found that, "All of the 26 failed thrifts made non-traditional, higher-risk investments and in doing so . . . violated laws and regulations and engaged in unsafe practices" (General Accounting Office, 1989b, p. 17). While deregulation made it legal for thrifts to invest in "non-traditional, higher risk" activities, regulations and laws were often broken in the process, either by extending investment activities beyond permissible levels or by compounding the level of risk by, for example, inadequate marketability studies or poor supervision of loan disbursement. In many respects, the factors that generate unlawful risk taking are similar to those highlighted in other analyses of white-collar crime. Most obviously, Sutherland (1949), Geis (1967), Farberman (1975), Hagan (1985), and others have cited the importance of the force of competition in the profit-making enterprise as a major reason for corporate crime. In his explanation of violations in the thrift industry, a high-ranking thrift regulator underlined the importance of such economic imperatives. Pointing to the provision of deposit insurance that protected the depositors' investments and the possibility of windfall profits for stockholders if risky ventures succeeded, he suggested that from this point of view, the thrift regulator had a fiduciary duty to try to maximize profits through "risky" schemes, given their immunity to any real risk via deposit insurance. This regulator told the authors, "I've had lawyers argue to me that they [thrift operators] had not only a right, but they had . . . a fiduciary responsibility to go forward [with risky deals]" (personal interview).[1]

In addition, the opportunity structure has been cited as a facilitating factor in the commission of corporate crime. For example, some analyses emphasize the ease with which these crimes can be committed as complementary to the profit motive in the production of such crime (Wheeler and Rothman, 1982). The infamous electrical company conspiracy of the 1940s and 1950s, which involved price-fixing in government contract bids, provides an excellent example (Geis, 1967).

The unlawful risk taking in the savings and loan industry, however, is distinct from such traditional corporate crimes. While "successful" corporate crime usually results in increased profits and long-term liquidity for the company, unlawful risk taking in the thrift industry is more like a "gamble"—and one with very bad odds. That is, unlike more traditional corporate and white-collar crimes in the industrial sector, these financial crimes often result in the *bankruptcy* of the institution.

One of the most critical factors found in failed thrifts was their extensive use of "acquisition, development, and construction" (ADC) transactions, often with related parties (General Accounting Office, 1989a). An extremely high degree of risk was assumed by the institution in these generous loans to developers for the purpose of acquiring property and constructing commercial developments. To compensate for this high degree of risk and the fact that thrifts often required little or no down payment on such loans, the thrifts hypothetically received a portion of the profits generated from the completed projects. If the developer defaulted, the thrift had only the property as an asset. The thrift's return on its investment, however, was dependent on the original project being completed, and subsequently turning a profit. In addition to ADC transactions, excessive investment in junk bonds has increasingly been uncovered as a significant factor in the collapse of a number of the largest thrifts. When accompanied by inadequate investment analysis, gross mismanagement, or other regulatory violations, this reckless dependence on junk bond investment fits clearly in this category of unlawful risk taking.

Deregulatory policies in the early 1980s gave legal authority to thrifts to pursue such deals, but many did so in ways that violated loan-to-one-borrower limits, and other such regulatory standards. The GAO has documented that a combination of poor underwriting, the large amounts of funds involved, excessive geographic concentrations of transactions—all coupled with violations of regulations—spelled disaster for the industry, especially in the southwest region of the country where real estate markets collapsed. In one case in California, a thrift lent $40 million to one borrower to build condominiums and a shopping center. No feasibility study was conducted, and examiners argue that if one had been done, it would have shown that the proposed site was already heavily overdeveloped. This transaction alone cost the thrift over $10 million (General Accounting Office, 1989a).

Collective Embezzlement

In its report on crime and fraud in financial institutions, the House Committee on Government Operations (1988, p. 34) concluded, "Usual internal controls do not work in this instance." The committee quoted the commissioner of the California Department of Savings and Loans: "We built thick vaults; we have cameras; we have time clocks on the vaults; we have dual control—all these controls were to protect against somebody stealing the cash. Well, you can steal far more money and take it out the back door. *The best way to rob a bank is to own one*" (quoted in U.S. Congress, House Committee on Government Operations, 1988, p. 34; emphasis in the original).

Collective embezzlement, also referred to here as "looting," refers to the siphoning off of funds from a savings and loan institution for personal gain, at the expense of the institution itself *and with the implicit or explicit sanction of its management*. The "robbing of one's own bank" is currently estimated to be the single most costly category of crime in the thrift industry, having precipitated a significant number of the largest insolvencies to date (U.S. Congress, House Committee on Government Operations, 1988, p. 41; General Accounting Office, 1989b, p. 19). For example, the GAO reports that of the 26 thrifts it studied, "almost all of the 26 failed thrifts made transactions that were not in the thrift's best interest. Rather, the transactions often personally benefitted directors, officers, and other related parties" (General Accounting Office, 1989b,

p. 19). The "collective embezzlement" described here, while perhaps not an entirely new form of white-collar crime, has yet to be closely studied. It is a hybrid form of corporate crime, consisting of crime *by* the corporation *against* the corporation.

Individual or traditional embezzlement is an increasingly common form of white-collar crime. The advent of computers and their proliferation in business makes access to funds easier than ever. The toll from such crime is considerable as well. Conklin (1977) notes that between 1950 and 1971 at least one hundred banks were made insolvent as a result of embezzlement. Moreover, in the mid-1970s commercial banks lost almost five times as much money to embezzlers as they did to armed robbers (Conklin, 1977, p. 7).

The traditional embezzler is usually seen as a lone actor stealing from a large organization. For example, in discussing various forms of white-collar lawbreaking, Sutherland noted that "the ordinary case of embezzlement is a crime by a single individual in a subordinate position against a strong corporation" (1983, p. 231). In his landmark study *Other People's Money*, Cressey (1953) examined the phenomenon of embezzlement, with particular emphasis on the processes by which a person is led to embezzle. He found that embezzlers were usually living beyond their means and had an "unshareable financial problem" that they attempted to resolve through "borrowing" funds. Three phases were identified in the process of becoming an embezzler: (1) an unshareable financial problem; (2) a realization of the opportunity for solving the problem; and (3) a rationalization of the act (only "borrowing it").

While the *act* of embezzlement is comparable to the collective siphoning off of thrift funds by management, the causes underlying it are distinct. In the case of collective embezzlement, the opportunity structure as affected by deregulation would seem to take primacy over the "problem-centered" motivation of Cressey's lone, underling embezzlers.

In his research on corrupt police departments, Sherman (1978) distinguishes between deviance *by* an organization and deviance *in* an organization by an individual or group. Deviance *in* an organization is comprised of those actions that directly harm the attainment of an organizational goal (such as making a profit). Traditional forms of employee crime, like theft of materials owned by an organization and embezzlement of funds, are offenses that fit this model. On the other hand, deviance *by* an organization involves "collective rule breaking" that helps achieve organizational goals. False advertising and price fixing are examples of this type of organizational deviance.

It is less clear how to categorize fraud and insider abuse by savings and loan operators. In cases of collective embezzlement of thrifts, the "operative goal" of executives was the diversion of funds for *personal* profit. Indeed, in many cases the *organizational* goal was to siphon funds to management, despite its effect on the organization (leaving the government to pay off the insured depositors). The deviance was "organizational" in the sense that the primary *purpose* of the thrift was to provide a "money machine" for management.[2] The formal goals of the organization merely comprised a "front" for the real goals of these money machines. It is thus a prime example of what Wheeler and Rothman (1982, p. 1406) called "the organization as weapon": ". . . The organization . . . is for white-collar criminals what the gun or knife is for the common criminal—a tool to obtain money from victims." The principal difference between Wheeler and Rothman's profile of the organization as weapon and the case of collective embezzlement presented here is that the latter is an organizational crime *against* the organization's own interests. In other words, the organization itself is *both weapon and victim.*

Numerous examples of this form of white-collar crime can be found in media and journalistic accounts of the S&L crisis, as well as in government investigations (General Accounting Office, 1989b; Pizzo et al., 1989; U.S. Congress, Committee on Government Operations, 1988). Furthermore, such looting is not confined to thrift operators. Some schemes required intricate partnerships with those outside the industry, including real estate developers and loan brokers (U.S. Congress, Subcommittee on Commerce, Consumer, and Monetary Affairs of the House Committee on Government Operations, 1987, p. 332). Thus, as new deregulatory policies opened the doors to higher risk investments of depositors' money, they simultaneously opened them to those both within and outside the industry who intended to embezzle funds. Not infrequently, the "gamblers" and the "swindlers" were the same people.

In one case in California, a 40-count indictment by a federal grand jury was returned against the former executive consultant of North America Savings and Loan in Santa Ana, Janet F. McKinzie, and five business associates, which charged that the failed financial institution had operated as a fraudulent enterprise almost since its inception in 1983. The case was the first on the West Coast that used racketeering laws (RICO) to bring charges against thrift executives who had looted more than $16 million from depositors in a systematic attempt to use the institution as a front for bogus real estate transactions. The defendants were accused of using part of the fraudulent earnings to make the thrift appear to have adequate capital long after it was insolvent. The remainder of the money was siphoned off to purchase expensive homes in Newport Beach, Rolls Royce automobiles, and other luxuries. A fifteen-month FBI investigation concluded that the failed thrift represented the worst case of insider fraud uncovered at a California S&L, and could be directly traced to the fraudulent activities of the institution's management (Murphy, 1989). On March 29, 1990, Janet McKinzie was found guilty of 22 of 26 counts, including racketeering, conspiracy, bank fraud, and interstate transportation of stolen property. The collapse of North America Savings and Loan will eventually cost taxpayers more than $120 million.

The major difference between such collective embezzlement and more traditional forms of organizational deviance and crime is that it involves the *intentional "looting" of the resources of the organization itself*. This form of white-collar crime differs from traditional embezzlement in that (1) it usually involves a network of individuals both directly and sometimes indirectly tied to the institution, and (2) it is an offense that eventually *leads to the total demise* of the organization itself, and is committed by its own executive officers.

Covering-Up

A considerable number of criminal charges leveled against fraudulent savings and loan institutions involve attempts to "cover-up" fraud and/or conceal insolvency in order to keep regulators at bay and keep the "money machine" open. This form of fraud may be the most pervasive and widespread criminal activity of thrift operators. Of the alleged 179 violations of criminal law reported in the 26 failed thrifts studied by the GAO, 42 were for such covering-up activity, constituting the single largest category of fraud (General Accounting Office, 1989b, p. 51). The same study also found that *every one* of the 26 failed thrifts had been cited by regulatory examiners for "deficiencies in accounting."

Cover-ups have been employed to a variety of ends by S&L

operators. First, they are used to produce a misleading picture of the institution's state of health, or more specifically, to misrepresent the thrift's amount of capital, as well as its capital-to-assets ratio. Second, deals may be arranged that include cover-ups as part of the scheme itself. For example, in cases of risky insider or reciprocal loans, a reserve account may be created to pay off the first few months (or years) of a loan to make it look current, whether or not the project has failed or was phony in the first place. Third, cover-ups may be used after the fact to disguise actual investment activity. Regulators (in responding to the crisis in the thrift industry in the early 1980s), may have inadvertently sent the wrong message to thrift operators when "regulatory accounting procedures" (RAP) were instituted. The new procedures included a complex formula that allowed for the understating of assets and the overstating of capital, which bolstered the image of financial health. The new RAP techniques provided a "gray area" within which thrift operators could commit fraud with little chance of detection, and within which deceptive bookkeeping seemed "normal."

In what may prove to be one of the most bizarre twists and major cover-ups in the S&L crisis, the House Permanent Select Committee on Intelligence announced in March 1990 that it will investigate alleged CIA involvement in the collapse of 22 failed S&Ls. The action grew out of a series of stories by a *Houston Post* reporter who purportedly found numerous links between organized crime figures engaged in savings and loan fraud and CIA operatives, involving gun running, drug smuggling, money laundering, and covert aid to the Nicaraguan Contras. One of the savings institutions tied to such activities was Silverado Savings in Denver, Colorado, where Neil Bush, son of the president, served on the board of directors until two months before regulators seized the thrift in December 1988.

Conclusion

We have argued here and elsewhere (Calavita and Pontell, 1990; 1991) that fraud was a pervasive and costly component of the thrift debacle. Our personal interviews with investigators lead us to the preliminary conclusion that much more fraud will be exposed as the RTC continues to sift through documents of seized institutions, and the FBI and Secret Service gear up for a long haul of investigations. Some observers still claim, however, that fraud does not account for very much in terms of total losses (Ely, 1990; White, 1991). For example, in a recent book on the crisis, Lawrence White devotes less than three pages to "fraud and criminal activity." While acknowledging that the regulatory climate of the 1980s brought new opportunities and capabilities for increased risk taking, and that carelessness and violations occurred, including lavish spending beyond reasonable business costs, White claims that popular depictions of the crisis have blown the "fraud factor" out of proportion. He notes:

> There is no question that rules violations did occur in many thrifts. The anecdotes highlight egregious cases that clearly warrant substantial civil and/or criminal penalties, and there will surely be further instances of insider abuse or other repugnant behavior that future investigations will reveal. *The bulk of the insolvent thrifts' problems, however, did not stem from such fraudulent or criminal activities. These thrifts largely failed because of an amalgam of deliberately high-risk strategies, poor business judgments, foolish strategies, excessive optimism, and sloppy and careless underwriting, compounded by deteriorating real estate markets.* These thrifts had little incentive to behave otherwise, and the excessively lenient and ill-equipped regulatory environment tolerated these business practices for far too long. (White, 1991, p. 117, emphasis in the original)

White's conclusion, though plausible, is suspect since he produces no data to support his claim. While he may not be an apologist for the excesses of the thrift industry, the behaviors he cites as responsible for insolvencies are precisely those types of business practices discussed earlier as vehicles for the perpetration of fraud and criminal activities. As Katz (1979) has noted in regard to "pure white-collar crime," it is extremely difficult to ascertain whether it ever took place, since evidence and intent can be well hidden within ordinary occupational and organizational structures. Moreover, as we have discussed, there is more than "anecdotes" to support the notion that criminal activity was widespread, and this is likely to be a central factor in the S&L debacle. The GAO study (1989a) cited here stands as the most comprehensive and rigorous scientific investigation to date of the nation's largest thrift failures, and its data demonstrating extensive fraud have yet to be directly challenged.

Edwin Sutherland (1983) believed that the diffusion of techniques for enacting illegal activities was facilitated by a learning process he termed "differential association." He also noted numerous factors that help explain the lenient response of government toward business violations as opposed to those of the lower classes, including general cultural homogeneity, specific common interests, linkages and investments, intimate personal relationships, the aspirations of persons in government to enter the business world, the role business plays in contributing to political campaigns, and the fact that business can promote or destroy different government initiatives and programs (Sutherland, 1983). Sutherland believed that these linkages protected business persons against negative definitions by the government.

In the case of the S&L crisis, the government may have seen the interests of business as identical to their own, trusting that S&Ls would do their best to use the deregulatory environment as an opportunity to make themselves financially healthy again. Furthermore, numerous studies have documented the substantial contributions that individual thrift operators and the U.S. League of Savings Associations made to members of Congress and the political pressure that accompanied these hefty contributions (Adams, 1990; Jackson, 1988; Mayer, 1990; Pizzo et. al., 1989). Not only the original deregulation that provided the opportunities for fraud, but regulatory lenience in the face of massive fraud and an escalating thrift crisis were undoubtedly the fallout of these massive campaign contributions and the implicit bribery or "folded lies" (Reisman, 1979) that they entailed.

The staggering financial losses incurred in the savings and loan crisis are due at least in part to widespread criminal activity, which was intentional and deliberate in nature.[3] As we have argued, the combination of selective deregulation of the industry combined with increased government insurance for deposits and the absence of effective oversight mechanisms provided an environment in which criminal activity proliferated (Needleman and Needleman, 1979). Moreover, government bailout schemes remain complicated by the fact that uncertainty still exists regarding the state of the industry and the general economy. Last year, S&Ls lost a record $19.2 billion, surprising authorities who had previously believed that the industry had already reached its low point (Rosenblatt, 1990b). Officials from the Office of Thrift Supervision believe that the current profit margin of the industry is "totally inadequate," which does not bode well for the future (Rosenblatt, 1990b).

Government efforts to recoup losses through the disposal of billions of dollars of assets from seized thrifts also deserve careful scrutiny in the future. The proposed manner of selling off these assets (much of it is in real estate) in local markets, could trigger another round of massive fraud by some of the same profiteers responsible for the original thrift insolvencies. Award-winning journalist Stephen Pizzo, in a nationally televised interview, predicted that the same criminals who looted thrifts into insolvency would use their ill-gained booty to buy up the assets of the insolvent institutions at bargain-basement prices. The limited capacity of the government to monitor the process leads some officials to believe that there will be a "couple of major embarrassments" as an unavoidable outcome (personal interview). It seems almost certain at this point that by the time the S&L crisis plays itself out, it will comprise the single largest set of white-collar crimes in history.

REFERENCES

Adams, J. (1990). *The big fix: Inside the S&L scandal.* New York: John Wiley and Sons, Inc.

Alt, K., and Siglin, K. (1990). *Memorandum on bank and thrift fraud to Senate Banking Committee members and staff,* July 25.

Bates, J. (1991). Dixon gets 5 Years for fraud in thrift collapse. *Los Angeles Times,* April 3, D2.

Calavita, K., and Pontell, H. N. (1990). "Heads I win, tails you lose": Deregulation, crime and crisis in the savings and loan industry. *Crime and Delinquency, 36* (3), 309–341.

Calavita, K., and Pontell, H. N. (1991). "Other peoples' money" revisited: Collective embezzlement in the savings and loan and insurance industries. *Social Problems, 38*(1), 94–112.

Conklin, J. E. (1977). *Illegal, but not criminal: Business crime in America.* New York: Spectrum Books.

Cressey, D. R. (1953). *Other people's money: A study in the social psychology of embezzlement.* Glencoe, Ill.: Free Press.

Crouch, G. (1990). McKinzie guilty of looting S&L. *Los Angeles Times*, March 30, 1.

Ely, B. (1990). *Crime accounts for only 3% of the cost of savings and loan mess.* Unpublished report.

Farberman, H. A. (1975). A criminogenic market structure: The automobile industry. *The Sociological Quarterly, 16*, 438–457.

Geis, G. (1967). The heavy electrical equipment antitrust cases of 1961. In M. B. Clinard and R. Quinney, eds. *Criminal behavior systems: A typology*, 140–151. New York: Holt, Rinehart and Winston.

General Accounting Office (1989a). *Failed thrifts. Internal control weaknesses create an environment conducive to fraud, insider abuse and related unsafe practices.* Statement of Frederick D. Wolf, assistant comptroller general, before the Subcommittee on Criminal Justice, Committee on the Judiciary, House of Representatives, March (GAO/T-AFMD-89-4).

———. (1989b). *Thrift failures. Costly failures resulted from regulatory violations and unsafe practices.* Report to Congress, June (GAO/AFMD-89-62).

Hagan, J. (1985). *Modern criminology: Crime, criminal behavior, and its control.* New York: McGraw-Hill.

Jackson, B. (1988). *Honest graft: Big money and the American political process.* New York: Alfred A. Knopf.

Johnston, O. (1990). GAO says S&L cost could rise to $500 billion. *Los Angeles Times*, April 7, 1, 28.

Katz, J. (1979). Legality and equality: Plea bargaining in the prosecution of white-collar and common crimes. *Law and Society Review, 13*, 431–459.

Kotz, D. M. (1989). S&L hell: Loan wolves howl all the way to the bank. *In These Times*, August 2–29, 20–21.

Kristof, K. M. (1990). American Continental bondholders may get tax writeoff on "Theft." *Los Angeles Times*, April 12, D5.

Lang, C. J. (1989). Blue sky and big bucks. *Southern Exposure, 17* (1), 20–25.

Mayer, M. (1990). *The greatest bank robbery ever: The collapse of the savings and loan industry.* New York: Charles Scribners' Sons.

Murphy, K. (1989). 6 are indicted in O. C. thrift case. *Los Angeles Times*, April 12, 1.

Needleman, M. L., and Needleman, C. (1979). Organizational crime: Two models of criminogenesis. *The Sociological Quarterly, 20*, Autumn, 517–539.

Pizzo, S., Fricker, M., and Muolo, P. (1989). *Inside job: The looting of America's savings and loans.* New York: McGraw-Hill.

Pontell, H. N., Jesilow, P. D., and Geis, G. (1982). Policing physicians: Practitioner fraud and abuse in a government benefit program. *Social Problems, 30,* 117–125.

———. (1984a). Practitioner fraud and abuse in medical benefit programs: Government regulation and professional white-collar crime. *Law and Policy, 6,* 405–424.

———. (1984b). Practitioner fraud and abuse in government medical benefit programs. Final Report and Executive Summary of Grant (82–1J-CX-0035) to the National Institute of Justice, U.S. Department of Justice, July.

Reisman, W. M. (1979). *Folded lies: Bribery, crusades, and reforms.* New York: The Free Press.

Resolution Trust Corporation. (1990). Report on investigations to date. Office of Investigations, Resolutions and Operations Division, December.

———. (1991). RTC review, *II* (1), January.

Rosenblatt, R. A. (1990a). 1,000 Bank, S&L fraud cases go uninvestigated, lawmaker says. *Los Angeles Times,* March 15, D1.

———. (1990b). S&Ls suffer $19.2 billion loss for worst year ever. *Los Angeles Times,* March 27, 1.

Sherman, L. W. (1978). *Scandal and reform: Controlling police corruption.* Berkeley: University of California Press.

Sutherland, F. H. (1949). *White collar crime.* New York: Dryden Press.

———. (1983). *White collar crime: The uncut version.* New Haven: Yale University Press.

U.S. Congress, House (1987). Committee on Government Operations. Subcommittee on Commerce, Consumer, and Monetary Affairs. Fraud and abuse by insiders, borrowers, and appraisers in the California thrift industry. Hearings before the subcommittee, June 13.

———. (1987). Committee on Government Operations. Subcommittee on Commerce, Consumer, and Monetary Affairs. Adequacy of federal efforts to combat fraud, abuse, and misconduct in federally insured financial institutions. Hearings before the subcommittee, November 19.

———. (1988). Committee on Government Operations. Combatting fraud, abuse and misconduct in the nation's financial institutions: Current federal reports are inadequate. Seventy-second report by the Committee on Government Operations, October 13.

———. (1989). Committee on the Judiciary. Prosecuting fraud in the thrift industry. Hearings before the committee, March 22–23.

———. (1989). Committee on Ways and Means. Budget implications and current tax rules relating to troubled savings and loan institutions. Hearings before the committee, February 22; March 2 and 15.

U.S. Congress, Senate (1989). Committee on Banking, Housing, and Urban Affairs. Problems of the federal savings and loan insurance corporation (FSLIC). Hearings before the committee, part 3, March 3 and 7–10.

————. (1989). Financial Institutions Reform, Recovery, and Enforcement Act of 1989. Report of the Committee on Banking, Housing, and Urban Affairs, April 13.

Wheeler, S., and Rothman, M. L. (1982). The organization as weapon in white collar crime. *Michigan Law Review*, *80* (7), 1403–1426.

White, L. J. (1991). *The S&L Debacle.* New York: Oxford University Press.

NOTES

1. Analyses of Medicaid fraud (Pontell et al., 1982; 1984a; 1984b) have similarly documented how the conflict between *government regulation and professional norms* relative to maximizing income results in an environment where fraud is bound to occur.

2. Wheeler and Rothman (1982, p. 1405) note the distinction in the literature between embezzlement and corporate crime, pointing out that this distinction suggests that "either the individual gains at the organization's expense, as in embezzlement, or the organization profits regardless of individual advantage, as in price fixing." The authors argue that this separation ignores cases where both organization and individual may benefit, as when an individual's career is advanced by crime perpetrated on behalf of the organization. What they neglect to notice, however, is the possibility of organizational crime in which the organization is a weapon for perpetrating crime against *itself*.

3. The similarity between savings and loan fraud and traditional robbery has recently been underscored in an announcement by the IRS that its tax rules may allow the holders of worthless uninsured bonds issued by American Continental Corporation (parent company of insolvent Lincoln Savings and Loan) to classify their losses as a "theft," rather than an investment loss (Kristof, 1990).

· 9 ·

The Space Shuttle *Challenger* Explosion

A Case Study of State-Corporate Crime

RONALD C. KRAMER

On January 28, 1986, the world was stunned by the explosion of the space shuttle *Challenger*. The *Challenger* exploded in midair, shortly after lift-off, sending six astronauts and schoolteacher Christa McAuliffe to their deaths. The major purpose of this paper is to tell the story behind the *Challenger* disaster. The decisions and actions that led to the explosion will be described, and the societal and organizational contexts within which those decisions and actions were made will be analyzed.

As this study will document, the *Challenger* disaster was the collective product of the interaction between a government agency, the National Aeronautics and Space Administration (NASA), and a private business corporation, Morton Thiokol, Inc., (MTI). Thus, the space shuttle tragedy falls into the special category of organizational misconduct that Kramer and Michalowski (1990) have identified as "state-corporate crime."

While considerable scholarly attention has been directed at both corporate crime and state crime,[1] almost no mention has been made in the literature of the fact that corporations and government agencies can and do act together to produce serious organizational transgressions. Despite this ubiquity, the structural relations between corporate and governmental organizations have been relatively peripheral to the study of organizational crime. Kramer and Michalowski (1990) have advanced the concept of state-corporate crime to fill this gap. They define state-corporate crimes as the "illegal or socially injurious actions that occur when one or more institutions of political governance pursue a goal in direct cooperation with one or more institutions of economic production and distribution" (1990, p. 3).

State-corporate crime is a form of organizational misconduct that occurs at the interstices of corporations and governments. Within a capitalist economy, such crimes involve the active participation of two or more organizations, at least one of which is in the civil sector and the other in the state sector. Thus, state-corporate crimes are the harmful consequences of a deviant interorganizational relationship between business and government.

There are many recent examples of state-corporate crime. They include the environmental, safety, and health violations that occurred at various nuclear weapons production facilities managed by private contractors for the U.S. Department of Energy; the coordinated criminal frauds involving defense contractors and U.S. military officials with key positions in the Pentagon's weapons procurement process; and the Iran-Contra crimes that resulted from interrelationships among the CIA, the National Security Council, and private arms suppliers. Another purpose of this paper is to demonstrate the utility of the concept of state-corporate crime by applying it to the specific case of the space shuttle *Challenger* explosion.

Toward an Integrated Theory of Organizational Misconduct

Any attempt to understand a form of organizational misconduct such as state-corporate crime must be grounded in an integrated theoretical framework that is capable of accounting for both the actions of actors and the context within which those actions become meaningful.

Three major theoretical approaches to the study of organizational deviance have been advanced over the years. The first is differential association theory as developed by Sutherland (1940, 1949). The second perspective is based on organizational theory and argues either that organizations are inherently criminogenic due to the performance emphasis on goals (Gross, 1978), or that organizations commit crime due to defective standard operating procedures (Hopkins, 1978). The third perspective locates the criminogenic forces in the wider political, economic structure of the society. Most U.S. analysts working from this perspective focus on the crime producing pressures for profit-maximization that are inherent in corporate capitalism (Barnett, 1981).

Although these three perspectives represent three distinctive approaches to the explanation of organizational misconduct, they can be brought together in a more powerful integrated theoretical model. A number of efforts at theoretical integration with respect to corporate crime (Braithwaite, 1989; Coleman, 1987; Finney and Lesieur, 1982; Vaughan, 1982), when taken together, suggest that theoretical integration in this area is best pursued by linking together the insights of differential association, organizational theory, and political economy. The resultant integrated theory would unite the three levels of social experience that constitute the dialectical totality of human life—the individual, the institutional, and the societal.

From this integrated perspective it can be argued that the structure, dynamics, and cultural meanings associated with a capitalist political economy in any particular society will shape the goals and means of both corporations and the state, as well as the constraints they face. The organizational level of analysis does two things. First, it links the internal structure of specific economic or political units with the external political, economic environment. Second, it shows how the work-related thoughts and actions of replaceable individuals who occupy positions in those units are shaped by the requirements of the positions they hold and by the procedures of the organization. Differential association, by focusing on individuals and the social definitions that give meaning to their world, enables us to examine the symbolic world derived from social interaction within bounded organizational niches.

An integrated theoretical model of organizational misconduct can be further fleshed out if these three levels of analysis are linked to three catalysts for action. These catalysts are (1) motivations or performance emphasis, (2) opportunity structure, and (3) the operationality of control. With these elements added, the model is designed to indicate the key factors that will contribute to or restrain organizational deviance at each intersection of a catalyst for action and a level of analysis.

The first catalyst for action is the emphasis on goal attainment. Political economies, organizations, and individuals all may place greater or lesser emphasis on the attainment of rationalized goals as the engine for social action.

The second catalyst for action suggests that organizational deviance is more likely in a society where legitimate means are scarce relative to goals. The likelihood increases for those organizations or organizational subunits where the allocation of means by the internal structure is inadequate relative to the organization's goals, and for those individuals who perceive blockage from legitimate means.

Finally, the operationality of social control at all three levels will serve as both an important restraint on organizational deviance and as a critical element in constructing symbolic frameworks that will operate at the societal, organizational, and personal levels as time passes. Thus, the integrated model is based on the hypothesis that criminal or deviant behavior at the organization level results from a coincidence of pressure for goal attainment, availability and perceived attractiveness of illegitimate means, and an absence of effective social control.

By its very nature, state-corporate crime directs us to examine the linkages between levels of analysis and catalysts for action. When the topic is profit-oriented violations of law by some business, it is possible—although not necessarily sufficient—to treat the crime as organizationally self-contained. When we examine injurious social actions that violate laws, regulations, or norms of prudent conduct and that are the result of concerted actions by organizations operating in different social spheres (for example, production versus governance), we must expand the frame of our analysis. The following discussion of the explosion of the space shuttle *Challenger* examines how this particular case of state-corporate crime emerged as the catalyst for action affected two separate organizations, and how these organizations, in turn, defined and redefined the operational environment for one another.

The Case of the *Challenger* Explosion

To understand more fully why the *Challenger* explosion constitutes state-corporate crime and to assess the ability of the integrated theoretical model of organizational crime to explain this interorganizational act, we will examine the following: First, the political history of the shuttle will be reviewed as part of the societal context within which the problem emerged. Second, the O-ring problem, the "fatal flaw," will be described. The creation of this fatal flaw places the emerging problem within its dual-organizational context. Third, we will discuss the process through which specific individuals made the concrete decisions that led to the tragic flight. Finally, the failure of various social-control mechanisms relating to the shuttle system will be evaluated.

Societal Context: The Politics of the Space Shuttle

NASA was a product of the cold war between the Soviet Union and the United States. In the 1950s, the cold war gave rise to an arms race and a related science and technology race between the two superpowers (Nieburg, 1966). The launch of the first *Sputnik* by the Soviet Union in 1957 caused a political firestorm in the United States that eventually resulted in the creation of NASA in 1958 (McDougall, 1985). The new space agency was put under civilian control, but found itself constantly battling the military's attempt to influence its direction and policies (Trento, 1987). The glory days of NASA came in the 1960s with the *Apollo* program and the race to the moon. During this period, NASA had generous budgets and unlimited political support. With these resources the agency was able to recruit top-notch scientists and technicians and cultivate a "can-do attitude" together with a serious commitment to safety and quality control (Lewis, 1988; Trento, 1987).

In the 1970s, however, the political and economic environment of NASA changed dramatically. Economic conditions caused a string of budget problems at the same time that political and public support for the agency also began to decline (Lewis, 1988; Trento, 1987). As the *Apollo* program wound down, NASA faced an uncertain future. This was the environment that shaped the development of the space shuttle program.

The idea of a reusable spacecraft that could provide frequent, economical access to space first surfaced in the late 1960s during the height of the *Apollo* program. In September 1969, a Space Task Force report to the president offered a choice of three long-range plans. In varying combinations these plans called for (1) a manned Mars expedition, (2) a lunar-orbiting space station, (3) an earth-orbiting station, and (4) a reusable space shuttle to link the orbiting station to Earth. For budgetary reasons, the Nixon administration scrapped the Mars project and the space platform, but ordered the development of the shuttle vehicle. As the President's Commission (1986) pointed out: "Thus, the reusable Space Shuttle, earlier considered only the transport element of a broad, multi-objective space plan, became the focus of NASA's near-term future" (p. 2).

The decision to go with only the shuttle component of the space plan forced NASA to put all of its eggs in one basket, so to speak, and significantly shaped NASA's goals in the post-*Apollo* era. But NASA's troubles were only beginning. Financial restrictions from the Office of Management and Budget would have a major impact on the design of the shuttle, and to win political support NASA would have to allow the air force to help plan the design of the shuttle to accommodate military missions.

NASA's original design for the new shuttle craft was changed several times due to the severe budget constraints. As Lewis (1988) notes, "From a long-term point of view, the 51-L disaster was the end product of budget compromises that required NASA to abandon its original design of a fully reusable spaceship and substitute a partly reusable vehicle at about half the development cost" (p. 54). As one critic put it, "They had to build the shuttle down to a price, not up to a standard" (Lewis, 1988, p. 54). As a result of the crimped budget, NASA decided to go with solid-fueled rockets, which were cheaper but more dangerous than liquid-fueled engines, and eliminate the escape hatch (Trento, 1987). As Easterbrook (1987) points out, "NASA's incremental decision to rely on solid boosters with no abort mechanisms meant that priceless human lives, several billion dollars and the whole of American space prestige would be wagered time and again on the proposition that when five used rocket engines fire simultaneously, nothing can go wrong" (pp. 53–54). It would be a design flaw in the solid rocket booster that would eventually cause the *Challenger* explosion.

Due to the low development cost imposed on NASA and military requirements the agency agreed to in order to win political support, the shuttle ended up being a hybrid machine created by a series of political compromises. But not only did NASA have to make critical design changes in the shuttle system due to budget considerations, military demands, and the lack of political support, it was also forced into making a purely economic justification for building the shuttle. Both OMB and Congress wanted an inexpensive and efficient, reusable spacecraft. In the desperate political struggle to save the shuttle program, and in the minds of many the agency itself, unrealistic predictions concerning the ability of the shuttle program to pay for itself were continually made by NASA officials (Lewis, 1988; Trento, 1987). NASA began to promise the impossible in order to build the shuttle and save the agency. To be cost effective the shuttle would have to be used frequently and for a variety of purposes. Thus, the myth of the omnibus shuttle was born. This would eventually lead NASA to shift all payloads, including all of the scientific ones, to the shuttle, take on commercial customers, and accommodate itself to further military demands (Trento, 1987).

The effort to make the shuttle a cost-effective, universal, launch vehicle put enormous pressure on NASA. Once the shuttle was finally approved and under development, pressure was placed on the agency to get the system operational and begin a heavy schedule of flights. As the President's Commission (1986) concluded, "The nation's reliance on the shuttle as its principal space launch capability created a relentless pressure on NASA to increase the flight rate" (p. 201).

This pressure increased dramatically in the 1980s under the Reagan administration. Ronald Reagan came into office just as the space shuttle program was preparing to launch its first test flight. In August of 1981, the president established an interagency review of U.S. space policy chaired by Dr. George Keyworth, the president's science advisor. The Keyworth group's meetings took place as NASA completed the first of four orbital test flights. The result of these deliberations was the Presidential Directive on National Space Policy. This directive was issued in conjunction with Reagan's first major speech on space, delivered at Edwards Air Force Base on July 4, 1982, the day the initial orbital tests concluded.

In this speech, and in the directive, Reagan announced a national policy to set the direction of the U.S. space program during the coming decade. As part of that policy, the president stated that the shuttle system "is the primary launch system for both national security and civil government missions" (President's Commission,

1986, p. 164). Reagan went on to declare the space shuttle fully operational and, thus, ready for a wide variety of important tasks.

The president's declaration that the space shuttle was "fully operational" exerted an enormous pressure on NASA. An operational system is one that has moved out of the research and development phase into routine operation. Problems and mistakes are expected and looked for in the development phase but are not expected or looked for in the operational phase. By the time something is operational, the bugs in the system are supposed to be worked out. Yet, this was not true of the shuttle according to a number of experts (Heaphy, 1986; Pike, personal interview). They argue that the system was still in the research and development phase and that the president prematurely labeled it operational. This was one of the major factors that led to the relentless pressure on NASA to launch shuttle missions on an accelerated schedule. As Jim Heaphy (1986), editor of *Space for All People*, points out, "After the president had so promptly and vigorously declared the shuttle fully operational, the atmosphere at NASA was no longer conducive to sober and rational assessment of the underfunded spacecraft's shortcomings" (p. 3). And, as John Pike, associate director for space policy with the American Federation of American Scientists, observed on the launch pressure experienced by NASA: "The blame lies with the administration, for they were clearly declaring the shuttle operational before, in fact, it truly was" (personal interview). The reports of the President's Commission and the House Committee on Science and Technology bear this out.

The Reagan administration was so eager for the system to become operational because they had developed some rather ambitious plans for the shuttle. One of their goals, which harkened back to the budget crisis years of the shuttle's development in the early 1970s, was for NASA to become economically self-sufficient. One way for NASA to do this was to become a commercial cargo hauler, primarily of communication satellites. Thus, the agency found itself under pressure to prove that the high costs of space exploration could be at least partially recouped through the commercial use of the shuttle (President's Commission, 1986; House Committee on Science and Technology, 1986). NASA succumbed to the pressure and decided to begin carrying paying customers as soon as possible (Mark, 1987; Trento, 1987).

The business of launching satellites for a wide variety of customers generated further pressures on NASA. For one thing, the agency had to compete with the European Space Agency's *Ariane* satellite launcher and, therefore, "had to make its shuttle missions look routine and dependable" (*The Nation*, 1986, p. 164). But the launching of commercial satellites also introduced new schedule problems and a demand for an increased flight rate that only an operational system could meet. As the President's Commission (1986) pointed out:

> Pressures developed because of the need to meet customer commitments, which translated into a requirement to launch a certain number of flights per year and to launch them on time. Such considerations may occasionally have obscured engineering concerns. Managers may have forgotten—partly because of past success, partly because of their own well-nurtured image of the program—that the Shuttle was still in a research and development phase. (P. 165)

In addition to these commercial concerns, NASA was increasingly being asked by the Reagan administration to use the shuttle for military purposes as well. As noted above, from the very beginning the civilian space agency had been an important element in the science and technology race that took place within the context of the military objectives and interests of the cold-war superpowers. It has also been pointed out that during the political struggle over the design of the shuttle NASA had to repeatedly accept design changes suggested by the air force in order to win military support for the program. But the pressure to militarize the space shuttle program increased greatly under the Reagan administration.

The administration was eager to declare the space shuttle operational because it had a number of "tasks related to national security" that it wanted carried out. In the 1982 Presidential Directive on National Space Policy (quoted in Heaphy, 1986, p. 3), NASA was instructed to "preserve United States preeminence in critical space activities." Keeping the shuttle on an accelerated flight schedule was deemed "vital and critical" to the national defense. The directive went on to say that "launch priority will be provided for national security missions."

Pressures on the shuttle program escalated even more the next year with the announcement of Reagan's "Star Wars" plan. The administration clearly understood that, whatever form the Strategic Defense Initiative would eventually take, the testing and development of the space missile defense system they desired would require an operational shuttle capable of making a very large number of flights on a regular basis. The militarization of space that was planned by the Reagan administration clearly put additional demands on an already overburdened and underfunded space agency.

NASA's organizational goals concerning the space shuttle program were clearly shaped by this political history. Political and economic structures outside of the organization influenced the final hybrid design of the spacecraft and pressured NASA to take on a variety of commercial, military, and scientific goals that dictated an accelerated launch schedule. This pervasive pressure to fly the shuttle and fly it often has been cited by every investigation into the *Challenger* disaster as one of the chief factors leading to the tragedy. As the House Committee on Science and Technology (1986) concluded:

> NASA's drive to achieve a launch schedule of 24 flights per year created pressure throughout the agency that directly contributed to unsafe launch operations. . . . The Committee, the Congress, and the Administration have played a contributing role in creating this pressure. Congressional and Administrative policy and posture indicated that a reliable flight schedule with internationally competitive flight costs was a near-term objective. Pressures within NASA to attempt to evolve from an R&D agency into a quasi competitive business operation caused a realignment of priorities in the direction of productivity at the cost of safety. NASA management and the Congress must remember the lesson learned from the *Challenger* accident and never again set unreasonable goals which stress the system beyond its safe functioning. (P. 22)

The Organizational Context: Creating the Fatal Flaw

The tremendous performance pressure exerted on NASA by the demands of an accelerated flight rate is a necessary but not solely sufficient condition to explain the *Challenger* explosion. This performance pressure could only be judged unreasonable if the organization did not have access to the resources that it needed to meet these demands.

Presumably, given enough resources and without encountering a major barrier or obstacle to goal attainment, NASA should have been able to carry out the shuttle flight schedule without violating any of its own safety standards or any of the external standards that were applied to the agency in this matter. However, as noted above, NASA was not provided with sufficient resources in the development phase during the early 1970s, which led to some serious design compromises, nor would the agency have the necessary resources to carry out the extremely ambitious flight schedule in the 1980s. The lack of spare parts, for example, was forcing NASA to cannibalize each shuttle when it returned from a mission in order to get another vehicle ready for launch.

While any number of things could have gone wrong with a shuttle flight and caused disaster, what did cause the explosion of the *Challenger* was a problem with the O-ring seal in the field joint of a solid rocket motor. The faulty design of the field joint manufactured by MTI was the fatal flaw that destroyed the *Challenger*. The President's Commission (1086) placed the blame for the flawed design, and the failure to act on information concerning the flaw, on both NASA and MTI:

> The genesis of the *Challenger* accident—the failure of the joint of the right Solid Rocket Motor—began with decisions made in the design of the joint and in the failure by both Thiokol and NASA's Solid Rocket Booster project office to understand and respond to facts obtained during testing. The Commission has concluded that neither Thiokol nor NASA responded adequately to internal warnings about the faulty seal design. Furthermore, Thiokol and NASA did not make a timely attempt to develop and verify a new seal after the initial design was shown to be deficient. (P. 148)

Information concerning the faulty seal design was a source of organizational strain within NASA and MTI. The problem with the field joint seal was a major barrier to the ability of NASA to fly its manifest and meet its flight-rate goals in a safe or legitimate manner. Since this operating problem came from a private contractor outside the space agency, it constitutes an external blockage of the ability of NASA to use legitimate means to achieve its goals concerning the shuttle. This problem also introduces the interaction between a private business and a government agency that is at the heart of the concept of state-corporate crime.

On November 20, 1973, the Thiokol Chemical Corporation (later to become Morton Thiokol, Inc.) was awarded a cost-plus contract valued at $800 million to manufacture solid rocket boosters for NASA's space shuttle project. An early test, called a hydroburst test, revealed that there was a problem with the field joint on the booster. As an MTI supervisor told the President's Commission (1986, vol. 5), "We discovered that the joint was opening rather than closing as our original analysis had indicated and, in fact, it was quite a bit" (p. 1435). As McConnell (1987) pointed out:

> The implications of this discovery were ominous. Without this pressure seal, the hot combustion gas could shoot through the putty and erode the O-rings. If this erosion was widespread, an actual flame path would quickly develop and the booster would burst at the joint, destroying the entire booster, and, of course, the space shuttle itself. (P. 118)

MTI did report this test effect to NASA, but the company said it did not believe that the joint rotation would cause problems and it did not schedule any additional tests on the joint-gap effect. A number of engineers at NASA's Marshall Space Flight Center, however, did express concern about the gap in a series of memos written in the late 1970s (President's Commission, 1986). One of these memos, written in 1978 by John Q. Miller, Marshall's chief of the Solid Rocket Motor Branch, argued that the MTI design was so dangerous that it could produce "hot gas leaks and resulting catastrophic failure" (President's Commission, 1986, p. 123). The project manager at Marshall, however, did not pass these memos on to MTI, and in the end "the alarming concerns of knowledgeable Marshall engineers did not result in a redesign of the SRB field joint before flights began" (McConnell, 1987, p. 119).

In September of 1980, the Shuttle Verification and Certification Committee certified the solid rocket motor for flight, and the field joint on the motor was classified on the shuttle critical items list as 1-R, or redundant, meaning that there was a backup in case of a failure. After the second test flight in November 1981, however, it was discovered that hot gas had penetrated the putty and damaged the primary O-ring in the field joint of the right booster. This information was also not passed on from Marshall to higher levels within NASA (President's Commission, 1986, p. 125). This was indicative of a major flaw in the organizational structure of NASA. There was a major communication problem between Marshall and the other units within NASA. The President's Commission (1986) said that it was "troubled by what appears to be a propensity of management at Marshall to contain potentially serious problems and attempt to resolve them internally rather than communicate them forward" (p. 104). Marshall tended to keep "bad news" and problems to itself, and this flaw in the communication system would repeatedly be in evidence in the shuttle project in the days before the *Challenger* explosion.

Following further O-ring tests in May 1982, Marshall finally accepted the conclusion that "Thiokol's dual O-rings did not provide a fully redundant system because the secondary O-ring would not always function after joint rotation following ignition" (Lewis, 1988, p. 74). Thus, in December 1982, the O ring seals were reclassified as "criticality 1," which meant that they did not meet the fail-safe definition of the Space Shuttle Program Requirements document (President's Commission, 1986). The O-rings were now considered to be a potential "single failure point due to the possibility of loss of sealing at the secondary O-ring because of joint rotation" that could result in "loss of mission, vehicle and crew due to metal erosion, burn through, and probable case burst resulting in fire and deflagration" (President's Commission, 1986, p. 126).

Despite the reclassification of the O-rings to criticality 1, no one at Marshall called for a halt in the program to fix the problem. The solid rocket managers believed that the secondary O-ring actually was redundant except in rare cases (Lewis, 1988). In March of 1983, NASA associate administrator L. Michael Weeks settled the issue of whether the shuttle should continue to fly in its current condition when he approved a wavier on the criticality 1 field joint. But as the shuttle program picked up speed, signs of O-ring erosion and damage became more marked and more frequent (President's Commission, 1986; Lewis, 1988). The managers at Marshall, however, continued to define the erosion of the O-rings to be an "acceptable risk" (McConnell, 1987, p. 120).

However the O-ring problem was slowly coming to the attention of higher level officials at NASA. As an outgrowth of a flight readiness review in April 1984, NASA deputy administrator Dr. Hans Mark issued a directive to Lawrence Mulloy at Marshall requesting a formal review of the field joint sealing process (President's Commission, 1986). Mulloy, in turn, had a letter sent to MTI asking for a formal review to identify the cause of the erosion, determine whether it was acceptable, and define necessary changes (President's Commission, 1986). MTI replied in May with a proposal, but its final response to this directive would not be completed for another fifteen months. In the meantime, the primary O-ring of a nozzle joint failed and hot gases badly scorched the secondary ring in an April 1985 *Challenger* flight. Even though the secondary O-ring had held that time, the obvious failure of a criticality 1 component forced Marshall to impose a launch constraint on all future flights until the cause could be analyzed and dealt with. However, this launch constraint, which meant that the shuttle could not fly unless the cause of the constraint were taken care of, would be waived for the next flight and each subsequent flight right up through the 51-L mission of the *Challenger*.

By the summer of 1985, "the engineers at Marshall and Thiokol most intimately involved with the boosters could no longer deny that they had a potentially catastrophic situation facing them" (McConnell, 1987, p. 121). The interaction between NASA and MTI over the O-ring problem increased substantially that summer. In July two MTI inspectors were sent to Marshall to discuss O-ring problems with engineers there. Meanwhile, engineers back at Thiokol were increasingly concerned about the O-rings and urged the company to move quickly to solve the problem. In a July 31, 1985, memo one engineer, Roger Boisjoly, pointed out that a failure of the field joint would result in "a catastrophe of the highest order— loss of human life" (President's Commission, 1986, p. 249). Boisjoly recommended setting up a team to work on the O-ring problem, and concluded by stating, "It is my honest and very real fear that if we do not take immediate action to dedicate a team to solve the problem, with the field joint having the number one priority, then we stand in jeopardy of losing a flight along with all the launch pad facilities" (President's Commission, 1986, p. 249).

Concern at NASA was also escalating. Richard Cook, a budget analyst at NASA, wrote a memo only days before Boisjoly's July memo, concerning the budget implications of the O-ring problem he had been requested to investigate. Cook warned that the budget impact could be immense. He also concluded that "there is little question, however, that flight safety has been and is still being compromised by potential failure of the seals, and it is acknowledged that failure during launch would certainly be catastrophic" (Cook, 1985, p. 1). That same month, July 1985, NASA officials quietly began to embark on a program to solve the problem of the leaky booster rocket seals. They ordered seventy-two new steel cases so they could install capture features, which would lock the seals tightly in place, in boosters already in use (Broad, 1986). The capture feature was called the "big fix" by Marshall engineers, but while they waited for the big fix to become available, they continued to fly.

With the proposed big fix and the events of late summer and early fall in 1985, McConnell (1987) argues that there was "irrefutable evidence that both Marshall and Thiokol realized that they were risking disaster by allowing shuttle flights to continue despite the chronic O-ring erosion" (p. 121). On August 19, 1985, MTI and Marshall engineers briefed NASA headquarters on the O-ring erosion problem. The briefing was "detailed" according to the President's Commission (1986, p. 140), and the conclusion presented by the engineers was that the seal was a critical matter and an accelerated pace was recommended to eliminate erosion, but it was safe to fly. In view of this high-level briefing the statement by the President's Commission that "those who made that decision (to launch) were unaware of the recent history of problems concerning the O-rings and the joint," seems very strange.

The next day MTI, noting that a leak at any of the joints would be catastrophic, announced the formation of an O-ring task force "to investigate the solid rocket motor case and nozzle joints, both materials and configurations, and recommend both short-term and long-term solutions" (President's Commission, 1986, p. 140). The task force, however, was plagued with resource problems and foot dragging on the part of top management during a period when the company was renegotiating its contract with NASA. As McConnell (1987) observes, "It might be reasonable to assume, therefore, that Thiokol was hesitant to have its engineering task force act too quickly on the booster redesign and by doing so expose the inherent weakness of the original field joint design to hostile Congressional scrutiny" (p. 181). Whatever the reason for the delays, Boisjoly and others on the MTI task force complained that they were being blocked in their efforts to accomplish the task (Boisjoly, personal interview; President's Commission, 1986; Lewis, 1988). Incredibly, without arriving at any solution to the problem, MTI requested to NASA that the O-ring problem be closed out—that is, considered resolved. On January 23, 1986, five days before the *Challenger* explosion, an entry was made in the Marshall Problem Reports that "the problem is considered closed" (Lewis, 1988, p. 88).

Information concerning the flawed design of the field joint seal was clearly a source of organizational strain at both NASA and MTI. Both organizations had clear knowledge of the serious nature of the problem and the possible consequences of a failure of the O-ring seals. To fix the serious problem, however, would require that the shuttle program be grounded, probably for a lengthy period of time. To do this would have greatly slowed down the space shuttle's flight schedule, cut into MTI's profits, and perhaps jeopardized the second phase of their lucrative contract with NASA. Because of the enormous pressures on NASA, a long delay was to be avoided at all costs. As Heaphy (1986) noted: "An environment had been created where anyone calling for a halt to the shuttle program for a safety design was opening themselves up to a charge of advocating economic collapse, nuclear destruction and communist control of Mars" (p. 3).

How did NASA and MTI respond to the strain? They responded by keeping the space shuttle flying, and at an accelerated pace at that. The problems with the seals were defined as "not serious" and as an "unavoidable" and "acceptable flight risk." Unsafe or illegitimate means were used to attain the organizational goals that had been established. These unsafe means were available simply because, as Commissioner Richard Feynman put it, "they got away with it last time." As Dr. Feynman (President's Commission, 1986) observed, the decision making was

a kind of Russian roulette . . . (the shuttle flies with O-ring erosion) and nothing happens. Then it is suggested, therefore, that the risk is no longer so high for the next flight. We can lower our standards a little bit because we got away with it last time. . . . You got away with it, but it shouldn't be done over and over again like that. (P. 148)

Actors in Context: The Decisions to Launch Flight 51-L

So far, data have been presented on the general performance pressure that NASA was subjected to with regard to the shuttle program and its flight rate goals, and the organizational strain caused by the O-ring problem that NASA resolved by continuing to fly an unsafe vehicle. In this section the focus shifts to the specific pressures and strains surrounding the flight of the *Challenger* on January 28, 1986.

Mission 51-L, with the space shuttle *Challenger*, was originally scheduled for launch December 23, 1985. Bad weather, however, had forced numerous delays of the previous mission, 61-C, a *Columbia* flight. The 61-C delays made it necessary to reschedule flight 51-L to January 23, 1986. 51-L itself would be postponed four times and scrubbed once for a variety of reasons. These launch delays wore exerting tremendous pressure on NASA and the shuttle launch schedule. The space agency had scheduled fifteen launches for 1986, its most ambitious schedule yet, and nineteen missions in 1987. As Lewis (1988) observes, "There was no question that launch delays during the unusually cold winter of 1985–86 in Florida were eroding NASA's ability to meet commercial and military satellite launch commitments" (p. 52).

There were also three important scientific missions that NASA planned to launch that spring. Two of these missions, the *Ulysses* and the *Galileo*, were dependent on the orbit of Jupiter. The other mission, the *Astro 1* observing mission for the appearance of Halley's comet, was also on a very tight time schedule. The *Challenger* 51-L launch, therefore, was time-critical. NASA had to get the *Challenger* launched and returned within a very short time frame so that the orbiter could be reconfigured for one of these scientific missions, and preparations could be made at the launch facility for the other time-critical missions.

The 51-L mission was also special because of the presence of teacher Christa McAuliffe. She was to be the first private citizen to ride into space, where she was scheduled to deliver a school lesson to millions of American students. McAuliffe had captured the hearts of many Americans who were following this shuttle flight much more closely than normal. Media attention was also high, and NASA had come in for some criticism from the news media for the numerous delays in late 1985 and early 1986. As Lewis (1988) notes, "News media critics tended to view launch delays caused by engineering problems as evidence of inadequate quality control, and caused by weather as indicative of excessive caution and lack of confidence" (p. 52).

For all of these reasons, NASA officials were feeling the heat as they rescheduled the 51-L flight for January 28, 1986. This date also presented NASA with an important opportunity. The president was scheduled to give the State of the Union address that night. There is evidence that NASA had suggested to the White House that the president include a reference to the shuttle program and the teacher Christa McAuliffe during the address (Cook, 1986, p. 20). According to former NASA budget analyst Richard Cook, a public-relations conscious agency like NASA saw this as an opportunity to counter media criticism and rally public support around the agency once again (personal interview). Cook argues that the timing of the State of the Union address created additional pressure within NASA to finally launch 51-L on the morning of January 28.

But as the pressured space agency prepared to launch the *Challenger*, another major strain arose in connection with the O-rings. The weather forecast for the morning of January 28 called for extremely low temperatures. At MTI in Utah, several Thiokol engineers became concerned when they heard about the low temperatures being predicted for launch time. They had evidence that suggested that the O-rings lost some of their resiliency in cold weather and that would make it even more difficult for them to seal out the hot gases when joint rotation occurred. During the afternoon of January 27, MTI engineers presented their concerns about the effects of cold weather on the booster seal joints to level III officials in the NASA readiness review process at Marshall and recommended that the launch be delayed again.

Late in the afternoon on January 27, a very significant interaction took place between MTI and NASA, one that would lead directly to the state-corporate crime of the *Challenger* explosion. That afternoon and evening, the now famous teleconference occurred between

MTI officials and Marshall officials. At this teleconference, which was also attended by senior executives and managers, MTI engineers presented their evidence on the effects of cold weather on the O-rings and the joint seal and recommended that NASA not launch the shuttle under the temperature of 53 degrees Fahrenheit. NASA's reaction to this information was swift and harsh (Boisjoly, personal interview). Lawrence Mulloy's response was "unusually heated" (McConnell, 1987, p. 196). He attacked MTI's data and their conclusions and accused them of trying to establish new launch commit criteria based on the 53-degree benchmark. It was at this point that Mulloy made his famous comment, "My God, Thiokol, when do you want me to launch, next April?" Another Marshall official said he was "appalled" at the MTI decision (President's Commission, 1986, p. 90). The mood of the teleconference quickly shifted and MTI officials found themselves on the defensive. NASA officials said they would not fly without the contractor's approval, but it was clear that they were bitterly opposed to the MTI conclusion. Pressure was brought to bear on MTI to reverse their no-launch recommendation.

After more discussion and debate it appeared that a stalemate had been reached. At this point, MTI requested a five-minute recess to caucus. Once off the net, one of the MTI executives said a management decision was required (Boisjoly, personal interview). When it appeared that the executives and managers intended to caucus alone, Boisjoly and another engineer physically intervened to restate their position (Boisjoly, personal interview). They argued vociferously against the launch for some time, but it became apparent that their arguments were having no effect. One of the MTI managers was told during the discussion to take off his engineering hat and put on his management hat (President's Commission, 1986). The engineering data and the pressure from a major client obviously caused MTI officials great strain in this situation. They resolved the situation by deciding to reverse the recommendation of their engineers and approve the launch of the *Challenger* the next morning, even though it was clear that their own engineers told them that it would not be safe to do so.

When MTI came back on line, they told NASA that while the cold weather was still a safety concern, on reassessment they found that the data were, indeed, inconclusive, and that they would now recommend that the launch proceed (President's Commission, 1986). Once the level III officials at Marshall had this recommendation, they did not communicate the engineering concerns of MTI regarding the cold weather effects on the O-rings to any higher level in the readiness review process despite the general history of problems with these seals that were well known to these higher level officials. Whether the communication of this information would have made any difference in the decision to launch cannot be known. Although the President's Commission found no evidence that level I and II officials did know of the MTI engineer's objections, Richard Cook believes that they did know of these concerns, but, given the enormous pressures to launch that day, it made no difference (Cook, personal interview).

Whether the level I and II NASA officials knew of the danger posed by the cold weather or not, clearly the level III managers at Marshall did have that knowledge. This information caused an organizational strain for this subunit of NASA. The individuals who occupied positions in this subunit were committed to a launch, but were presented with data that indicated that they did not have safe means to accomplish the task. Rather than change the goal and delay the flight, these managers resolved the strain by using illegitimate, that is unsafe means, that were available to them, the authority to authorize the flight at their level. The deviant nature of the interaction between MTI and Marshall on the night before the *Challenger* exploded was later described by two MTI officials in testimony before the President's Commission. Both Roger Boisjoly, the engineer, and Robert Lund, the manager, testified that there was an almost total reversal of the normal relationship between Marshall and MTI that night. Rather than having to prove to NASA that the shuttle was safe to fly, the contractor was being bullied to prove beyond a doubt that it was dangerous. As Boisjoly (President's Commission, 1986) put it,

> One of my colleagues that was in the meeting summed it up best. This was a meeting where the determination was to launch, and it was up to us to prove beyond a shadow of a doubt that it was not safe to do so. This is in total reverse to what the usual is in a preflight conversation or a flight readiness review. It is usually exactly opposite that. (P. 93)

A Critical Catalyst for Action:
The Silent Safety System

Given the strong performance emphasis at NASA, it is easy to see how the organizational strains that arose from the design flaw of MTI's solid rocket booster field joint pushed the space agency toward an illegitimate solution to the problem. Could these strains, however, have been checked or handled adequately by social control mechanisms? Would stronger social controls, both external and internal to NASA, have been able to prevent the tragic flight of 51-L? The data seem to suggest that as a real possibility.

One point that has emerged quite clearly out of the various investigations of the space shuttle program is the fact that NASA was not subjected to any strong oversight by any external control agency. Most organizations, public or private, are subjected to a variety of control mechanisms in their external environment. Corporations, for example, are subject to the criminal justice system, a wide variety of regulatory agencies, the media, labor unions, consumer and environmental groups, and public opinion. While these external controls are generally quite weak and ineffective, their sheer numbers guarantee at least a modest measure of oversight.

Governmental agencies like NASA are subjected to far fewer external controls as a general rule. Congress serves as the primary control agent for these organizations, with the media and public opinion in the environment as well. Of all the government agencies, NASA is one that has received a virtually free ride in terms of oversight and control over the years. The National Aeronautics and Space Act of 1958 allocated broad oversight responsibilities to the Congress and to the National Aeronautics and Space Council. Both of these bodies lacked the technical expertise, and, due to other responsibilities, the capacity for monitoring NASA activities (Vaughan, 1988).

Congressional oversight has been particularly lacking. As Representative Robert Roe of the House Committee on Science and Technology recently observed, "Congress has been too shy in finding fault with NASA. . . . As a result of the *Challenger* accident, Congress and NASA must begin a new era, one in which Congress must apply the same strong oversight to NASA that it does to any other government agency" (Benedict, 1986, p. 4). And, as Representative Manuel Lujan, the senior Republican on the Science and Technology Committee, has confessed, "As a committee, we may have been too trusting when NASA gave us glowing reports about the space shuttle program" (Benedict, 1986, p. 4).

As with congressional oversight, NASA has generally been given favorable treatment in the media and has been held in high esteem by the public. The excitement and romance of space travel, its high entertainment value, and the genuine successes of NASA have all combined to produce public approval of the space agency and its worship by the media, especially television. McConnell (1987) confesses that journalists covering NASA were taken in by the plush nature of the assignment and the skillful manipulations of the public relations staff, and did not do their job correctly. Despite their carping about launch delays (Lewis, 1988), the media did not ask the tough questions, probe behind the press releases, or investigate the agency as thoroughly as they should have (Lindee and Nelkin, 1986; Mann, 1986; McConnell, 1987). A more sober, objective, and critical stance toward NASA and the issue of safety on the part of the media, which we did witness in the coverage of the agency in the aftermath of the disaster, may have been able to exert some counterbalancing pressures on NASA before the explosion.

Given the lack of external social control over the space agency, the responsibility for close surveillance was left to NASA itself. As Vaughan (1988) points out, "The space agency, from its inception, was to guide its own regulation" (p. 6). This self-regulation was inadequate. As Vaughan (1988) notes, NASA's efforts at self-regulation concerning safety and quality control were marked with a variety of problems:

> The organizational response was characterized by poor communication, inadequate information handling, and failure to comply with regulations instituted to insure safety. Moreover, the regulatory system designed to oversee the safety of the shuttle program failed to identify and correct program management and design problems related to the O-rings. NASA insiders referred to these omissions as "quality escapes": failures of the program to preclude an avoidable problem. (P. 3)

One major social control problem within the organizational structure at NASA was the absence of an effective communication system

(Brody, 1986). A strong communication system is essential to handle the problems of coordination and control. Without effective vertical and horizontal communication, top management may experience authority leakage and lose control over subunits within the organization. According to the President's Commission (1986), "Failures in communication that resulted in a decision to launch 51-L based on incomplete and sometimes misleading information" (p. 82) was a contributing cause of the shuttle disaster. The tendency at Marshall toward management isolation in particular was cited by the presidential commission as a major factor in the breakdown of communication at NASA. This is ironic since the Marshall Space Flight Center in the 1960s was lauded as having an extremely effective communication system (Thompkins, 1977; 1978).

Another internal social control problem was the reduction in the safety program at NASA since *Apollo* (Perrow, 1986) and the lack of independence for those safety personnel who did remain (Vaughan, 1988). The President's Commission (1986) devoted an entire chapter of its report to the "silent safety program" at NASA. The commission found that the safety, reliability, and quality assurance work force at NASA had been reduced, and that this reduction had seriously limited NASA's capability in these vital functions which, in turn, adversely affected mission safety. As the commission (1986) noted,

> The unrelenting pressure to meet the demands of an accelerating flight schedule might have been adequately handled by NASA if it had insisted upon the exactingly thorough procedures that were its hallmark during the *Apollo* program. An extensive and redundant safety program comprising interdependent safety, reliability and quality assurance functions existed during and after the lunar program to discover any potential safety problems. Between that period and 1986, however, the program became ineffective. This loss of effectiveness seriously degraded the checks and balances essential for maintaining flight safety. (P. 152)

While there had been a reduction in the overall safety program at NASA, there still remained myriad safety, reliability, and quality assurance units within the overall structure. The ability of these units to act as social control mechanisms, however, was seriously eroded by their lack of independence within the structure. Both Kennedy and Marshall had placed safety personnel under the supervision of the very offices and activities whose efforts they are to check and control. This structural flaw was described well by the President's Commission (1986):

> In most cases, these organizations report to supervisors who are responsible for processing. The clear implication of such a management structure is that it fails to provide the kind of independent role necessary for flight safety. At Marshall, the director of Reliability and Quality Assurance reports to the director of Science and Engineering who oversees the development of shuttle hardware. Again, this results in a lack of independence from the producer of hardware and is compounded by reductions in manpower, the net bringing about a decrease in effectiveness which has direct implications for flight safety. (P. 153)

Still another social control problem within the internal structure at NASA was the erosion of norms supporting the use of legitimate means to accomplish organizational goals. Braithwaite (1989) argues that the internal culture of the organization is a critical factor in either promoting or controlling organizational crime. At NASA, an internal culture had developed in which safety and technical considerations were often downplayed. As former NASA employee Don Eyles (1986) notes, and the research of Thompkins (1977; 1978) supports, the normative environment at NASA was quite different during the *Apollo* era. The erosion of normative supports for the safest possible means to carry out the agency's missions removed one of the strongest social control mechanisms that can exist within an organization.

According to Vaughan (1988), in the final analysis, overall regulatory effectiveness at NASA, both internally and externally, was affected by the autonomy and interdependence of the agency and its regulators. Her analysis of the three primary safety units at NASA shows that failure was built into the space agency's system.

Conclusion

This essay had three objectives. First, it told the story behind the explosion of the space shuttle *Challenger*, describing the decisions and actions that led to the tragedy and the societal and organizational contexts within which these decisions and actions were taken. Second, it demonstrated the utility of the concept of state-corporate crime by applying it to the specific case of the *Challenger* explosion. Finally, the data from this case study gave some empirical support to the integrated theoretical model sketched out here and its ability to explain organizational misconduct.

As the story of the *Challenger* case reveals, the explosion of the shuttle was not an "accident." While the technical cause of the explosion was the failure of the O-ring seal in a field joint of a solid rocket booster, the essay describes in some detail the decisions and actions of NASA and MTI concerning the flawed design of the field joint and the safe launching of the shuttle that were the actual causes of the disaster. To make these decisions and actions understandable, the historical, political, and organizational contexts within which the social actors of NASA and MTI were operating were also analyzed.

The study also documents that the *Challenger* explosion was the collective product of the interaction between a government agency (NASA) and a private business corporation (MTI) and thus can be viewed as an instance of state-corporate crime. This disaster cannot be attributed solely to the actions of one organization. The misconduct occurred as an institution of political governance pursued a goal in direct cooperation with an institution of economic production. Thus, it is a prime example of the phenomenon of state-corporate crime that is emerging as a major problem in increasingly complex and interrelated political economies around the world (Perrow, 1986). It is hoped that the concept of state-corporate crime will direct further attention to the structural relations between corporate and governmental organizations and to the importance of interorganizational relationships and organizational sets in the study of organizational misconduct.

Finally, the data presented here provide a good measure of empirical support for the integrated theoretical model of organizational crime that appears to be emerging in the literature. The *Challenger* case study provides general support for the hypothesis that criminal or deviant behavior at the organizational level results from a coincidence of pressure for goal attainment, availability and perceived attractiveness of illegitimate means, and an absence of effective social control. In this case, the external political pressure on NASA and the internal organizational motivation of the agency combined to create an unreasonable launch rate schedule which placed enormous goal attainment pressure on the organization. When information about the faulty design of the solid rocket booster and the potential effects of cold weather on the O-rings was received by NASA, the agency could no longer launch the shuttle safely according to its own organizational standards. NASA, however, with the concurrence of MTI, made the decision to keep flying the shuttle fleet, and specifically to launch the *Challenger* on January 28, 1986, despite the lack of safe means. The absence of effective social control mechanisms at NASA, both external and internal, has been well documented. Thus, all three catalysts for action that are indicated by the integrated theoretical model were present in this case, allowing us, at this point, to have greater confidence in the ability of this model to help us understand organizational miscon-duct like that responsible for the *Challenger* explosion.

REFERENCES

Barak, G. (1990). Crime, criminology and human rights: Towards an under-standing of state criminality. *The Journal of Human Justice, 2*, Au-tumn, 11–28.

———. *Crimes by the capitalist state: An introduction to state criminality.* Albany, N.Y.: State University of New York Press.

Barnett, H. C. (1981). Corporate capitalism, corporate crime. *Crime and Delinquency, 27*, January, 4–23.

Benedict, H. (1986). Congress plans to watch NASA. *Detroit Free Press*, June 11, 4A.

Boisjoly, R. (1988). Personal interview, February 2.

Box, S. (1983). *Power, crime and mystification.* London: Tavistock.

Braithwaite, J. (1984). *Corporate crime in the pharmaceutical industry.* London: Routledge & Kegan Paul.

———. (1989). Criminological theory and organizational crime. *Justice Quarterly, 6*, 333–358.

Broad, W. (1986). NASA had solution to key flaw in rocket when shuttle exploded. *New York Times*, September 22, 1.

Brody, M. (1986). NASA's challenge: Ending isolation at the top. *Fortune*, May, 26–28.

Chambliss, W. (1988). *On the take: From petty crooks to presidents*, (rev. ed.). Bloomington: Indiana University Press.

——. (1989). State-organized crime. *Criminology*, *27*, 183–208.

Chomsky, N. (1987). *On power and ideology*. Boston: South End Press.

——. (1988). *The culture of terrorism*. Boston: South End Press.

Clinard, M. B. (1990). *Corporate corruption: The abuse of power*. New York: Praeger.

Clinard, M. B., and Yeager, P. C. (1980). *Corporate crime*. New York: Free Press.

Coleman, J. W. (1987). Toward an integrated theory of white-collar crime. *American Journal of Sociology*, *93*, 406–439.

——. (1989). *The criminal elite: The sociology of white collar crime* (2d ed.). New York: St. Martin's Press.

Cook, R. (1985). Problem with SRB seals. Internal NASA Memo, July 23.

——. (1986). The Rogers Commission failed: Questions it never asked, answers it didn't listen to. *The Washington Monthly*, November, 13–21.

——. (1988). Personal interview, January 29.

Cullen, F. T., Maakestad, W. J., and Cavender, G. (1987). *Corporate crime under attack: The Ford Pinto case and beyond*. Cincinnati: Anderson Publishing.

Easterbrook, G. (1987). Big dumb rockets. *Newsweek*, August 17, 46–60.

Ermann, M. D., and Lundman, R. J. (1982). *Corporate deviance*. New York: Holt, Rinehart and Winston.

——. (1987). *Corporate and governmental deviance: Problems of organizational behavior in contemporary society*, (3rd ed.). New York: Oxford University Press.

Eyles, D. (1986). At NASA where was "what if"? *New York Times*, March 12.

Finney, H. C., and Lesieur, H. R. (1982). A contingency theory of organizational crime. In S. B. Bacharach, ed. *Research in the sociology of organizations*, vol. 1, 255–299. Greenwich, Conn.: JAI Press.

Frankel, M. (1989). *Out of the shadows of night: The struggle for international human rights*. New York: Delacorte Press.

Frappier, J. (1984). Above the law: Violations of international law by the U.S. government from Truman to Reagan. *Crime and Social Justice*, *21–22*, 1–36.

Geis, G. (1984). White-collar and corporate crime. In Robert Meier, ed. *Major forms of crime*. Beverly Hills: Sage.

————. (1988). From deuteronomy to deniability: A historical perlustration on white-collar crime. *Justice Quarterly, 5*, March, 7–32.

Giddens, A. (1987). *Social theory and modern sociology*. Stanford: Stanford University Press.

Goff, C., and Reasons, C. (1978). *Corporate crime in Canada: A critical analysis of anti-combines legislation*. Scarborough, Ontario: Prentice-Hall of Canada, Ltd.

Green, G. (1990). *Occupational crime*. Chicago: Nelson-Hall.

Gross, E. (1978). Organizational crime: A theoretical perspective. In N. K. Denzin, ed. *Studies in symbolic interaction*, 55–85. Greenwich, Conn.: JAI Press.

————. (1980). Organizational structure and organizational crime. In G. Geis and E. Stotland, eds. *White-collar crime: Theory and research*, 52–76. Beverly Hills: Sage.

Halperin, M. H., Berman, J., Borosage, R., and Marwick, C. (1976). *The lawless state: The crimes of the U.S. intelligence agencies*. New York: Penguin Books.

Heaphy, J. (1986). *Challenger's* trial of blame. *In These Times, 10*, June 25-July 8, 3.

Herman, E. S. (1982). *The real terror network: Terrorism in fact and propaganda*. Boston: South End Press.

Hills, S. L. (1987). *Corporate violence: Injury and death for profit*. Totowa, N.J.: Rowman & Littlefield.

Hochstedler, E. (1984). *Corporations as criminals*. Beverly Hills: Sage.

Hopkins, A. (1978). The anatomy of corporate crime. In P. R. Wilson and J. Braithwaite, eds. *Two faces of deviance: Crimes of the powerless and powerful*. Brisbane, Australia: University of Queensland Press.

Kelman, H. C., and Hamilton, V. L. (1989). *Crimes of obedience*. New Haven: Yale University Press.

Kramer, R. (1989). Criminologists and the social movement against corporate crime. *Social Justice, 16*, 146–164.

Kramer, R. C., and Michalowski, R. J. (1990). State-corporate crime. Paper presented at the annual meeting of the American Society of Criminology, November, Baltimore, Maryland.

Lewis, R. S. (1988). *Challenger: The final voyage*. New York: Columbia University Press.

Lindee, S., and Nelkin, D. (1986). *Challenger*: The high cost of hype. *Bulletin of the Atomic Scientists*, November, 16–17.

McConnell, M. (1987). *Challenger: A major malfunction*. Garden City, N.Y.: Doubleday & Company, Inc.

McDougall, W. A. (1985). *The heavens and the earth.* New York: Basic Books.

Mann, P. (1986). The NASA story we missed. *Bulletin of the Atomic Scientists,* November, 18.

Mark, H. (1987). *The space station: A personal journey.* Durham, N.C.: Duke University Press.

Michalowski, R. J. (1985). *Order, law, and crime.* New York: Random House.

Michalowski, R. J., and Kramer, R. C. (1987). The space between laws: The problem of corporate crime in a transnational context. *Social Problems, 34,* 34–53.

Mokhiber, R. (1988). *Corporate crime and violence: Big business power and the abuse of the public trust.* San Francisco: Sierra Club Books.

Nation, The (1986). The lethal shuttle. *The Nation, 232,* February 22, 193.

Nieburg, H. L. (1966). *In the name of science.* Chicago: Quadrangle Books.

Perrow, C. (1986). Risky systems: The habit of courting disaster. *The Nation, 242,* October 11, 347–356.

Pike, J. (1988). Personal interview, January 29.

Poveda, T. (1990). *The F.B.I. in transition.* Pacific Grove, Calif.: Brooks/Cole Publishing Company.

President's Commission on the Space Shuttle *Challenger* Accident (1986). *Report of the Presidential Commission on the space shuttle Challenger accident,* Vols. I, II, III, and IV. Washington, D.C.: U.S. Government Printing Office.

Roebuck, J., and Weeber, S. (1978). *Political crime in the United States.* New York: Praeger.

Simon, D. R., and Eitzen, S. D. (1990). *Elite deviance,* 3rd ed. Boston: Allyn and Bacon.

Snider, L. (1987). Towards a political economy of reform, regulation, and corporate crime. *Law & Policy, 9,* 37–68.

Stockwell, J. (1991). *The praetorian guard: The U.S. role in the new world order.* Boston: South End Press.

Sutherland, E. H. (1940). White collar criminality. *American Sociological Review, 5,* 1-12.

———. (1949). *White collar crime.* New York: Dryden Press. (Re-issued by Holt, Rinehart and Winston, New York, 1961).

Thompkins, P. (1977). Management qua communication in rocket research and development. *Communication Monographs, 44,* 1–26.

Thompkins, P. (1978). Organizational metamorphosis in space research and development. *Communication Monographs, 45,* 110–118.

Tilly, C. (1985). War making and state making as organized crime. In P.

Evans, D. Rueschemeyer, and T. Skocpol, eds. *Bringing the state back in*. Cambridge: Cambridge University Press.

Trento, J. J. (1987). *Prescription for disaster: From the glory days of* Apollo *to the betrayal of the shuttle*. New York: Crown Publishing.

U.S. Congress, House (1986). Committee on Science and Technology. Investigation of the *Challenger* accident. Washington, D.C.: Government Printing Office.

Vaughan, D. (1982). Toward understanding unlawful organizational behavior. *Michigan Law Review, 80*, June, 1377–1402.

———. (1983). *Controlling unlawful organizational behavior: Social structure and corporate misconduct*. Chicago: University of Chicago Press.

———. (1988). *Autonomy, interdependence, and social control: NASA and the space shuttle* Challenger. Unpublished manuscript, Department of Sociology, Boston College.

Wickman, P., and Daily, T. (1982). *White-collar and economic crime*. Lexington, Mass.: Lexington Books.

Yeager, P. C. (1987). Structural bias in regulatory law enforcement: The case of the U.S. Environmental Protection Agency. *Social Problems, 34*, 330–344.

NOTES

I would like to thank Ray Michalowski for the important contributions he made to the final revision of this essay. I would also like to thank Jim Jaksa, Mike Pritchard, and the Center for the Study of Ethics in Society at Western Michigan University for their encouragement of this project.

1. This literature is cited in the references above.

· 10 ·

Moving Backstage

Uncovering the Role of Compliance
Practices in Shaping
Regulatory Policy

NANCY REICHMAN

Sutherland's address (1940) before the American Sociological Society focused attention on the significance of "white-collar" criminality. Since then we have sought to identify ways in which white-collar offenses and offenders can be distinguished from their street-level counterparts. We have identified the criminogenic characteristics of particular industries in an effort to explain why violations are located there. We also have come some distance in understanding our responses to white-collar crime, its detection, prosecution, and sanctioning. Yet there is still much to be done to develop an appreciation of how business discourse and practice actively participate in the construction of regulatory violations and pattern their distribution.

I offer this essay as one effort to explicate the business sector's influence on the definition and distribution of white-collar crime within specific regulatory contexts. I argue that business actors influence the distribution of white-collar crime not only through their influence on the enactment and administration of law, but also through their relative abilities to define what regulatory law is, how it is violated, and enforced. Typically, when studies have considered private-sector influence on the behavior of law, they have examined how business interests and activities affect the detection of offenses, the application of sanctions, and the potential deterrent effect of enforcement initiatives.

To fully understand patterns of regulatory behavior, including the patterns of violations and sanctions we observe, we must move "backstage" in the regulatory drama to explore how everyday business transactions organize a firm's compliance with regulatory rules. Legal action is not simply a reaction or alternative to the threat of a legal sanction (see also Yeager, 1990). Regulatory enforcement policy emerges out of the informal arrangements, tacit agreements, and pressures for conformity that provide legal significance to behavior quite apart from regulatory action. Thus, we must extend the criminological program to look beyond the relationship between regulator and regulated, and locate regulatory policy and practice within the complex networks of clients, legal and accounting personnel, and market competitors that offer authority and legitimacy for business activity (see Stone, 1975; Vaughan, 1983; Stenning et al., 1990; Manning, 1987; and Yeager, 1990 for different discussions of how regulatory law is embedded in the complexity of social life). And, most importantly, once we have identified the inter- and intraorganizational correlates of business authority, we must begin to consider how variation in the organization of compliance affects the observation of regulatory violations and the distribution of regulatory enforcement actions.

I argue here that the shape of regulatory policy, including the distribution of regulatory violations, can be linked to the patterns of cultural authority that develop within a particular business sphere. Following Starr (1982, p. 13), cultural authority is defined as the authority to construct reality through definitions of fact and value. It is the ability to interpret, diagnose, and persuade, not necessarily the ability to command action (the latter he refers to as "social authority"). One manifestation of cultural authority is the ability to assign legal significance to business activities. I call this kind of cultural authority "regulatory authority." Regulatory authority relates to the relative power of firms to embed their compliance in larger social networks that allow them to authenticate their actions while marginalizing and discrediting the actions of others. It is the authority to set the rules, to define the winners and losers, and to change the definitions of the regulation game (Meidinger, 1987, p. 357). Business firms acquire regulatory authority through the accumulation of juridical capital (Bourdieu, 1987). They build legitimating social networks by purchasing the "legal" authority of other professional groups—for example, lawyers and accountants. Regulatory authority converts into business privilege when the norms, values, beliefs, and justifications associated with a particular regulatory culture become status indicators that differentiate core and periphery firms.

Efforts to model variation in compliance practice and the construction of regulatory authority offer to elaborate arguments of systematic bias in regulatory law enforcement. Observations of bias (systematic differences in the amount and type of enforcement) have been linked to the characteristics of offenses, the technical abilities and interests of regulatory agencies (Shapiro, 1984),[1] the situational "politics" of regulatory action (Bardach and Kagan, 1982), as well as to the attributes of the regulated entities themselves (for example, their size, economic clout, technical prowess [Yeager, 1987], personal background [Shover, 1980], and legal competence [Galanter, 1974]).[2] I suggest that neither the situated politics of regulatory actions, nor the attributes of parties to the regulatory process are sufficient for understanding systematic variation in regulatory practice. Patterns of enforcement cannot be understood without attending to structural differences in the inter- and intraorganizational relationships that provide meaning for regulatory compliance (and, thus, its noncompliance). Understanding variation in how regulated firms and their employees "manage" or negotiate the substance of law—that is, a firm's regulatory authority—may tell us a great deal about where we might expect to find rule-breaking behaviors.

In the remainder of this essay, I weave a model of regulatory authority and its effect on regulatory policy and practice around the context of deal making in the securities industry. The mobilization of regulatory law in the securities industry depends on a vast interorganizational network of stock issuers, brokers, independent gatekeepers (lawyers, accountants, and the like), regulators, and investors who transcend the form and content of their constituent agencies to create a shared, albeit temporary and contingent, "regulatory authority." I hypothesize that this authority has significant influence on the interpretation of business practice as conforming or not conforming to regulatory law. (See the discussion of legal networks in O'Malley [1989] or regulatory communities in Meidinger [1987].)

The Construction of Regulatory Meanings

As observers of the regulatory process have shown time and again, regulatory rules, despite (or because of) the minutia of detail, command wide discretion in their application. A certain amount of rule ambiguity is necessary because of the nearly impossible task of standardizing performance (Bardach and Kagan, 1982), an acute problem in many business contexts where innovation and outperformance is the raison d'etre.[3] The vast case law associated with regulatory programs provides continuing testimony for the need to interpret regulatory rules. Rule ambiguity is considered to be an important factor in regulatory accommodation. (See, for example, Diver's [1989] discussion of the effect of rule imprecision on, among other things, compliance with regulatory rules.)

Indeed, the past decade of regulatory scholarship has sought to show how regulatory policy is situationally constructed in the context of regulatory rule ambiguity (Hawkins and Thomas, 1984; 1989). Studies have shown how regulators cajole, persuade, and negotiate compliance with regulatory rules (Bardach and Kagan, 1982; Lynxwiler, Shover, and Clelland, 1983; Hawkins, 1984; Scholz, 1984; Braithwaite et al., 1987; Ayres and Braithwaite, 1989; Hawkins and Thomas, 1989). Kenneth Mann's (1985) study of attorneys who represent white-collar crime defendants offers a different twist on the dilemma of ambiguity. His work shows how attorneys, through a variety of information strategies, retroactively structure facts and reinterpret rules so that behavior is seen as fitting within the law. In this way, ambiguity limits the reach of formal legal process.

The regulatory agency/law enforcement perspective that has organized much of the regulatory scholarship about the consequences of rule ambiguity produces a somewhat myopic vision of regulatory practice. While we recognize that regulated entities may transform regulations by pressuring legislatures and regulatory agents to pass laws and enforce them in particular ways, we often overlook how the day-to-day activities of regulated actors shape and modify the rules that organize and provide meaning for business practice.[4] As Manning (1989, p. 51) observed, it is "interpreted meaning, not information, [that] is the basis for regulation." Legal interpretation arises not only in response to, or in the context of, official legal action, but out of the interpretations of behavior and organizational constraints offered by the networks of social agents and institutions in which everyday transactions are embedded.[5] Organizations regulated by law collectively create, modify, and undermine the very regulatory structures through which their work is organized. It is in this sense that we can define organizations as dual creations, governed by rules yet transformed from within as organizational actors adapt and reconstruct the regulations that constitute organizational life (see Giddens's [1986] conceptualization of structures as creations and constraints of social action and Burk's [1988] description of regulated financial markets).

Extending the white-collar crime paradigm to include the day-to-day compliance practices and the social construction of legal meaning is consistent with a movement in the sociology of law to understand how law is shaped by, and in turn shapes, social phenomena (Merry, 1989; Harrington and Merry, 1988; Yngvesson, 1988; Silbey and Sarat, 1987, as well as many others). The "force of law" (Bourdieu, 1987) is not simply imposed by external agencies. It is "simultaneously separate and immanent, imposed and participatory" (Yngvesson, 1988, p. 412), a product and producer of conflicts over authorized or legitimized interpretations of legal texts and regulatory practice.

As described by Rafter (1990), this constructionist approach to legal "meanings" should not be equated with more subjective accounts of negotiated order in which individuals' rule-breaking behavior is explained in terms of the way largely atomistic actors construct symbolic understandings of themselves and the situations they face. (See Coleman's [chapter 2] discussion of classic treatments of the social psychology of white-collar crime.) The constructionist approach to legal behavior advanced here recognizes that legal meanings are powerful ideologies that both reflect and reinforce relations of power, conditions of hierarchy, and historical circumstance. Our task then is to

> illustrate how particular ways of seeing the world come to be constituted, how they achieve hegemony through particular practices and discourses, what institutional conditions and social forces serve to maintain such discourses as authoritative, and how people cope with and represent to themselves their ongoing *struggle* to make the world conform to their conventional understandings and expectations of it. (Coombe, 1989, p. 111)

As we move the criminological focus to include the constitution and reproduction of regulatory meanings through organizational practice, we bring organizational theory into the study of white-collar crime in ways that it has not been in the past. Typically, when white-collar crime theorists bring organizational theory into their work they focus on the criminogenic characteristics of organizational structures, in particular, their goals and opportunity structures. Organizational environments, including regulatory environments, enter into these models as constraints on organizational action, which create pressures to violate the law or opportunities to neutralize social controls. (See the discussions by Vaughan and Kramer [chapters 5 and 9], and for their more classic treatments, Vaughan, 1983, and Kramer, 1982.)

A different view of organizational environments and their relationship to white-collar crime considers the environment, including state regulatory policy as enacted by organizations. According to this perspective, regulation is not simply a constraint on organizational action. Organizations interact with their regulatory environments—shaping as well as being shaped by them.[6] And because organizations do not operate in political or social vacuums, "The structure of relations rather than the individual organizations are the units of analysis" (Mizruichi and Schwartz, 1987, p. 3).

Organizational theorists use the term "organizational field" to describe the set of organizations that constitute a recognized area of institutional life. Within fields there is a tendency for "institutional isomorphism," a kind of structural and cultural convergence that provides a "map" for behavior (DiMaggio and Powell, 1983). Specifying the organizational fields that influence or "map" the regulatory program is an important step in developing theory about business influence on regulatory policy. Nonetheless, as Fligstein (1990) observed, it is important that as we do so we also remember that

> organizational fields are not generally benign and cooperative arrangements held in place by a sense of duty or honor, although the rhetoric and ideology of their proponents might lead one to think so. Instead, they are set up to benefit their most powerful members. These firms have often organized the rules and have the power to enforce them. The most important determinants of that power are the size of the firms and the ability of actors in them to

prevent other organizations from entering their fields. (P. 6)

Although Fligstein sees the common barriers to entry in terms of the economic factors of production (patents, technologies, investments, and the like), we might also ask whether firms use their abilities to influence regulation and construct cultural (or normative) barriers as well. If so, this might help predict where business influence on regulatory programs is most likely to occur.

Borrowing from the insights of the organizational theory outlined above, I suggest that businesses influence regulatory policy not only through pressure on legislation and the administration of justice, but by their participation in the organizational fields that "enact" regulatory policy through daily practice. In short, organizational policies and practices constitute and reproduce regulatory meanings and structures. And since firms differ in their position and power within fields, it may be possible to distinguish firms by the amount of regulatory authority they can generate.[7] Firms with high levels of regulatory authority may take command of the rules of the game in ways that marginalize, if not discredit, the actions of more subordinate members of their field. If so, the organization of compliance may be linked to the definition of regulatory meanings and the distribution of white-collar crime.

In the following section I use aspects of the securities business to illustrate why the study of business influence on regulatory process requires a deep understanding of the networks of interpersonal and organizational relations in which compliance activities are embedded.

The Securities Case

To illustrate the importance of moving to the "backstage" of compliance (that is, to the ordinary transactions where law "happens"), I draw from my preliminary observation of regulatory compliance in the securities industry. The securities industry provides a particularly apt arena for studying the organizational dimensions of compliance. It is hard to think of another setting in which so many different interests, agency relationships, and gate-keeping functionaries are required to intersect. Nor can one think of a business arena where the compliance function has been so clearly institutionalized, in part a response to the myriad conflicts of interests and risks of agency relationships that are found there. And, at no other time is the effort to link our understanding of white-collar crime and regulatory processes more important. The stock market "crashes" in 1987 and 1989, and insider-trading scandals have raised public fears about the fates of individual investors in a market that appears rigged against them (Reichman, 1989, forthcoming).

Regulatory Context

The corpus of statutory rules regulating the market is vast, technically complex, and enjoys a complicated history (see, for example, Seligman, 1982; and Burk, 1988, as well as others). The Securities Act of 1933, the Securities Exchange Act of 1934, and the Investment Company Act of 1940 lay the foundation for half a century of rule making in the securities industry.[8] These rules, among other things, (1) established a reporting protocol for disclosure of "material" information, (2) constructed barriers to participation that protected individuals from manipulative and fraudulent agents, (3) prohibited market manipulations, (4) bolstered procedures for maintaining an orderly market, (5) set limits on outright speculation, and (6) insulated participants from the effects of market collapse. A regulatory agency, the Securities and Exchange Commission, was created to ensure that these objectives were met.

Rules that mandate disclosure of "material" information about a securities offering have been cornerstones of SEC enforcement activities for decades, and thus are useful foci for our understanding of how compliance practices shape enforcement action. They are rules that tend to get enforced. Shapiro (1984) found, for example, that misrepresentations and registration violations were the most "popular" offenses in her sample. More importantly, these rules have been a source of normative debate (and substantive ambiguity) from their inception. They are important texts for regulatory interpretation. [9]

Disclosure rules require stock issuers to file a registration statement with the SEC and to use a particular circular, a prospectus, for offering their stock. These rules provide a set of explicit conventions by which actors can make judgments about their investments. The keystone to these regulations is the revelation of all matters "material" to an investor's decisions (Howell, Allison, and Hentley, 1985, p. 1109). Registration statements include, among other things, information about the organization, financial structure and nature of the business, balance sheets, and profit-and-loss statements for a three-year period, as well as discussion about the significant risks facing the industry and the particular organization. Continuous updating of registration statements with annual and quarterly reports (10-Ks and 10-Qs, respectively) is mandatory. Although the SEC evaluates the sufficiency and accuracy of statements made in the registration and prospectus, it does not rule on the merits of the offering. Federal rules merely provide a reporting protocol to aide investors as they attempt to sort out the worthiness of stock offerings. Some states include a merit review as part of their regulatory program as well.

Compliance Networks

Even an overly simplified illustration of how securities products are "made" and then distributed to the public can demonstrate why our understanding of regulatory behavior needs to expand beyond the sights of regulatory agencies to include a wide range of actors and activities that directly and indirectly participate in generating meaningful compliance with rules about disclosure. A diagram of the actors that will be described can be found in figure 1.

As the term is conventionally used, "security" refers to the legal representation of the right to receive some prospective benefit (or loss) from corporate activities. It is, in essence, the corporation's promise of a future "piece of the action," given in return for an investor's willingness to provide capital today (Sharpe, 1985).[10] Securities are issued to raise capital. A family-owned manufacturing company, Jones Inc., that wishes to expand its widget-making capabilities but cannot finance the expansion on its own, might decide to open up ownership of the company by *issuing* a type of security—common stock or public shares of ownership.

Having made their decision to "go public," the Jones family chooses an investment bank to help structure and finance their stock offering. *Investment bankers* mediate the flow of assets be-

FIGURE 1 · Constellation of Actors Creating and Selling Security Products

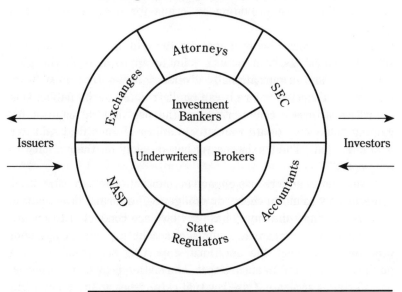

tween *issuers*, those who want to sell pieces of their action, and potential *investors*, companies, institutions, and individuals who wish to purchase a piece of it.[11] The prospectus that describes the "deal," or security offering, is constructed by an investment bank's team of lawyers, accountants, and bankers, and a similar team of legal and financial professionals hired by the company issuing stock. As noted earlier, Securities and Exchange Commission rules, state regulations, and the rules of self-regulatory organizations mandate full disclosure of material facts about the corporation and its stock offering. Still, there is plenty of room for interpretation as issuers and investment bankers haggle over exactly what details should appear in the prospectus and precisely what language should be used to describe them. Lawyers and accountants might debate whether certain items, such as outstanding lawsuits against a company, qualify or not. In the case of outstanding litigation against Jones Inc., for example, lawyers might provide opinions about the likelihood of a judgment against Jones, and accountants might debate whether the penalties that would accrue are material to Jones's future operation. Whatever the outcome of the negotiations between the investment bank and the issuing corporation, decisions about whether and what to disclose must still pass muster with the SEC, the state regulators, stock exchanges, and professional standards boards—each providing an arena for further debate and negotiation.[12]

Additional (local) counsel may be brought in to negotiate the special "issues" associated with gaining approval from the geographically and organizationally diverse agencies that must "sign off" on a prospectus before it can be distributed to the public. One securities attorney commenting on the use of local counsel for gaining "blue-sky" (state regulatory) approval for a deal said, for example, that "Their existence is based solely on their ability to schmooze."

Investment bankers also engage accountants, lawyers, and other professionals to aid in their "due diligence," a formal investigation into the issuing company. These reviews are conducted to ensure that the issuing company has sufficient accounting and management procedures to meet the additional reporting requirements of a public company and to ensure that information provided in a security offering is accurate. Case law that establishes an investor's right to sue if losses arise because bankers failed to perform this important duty supports the expectation that investment bankers will probe for mis- and malfeasance in the issuer's statements before distributing the securities products.[13] Similarly, SEC Rule 2(e) provides a mechanism for suspending from practice before the commission lawyers, accountants, and other professionals who fail to perform reasonable due diligence, fail to comply with GAAS and GAAP (government accounting standards), or fail to uncover and disclose material facts about an issuer.

In many cases, investment bankers also *underwrite* the offering. This means that they agree to purchase some or all of the securities and then distribute them. Underwriters can be thought of as the wholesalers of the securities product. It is their job to establish the price of the offering. In our example, ABC Securities helps Jones, Inc., construct an offering to sell one hundred shares of stock, and then buys the one hundred shares for future sales. In another case involving a larger distribution of the securities product, it might be necessary to assemble a syndicate of underwriters to purchase the security for later distribution to the public.

The possibility of deal syndications creates an additional web of entanglement and obligations that may induce an investment bank to conform to its peers at the expense of either its clients' or regulators' interests. Bankers must price a security so that it sells *and* provides sufficient revenue for the interests involved in its distribution. Underwriting, thus, creates different and sometimes contradictory risks (to a firm's reputation as well as its finances) for investment banks and their clients.

Finally, the actual trading of stock is realized by brokers. *Brokers* are agents who effect transactions for the account of other investors. Thus, if I wanted to purchase Jones, Inc. stock, I would ask my broker to purchase it for me at a particular price. Institutions (mutual funds, pension plans, corporations) use special brokers to place their market orders. In some cases, these institutional investors trade directly in the marketplace. As agents for investors, brokers are bound by the law of agency and SEC rules that say, among other things, that they must know their clients, know their products, and trade fairly (refrain from, for example, manipulating the price of stocks, churning accounts, using bait-and-switch tactics, selling unregistered securities, and the like). As employees of securities firms, brokers are bound by the organizational constraints of their firms. As commission salespersons, they are out to make a sale.

In short, creating and distributing a securities product combines a diverse set of actors and organizations into a single network organized around a particular, regulated product. Each actor has to be both responsive to the deal and also to the larger constellation of actors that embed his or her work. My preliminary research suggests that firms organize these relationships in different ways. Explicating these differences and their effect on compliance practice and the distribution of regulatory violations is of great theoretical import.

Observations of structural bias in SEC enforcement action raise important questions about how variations in compliance practices might affect regulatory law enforcement. Shapiro (1984), for example, notes that "the organizations subject to SEC investigation are not corporate giants that have been around for a long time; they are very young and very small" (p. 41). Further support for enforcement bias can be found in Ewick's (1985) study of SEC sanctioning. She found that, in the case of organizational offenders, the most severe sanctions were reserved for firms that were financially or organizationally moribund.

Similarly, task force reports (for example, NASAA, 1989) supporting increased enforcement of penny-stock fraud suggest that there are important industry differences between the compliance practices of firms that specialize in penny stocks and the practices of firms that offer more prestigious stock products. Regulatory processes, standard in other markets, apparently do not reach the penny-stock market, and, if they do, fail to meet their control objectives.[14] The persistence of fraud is often implicitly linked to the attributes of those who sell penny stocks. While not entirely discounting the "bad apple" theory of lawbreaking, I think it is important to ask whether differences in the social production of compliance (or noncompliance) have a more structural foundation.[15] Small, penny-stock firms may find themselves more likely to be classified as violators because they cannot "authoritatively reinterpret (within limits) what the rules mean" (Clegg, 1989).[16] Regulatory traditions that reify the marginality of penny-stock trading may relegate that sector of the market as the one where delinquency is "allowed" to flourish, and, in effect, privilege other sectors. This may occur because regulatory programs leave the interpretation of regulatory rules to the networks of regulated entities, only some of which have the power to make those interpretations, and only some of which are listened to when they do.

Toward a Model of Regulatory Authority and White-Collar Crime

In this section of the essay, I offer a model of regulatory authority that may help explicate differences in compliance practices and their effect on regulatory process. Once again, regulatory authority refers to the ability to assign legal significance to one's action, to set the rules of the game, and to define winners and losers in regulatory negotiations. The model is speculative and should be understood as a framework for future empirical work.

Faced with regulatory ambiguity, securities firms and their agents play important roles in constructing meaning for their dealmaking activities. Regulatory compliance is a fluid process (Hawkins, 1984) that involves negotiated interpretations of both rules and facts. From the perspective of the regulated entity, rule-oriented negotiations involve efforts to show that the rules don't apply, or don't apply in traditional ways, to the deals that investment bankers construct. For example, an investment banking firm might try to convince the SEC that the acquisition of a failed savings and loan institution is not the acquisition of an ongoing business, and, thus, should not be subject to historical financial disclosure. In this case, the jurisdiction of the rule is the subject of the negotiation. Fact-oriented negotiations involve efforts to change deal facts to fit within accepted rule structures. Attempts to construct deals so that they fit within the rule parameters or decisions to omit deal facts on the deal prospectus might be so regarded. To avoid complex regulatory requirements, for example, companies issuing a limited partnership might choose not to specify the assets that the partnership intends to purchase.

Regulators respond to these efforts at interpretation in a number of ways that depend on the gap between the regulators' impression of the rules or facts and the interpretation offered by the regulated entity, and on regulators' judgments about the motives for interpretation. (For an excellent discussion of the variegated response to suspected deviance, see Hawkins, 1984.) Regulators may reject all efforts at interpretation, in essence playing the game "by the book," regardless of the situation and contingencies encountered. Regulators may accept the interpretation as legitimate or purposeful from a public policy point of view. Or, finally, regulators may perceive the interpretations as willful attempts to get around the rules and, thus, regard them as legally implausible readings of the situations at hand.

I suggest that regulatory response is shaped by (and in turn shapes) the regulatory authority of regulated entities. Firms mobilize their power to shape regulatory response by embedding their activities within a network of interorganizational relations that authenticate and legitimate their actions. I hypothesize that three aspects of embeddedness condition the interplay of regulatory authority and regulatory response: (1) professional embeddedness, (2) structural embeddedness, and (3) cultural embeddedness. Each will be briefly discussed below.

1. *Professional embeddedness* refers to the ability to embed compliance practices within an interprofessional coalition that offers

different legitimizing perspectives on compliance practice. Business organizations that can embed their compliance activities within the legitimation structures of other professional groups are more likely to exercise authority over the regulatory process than business organizations that cannot situate their activities within a professional network. As noted earlier, Bourdieu (1987) argues that the "force of law" relates to ongoing professional struggles over the legal significance of everyday behavior. Regulatory authority flows to those who can accumulate the greatest number of these professional resources. The professional groups that are pivotal in the case of securities work are accountants, lawyers, and even regulators who can form coalitions of regulatory practice and meaning. There are two methods for securing professional embeddedness. The first involves purchasing professional authority by contracting with the "big" law firm or accounting firm to take advantage of its authority and influence. The second way to secure professional legitimation is through the transfer of personnel. This form of professional embeddedness includes actions such as bringing in a former SEC enforcement attorney to head the compliance department for a firm, or hiring in-house counsel with previous SEC experience. Whichever way it is accumulated, the more professional "capital" a firm acquires, the greater its regulatory authority and the more influence it will have on defining regulatory practice and policy.

2. *Structural embeddedness* refers to the contextualization of economic exchange in patterns of ongoing interpersonal relations (Granovetter, 1985). This kind of embeddedness is important for its perceived social control (self-regulatory) benefits. Researchers have argued that the reciprocal obligations of "doing deals" and threats to reputation offer important social constraints in modern business contexts (Macaulay, 1963; Granovetter, 1985; Leifer and White, 1987; Eccles and Crane, 1988; as well as others). To the extent that regulatory policy incorporates this notion, firms that can build their compliance activities within such networks (for example, incorporating continuing relationships with clients or other financial institutions in compliance programs) may be less carefully scrutinized by regulatory agents. The assumption here is that an organization's business reputation is a reasonably reliable source of control and that state attention should be reserved for more marginal firms that

do not offer this alternative, that is, where customers or suppliers are less likely to monitor the activities of firms.

3. *Cultural embeddedness* refers to the extent that firms can participate in constructing the collective understandings that shape more general economic strategies and goals. (See the discussion in Zukin and DiMaggio, 1990.) Here the concern is with a firm's ability to participate in shaping definitions of integrity, reasonableness, success, fairness, and justice. It is not simply that "the *subcultures* of Wall Street rationalize exploitative behavior as that which made America great," as Braithwaite (chapter 3) suggests (my emphasis). To the extent that businesses participate in perpetuating general cultural values such as "greed is good," they may also play significant roles in constructing the normative agenda for regulatory programs. Firms that can achieve this kind of cultural embeddedness are likely to be those with access to media (popular culture) and those that can locate their actions within a "tradition of service" by placing key personnel on professional task forces, presidential commissions, and the like that "investigate" industry wrongdoing. Cultural embeddedness provides a way to control the normative agenda, but does so in ways that mask the power and authority of key players.

The regulatory authority built by embedding the practice of social compliance within structured interorganizational networks can be linked to the definition and distribution of regulatory enforcement actions in two ways. Regulatory authority, derived from the organization of compliance practice, is positively correlated with the likelihood that regulated entities will offer rule-centered interpretations of their behavior and with the likelihood that these interpretations will be accepted as legitimate. Regulatory acceptance reproduces regulatory authority for regulated entities. The following hypotheses are proposed.

> The greater the regulatory authority of a given firm, the more likely that regulatory negotiation will focus on rules rather than facts.

When firms can locate their compliance practices within a complex interorganizational network of attorneys, accountants, regulators, and clients, they will be more likely to offer rule-centered negotiations than fact-centered ones. This is because they are able to mobilize the necessary interorganizational alliances to challenge the rules of the game. But it is also because interpretations of fact may be too visible and costly. These are the firms whose actions are most actively scrutinized by other professional organizations, clients, and investors, and, thus, discrepancies in deal facts may be regarded as too blatant or obvious. More subtle, yet more powerful, rule interpretations may be preferred. (See the discussion in Gross, 1980, that refers to the effect of organization set on organizational misconduct.) By way of contrast, the more marginal firms who cannot mobilize the resources to change the rules may be more likely to engage in fact-centered negotiations. The activities of these small firms may be less keenly scrutinized by their peers and their clients, so some manipulation of fact may be possible. (Although, for this reason, they may be more subject to regulatory enforcement initiatives.)

> The greater the regulatory authority of a given firm, the more likely that its interpretations of rules and facts will be accepted as legitimate exercises of public policy.

Hawkins (1984, p. 127) argues that the issue of compliance is ultimately evaluated in moral terms. The perception of the regulated entity as reasonable is a predictor of a regulator's willingness to negotiate interpretations. (See also, Ayers and Braithwaite, 1989; Kagan and Scholz, 1984; and Shover et al., 1984.) The construction of regulatory authority is an important component of the image of a regulated entity as a moral, reasonable actor. Firms that have a significant amount of regulatory authority, therefore, are more likely to find that their interpretations of facts and rules are accepted as legitimate public policy. Firms with limited regulatory authority are more likely to find their interpretations perceived as willful, self-interested manipulations of fact and law.

Conclusion

I have proposed that our understanding of regulatory behavior, including the definitions and distribution of regulatory violations, would benefit from efforts to extend the criminological enterprise to the everyday practices that set regulatory programs into motion. Compliance is a process that deserves our attention, not simply as an alternative or corrective to the activities of regulatory agencies, but as an important regulatory process in its own right. I have suggested that we must examine how regulated actors interpret, implement, and modify regulatory rules. Looking at regulation from the backstage of compliance promises a more contextual understanding of regulatory behavior since it permits us to consider how regulated firms structure the interpretation of their behavior.

I have introduced the concept of regulatory authority to describe how business firms influence the regulatory program. Regulatory authority, I have argued, is a product of the social organization of compliance. Firms that accumulate significant amounts of juridical capital (for example, by buying the cultural authority of different professional groups) and that can embed their compliance practices within ongoing networks of professional and social relations are likely to exercise significant regulatory authority. They use that authority to define the shape of regulatory programs. I have suggested that regulatory authority might determine when, how, to what extent, and with what consequences regulators scrutinize business transactions. Understanding differences in firms' abilities to construct regulatory authority, that is differences in the social organization of compliance, may provide insight into how business influences the definition and distribution of white-collar crime. Firms that can command high levels of regulatory authority are most likely to take control of the rules of the game in ways that authenticate their actions at the same time that they marginalize, if not discredit, the actions of more subordinate members of their community.

REFERENCES

Abolafia, M. Y., and Kilduff, M. (1988). Enacting market crisis: The social construction of a speculative bubble. *Administrative Science Quarterly, 33*, 125.

Ayres, I., and Braithwaite, J. (1989). Tripartism, empowerment and game—theoretic notions of regulatory capture. Paper presented at the annual meeting of the Law and Society Association, Madison, Wisconsin.

Bardach, E., and Kagan, R. A. (1982). *Going by the book: The problem of regulatory unreasonableness.* Philadelphia: Temple University Press.

Barnett, H. C. (1981). Corporate capitalism, corporate crime. *Crime & Delinquency, 3,* 171.

Baron, J. N., and Bielby, W. B. (1980). Bringing the firms back in: Segmentation and the organization of work. *American Sociological Review, 45,* 737.

Baron, J. N., and Bielby, W. B. (1984). The organization of work in a segmented economy. *American Sociological Review, 49,* 454.

Bourdieu, P. (1987). The force of law: Toward a sociology of the juridical field. *Hastings Law Journal, 38,* 805.

Braithwaite, J. (1984). *Corporate crime in the pharmaceutical industry.* London: Routledge & Kegan Paul.

———. (1985). *To punish or persuade: Enforcement of coal mining safety.* Albany: State University of New York Press.

Braithwaite, J., and Fisse, B. (1987). Self regulation and the control of corporate crime. In C. Shearing and P. Stenning, eds. *Private Policing,* 221–247. Beverly Hills: Sage.

Braithwaite, J., Walker, J., and Grabosky, P. (1987). An enforcement taxonomy of regulatory agencies. *Law and Policy, 9,* 323.

Burk, J. (1988). *Values in the marketplace: The American stock market under federal securities laws.* New York: Walter de Gruyter.

Clegg, S. (1989). *Frameworks of power.* Newbury Park, Calif.: Sage Publications.

Cohen, S. (1985). *Visions of social control: Crime punishment and classification.* New York: Basil Blackworth.

Coleman, J. W. (1992). The theory of white-collar crime: From Sutherland to the 1990s. (This volume.)

Coombe, R. J. (1989). Room for maneuver: Toward a theory of practice in critical legal studies. *Law and Social Inquiry, 14,* 69.

DiMaggio, P., and Powell, W. W. (1983). The iron cage revisited: Institutional isomorphism and collective rationality in organizational fields. *American Sociological Review, 48,* 147.

Diver, C. S. (1989). Regulatory precision. In K. Hawkins and J. Thomas, eds. *Making regulatory policy,* 199–232. Pittsburgh: University of Pittsburgh Press.

Eccles, R. G., and Crane, D. B. (1988). *Doing deals: Investment banks at work.* Boston: Harvard Business School Press.

Ewick, P. (1985). Redundant regulation: Sanctioning broker-dealers. *Law and Policy, 7,* 423.

Fifty years of federal securities regulation: Symposium on contemporary problems in securities regulation (1984). *Virginia Law Review, 70,* (entire).

Fligstein, N. (1990). *The transformation of corporate control.* Cambridge, Mass.: Harvard University Press.

Galanter, M. (1974). Why the "haves" come out ahead: Speculation on the limits of legal change. *Law and Society Review, 9,* 95.

Giddens, A. (1986). *The constitution of society.* Berkeley: University of California Press.

Glasberg, D., and Schwartz, M. (1983). Ownership and control of corporations. *Annual Review of Sociology, 9,* 311.

Granovetter, M. (1985). Economic action and social structure: The problem of embeddedness. *American Journal of Sociology, 91,* 481.

Gross, E. (1980). Organizational structure and organizational crime. In G. Geis and E. Stotland, eds. *White-collar crime: Theory and research,* 52–77. Beverly Hills: Sage.

Gunningham, N. (1987). Negotiated non-compliance. *Law and Policy, 9,* 69.

Harrington, C., and Merry, S. (1988). Ideological production: The making of community mediation. *Law and Society Review, 22,* 709.

Hawkins, K. (1984). *Environment and enforcement: Regulation and the social definition of pollution.* New York: Oxford University Press.

———. (1989). "FATCATS" and prosecution in a regulatory agency: A footnote on the social construction of risk. *Law and Policy, 11.*

Hawkins, K., and Thomas, J. M. (1984). *Enforcing regulation.* New York: Kluwer-Nijhoff Press.

Hawkins, K., and Thomas, J., eds. (1989). *Making regulatory policy.* Pittsburgh: University of Pittsburgh Press.

Howell, R. A., Allison, J. R., and Hentley, N. T. (1985). *Business law.* New York: Dryden Press.

Kagan, R. A., and Scholz, J. T. (1984). The criminology of the corporation and regulatory enforcement strategies. In K. Hawkins and J. M. Thomas, eds. *Enforcing regulation,* 67–95. New York: Kluwer-Nijhoff.

Kramer, R. C. (1982). Corporate crime: An organizational perspective. In P. Wickman and T. Daily, eds. *White-collar and economic crime,* 75–94. Lexington, Mass.: Lexington Books.

———. (1992). The space shuttle *Challenger* explosion: A case study of state-corporate crime. (This volume.)

Leifer, E. M., and White, H. C. (1987). A structural approach to markets. In M. S. Mizruichi and M. Schwartz, eds. *Intercorporate relations: The structural analysis of business,* 85–108. New York: Cambridge University Press.

Lynxwiler, J., Shover, N., and Clelland, D. A. (1983). The organization and impact of inspector discretion in a regulatory bureaucracy. *Social Problems, 30,* 425.

Macaulay, S. (1963). Non-contractual relations in business: A preliminary study. *American Sociological Review, 28,* 55.

Mann, K. (1985). *Defending white-collar crime: A portrait of attorneys at work.* New Haven: Yale University Press.

Manning, P. K. (1987). Ironies of compliance. In C. Shearing and P. Stenning, eds. *Private policing,* 298–316. Beverly Hills: Sage.

―――. (1989). The limits of knowledge: The role of information in regulation. In K. Hawkins and J. N. Thomas, eds. *Making regulatory policy,* 49–87. Pittsburgh: University of Pittsburgh Press.

Meidinger, E. (1987). Regulatory culture: A theoretical outline. *Law and Policy, 9,* 355.

Merry, S. E. (1989). *Getting justice or getting even.* Chicago: University of Chicago Press.

Mizruichi, M. S., and Schwartz, M. (1987). *Intercorporate relations: The structural analysis of business.* New York: Cambridge University Press.

Nash, Gerald D. (1964). Government and business: A case study of state regulation of corporate securities, 1860–1933. *Business History Review, 38,* 144.

North American Securities Administrators Association (NASAA) (1989). The NASAA report on fraud and abuse in the penny stock industry. Washington, D.C.: NASAA.

O'Malley, P. (1989). Legal networks and domestic security. A paper presented at the annual meeting of the Law and Society Association, Madison, Wisconsin.

Palay, T. M. (1985). Avoiding regulatory constraints: Contracting safeguards and the role of informal agreements. *Journal of Law, Economics, and Organization, 1,* 155.

Rafter, N. H. (1990). The social construction of crime and crime control. *Journal of Research in Crime and Delinquency, 27,* 376.

Reichman, N. (1989). Breaking confidences: Organizational influences on insider trading. *The Sociological Quarterly, 30,* 185.

―――. (forthcoming). Regulating risky business. *Law and Policy.*

Scheppele, K. L. (1988). *Legal secrets: Equality and efficiency in the common law.* Chicago: University of Chicago Press.

Scholz, J. T. (1984). Cooperation, deterrence and the ecology of regulatory enforcement. *Law and Society Review, 18,* 179.

Seligman, J. (1983). The historical need for a mandatory corporate disclosure system. *Journal of Corporation Law, 9,* 45.

―――. (1982). *The transformation of Wall Street: A history of the Securi-*

ties and Exchange Commission and modern corporate finance. Boston: Houghton Mifflin Company.

Shapiro, S. P. (1984). *Wayward capitalists: Targets of the Securities and Exchange Commission.* New Haven: Yale University Press.

———. (1987a). The social control of impersonal trust. *American Journal of Sociology, 93,* 623.

———. (1987b). Policing trust. In C. Shearing and P. Stenning, eds. *Private policing,* 194–220. Beverly Hills: Sage.

———. (1990). Collaring the crime, not the criminal: Reconsidering white-collar crime. *American Sociological Review, 55,* 346.

Sharpe, W. F. (1985). *Investments.* Englewood Cliffs, N.J.: Prentice Hall.

Shover, N. (1980). The criminalization of corporate behavior: Federal surface coal mining. In G. Geis and E. Stotland, eds. *White-collar crime,* 98–125. Beverly Hills: Sage.

Shover, N. Lynxwiller, J., Groce, S., and Clelland, D. (1984). Regional variation in regulatory law enforcement: The Surface Mining Control and Reclamation Act of 1977. In K. Hawkins and J. Thomas, eds. *Enforcing regulation,* 121–146. New York: Kluwer-Nijhoff.

Silbey, S. S. (1990). On the relationship of state theory to sociolegal research: The example of minor dispute processing. In S. S. Silbey and A. Sarat, eds. *Studies of law, politics and society,* 67–75. Greenwich, Conn.: JAI Press.

Silbey, S. S., and Sarat, A. (1987). Critical traditions in law and society research. *Law and Society Review, 21,* 165.

Starr, P. (1982). *The social transformation of American medicine.* New York: Basic Books.

Stenning, P., Shearing, C., Addario, S., and Condon, M. (1990). Controlling interests: Two conceptions of order in regulating a financial market. In M. L. Friedland, ed. *Securing compliance: Seven case studies,* 88–118. Toronto: University of Toronto Press.

Stevenson, R. A., and Jennings, E. H. (1984). *Fundamentals of investments.* New York: West Publishing Company.

Stigler, G. (1964). Public regulation of the securities market. *Journal of Business, 37,* 37.

Stone, C. D. (1975). *Where the law ends: The social control of corporate behavior.* New York: Harper & Row.

Sutherland, E. H. (1940). White collar criminality. *American Sociological Review, 5,* 1.

Vaughan, D. (1983). *Controlling unlawful organizational behavior: Social structure and corporate misconduct.* Chicago: University of Chicago Press.

———. (1992). The macro-micro connection in white-collar crime theory. (This volume.)

Yeager, P. C. (1987). Structural bias in regulatory law enforcement: The case of the U.S. Environmental Protection Agency. *Social Problems*, *34*, 330.

―――. (1990a). *The limits of law: The public regulation of private pollution.* New York: Cambridge University Press.

―――. (1990b). Realms of reason: Notes on the division of moral labor in corporate behavior. Paper presented at the Edwin Sutherland Conference on White-Collar Crime: Fifty years of research and beyond. Bloomington, Indiana.

Yngvesson, B. (1988). Making law at the doorway: The clerk, the court, and the construction of community in a New England town. *Law and Society Review*, *22*, 409.

Zukin, S., and DiMaggio, P. C. (1990). Introduction. In S. Zukin and P. C. DiMaggio, eds. *Structures of capital: The social organization of the economy*, 1–36. New York: Cambridge University Press.

NOTES

1. Shapiro (1984) notes that "the social organization of illicit activities determines the way they are detected, and, therefore, . . . different strategies of intelligence catch different kinds of securities offenses" (p. 167). Strategic choices about appropriate intelligence gathering, therefore, are important determinants of the enforcement "catch."

2. Regulatory bias is actualized in a number of ways. First, regulatory law favors larger business that can better afford the increased costs of compliance (Barnett, 1981). Indeed, historically, large firms have "welcomed" regulation and have even influenced the drafting of regulatory rules. This is because regulations can provide the modicum of certainty necessary for business development. The higher unit costs of compliance imposed on smaller firms has the positive benefit of reducing competition from those firms. A second manifestation of bias is seen in the situational contexts of regulatory action. Powerful corporate offenders are better able to mobilize sufficient political, economic, technical, and legal resources to thwart or neutralize regulatory action than their smaller counterparts (Shover et al., 1984). In this paper I suggest that regulatory bias is due not only to the static attributes of regulated firms, but also to their "organizational place" and the constellations of roles, interests, and liabilities that compete and interact with law to constrain organizational life (Stone, 1975).

3. The ambiguity of rules creates a variety of problems for regulatory agents, often discussed in terms of regulators' legal risks, that is, uncertainty of successful prosecution should official legal action be invoked (see, for example, Hawkins, 1989).

4. Braithwaite's (1985) interviews with coal-mining company executives

about the characteristics of their internal compliance systems and his study of the pharmaceutical industry (1984) are some of the important exceptions. See also Yeager's (1990) suggestion to "extend the conventional criminological paradigm . . . by inspecting the ways in which rules of morality are perceived and enacted in corporate bureaucracies."

5. Moving to the backstage of regulatory activity—that is, to the patterned interactions that construct regulatory policy—implies an expanded notion of state power. As Cohen (1985) notes, locally produced understandings of law-abiding or non-law-abiding behavior can increase the reach and intensity of state control. (See Silbey [1990] for a related discussion.)

6. For a discussion of how financial institutions "enact" their regulatory environments, see Burk (1988) and Abolafia and Kilduff (1988).

7. Baron and Bielby (1980, 1984) argue that firms within an industry sector are stratified by the degree of task differentiation, the vitality of internal labor markets, and types of control systems that operate. I am suggesting that the organization of compliance may be another important status indicator.

8. State governments were responsible for the early statutory regulation of securities trading. Laws of incorporation set conventions by which potential investors could assess their risk by requiring certain kinds of financial disclosures. Commissions were established to review new stock issues (Nash, 1964). In 1911 Kansas enacted the first so-called "blue-sky" law that required state licensing of securities sold within a state. "The objective was to curb fraudulent securities transactions by refusing licenses for worthless securities and to the swindlers willing to peddle them" (Burk, 1988, p. 170). The states continue to play an important, albeit quite variable, role in securities regulation today.

9. A cursory review of business and legal periodicals reveals that there is substantial debate about the normative utility of disclosure rules. At one end of the debate are those who argue that the market itself provides incentives for corporations to voluntarily disclose information sufficient to protect all but the most gullible investors. (For a classic statement see Stigler, 1964.) Others argue that disclosure rules are important to maintain adequate disclosure and historically have served the investor and the market well (Seligman, 1983). For contemporary refinements and elaboration of the debate, see "Fifty Years of Federal Securities Regulation" (1984).

10. In theory, those who purchase stock become the "owners of the corporation," or the owners of the corporation's assets. In practice, this is hardly the case (Glasberg and Schwartz, 1983).

11. Eccles and Crane (1988) offer one of the few systematic studies of investment banking activities. Their work examines the management system that coordinates the flexible and changing network structure of

investment banks. Interestingly, regulation and regulatory networks are not discussed as part of the internal and external ties that require strategic management.

12. Note that the criteria for approval may not be the same.

13. Because of their role as mediator between issuers and investors, bankers often stand in an uneasy relationship with their clients. As one investment banker told me, "Entrepreneurs expect to give up some control of their company to their public shareholders. What they don't expect is that they also give up control to the brigade of legal, accounting, and financial experts who must approve every step they now take." Bankers have to create a product that will sell, and thus, they have to be concerned with the regulatory, marketing, and retail aspects of their deals as well as the interests of their clients.

14. One reason for this market's vulnerability to fraud and abuse is that neither penny-stock investors nor regulators can effectively monitor the price quotations. The computer-guided market surveillance that watches other equity markets does not reach here.

15. Another explanation for penny stock fraud locates the problem in the character of the market itself. "The stocks have no chance of going up (in the absence of manipulation), because there are too many shares outstanding . . . the amount of buying that would have to take place in these companies is almost impossible, and therefore the stocks can't rise. If they rise, it's done artificially" (NASAA, 1989, p. 29).

16. Although we may observe both more violations *and* more enforcement in a particular sector, it is not clear that we see more enforcement *because* there are more violations. The same social processes that breed opportunities to violate may also engender more opportunities and/or incentives to mobilize formal legal actions.

· 11 ·

Community Context and the
Prosecution of Corporate Crime

MICHAEL L. BENSON

FRANCIS T. CULLEN

WILLIAM J. MAAKESTAD

It has become something of a sociological truism that white-collar offenders commit their crimes because they are unlikely to be punished (Coleman, 1990). Although it is widely accepted that white-collar and especially corporate white-collar offenders are less likely to be punished for their crimes than other criminals, only recently has much attention been paid to the factors that influence this differential application of the law. In the past decade, investigators have studied virtually all stages of the law enforcement process as it applies to white-collar offenses from the creation of a regulatory agency (Shover, Clelland, and Lynxwiler, 1986) to the sentencing of white-collar offenders (Hagan, Nagel-Bernstein, and Albonetti, 1980; Wheeler, Weisburd and Bode, 1982; Benson and Walker, 1988; Weisburd, Waring, and Wheeler, 1990). This research suggests that, as with other crimes, white-collar law enforcement is influenced by the community context in which it occurs.

The influence of community context on law enforcement with respect to ordinary street crime is well known. For example, some police agencies employ a legalistic approach to law enforcement; others use a watchman or service style (Wilson, 1968). Judges in rural communities sentence blacks differently than do judges in urban areas (Myers and Talarico, 1987; Hagan, 1977; Pope, 1975). These styles of enforcement are largely shaped by the norms, concerns, and activities of local communities (Wilson, 1968).

Community context also influences the agencies and organizations that respond to white-collar crime (Hagan et al., 1982). For example, the caseloads, enforcement priorities, and investigative strategies of regional offices of the Securities and Exchange Commission vary significantly (Shapiro, 1984). Shover et al. (1986) show that the Federal Office of Surface Mining adopted more stringent enforcement strategies in Appalachian states than in western states. Others have shown that contextual factors influence how regulatory agencies select and process cases (Bardach and Kagan, 1982; Feldman and Zeckhauser, 1978). Studies of the sentencing of white-collar offenders also reveal substantial variation in sentence severity among districts and over time (Benson and Walker, 1988; Hagan and Palloni, 1986; Hagan and Parker, 1985; Nagel and Hagan, 1982; Wheeler et al., 1982; Hagan et al., 1980). In response to local conditions, regulatory and criminal justice agencies develop different enforcement styles to combat white-collar crimes.

The notion that contextual factors influence reactions to white-collar crime is increasingly recognized. Little effort has been made, however, to link this fact to broader sociological theories of societal reactions to crime. These theories hold that threats to social and economic stability influence societal reactions to ordinary street crime (Box and Halo, 1982; Jankovic, 1977).

In this paper, we argue that there is also a relationship between economic conditions and reactions to white-collar crime. We extend recent work on reactions to white-collar crime by developing and testing a contextual theory of prosecutorial activity against corporate crime. The theory focuses on how community context influences corporate-crime prosecution rates. Data gathered from a national survey of district attorneys are used to estimate a causal model based upon the theory. Specifically, we assess the influence of the characteristics of local prosecutors' offices and their surrounding communities on prosecutorial activity against corporate crime. Our goal is to determine whether the level of prosecutorial activity varies with type of office and type of community. Before turning to the theory, we briefly explain our decision to focus on local prosecutors and corporate crime.

The Office of Prosecuting Attorney

Although it is tempting to think of criminal laws as clear and precise proscriptions with unambiguous behavioral referents, those who must apply them to events of everyday life know otherwise. The demarcation between lawful and unlawful conduct often is not obvious. When does a public altercation between two acquaintances become disorderly? At what point does communication between two companies about prices or markets become a criminal conspiracy? These questions cannot be answered without careful scrutiny of situational elements of individual cases. The lesson is clear: Legal actors must exercise judgment as they apply the law to ambiguous and ever-changing events. Discretion is an unavoidable component of "law in action" (Friedman, 1975).

Discretion is especially important with respect to white-collar offenses committed by corporations and other business entities. Although potentially prosecutable, many corporate offenses are not brought into the criminal justice system. Rather, they are filtered out of the system and dealt with by special noncriminal procedures administered by regulatory agencies (Sutherland, 1983). A key decision maker in this screening process is the prosecutor.

Prosecutors function as perhaps the most important gatekeepers in the legal system. Because of their discretionary authority to decline to prosecute, they determine whether and how often offenses are brought under the criminal law. Since most local prosecutors are locally elected officials, they must be sensitive to local community and political pressures. Their day-to-day approach to enforcement largely reflects the concerns and priorities of their constituencies and local communities (Bequai, 1978; Cole, 1980, 1970). Hence, the office of prosecuting attorney is an important site in which to investigate how community characteristics influence reactions to corporate crime.

Corporate crime is usually regarded as the domain of federal prosecutors. However, since the early 1970s local prosecutors have become increasingly active in this area (Benson, Cullen, and Maakestad, 1990; Cullen, Maakestad, and Cavendar, 1988; Edelhertz and Rogovin, 1980). Little is known about the distribution of local corporate-crime prosecutions as previous investigators have relied on case study methods (Cullen et al., 1988; Gurney, 1985; Schudson, Onellion, and Hochstedler, 1984). There is, however, suggestive evidence that community context influences local prosecutorial reactions to corporate crime. A study of California district attorneys found that population size of jurisdiction influenced how prosecutors perceive decision-making constraints in corporate-crime cases (Benson, Cullen, Maakestad, and Geis, 1988). In contrast to their counterparts in large districts, prosecutors in small districts were more likely to be constrained by lack of resources and the availability of alternative remedies. They were also more sensitive to the potential impact of corporate prosecutions on the local economy.

The Data and the Theory

Data for this analysis are drawn from a study of local prosecutors and corporate crime in the United States. As part of this project, a national survey of district attorneys was conducted during the spring of 1989.

Using a mailing list provided by the National District Attorneys Association (NDAA), we sent questionnaires to every district attorney whose jurisdiction is located in a metropolitan statistical area $(N = 632)$.[1] After a follow-up postcard and two other mailings, the final response rate was 66 percent $(N = 419)$. The mail survey focused on prosecutors' experiences with and attitudes toward corporate crime. Directions on the survey defined corporate crime as "a violation of a criminal statute either by a corporate entity or by its executives, employees, or agents acting on behalf of and for the benefit of the corporation, partnership, or other form of business entity." We noted explicitly that this "definition excludes crime committed by an employee against an employer for the purpose of personal gain, such as embezzlement or theft."

The dependent variable for this analysis is the level of prosecutorial activity against corporate crime. To measure level of activity, we asked respondents how often their offices typically prosecuted nine types of corporate crimes: consumer fraud, insurance fraud, securities fraud, tax violations, false claims, illegal payments, workplace-related offenses, environmental offenses, and unfair trade practices. Assigned ordinal ranks and summed, the item responses (never, less than 1 per year, 1 to 3 times per year, more than 3 times per year) form a scale of "prosecutorial activity."[2] Although this set of offenses is not comprehensive, it does provide a broad and heterogeneous sample of offenses commonly committed in a wide variety of industries and businesses.

A direct count of the actual number of corporate prosecutions conducted would be a more valid indicator of prosecutorial activity, but such information unfortunately is not readily available. A question on the survey asking about the exact number of corporate prosecutions the respondents' offices conducted in 1988 generated a sizeable number of nonresponses. Apparently, local prosecutors do not keep easily accessed records on corporate cases. The prosecutorial activity scale correlates strongly with the question on number of prosecutions among those respondents who answered it.

The contextual model that we are proposing assumes that two sets of factors influence prosecutorial activity: (1) the characteristics of prosecutors' offices and (2) the social and economic characteristics of their local communities. These factors frequently are cited to explain why most illegal corporate conduct does not result in criminal prosecution.

It is well known that successful application of the criminal law in corporate cases is difficult (Stone, 1975; Shapiro, 1984; Rakoff, 1985; Levi, 1987). The detection and investigation of corporate crimes pose special problems for prosecutors. Because of their technical and legal complexity, corporate crimes require more investigative and prosecutorial resources and greater technical expertise than street crimes. Case studies of corporate crime suggest that local prosecutors often have inadequate organizational resources to overcome these obstacles (Cullen et al., 1988; Schudson et al., 1984; Vaughan, 1983). Accordingly, one factor that must be included in our model is the level of prosecutorial resources and expertise.

As an indicator of prosecutorial resources, we used the number of full-time attorneys in the office. Expertise was operationalized as a dummy variable indicating whether the office has a special unit devoted to white-collar or economic-crime prosecutions.

Resources, however, are not self-activating. Unless district attorneys are motivated to use them against corporate crime, neither will lead to more corporate prosecutions. Certain attitudes toward corporate crime may keep prosecutors from conducting such prosecutions. For example, if prosecutors regard alternative civil or administrative remedies as appropriate in cases of corporate wrongdoing, they will be less inclined to expend resources on corporate criminal prosecutions. Similarly, prosecutors may not favor criminalization of corporate wrongdoing. Attitudes toward alternative remedies and criminalization make up what can be called the office culture regarding corporate crime. Our theory assumes that the level of activity against corporate crime should be positively associated with the level of support for criminal prosecution in the office.

Office culture regarding alternative remedies was measured by three items, asking to what extent the respondent's willingness to prosecute would be limited if federal or state regulatory agencies or private parties initiated action against a corporate offender (definitely would be limited, probably would, probably would not, definitely would not). Assigned ordinal ranks and summed, these items form an "alternative remedy" scale.[3] Attitude toward criminalization as a means of controlling corporate crime was measured by a question asking how useful tougher criminal penalties would be as a method of improving corporate compliance with the law (not very useful, somewhat useful, very useful).

Each questionnaire represents the opinion of only one person; hence, our measures of office culture admittedly are less than perfect. However, directions on the questionnaire specified that it be completed by the district attorney or a person with experience in prosecuting corporate offenses. Preliminary analysis indicates that these instructions were followed. The respondents had an average of ten and a half years on the job and only three questionnaires were filled out by nonattorneys. Thus, we have some confidence that the responses come from individuals knowledgeable of office policies and practices regarding corporate crime.

Our attention now shifts to the community context within which the office of prosecuting attorney operates. To gather data on context we used the County and City Data Book, 1988 (Bureau of the Census, 1988). Two aspects of community context are especially important: legal culture and economic structure.

Communities establish the legal culture within which agencies operate. Following Friedman (1975), we define legal culture as a set of community-based norms, values, and understandings about when and how legal actors should carry out their official responsibilities (compare Galanter, 1986). This culture influences the priorities and practices of legal agencies because these agencies need external justification (Friedman, 1985). In our theory, variation in legal culture influences variation in official responses to corporate crime.

Historically, the South has held conservative attitudes regarding regulation of economic activities. Unions are weaker in the South and government regulation is generally less intrusive in southern than nonsouthern states. The probusiness, antigovernment attitudes of southerners suggest that southern legal culture regards criminalization of corporate behavior with suspicion. Hence, we expect that region of the country significantly influences prosecutorial activity. Region of the country is operationalized as a dummy variable indicating whether the respondent's jurisdiction is located in a southern or nonsouthern state.

Unlike ordinary crimes, corporate crimes are committed by actors who may make valuable economic contributions to communities. Communities vary in the degree to which they can be harmed by enforcement action directed against these potentially important economic entities. If enforcement causes a corporate perpetrator to relocate to another community, it may have significant negative effects for local tax revenues and employment (Moore, 1987). Thus, in corporate-crime cases more than in other criminal cases, it is assumed that legal actors are sensitive to the potential impact of their decisions on the local economy (Jowell, 1986). This suggests that local responses to corporate crimes are influenced by local economic conditions. Where the potential external costs of corporate criminal prosecutions are great, enforcement will be less.

Two important dimensions of local economies are strength and specialization. Strength of economy refers to a community's general level of wealth. Specialization refers to the extent to which a community is dependent on a particular employer or type of employer for its economic well-being. We expect that where the local economy is weak or dominated by a few large employers community demands for corporate crime control will be reduced.

Overall strength of economy is operationalized as the ratio of local per capita income to national per capita income. To assess economic specialization we use a measure developed by economists called the Location Quotient (LQ). LQ can be used to measure whether a region's employment is over- or underrepresented in a particular industry relative to the national industrial distribution of employment (Isard, 1960, pp. 123–126). The formula for LQ is

$$LQ_{ij} = 100 * (E_{ij}/E_{usi})/(E_j/E_{us})$$

where

E_{ij} = employment in industry "i" in region "j"
E_j = total employment in region "j"
E_{usi} = total employment in industry "i" in U.S.
E_{us} = total employment in U.S.

If LQ is greater than 100, then industry "i" is overrepresented in region "j" relative to the national industrial distribution of employment.

In preliminary analyses, we experimented with LQs for different industries (retail, financial, service, and other) before deciding to use the LQ for manufacturing employment as our measure of economic specialization. Our decision to focus on manufacturing employment is somewhat arbitrary. Our rationale was that the manufacturing sector of the economy in the United States generally is in a state of decline. The theory that we are proposing predicts that communities economically dependent upon weak industries will be less willing to control business activity tightly. Using the LQ for manufacturing as our measure of economic specialization permits us to investigate this prediction.

The model includes two other contextual variables: population size and crime rate. We assume that population size roughly correlates with the number of businesses in a jurisdiction. Hence, it serves as proxy control for the number of offenders and offenses. Crime rate is included because street crimes make competing demands on office resources and because some research indicates that the crime rate influences the size of social control agencies (Chamlin, 1989). Crime rate is the number of crimes known to the police per 100,000 people.

FIGURE 1 · Casual Model of Prosecutorial Activity
Against Corporate Crime

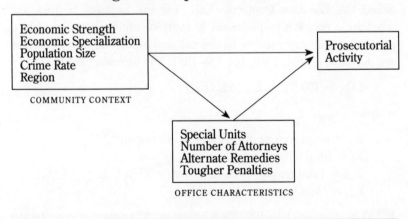

Figure 1 presents in schematic form our theory of prosecutorial activity.

Analysis

We use ordinary least squares (OLS) regression to estimate our contextual model of prosecutorial activity against corporate crime. Unfortunately, our theory is not sufficiently developed to permit a deductive model-testing approach. Rather, we estimate a series of equations to determine inductively the important causal linkages between the variables. To identify significant paths in the model, the endogenous variables (office characteristics) are regressed on the exogenous variables (community context). Paths less than .10 in significance or weaker than .10 in strength are deleted from the model, and the equations are reestimated.[4] The final equations include only paths significant at .05. The same rules apply to the dependent variable.[5]

Table 1 presents descriptive information on the variables and their zero-order correlations with the dependent variable.

Results

Before turning to the path analysis, we briefly discuss the zero-order correlations of the independent variables with the activity scale (see table 1). The signs for all variables are in the expected direction. The office characteristics that we predicted would be directly related to activity (attorneys, special units, and procriminalization attitudes) have positive signs. The sign for the alternative remedies scale, as predicted, is negative. Among the contextual variables, population, crime rate, economic strength, and region have positive signs, while economic specialization in manufacturing is negatively related to activity. The strongest correlations involve number of attorneys, special units, and population size.

Figure 2 depicts the estimated causal model for prosecutorial activity and shows the standardized path coefficients, that is, the B coefficients.

The model shows that activity against corporate crime is largely determined by the characteristics of prosecutors' offices. The avail-

TABLE 1 · Descriptive Statistics

VARIABLES	MEAN	ST. DEV.	CORRELATION WITH ACTIVITY
Special units	.24	.43	.51
Number of attorneys	21.96	35.13	.55
Alternative remedies	8.06	2.04	−.19
Criminalization	1.99	.76	.18
Population size (log)	12.02	1.08	.51
Crime rate	4485.08	2051.19	.33
Economic strength	.98	.19	.28
Economic specialization	106.35	51.32	−.19
Region	.61	.49	.09
Activity	6.53	5.24	———

ability of resources (number of attorneys) and expertise (presence of special unit) exert strong, positive, and independent effects on activity. The standardized coefficients (B) are .29 and .25, respectively. Office culture, as measured here, appears to have a relatively weak effect on activity. The effect of alternative remedies is in the expected negative direction but is small compared to other office variables (B = −.10). Contrary to expectations, attitude toward criminalization of corporate offenses does not influence activity. The weak effect of alternative remedies and the lack of effect by criminalization may result from their lack of validity as measures of office culture.

Among the contextual variables, only population size directly influences activity (B = .14). It also has indirect effects, which can be calculated by multiplying the coefficients on the paths that lead from population to activity. For example, the indirect effect of population size on activity via number of attorneys is .21 (.71 x .29). Its indirect effects via special units and alternative remedies are .13 (.53 × .25) and .01 (−.11 × −.10), respectively.

FIGURE 2 · Estimated Model of Prosecutorial Activity
Against Corporate Crime

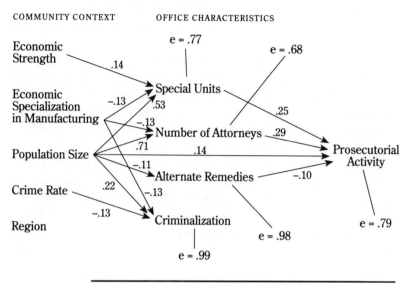

The other dimension of community context that indirectly influences activity is economic structure. Increases in overall economic strength increase the probability that a jurisdiction has a special unit (B = .14). Thus, economic strength exerts an positive indirect effect on activity via special units (.14 × .25 = .04). In contrast, degree of specialization in manufacturing is negatively related to both the number of attorneys and special units. Its indirect effect on activity via these variables is negative.

Contrary to the predictions of the theory, crime rate and region of the country have no effect on activity. Indeed, the only significant path emerging from these variables links crime rate to criminalization (B = −.13), indicating that in high crime-rate jurisdictions prosecutors are less inclined to believe that tougher criminal penalties would be useful as a means of securing corporate compliance with the law. Recall that region (nonsouthern versus southern) is meant to index community legal culture regarding state control of business activity. We predicted that prosecutors would be more active in liberal (nonsouthern) as opposed to conservative (southern) communities. Empirical results do not support this prediction. The lack of an effect by region may indicate only that it is a poor indicator of the underlying dimension of legal culture incorporated in our theory.

Considered as a whole, the final causal model can be interpreted as follows. Prosecutorial activity against corporate crime is largely determined by the characteristics of prosecutors' offices. As resources and expertise increase so does the level of activity. Two dimensions of community context, however, exert strong influence on office characteristics: population size and economic structure. Prosecutors who serve large, economically healthy communities have greater resources than their counterparts in small, economically depressed communities. Hence, the former are more active than the latter. If our assumption is correct that population size controls (roughly) for the amount of corporate crime, then we can say that economic structure exerts an independent effect on activity via its effect on resources and expertise. This latter finding may have important implications for a contextual theory of corporate-crime control.

The Context of Corporate-Crime Control

Contextual explanations postulate that the behavior of some unit of analysis, a person or an organization, is explained, at least in part, by the characteristics of its environment (Stinchcombe, 1987). Radical and conflict theorists have applied this logic to the institutions charged with controlling street crime. They argue that these institutions—police, courts, and prisons—are influenced by the communities in which they are located. The same logic can be applied to the organizations that respond to corporate crime.

Radical and conflict theorists focus on the relation between the economic order and the state's control apparatus. They contend that coercive control by the state is a function of perceived threats to social and economic stability (Box and Hale, 1982; Jankovic, 1977). In theory, social elites fear disadvantaged minority groups and the unemployed. Where these subject populations are large or growing, elites perceive them as threats to order. In response to these perceived threats, the panoply of control institutions—police, courts, and prisons—becomes more coercive. Empirical investigations have focused, with generally favorable results, on the relations between unemployment and imprisonment rates (Inverarity and McCarthy, 1988) and between minority group size and police per capita (Liska, Lawrence, and Benson, 1981; Jackson and Carroll, 1981). For our purposes the theoretically important point is that as economic conditions worsen the general level of control directed against disadvantaged groups increases.

While less direct than conflict theorists, white-collar crime theorists also posit an implicit relation between the economic order and the activities of social control institutions. The relation, however, is the opposite of that proposed by conflict and radical theorists: poor economic conditions reduce state control of business activity because of the state's interest in nurturing economic growth. For example, Simpson (1987) argues that during economic downturns enforcement of federal antitrust law becomes more lenient as the government seeks to simulate business activity.

What happens when economic conditions improve has rarely been explicitly considered by white-collar crime theorists. Empirical results of the present investigation suggest that economic health may be associated with more vigorous efforts to control corporate and business activity. Prosecutors whose offices are located in communities with high per capita incomes are more likely to have a special unit devoted to white-collar or economic crime and to conduct more corporate prosecutions than their counterparts in poorer communities.

It would appear that poor or deteriorating economic conditions lead to more coercive control efforts directed against street crime and less coercive efforts against corporate crime. The opposite occurs when the economy improves. What accounts for the latter relationship?

The most straightforward explanation is that economically healthy communities simply have more corporate crime than economically depressed communities. The number of prosecutions reflects nothing more than the number of offenses available to be prosecuted. Although such an explanation cannot be dismissed without further investigation, we believe that at best it is only partially correct. More general social processes involving social organization and power also must be considered.

As we noted at the outset this paper, it is widely accepted that business offenders commit their crimes because they are unlikely to be punished. To explain the general lack of societal reaction against corporate crime, most observers cite the vast economic and political power of the business class. It is important to recognize, however, that the balance of power between the business class and other sectors or interests in society may vary over time and place. A fully developed theory of societal reactions to corporate crime must recognize not only the power of corporate offenders but also countervailing sources of power in the community.

Just as communities may be more or less organized against street crime, they also may be more or less organized against corporate crime. When general economic conditions are good, communities may perceive less threat from street crime and be able to afford greater control of corporate crime. Equally important, economically strong communities may not be willing to tolerate corporate misconduct for the sake of jobs. The trade-offs between economic growth and worker safety, environmental pollution, or corrupt financial activities may appear less necessary and less palatable. Large, economically well-off communities may develop legal cultures less tolerant of corporate misconduct than economically depressed communities. In response to local legal culture, prosecutors in well-off communities may devote more resources to investigating and prosecuting corporate crime than their counterparts in poorer communities.

Our data only permit us to take a cross-sectional look at the relation of economic structure to corporate crime prosecutions. The obvious next step is to investigate this relation over time. If our theory is correct, we would expect that local corporate crime prosecution rates will rise and fall with economic trends in communities. More generally, as the overall wealth of a society rises, we would expect gradual increases in the level of controls placed on business activity.

We have provided, at best, only a preliminary effort toward a theory of reactions to corporate crime. The analysis did not support many of the theory's predictions. Although a step in the right direction, the theory clearly needs further development and specification. The indicators used here for important underlying constructs—office culture, community legal culture, and economic structure—are less than ideal. Nevertheless, empirical results of our work are sufficiently in line with theoretical expectations to warrant further consideration.

REFERENCES

Bardach, E., and Kagan, R. A. (1982). *Going by the book: The problem of regulatory unreasonableness*. Philadelphia: Temple University Press.

Belsay, D. A., Kuh, E., and Welsch, R. E. (1980). *Regression diagnostics*. New York: John Wiley.

Benson, M. L., Cullen, F. T., and Maakestad, W. J. (1990). Local prosecutors and corporate crime. *Crime and Delinquency, 36*, 356–372.

Benson, M. L., Maakestad, W., Cullen, F., and Geis, G. (1988). District attorneys and corporate crime: Surveying the prosecutorial gatekeepers. *Criminology, 26*, 501–514.

Benson, M. L., and Walker, E. (1988). Sentencing the white-collar offender. *American Sociological Review, 53*, 294–302.

Bequai, A. (1978). *White-collar crime: A 20th century crisis*. Lexington, Mass.: Lexington Books.

Box, S., and Hale, C. (1982). Economic crises and the rising prisoner population in England and Wales. *Crime and Social Justice, 17*, 20–35.

Bureau of the Census (1988). *County and City Data Book, 1988, Files on Diskette* (machine-readable data file). Washington, D.C.: The Bureau of the Census.

Chamlin, M. B. (1989). A macro social analysis of change in police force size, 1972–1982: Controlling for static and dynamic influences. *The Sociological Quarterly, 30*, 615–624.

Cole, G. F. (1970). The decision to prosecute. *Law and Society Review, 4*, 313–343.

——. (1980). Prosecution. In G. F. Cole, ed. *Criminal Justice*, (3rd ed.), 147–154. North Scituate, Mass.: Duxbury Press.

Coleman, J. (1990). The theory of white-collar crime: From Sutherland to the 1990s. Paper presented at the Edwin Sutherland Conference on White-Collar Crime, May, Bloomington, Indiana.

Cullen, F. T., Maakestad, W. J., and Cavender, G. (1987). *Corporate crime under attack: The Ford Pinto case and beyond*. Cincinnati: Anderson Publishing.

Edelhertz, H., and Rogovin, C. (1980). Symposium background. In H. Edelhertz and C. Rogovin, eds. *A national strategy for containing white-collar crime*, 11–17. Lexington, Mass.: Lexington Books.

Feldman, L. H., and Zeckhauser, R. J. (1978). Some sober thoughts on health care regulation. In C. Argyris, ed. *Regulating business: The search for an optimum*, 103–111. San Francisco: Institute for Contemporary Studies.

Friedman, L. M. (1975). *The legal system*. New York: Russell Sage Foundation.

————. (1985). On regulation and legal process. In R. G. Noll, ed. *Regulatory policy and the social sciences*, 111–135. Berkeley: University of California Press.

Galanter, M. (1986). Adjudication, litigation, and related phenomena. In L. Lipson and S. Wheeler, eds. *Law and the Social Sciences*, 151–257. New York: Russell Sage Foundation.

Gurney, J. (1985). Factors influencing the decision to prosecute economic cases. *Criminology*, *23*, 609–628.

Hagan, J. (1977). Criminal justice in rural and urban communities: A study of the bureaucratization of justice. *Social Forces*, *55*, 597–612.

Hagan, J., Nagel-Bernstein, I. H., and Albonetti, C. (1980). The differential sentencing of white-collar offenders in ten federal district courts. *American Sociological Review*, *45*, 802–820.

————. (1982). The social organization of white-collar sanctions: A study of prosecution and punishment in the federal courts. In P. Wickman and T. Dailey, eds. *White-collar and economic crime*, 259–275. Lexington, Mass.: Lexington Books.

Hagan, J., and Palloni, A. (1986). "Club Fed" and the sentencing of white-collar offenders before and after Watergate. *Criminology*, *24*, 603–622.

Hagan, J., and Parker, P. (1985). White-collar crime and punishment: The class structure and legal sanctioning of securities violations. *American Sociological Review*, *50*, 302–316.

Inverarity, J., and McCarthy, D. (1988). Punishment and social structure revisited: Unemployment and imprisonment in the United States, 1948–1984. *Sociological Quarterly*, *29*, 263–280.

Isard, W. (1960). *Methods of regional analysis: An introduction to regional science*. Cambridge, Mass.: The M.I.T. Press.

Jackson, P. I., and Caroll, L. (1981). Race and the war on crime: The sociopolitical determinants of municipal expenditures in 90 non-southern U.S. cities. *American Sociological Review*, *46*, 290–305.

Jankovic, I. (1977). Labor market and imprisonment. *Crime and Social Justice*, *8*, 17–37.

Jowell, J. (1986). Implementation and enforcement of law. In L. Lipson and S. Wheeler, eds. *Law and the social sciences*, 287–318. New York: Russell Sage Foundation.

Levi, M. (1987). *Regulating fraud: White-collar crime and the criminal process*. London: Routledge.

Liska, A. E., Lawrence, J., and Benson, M. (1981). Perspectives on the legal order: The capacity for social control. *American Journal of Sociology*, *87*, 412–426.

Moore, C. A. (1987). Taming the giant corporation? Some cautionary remarks on the deterrability of corporate crime. *Crime and Delinquency, 33,* 379–402.

Myers, R. H. (1986). *Classical and modern regression with applications.* Boston: Duxbury.

Myers, M., and Talarico, S. M. (1987). *The social contexts of criminal sentencing.* New York: Springer-Verlag.

Nagel, I., and Hagan, J. (1982). The sentencing of white-collar criminals in federal courts: A socio-legal exploration of disparity. *Michigan Law Review, 80,* 1427–1465.

Pope, C. E. (1975). *Sentencing of California felony offenders.* National Criminal Justice Information and Statistics Service. Washington, D.C.: U.S. Department of Justice.

Rakoff, J. S. (1985). The exercise of prosecutorial discretion in federal business fraud prosecutions. In B. Fisse and P. A. French, eds. *Corrigible corporations and unruly law,* 173–186. San Antonio: Trinity University Press.

Schudson, C. B., Onellion, A. P., and Hochstedler, E. (1984). Nailing an omelet to the wall: Prosecuting nursing home homicide. In E. Hochstedler, ed. *Corporations as criminals,* 131–146. Beverly Hills: Sage.

Shapiro, S. P. (1984). *Wayward capitalists: Targets of the Securities and Exchange Commission.* New Haven: Yale University Press.

Shover, N., Clelland, D. A., and Lynxwiler, J. P. (1986). *Enforcement or negotiation.* Albany: State University of New York Press.

Simpson, S. (1987). Cycles of illegality: Antitrust violations in corporate America. *Social Forces, 65,* 943–963.

Stinchcombe, A. L. (1987). *Constructing social theories.* Chicago: University of Chicago Press.

Stone, C. D. (1975). *Where the law ends: The social control of corporate behavior.* New York: Harper & Row.

Sutherland, E. H. (1983). *White collar crime: The uncut version.* New Haven: Yale University Press.

Vaughan, D. (1983). *Controlling unlawful organizational behavior: Social structure and corporate misconduct.* Chicago: University of Chicago Press.

Weaver, S. (1980). Antitrust division of the Department of Justice. In J. Q. Wilson, ed. *The politics of regulation,* 123–151. New York: Basic Books.

Weisburd, D., Waring, E., and Wheeler, S. (1990). Class, status, and the punishment of white-collar criminals. *Law & Social Inquiry, 15,* 223–243.

Wheeler, S., Weisburd, D., and Bode, N. (1982). Sentencing the white-collar offender: Rhetoric and reality. *American Sociological Review, 47,* 641–659.

Wilson, J. Q. (1968). *Varieties of police behavior*. Cambridge: Harvard University Press.

NOTES

This research was supported by grant #88-IJ-CX-0044 from the National Institute of Justice. Points of view or opinions in this essay are those of the authors and do not necessarily reflect the official position or policies of the Department of Justice.

1. We also surveyed a random sample of 410 prosecutors located in rural districts. Preliminary analyses indicated that rural prosecutors conduct few corporate-criminal prosecutions, so we deleted them from this analysis.

2. The scale has an alpha reliability of .85, which indicates that the items in the scale are strongly intercorrelated and that it is reasonable to assume they are indicators of a single underlying construct.

3. The alternative remedies scale has an alpha reliability of .84.

4. The coefficients for the variables included in the reduced model were not substantially affected by this procedure. Their signs remained the same and their sizes were only slightly changed after the insignificant variables were deleted.

5. At each stage of the analysis, collinearity diagnostics (Belsay, Kuh, and Welsch, 1980) were used. There is some evidence of multicollinearity in the equation for activity. The condition number, 46.27, is above the suggested cutoff of 30, but it is mainly associated with the intercept. The largest variance inflation factor (VIF) is 2.36, which indicates that none of the variable coefficients are adversely affected by multicollinearity (Myers, 1986, p. 219).

· I V ·

SANCTIONING

· 12 ·

Corporate-Crime Deterrence and Corporate-Control Policies

Views from the Inside

SALLY S. SIMPSON

Deterrence is a familiar and well-researched concept in the conventional crime literature (Paternoster, Saltzman, Chiracos, and Waldo, 1983; Paternoster, 1987; Gibbs, 1975; Grasmick and Green, 1980; Nagin, 1978; Tittle, 1980; Williams and Hawkins, 1986, 1989). The idea that people fear punishment and will adjust their behaviors accordingly is at the heart of the deterrence question (Gibbs, 1975). Whether deterrence actually works or how it works is equivocal (Paternoster, 1987; Williams and Hawkins, 1986). Yet Tittle (1980) points out that in spite of evidence to the contrary, many criminal justice professionals and laypersons believe deterrence works.

Certainly in the area of corporate misbehavior, debates are raging as to whether more severe sanctions are necessary to stem the tide of unethical and illegal conduct and whether such sanctions offer greater general or specific deterrence (compare Gruner, 1988; U.S. Sentencing Commission, 1988; 1989). There is further disagreement as to whether the more appropriate sanction target is the company (Becker, 1968; Block, Nold, and Sidak, 1981; Elzinga and Breit, 1976; Posner, 1980) or the individual decision maker (Coffee, 1980; 1981; Schlegel, 1990). Yet given the general interest in corporate-crime deterrence, it is ironic that there is so little research on the subject. This may be a function of our lack of knowledge of how managers understand their environments and make decisions in them. As Cullen, Maakestad, and Cavender (1987, pp. 349–350) note, scholarship in this area is overly simplistic:

> Although a burgeoning literature on corporate crime and its control has been produced in recent years, relatively little of this research has sought to interview or survey executives to see how they view and negotiate the ethically questionable situations they encounter. Instead, much of this literature contains implicitly an oversocialized conception of the corporate manager—the notion that the conditions of organizational life turn even the most moral individuals into profit-seeking sociopaths.

The goal of this research is to address some of these deficits. Specifically, I examine the applicability of a deterrence model for corporate crime by examining the circumstances and choices that guide managers as they "view and negotiate ethically questionable situations." Additionally, managers are queried about the perceived and potential deterrent effects of internal and external control systems (Braithwaite, 1985).

Background Research

When applied to the study of corporate crime, the concept of deterrence loses its empirical grounding and, to some degree, its theoretical precision. Few studies systematically examine the deterrent effects of corporate legal sanctions. Consequently, much work in this area is mere speculation.[1] For instance, Chambliss (1967) suggests that corporate executives should be more amenable to deterrence strategies because they are not committed to a criminal lifestyle and their crimes are more rational, that is, instrumental as opposed to expressive. Thus, corporate personnel are assumed to value conformity at the same time that they weigh the costs of crime relative to its possible benefits (see, for example, Cornish and Clarke, 1986). Presumably, if crime costs are perceived as severe and certain, managers will avoid the pain of legal discovery and processing (Braithwaite and Geis, 1982).

Deterrence theorists distinguish the relative contributions of informal (stigmatic, attachment, and commitment costs) and formal legal sanctions to crime deterrence. The traditional deterrence position states that only formal legal sanctions can be considered as components of deterrence (see Andenaes, 1974, Paternoster, 1987, and Williams and Hawkins, 1986, for reviews of competing positions and collaborating evidence). Informal sanctions are best understood as extralegal, within a broader context of social control.

Such distinctions are absent in studies of corporate misconduct, perhaps due to a dominant concern with corporations as criminal actors. Yet because individuals make decisions that are attributable to companies, presumably both formal and informal sanctions will affect participation in unethical/illegal conduct. Informal sanctions will matter because the potential costs of crime, whether discovered or not, can damage one's self-esteem and self-respect. Discovery could result in rejection by significant others, a loss of employment opportunities, and so on. Formal costs are also likely to be salient because some legal consequences (particularly jail) can be frightening to otherwise "conforming" and inexperienced offenders.

Though there is little study of corporate-crime deterrence per se (recent exceptions include Braithwaite and Makkai, 1991; Simpson and Koper, 1992), a number of scholars are learning more about how managers confront ethical dilemmas in their day-to-day work life. Corporate decisions appear to involve more than rational choices—they have moral components as well (Etzioni, 1988). At issue is how the moral is defined and incorporated into the decision process. Kram and her colleagues (1989) find that in situations where individual morality and business concerns clash, the former typically is relegated to the nonbusiness (and therefore irrelevant) sphere. Similarly, in the corporate world examined by Jackall (1988, p. 101), there is little room for personally held convictions and principles.[2] Instead, morality is situational, always in flux, changing along with social relations and networks within the organization.

Language plays an important role in mediating the tension between the edicts of morality and the lived experience of business. Through language, moral codes are turned into pragmatic and "neutralizing" vocabularies.

> Dichotomous modes of thinking like "cost-benefit analysis" are to some extent conceptual paradigms of functional rationality. They help managers apply a thoroughly secular, pragmatic, utilitarian calculus even to areas of experience

· 291

that, in their private lives, they might consider sacred. (Jackall, 1988, p. 127)

Both studies note the tension between what managers are paid to do (that is, think and act rationally) and their individually held conceptions of what is right, ethical, and moral. The goal of this research is less a "test" of a deterrence doctrine than it is an exploration of how corporate actors make sense of illegality when it occurs and whether and from what source they perceive punishment risks.

Data and Methods

Questions about ethical dilemmas, rational choice, and organizational compliance systems were asked of fifty-nine top and middle managers representing three large U.S. manufacturing corporations. All interviews were conducted by this author. A conversation format was followed with the above themes guiding discussion. Respondents were lead into the subject matter with the following inquiry (or a variation thereof): "Do you know of any situation in the past where someone made a decision that was unethical? Can you describe this situation?"[3]

Questions leading into the topic of rational choice decision making took one of two forms. Respondents were asked whether they believed a rational calculus was employed by *others* when illegal conduct occurred (for example, within their company or in relatively famous cases of corporate crime, such as the Ford Pinto case) or how *they* (the respondents) would make a decision under similar kinds of conditions. Finally, respondents were queried about the kinds of corporate control systems that were in place at the time of the interviews. Specifically, I was interested in questions of visibility, fairness, and deterrence and whether perceptions varied across respondents in different areas and at different levels in the company.

The selection of firms and respondents for study followed the logic of purposive sampling. Firms were selected, in part, if they had recently undergone major structural and/or strategic changes.[4] Within these firms, a range of top and middle management from different functional areas and SBUs (Standard Business Units) are represented. Selection criteria for respondents varied. Specific individuals—such as CEOs and executive vice presidents—were targeted across firms. Then, within each company various representatives were selected from different subunits of interest, such as sales and marketing.[5]

All respondents were assured confidentiality (not as to identity, because a master list of participants was known within the organization, but as to responses) and, with their permission, their responses were tape-recorded. Interviews varied in length between forty minutes and two hours.

There are several reasons to be cautious about the veracity and potential bias of responses. First, many respondents are hand-picked by the corporate staff. An "organization line," if there is one to present, is more apt to emerge from this type of selection process. Second, respondents may feel uncomfortable talking about their or their organizations' participation in unethical conduct—particularly when top management can identify who participated in the study and their responses are tape-recorded.

No doubt, under these conditions some managers were less than candid. However, I found respondents to be refreshingly frank about their companies' *past* illegality and, if appropriate, their role in it. Most were comfortable talking about the more famous cases of corporate misconduct and assessing how each firm responded to it. Moreover, judging from the degree of emotion and thoughtfulness that accompanied many responses, these issues are of greater concern to managers than outsiders might imagine. Thus, I believe that these data are relatively accurate representations of manager perceptions and beliefs about illegality—at least within these companies.

Obviously, generalizations about managerial decision making or effective versus ineffective systems of control are not possible from this type of sample. However, the data offer insights into how managers cope with conflicting demands, where pressures to violate ethical conduct norms come from, and the ways in which organizations can encourage (and perhaps unintentionally discourage) ethical choices. As Jackall (1988, p. 5) neatly summarizes, "Only an understanding of how men and women in business actually experience their work enables one to grasp its moral salience for them." Our first goal then is to assess how managers think about unethical conduct, particularly in terms of its causes and mechanisms for control.

Views from the Inside:
Images of Offense and Offender Type

For most respondents, the image of the unethical manager is negative and disreputable. Viewed as little different than "common" criminals, these offenders are seen as inherently bad, inadequately socialized, immoral, and troublesome. A middle-level manager at Firm B succinctly characterizes this view.

> My personal belief is that there are ethical people and there are unethical people and that if I hire Dave or somebody else who's unethical, I can tell them about the corporate policy all I want and it won't make any difference to him. I think it probably starts somewhere around potty training. You're either ethical by the time you're five or you're not ethical.

When pressed on the type of acts these managers are most apt to commit, respondents typically describe personal gain offenses—embezzlement, accepting gratuities, graft, in addition to more conventional offending (such as theft).[6] Unethical managers are believed to be more amenable to deterrence because they are seen as more calculating in their unethical conduct. As one manager summarized, "Unethical people will comply only if some kind of pain is involved."

In these respondents' minds, disreputable managers are clearly distinguishable from reputable managers who cross the boundary of ethical conduct but with less culpability. Such offenders make "mistakes"; they "accidentally" cut corners when costs are too high, or manipulate tax and/or other financial documents in a "misguided belief that they are doing it to save the company."[7] As one respondent put it, "There's certain things you do. You'll bend the rules a bit. In your own mind you're not violating the law, you're bending a rule."

As is obvious from the use of neutralizing language, when reputable managers do offend, their acts of deviance are more forgivable—perhaps because respondents (particularly middle managers) can empathize with the circumstances under which such acts of deviance occur. The matter is more often framed as an organizational problem and less as one of individual responsibility. Thus, like Benson's (1985) white-collar criminals who avoid a "criminal" label through elaborate denial mechanisms, managers also neutralize offender blameworthiness, but selectively. Only corporate offenses are structured and organizationally situated in ways that allow neutralization.

In sum, managers selectively apply a deterrence framework depending on who the offender is and the nature of her or his offense. They distinguish peers who are deserving of severe sanctions from those who need treatment or rehabilitation. The former—the personal gain profiteers—deserve swift and certain punishment. Every company, no matter how ethical, will be vulnerable to these offenders. As one executive vice president put it, "You're always going to have some of those people . . . but individuals who have that kind of [rational] calculus don't belong." Conversely, those who offend for "the good of the company" are viewed less harshly. The behavior may be unacceptable, but its causes are understandable. And, depending on who is perceived as being at fault (that is, the individual or the organization), nonpunitive remedies are more likely to be promoted.

Costs and Benefits of Crime: Are Managers Rational Calculators?

At the core of the rational choice perspective is the assumption that persons make conscious decisions based on the relative costs and rewards of a particular line of action. Legal sanctions, in the vernacular of rational choice, are a "cost" to be weighed and factored into any decision that is illegal. As noted previously, it is assumed that corporate offenders are especially suited for deterrence because of the rational nature of their deviant activities and their lack of commitment to a criminal lifestyle (Chambliss, 1967; Braithwaite and Geis, 1982; Cullen et al., 1987). Thus, the extent to which deterrence theory is applicable to corporate illegality depends, in large part, on the degree to which managers calculate and assess the relative benefits and costs of decisions (see also Schlegel, 1990).

Among managers in this study, the majority replied "no" when asked whether decision makers rationally assess benefits and consequences when confronting unethical possibilities. A good example is Ted, who sees deviance as part of an unconscious process:

> First you put your little toe in, and then all of a sudden you've got your whole foot in and before long you're up to your waist. You start and then all of a sudden . . . rationalization is a wonderful process!

However, some do believe that while choices and decision outcomes may not be as broadly rational as management would like the general public to believe, decision makers do weigh various factors when ethical dilemmas are confronted. What counts as costs and benefits, however, are calibrated quite differently. Some costs are best understood as "organizational," while others combine more subjective and personal components.

Key ethical choices are rarely framed in *narrowly* utilitarian business terms, even among those whose job it is to do so. A reliability manager, for whom cost-benefit calculations are part and parcel of her job description, illustrates this point:

> In my old job we had to do this [quantitative analysis] on [safety] campaigns. Those are the kind [of decisions] that make you stay awake at night because your moral feelings say, God, it shouldn't matter if the cost were fifty billion dollars because you ought to save a life.

Even among respondents who feel that some form of rational calculus occurs when ethically questionable situations are confronted, few (28 percent) assess risk in solely economic terms (that is, costs to the company of compliance with law versus violation). Like Jackall's managers, these respondents use neutralizing language to disguise the moral components of their decisions:

> When you're in a survival mode, your stripes change. It's human nature. There are no purists in a survival mode and its very easy to be absolutely ethical when you're profitable

and everybody is. And as soon as you're on the threshold, . . . then all of the shortcuts come out of the woodwork and we give them titles, "entrepreneur of risk," "risk analysis." We give them all kinds of fancy things to accommodate and legitimize the decision-making process.

Managers who hold these opinions primarily are located lower in the corporation, perhaps because economic pressures are more keenly felt among those responsible for policy implementation than among policymakers. This is certainly true for the middle managers interviewed by Clinard (1983). Top executives, on the other hand, are more sensitive to personal risk factors.

Another organizational level cost that factors into a few decisions is how the firm's public image and reputation will be affected by the disclosure of unethical conduct (Fisse and Braithwaite, 1983). However, while most respondents feel their firms are more sensitive to ethical issues these days because the general public expects greater social responsibility from business, surprisingly few incorporate these considerations into their decision-making processes. Of the two respondents who do mention it, the perceived stigmatic consequences of unethical conduct offer a clear deterrent. An attorney at Firm A explains, "Everyone knows what happens when you cross the line. We don't need any more examples." In the same company, another manager points specifically to how negative publicity hurts in the marketplace: "I think that unethical decisions ultimately come back to hurt the company. It isn't worth it. Ever!"

Managers also cite individual costs and rewards (formal and informal) as influential over decision outcomes. For six respondents, legal-sanction risk clearly weighs in their calculations. On one occasion an executive vice president at Firm B was called before the grand jury. The experience was so traumatic he "never wanted to go through that again." Another claims that fear of punishment is what keeps him law abiding, "no matter how ridiculous" the law:

For example, not complying with health and safety standards. That's a prosecutable offense no matter how ridiculous. I wouldn't call that [noncompliance] unethical, because it is a senseless standard, but I would comply because of personal fear of prosecution.

However, fear of jail (with the exception of the grand jury experience, the only legal sanction mentioned by managers as a personal deterrent) was often coupled with other costs. Some of these "costs" are articulated with rational and pragmatic language (Jackall, 1988), such as, "I wouldn't price fix because it's bad business and I don't want to go to jail." Others offer moral considerations, especially when human lives are at stake.[8] For example, a supervisor explains why he will not compromise on safety regulations:

> If there was a disaster or one of the men got hurt, and you know, morally you think about it and legally it's one thing under the Health and Safety Act. I am criminally liable.
>
> Q: Which do you think people think is more important, the criminal or the moral on that?
>
> Myself, the moral on that. . . . I tell my people, morally I don't want anyone hurt. My father had . . . two people work for him that were killed and I saw how it affected him. It took him years to get over it. Deep down he questioned himself, should he have done something different? And, I've had two of my employees killed and I keep thinking back, "What could I have done differently?"

Like the findings from more traditional deterrence studies, informal costs and benefits appear to influence corporate executives and managers more than formal legal sanctions. But it is not always easy for managers to distinguish one from the other. "I have this battle as to am I doing something to do what's right or am I afraid of getting caught? . . . It doesn't really matter, the outcome is the same. But it bothers me a little."

Respondents who identify subjective factors as influencing their decision making are most likely to weigh career and/or monetary gains against the negative impact on family and friends, damage to reputation, self-respect, and trust. One attorney suggests that individual subjectivity colors all corporate decisions:

> There are always subjective factors. "Will this help me with my career?" "How am I going to look?" But if everything is working the way it's supposed to, what's good for the

company, what is ethical, what is legal, and what is good for you as an employee—those all ought to converge pretty close to one another.

At the broad-stroke level, these data offer little support for a strict utilitarian model. Nor does deterrence in the traditional sense of fearing legal sanctions play a major role in the decision-making process. A majority of respondents discount the likelihood of a rational calculus occurring when illegal opportunities are confronted.[9] They believe that people act ethically not out of fear of sanction, but because it is the "right thing to do." Among those who believe that some rational choice is involved when unethical conduct is contemplated, most perceive informal costs to be more salient than legal ones (40 percent versus 25 percent, respectively).[10]

Extralegal sanctions may be more salient for managers because the latter are rarely applied and, if invoked, are generally lenient.[11] However, it is not clear that informal sanctions are any more certain. Yet they appear to matter more. In this next section, we examine the implications of these findings for corporate-crime control. Specifically, we examine how corporate compliance systems may offer educative and deterrent effects separate from formal legal sanctions.

Facilitating Corporate-Crime Control

Alternatives to the Legal Sanction[12]

Coffee (1981) argues that corporate deterrence is increased through a combined force of legal and internal remedies. However, there are several pragmatic problems with such a model. First, from what little data exist, legal remedies are rarely invoked and punishments are relatively meager (compare Cohen, 1989; U.S. Sentencing Commission, 1989). Moreover, the dominant economic model of deterrence assumes that the corporation is the sanction target. Coffee (1980) believes the more appropriate and deterrable target to be the individual who is responsible for the misconduct. Yet it is extremely difficult for the legal system to ferret out the culpable manager from the innocent, the minion from the mastermind. Putatively, that is a less difficult task for insiders. Given these difficulties, corporate compliance systems may be the best available weapon against corporate crime and preferable if "violations and sanctioning violators are so complex and protracted or so costly that they are regarded as inadequate remedies for continuing harm" (Reiss, 1984, p. 26).

Compliance and deterrence, as two distinct types of social control, have different aims. The former is preventative, the latter postmonitory (Reiss, 1984). Corporate compliance systems can be both. Deterrence may be achieved through sanctions levied by the company against the wrongdoer (for example, dismissal, demotion, or other disciplinary action). Prescriptive remedies, on the other hand, are nonpunitive. Through policies, programs, and informal mechanisms, they provide support and direction for managers who must make ethical choices. However, not all compliance systems are effective. Some are mere window dressing to pass the inspection of interested outside parties (usually the U.S. government). Others, while more powerful internally, are ineffectual. Our goal is to use the perceptions of managers and top executives to identify the strengths and weaknesses of the various compliance systems.

Assessing Corporate Control Systems

Across firms, managers generally believe their companies are ethical. Summarizing the sentiments of most respondents in his firm, an executive vice president claims, "I've always thought that [Firm A] was an ethical company. Highly ethical company. Its morals, its policies, and its procedures are of the highest order." At Firm B, the attitudes are similar. "By the time I started at the company, there was always an emphasis on integrity, integrity, integrity."[13] Respondents at Firm C candidly acknowledge that they have only recently found their ethical and moral direction:[14]

> Throughout the course of the last fifteen years, there have been a couple of things take place in this company that have driven us to the point where we are almost legalized as managers from an ethical standpoint. We literally have a manual [of] employee guidelines that stipulate what our rules are. . . . And, we have to sign a statement every year that says we have adhered to and know of no instance where anyone else has not adhered to our guidelines for proper action, both domestically and internationally.

In spite of the claims and some evidence to the contrary, my interviews uncovered some illegal and unethical *organizational* conduct at all companies. Thus, it makes sense to examine how individual managers perceive "effective" systems of control along with various threats to their success. When managers were queried about specific aspects of their self-regulatory systems, it became clear that across and within companies there are significant differences in perceptions of system (1) visibility and (2) fairness.

Visibility

For the most part, managers feel as though their respective compliance systems are well publicized and communicated. Policies/procedures are seen as permeating the informal culture of the corporation (good news for the compliance side of social control).[15] Fewer respondents, however, believe that the consequences associated with violations were equally well disseminated (bad news for deterrent effects). Visibility seemed to vary according to violation type. For instance, offenders who violate criminal law are more apt to be used as an example. "I could count on one hand almost the major problems we've had [like] price fixing, kickbacks, and things like that. Those things are publicized. 'John Jones got fired for being on the take.' . . . Everybody knows what the consequences are." More commonly, however, outcomes are perceived as invisible. "They do try to hide it. But I think that's wrong. They ought to make it visible."

There are organizational reasons for keeping violations secret. First, organizations are vulnerable to liability suits from employees who have been sanctioned—wrongful discharge, sullied reputations, and the like:

> If I were to be critical of anything, . . . in *any* breach of illegal or unethical conduct, we should disclose as much as possible without subjecting ourselves to a liability problem. Historically, as a company we have chosen to deal with those situations, regardless of the level, in a very secretive way.

Second, because almost all firms are concerned with image, the appearance of management impropriety raises questions about misplaced trust. Further, secrecy may be an organizational imperative.

Jackall (1988, p. 131) describes the tension between openness and trust. "One retains the trust and confidence of others only by displaying the kind of reputation for discretion that leads to social acceptance in the first place."

Fairness

Perceptions of impartiality vary across the organizational hierarchy. Top executives believe their compliance systems treat all offenders equally. "If we found instances of wrongdoing, we'd come down very hard on [offenders]." But middle managers see discrepancies in who is investigated, who is punished, and what that punishment might be:

> The severity of punishment has always seemed to be in direct relationship to the position. The higher the position, the less severe the consequences. So, in that regard, it seems to me that some of the most serious abuses that I have observed occurred when a person reaches a level where he feels as though he is above the rules.

Another observes that investigations rarely implicate higher-ups. "You would think that for certain instances that . . . people in leadership roles would have had more responsibility than they did, or would have had to pay more consequences than they did." One manager notes that even if higher-ups are implicated, the consequences for misconduct may be quite different. "Oh yea, you're young, you're fired; but if you've been here awhile, well, good old Harry took a special early retirement. He was sixty anyway."

If internal compliance systems are perceived as secretive and discriminatory, the potential for deterrence breaks down since it is hard for individuals to calculate sanction probabilities. But, perhaps more consequentially, so does compliance. Employees are apt to lose respect and trust for the system and those that administer it. Thus, even with a sophisticated and complex system in place, more rather than less unethical conduct may result.

Conclusions

Within the parameters of the deterrence debate, most scholars believe that more severe and certain punishment will deter corporate violators (Cullen et al., 1987; Coffee, 1980; Elzinga and Breit, 1976; Becker, 1968) and that policy should focus on (1) how to increase surveillance capacities, (2) determining to what level sanctions should be raised (higher fines, incarceration), and (3) how to eliminate the inconsistencies in punishment that currently exist. But too much of the corporate-crime deterrence debate centers on the role of external regulation and sanction (whether these are criminal, civil, or regulatory), diverting attention away from a powerful weapon in the battle against corporate misconduct.

Quizzing managers about the ethical choices they make while on the job leads one to conclude that managers do not, for the most part, think in deterrence terms. And, when they do, the salience of formal legal sanctions is revealed when managers contemplate traditional occupational offenses like embezzlement, bribery, employee theft, and so on, not corporate offenses. Moreover, as these data and critics of the rational-choice model of corporate decision making suggest (Byrne and Hoffman, 1985), many organizational decisions are irrational.[16] For these reasons, there may be better ways to accomplish corporate-crime control than through legal means alone.[17]

Supplementing a formal sanction model is the idea of self-regulation (Braithwaite, 1982). Corporate self-regulation assumes that managers take the notion of corporate responsibility seriously (Braithwaite, 1985) and put into place internal sanctions and processes that are both disciplinary and persuasive. Since managers describe themselves as law-abiding and they profess to be unhappy when working in an environment that forces them to compromise their ethical standards (assuming what they say is true), visible and fair corporate compliance systems make ethical compromises less likely and improve the chances of prosocial outcomes.

REFERENCES

Andenaes, J. (1974). *Punishment and deterrence.* Ann Arbor: University of Michigan Press.

Becker, G. S. (1968). Crime and punishment: An economic approach. *Journal of Political Economy, 76,* 169–217.

Benson, M. L. (1985). Denying the guilty mind: Accounting for involvement in a white-collar crime. *Criminology, 23,* 583–607.

Block, M. K., Nold, F. C., and Sidak, J. G. (1981). The deterrent effect of antitrust enforcement. *Journal of Political Economy, 89,* 429–445.

Braithwaite, J. (1982). The limits of economism in controlling harmful corporate conduct. *Law and Society Review, 16*, 481–506.

——. (1985). Taking responsibility seriously: Corporate compliance systems. In B. Fisse and P. A. French, eds. *Corrigible corporations and unruly law*, 39–61. San Antonio: Trinity University Press.

Braithwaite, J., and Geis, G. (1982). Theory and action for corporate crime control. *Crime and Delinquency, 28*, 292–314.

Braithwaite, J., and Makkai, T. (1991). Testing an expected utility model of corporate deterrence. *Law and Society Review, 25*, 7–39.

Byrne, J., and Hoffman, S. M. (1985). Efficient corporate harm: A Chicago metaphysic. In B. Fisse and P. A. French, eds. *Corrigible corporations and unruly law*, 101–136. San Antonio: Trinity University Press.

Chambliss, W. J. (1967). Types of deviance and the effectiveness of legal sanctions. *Wisconsin Law Review*, summer, 705–719.

Clinard, M. B. (1983). *Corporate ethics and crime: The role of middle management*. Beverly Hills: Sage.

Clinard, M. B. and Quinney, R. (1973). *Criminal behavior systems*. (2d ed.). New York: Holt, Rinehart and Winston.

Coffee, J. C., Jr. (1980). Corporate crime and punishment: A non-Chicago view of the economics of criminal sanctions. *American Criminal Law Review, 17*, 419–476.

——. (1981). No soul to damn: No body to kick: An unscandalized inquiry into the problem of corporate punishment. *Michigan Law Review*, January, 386–459.

Cohen, Mark A. (1989). The role of criminal sanctions in antitrust enforcement. *Contemporary Policy Issues, 7*, 36–46.

Cornish, D. B., and Clarke, R. V., eds. (1986). *The reasoning criminal: Rational choice perspectives on offending*. New York: Springer-Verlag.

Cullen, F. T., Maakestad, W. J., and Cavender, G. (1987). *Corporate crime under attack: The Ford Pinto case and beyond*. Cincinnati: Anderson Publishing.

Elzinga, K. G., and Breit, A. (1976). *The antitrust penalties: A study in law and economics*. New Haven: Yale University Press.

Etzioni, A. (1988). *The moral dimension: Toward a new economics*. New York: Free Press.

Fisse, B., and Braithwaite, J. (1983). *The impact of publicity on corporate offenders*. Albany: State University of New York Press.

Gibbs, J. P. (1975). *Crime, punishment, and deterrence*. New York: Elsevier Press.

Grasmick, H. G., and Green, D. E. (1980). Legal punishment, social disapproval and internalization as inhibitors of illegal behavior. *The Journal of Criminal Law and Criminology, 71*, 325–335.

Gruner, R. (1988). To let the punishment fit the organization: Sanctioning corporate offenders through corporate probation. *American Journal of Criminal Law, 16,* 1–106.

Jackall, R. (1988). *Moral mazes: The world of corporate managers.* New York: Oxford University Press.

Klepper, S., and Nagin, D. (1989). Tax compliance and perceptions of the risks of detection and criminal prosecution. *Law and Society Review, 23,* 209–240.

Kram, K. E., Yeager, P. C., and Reed, G. E. (1989). Decisions and dilemmas: The ethical dimension in the corporate context. In J. E. Post, ed. *Research in corporate social performance and policy.* Vol. 11. Greenwich, Conn.: JAI Press.

Nagin, D. (1978). General deterrence: A review of the empirical evidence. In Deterrence and incapacitation: Estimating the effects of criminal sanctions on crime rates. Report of the Panel on Research on Deterrent Incapacitative Effects, NAS, Washington, D.C.

Paternoster, R. (1987). The deterrent effect of the perceived certainty and severity of punishment: A review of the evidence and issues. *Justice Quarterly, 4,* 173–217.

———. (1989). Decisions to participate in and desist from four types of common delinquency: Deterrence and the rational choice perspective. *Law and Society Review, 23,* 7–40.

Paternoster, R., Saltzman, L., Chiracos, T., and Waldo, G. (1983). Perceived risk and social control: Do sanctions really deter? *Law and Society Review, 17,* 457–479.

Posner, R. (1980). Optimal sentences for white-collar criminals. *American Criminal Law Review, 17,* 409–418.

Reiss, A. J., Jr. (1983). The policing of organizational life. In M. Punch, ed. *Controls of the police organizations,* 78–97. Cambridge: MIT Press.

———. (1984). Selecting strategies of social control over organizational life. In K. Hawkins and J. M. Thomas, eds. *Enforcing regulation,* 23–35. Boston: Kluwer-Nijhoff.

Schlegel, K. (1990). *Just desserts for corporate criminals.* Boston: Northeastern University Press.

Simpson, Sally S. and Koper, Christopher S. (1992). Deterring corporate crime. Forthcoming (August). *Criminology, 30.*

Stone, C. D. (1975). *Where the law ends: The social control of corporate behavior.* New York: Harper & Row.

Tittle, C. (1980). *Sanctions and social deviance: The question of deterrence.* New York: Praeger.

U. S. Sentencing Commission (1988). Discussion materials on organizational sanctions (July). Washington, D.C.

———. (1989). Sentencing guidelines for organizational defendants (preliminary draft, November 1). Washington, D.C.

Victor, B., and Cullen, J. B. (1988). The organizational bases of ethical work climates. *Administrative Science Quarterly, 33*, 101–125.

Williams, K. R., and Hawkins, R. (1986). Perceptual research on general deterrence: A critical review. *Law and Society Review, 20*, 545–572.

———. (1989). The meaning of arrest for wife assault. *Criminology, 27*, 163–181.

NOTES

This research was funded while the author was a Post-Doctoral Research Fellow at the Harvard Graduate School of Business Administration. The author is grateful to Dean John McArthur and the Division of Research for their support. Thanks also to Amitai Etzioni, Rosabeth Moss Kanter, and Charles Wellford for their helpful comments and to Chris Koper and Michelle Harmon for assistance in preparing the data.

1. Simpson and Koper, 1992, Block, Nold, and Sidak, 1981, and Braithwaite and Makkai, 1991 empirically test a deterrence perspective for corporations.

2. I found similar results in my interviews. When asked to respond to a number of questions that tapped ethical work climates (see Victor and Cullen, 1988), managers often reframed questions so that individual and corporate values did not conflict.

3. The choice to ask about "unethical conduct" instead of crime or illegality was guided by two concerns: (1) that respondents would shy away from truthfully answering questions that could criminally implicate either themselves or the company; and (2) that respondents, rather than the interviewer, define what constituted unethical conduct. It was at least as interesting to see how managers framed the terms as it was to learn how they made sense of them. In each instance where a manager defined unethical conduct as "occupational" crime, they were asked whether their interpretations were also appropriate for "corporate" crime—with examples given (see Clinard and Quinney, 1973).

4. These data are drawn from a research project that examines the effect of top-down changes in corporate strategy and structure on managerial decision making. Thus, sampling strategies reflect these concerns. There is some concern that respondents' comments and opinions will be affected by the changes that are occurring around them. There is no question that the disruptions to organizational structure and its impact on the informal culture were salient in the minds of those interviewed. In fact, most of my questions not dealing specifically with unethical conduct addressed the impact of change on corporate structure, culture, and intraorganizational relations. However, there is no

reason to suspect a priori that answers will be affected in any particular direction or any more than a company that is experiencing, say, profit squeeze or a change in management.

5. On occasion, things did not work out as smoothly as originally planned. Sometimes respondents were unavailable on interview days. When this occurred another manager in the desired functional or SBU area was substituted.

6. The fact that respondents would define unethical conduct as "occupational" rather than "corporate" crime (Clinard and Quinney, 1973) is not surprising. This position accurately captures a managerial worldview that sees offenses perpetrated for personal gain as "criminal" (therefore unethical), while those done for the benefit of the corporation are not. Most violations of regulations/administrative law are illegal, but not criminal (*mala prohibita* as opposed to *mala in se*). Not surprisingly, personal gain offenses are viewed as more serious, more costly to the firm, and requiring greater punishment.

7. When managers discuss occupational crime, it's not the act that is defined as bad, but the actor. The converse is true of corporate illegality.

8. Paternoster (1989) finds deterrence/rational choice models of delinquency offending to be offense specific. It is reasonable to suspect such variation among corporate actors as well.

9. When asked whether people act ethically because they fear punishment (certainty, celerity, and severity of legal sanctions), one respondent replied (only slightly tongue-in-cheek): "You mean what keeps me straight? None of those things. I was a Boy Scout!"

10. The little evidence that is available from these interviews offers more support for general than specific deterrence. None of the executives or managers I interviewed had served jail time for criminal offenses, and only one had experience before a grand jury. Thus, perceptions of sanction risk were based on their knowledge of what happened to others. And many could relay stories about someone they knew or a company they knew about that had been sanctioned in some way for violation of law.

11. In a study of taxpayer noncompliance, Klepper and Nagin (1989, pp. 237–238) find taxpayers to make "calculated decisions of weighing the benefits and costs of noncompliance, but their calculations *appear to conform loosely to the institutional realities of the enforcement process* [emphasis added]." This may also be true for corporate managers. If the risk of legal sanction is minimal, formal social control may not weigh heavily in the decision-making process.

12. Williams and Hawkins (1986) argue that it is conceptually imprecise to assess extralegal and legal sanctions separately. In fact, the former may be a consequence of the latter. While this is an intriguing theoretical notion, these data are not conducive to the sort of analysis neces-

sary to tease out the separate and multiplicative effects. See Paternoster (1987) for an insightful criticism of these ideas.

13. This firm has one of the lowest accident rates in its industry.

14. In one of the firms, this perception is tied explicitly to the current management. Prior to this CEO's tenure, the firm was family controlled. As such, "the exterior boundaries [of ethical behavior] were drawn by the family. It is clear that the family was involved in pushing into certain areas. . . . I think there could have been (and I was not there so this is conjecture) an assumption [that] what was desired by the family was in fact the boundaries—and if they wanted to push into an area, that the boundaries had been moved." Using criminal and regulatory compliance records as an indicator of whether and where the family pushed (particularly during the 1970s), it is safe to conclude that the ethical boundaries of this firm were pretty fluid.

15. What comprises the internal compliance system varies greatly by corporation. For instance, one firm did not have a code of ethical conduct. Another required all managers to sign a document yearly testifying that they did not violate any law or policy or know of any other employee who did. Similar diversity was uncovered by Braithwaite (1985).

16. The broader study from which this research is drawn finds that many corporate decisions are made "on gut instinct" or "by the seat of my pants." Some decisions are more calculated than others, but these are strategic not routine. Everyday decision making can be routine and monotonous or, during periods of crisis, somewhat chaotic and irrational.

17. See Stone (1975) for other compelling reasons why the law cannot control corporate crime.

· 13 ·

Corporate Criminal Liability
and the Comparative Mix of Sanctions

STEVEN WALT

WILLIAM S. LAUFER

Theories of corporate criminal law are concerned with answers to the following three, simply put questions: (1) can corporations be included in the class of persons for normative or positive purposes?; (2) what justificatory or explanatory role, if any, should the notion of personhood play in corporate criminal law theory?; and (3) what limits are placed on the disparity in sanctions applied to corporations and individuals, whatever the status of corporate personhood may be? The first question is one of ontological *status*; the second is one of *theoretical usefulness*, whether normative or explanatory. The third question is a specific instance of the second and is limited to theories of sanctions.

Theorists have been exercised principally by the question of ontological status. Two sides divide over the answer to the question of corporation-personhood inclusion. One side argues that the poverty of theory in corporate crime research may be attributed to the "fictionalizing" of crimes committed by corporations (Cressey, 1988). Corporations have been given a life and a moral personhood that blurs the distinction between crimes attributable to persons and those attributable to the corporate entity. By giving a corporation an ontological status as an intending and acting entity, the notion of a person is denuded. Unlike people, corporations have no personality, no conscience, and no shame (compare Ladd, 1970; Donaldson, 1982; Held, 1986). As one New York court observed a

· 309

century ago: "A corporation, as such, has no human wants to be supplied. It cannot eat, drink, or wear clothing, or live in houses" (*Darlington v. The Mayor*, 1865).

Scholars on another side of the debate claim that corporations are metaphysical (real) persons. They can act, have intentions, commit crimes, and suffer from punishment (Braithwaite and Fisse, 1990). French (1979) has argued, for example, that corporations are full-fledged moral persons that exhibit intentionality. Others make weaker claims while still finding personhood (Manning, 1984; Ozar, 1985). The claims have been based on the linguistic or conceptual propriety of ascribing personhood to corporations.

The debate is not new. Nor are the attendant arguments particularly novel. Similar arguments appeared in a host of judicial opinions at the turn of this century. Judges extended the liability of corporations in decisions on the law of nuisance, on questions regarding corporate nonfeasance versus misfeasance, and on the extension of corporate penal liability to common law crimes requiring intent (Bernard, 1984; Brickey, 1984; Comment, 1990). Moreover, issues relating to corporate-personhood inclusion appeared during the American Law Institute's proceedings prior to the codification of the Model Penal Code (Mueller, 1957).

We contend that the enduring debate is misguided. The ontological question of corporate-personhood inclusion cannot be addressed without addressing the question of the theoretical usefulness of the notion of personhood. Elsewhere we have argued for the theoretical dispensibility of personhood in assigning criminal liability and imposing sanctions (Walt and Laufer, 1991). Personhood does not matter. Below we very briefly rehearse arguments for this conclusion (sections 1–2). The conclusion poses serious concerns about the available mix of comparable sanctions applied to corporations and individuals. We therefore address the third question identified above: the limits on disparity in available sanctions as between corporations and individuals (section 3). A proposal follows, utilizing a number of incapacitative corporate sanctions to serve as a proxy for corporate imprisonment (sections 4–6).

Corporate Personhood

Corporations and individuals, while not necessarily sharing common features, can both be persons. Evidence in support of this may be found by considering the following claims: (a) there may very well be a class of persons that includes entities other than individuals; (b) the features shared by individuals that give rise to a presumption of personhood may in fact be shared by corporations; (c) corporations exhibit preferences and engage in rational choice in a manner consistent with a finding of rationality; (d) in certain situations, for certain kinds of decisions, an individual may in fact be a corporation—a small collective with different goals and preferences, exhibiting planning and strategic behaviors; and (e) corporate-personhood inclusion ultimately is an empirical issue. Studies grounded in theories of the firm support the inclusion (Cyert and March, 1963; Alchian and Demsetz, 1972; Jensen and Meckling, 1976; Fama, 1980; Easterbrook, 1984; Winter, 1986). Note that claims (a) through (e) are based on the explanatory treatment of the corporation as a person.

The Irrelevance of Personhood

The basic premises of American criminal law, mens rea, *actus reus*, concurrence, causation, penalty, and harm, do not require reference to personhood. With few exceptions, these preconditions of liability may be satisfied by any entity causing a harmful and unlawful act, voluntarily and with a culpable mental state. Of course, statutory law can and does limit a corporation's liability. For example, for certain common law offenses, some state criminal codes restrict liability to "human beings." Others explicitly exclude corporations from liability for certain offenses, carrying particular sanctions. But these are merely legislative restrictions that address perceptions about the boundaries of corporate liability. They do not address corporate personhood. It is not in virtue of being a person that criminal liability attaches. It is in virtue of possessing the complex, relational property of causing-harm-voluntarily-with-a-culpable-state-of-mind-and-without-excuse (Walt and Laufer, 1991). Personhood also is irrelevant for the purposes of establishing moral responsibility. Whether corporations have or do not have rights or responsibilities is not contingent upon personhood. Rather, it is contingent upon the nature of the properties that moral persons share (compare Zimmerman, 1988). This may include the capacity for choice or voluntary action, as well as the presence of desires and beliefs (Manning, 1984). It does not require the presence of emotive or affective capabilities (DeGeorge, 1987; Wolf, 1985). The requirement confuses the fact of responsibility with empathic states contingently associated with responsibility. Acting in a morally responsible manner may be incidental to an awareness and sensitivity to the feelings of others. What is required is an awareness of and conformity to moral norms. Reference to the features of an entity (for example, corporate ethics codes, social audits, and ethics committees), rather than to its personhood, is needed (compare Hoffman, 1986). Justificatory parsimony suggests that reference to personhood be dispensed with.

Disparity in the Mix of Sanctions

The conclusion that features of entities, rather than personhood, are essential for determining criminal or moral responsibility has significant consequences for corporate criminal law. If personhood is inessential for the purpose of ascribing responsibility, then differential liability and availability of sanctions for corporations and individuals must be examined. An examination suggests that (1) equal liability should be assessed for like offenses committed in like circumstances; (2) while different forms of sanctions (that is, any particular mode of punishment) may be rendered, the type and extent of sanction should reflect equal liability; and (3) the mix of available sanctions (the category of sanction) should be comparable for corporations and individuals in order to ensure that equal liability results in sanctions that communicate a comparable content.

Von Hirsch (1976), in elaborating on a desert theory, suggests the now commonly accepted requirement that equivalent offenses require equivalent assessment of blameworthiness or liability (Schlegel, 1990; Gross, 1979). This is an unexciting truth. But desert theory is not principally concerned with liability, whether equal or unequal. As Von Hirsch notes, the concern is with the equitable nature of allocating sanctions. Thus, in allocating sanctions, serious as well as less serious crimes merit proportionate sanctions. The requirement is a corollary of an Aristotelian principle of fairness: Similar offenses are to be treated similarly in proportion to the degree of similarity between them.

The irrelevance of personhood in corporate criminal law presents problems concerning the equitable nature of liability and sanctions. Our focus here, like that of desert theorists, is on the latter. We are concerned with the specific question, To what extent is an inequitable disparity justified in the mix of sanctions available to corporations and individuals?

The question is important because punishment is a symbolic expression of condemnation and blame (Feinberg, 1965; Mac-Cormick, 1982). As H. M. Hart (1958) has noted: "What distinguishes a criminal from a civil sanction and all that distinguishes it, it is ventured, is the judgment of community condemnation which accompanies . . . its imposition" (p. 404). Thus, the possibility of a sanction to exact punishment, rather than serve as a mere penalty, depends upon it communicating condemnation. One concern is that an inequitable disparity in the mix of sanctions may be such that a truncated selection of sanctions for corporations fails to express the attitudes of indignation and condemnation necessary for criminal punishment. In other words, a truncated selection of sanctions may be seen by a corporate offender, for example, merely as an imposition of penalties. Feinberg (1965) has characterized penalties as "price tags attached to certain types of behavior that are generally undesirable, so that only those with especially strong motivation will be willing to pay the price" (p. 27). Many commentators view the imposition of fines on corporations as often nothing more than a price of doing business (compare Elkins, 1976; Coffee, 1977, 1980; Fisse, 1983).

A second concern was expressed by judges as early as the turn of the century. It is a concern grounded in a requirement that laws be uniformly applied. In articulating the permissible differences between sanctions for corporate officers and other noncorporate offenders, the Supreme Court of California held that "the effect of general laws shall be the same to and upon all persons who stand in the same relation to the law" (*Ex Parte Sohncke*, 1912). This is not to say, of course, that federal and state sentencing laws must treat individuals and corporations identically. But their communicative effect must be comparable. They must allow for the *same* communication of condemnation. This was the essence of the holding in *State v. Central Lumber* (1909), where the court ruled that the mix or classification of sanctions for corporations and individuals can be made comparable in much the same way "as there can be different punishments imposed as against different individuals, if such distinction in punishment is based upon reasonable grounds bearing relation to the crime and nature and condition of parties" (p. 513).

When is there an inequitable disparity in the mix of sanctions? When corporate and individual offenders, having committed the same offense under similar circumstances, are subject to qualitatively different "mixes of sanctions." An array of available forms of punishments constitutes a mix of sanctions. Mixes of sanctions are qualitatively different when they differ as to their communicative content. The qualitative difference concerns the "semantic value" of harsh treatment. If judges must by necessity give priority to one sanction over another, then there may be inequitable disparity. In the limiting case, inequitable disparities may be such that prices, not sanctions, are being assessed. Harsh treatment then may lose its character as a *sanction*.

Virtually all federal statutes, including those prohibiting mail fraud, antitrust violations, securities violations, and tax evasion, have separate sentencing provisions for individual and corporate violators (see, for example, Clinard and Yeager, 1980). Following the passage of the Sentencing Reform Act of 1984 (SRA), individuals may receive fines, probation, or imprisonment. Judges may sentence corporations to probation or assess a fine. Imprisonment is not an available sanction for corporations. Individuals and corporations both may be subject to forfeiture, restitution, and notice to victims. Hence, the SRA includes different forms of punishment for individuals and corporations.

What practical effect does this have on two similarly situated offenders, one corporate and one individual? Consider that the Sherman Act, which prohibits monopolies, contracts, or conspiracies in restraint of trade, provides the following sanctions for individuals: imprisonment for not more than three years or fines of not more than $100,000. The penalties for corporations are fines of not more than $1,000,000. In order to provide judges with greater flexibility in condemning acts committed by corporations, we will consider the wisdom of fashioning organizational sanctions that will serve as proxies for the individual sanctions of imprisonment.

It is critical to note here that these proxies are not intended to promote sentencing based upon an incapacitative theory of punishment. At least, no more so than imprisonment of individuals promotes incapacitative theory. The most recent U.S. Sentencing

Commission Draft Guidelines for the Sentencing of Organizations (November 1990) offers four penal theories in support of punishment: just punishment, deterrence, protection of the public, and rehabilitation. These are identical to the goals set for sentencing individuals. Incapacitative sanctions, or sanctions designed to restrain organizational offenders, may serve any one of these goals. Sanctions effectuating these goals must satisfy two constraints: their mix must not be such that they lose their character *as* sanctions, and they must be equitably applied. Corporate imprisonment as an element in the mix of sanctions satisfies both constraints.

Corporate Imprisonment

The idea that corporations should be on equal footing with respect to liability and allocation of sanctions is certainly not new. Nearly eighty years ago, Richberg (1912) asked the question "Should it not be the effort of all legislation dealing with corporations, to place them in as nearly as possible on a plane of equal responsibility with individuals, subject to similar legal restraints and punishments?" (p. 512). Richberg posed this question toward the end of a proposal for an innovation in corporate sanctions—the imprisonment of a criminal corporation. He advocated placing corporations sentenced to a term of imprisonment in the control of marshal receivers (as compared to civil receivers). While in the custody of these federal surrogates, corporate illegality would be confined, exposed, and cured. Portions of the profits derived from the corporation during the period of incapacitation could be given to the state.

Richberg justified his proposal by claiming that the publicity surrounding the disclosures of illegality, as well as the disclosures themselves, would serve a purpose. The public would be well informed as to the nature and extent of the offense, and the corporation would suffer a penalty from the public disclosure. He further argued that receivership would allow for speedy investigations. Finally, as stated earlier, Richberg considered the question of equity. In effect, he asked whether there is an acceptable mix of sanctions as between individuals and corporations.

It is fair to say that Richberg's call for reform has so far failed.

Over the last eighty years, legal commentators, legislators, as well as judges have rejected the notion that corporations may be subjected to government-sanctioned restraint (Gruner, 1988). In 1973, Congress and the Senate considered corporate "quarantine" in early versions of the Crime Control Act (S. 1400, sec. 1–441 [c]). If it had survived, this sanction would have given courts the discretion to suspend a convicted corporation's right to engage in interstate or foreign commerce. The length of suspension would approximate a term of imprisonment for a similarly situated individual offender. Corporate quarantine has been labeled "draconian" and far less preferable to fines or limited adverse publicity (Comment, 1979). Moreover, there is a concern about externalities associated with sanctions (Comment, 1990a). To what extent would employees, the community, and innocent customers or lenders suffer during a period of quarantine? Rush (1986) adds to this list, suggesting that stock prices may plummet, consumers deprived of products and services, judgment creditors forced to receive little at bankruptcy proceedings, and quarantine sanctions an "administrative nightmare" to oversee.

Courts have uniformly agreed with these commentators, often citing the presence of externalities and sometimes assuming that corporations cannot be imprisoned because they cannot be incarcerated in a correctional facility. (Melrose Distillers, Inc. v. U.S., 1958, 1959; compare Comment 1979, p. 1365). This was so until only recently when a U.S. District Court revisited Richberg's proposal. In 1988, Judge Daumar of the Eastern District of Virginia ruled that a corporation could be imprisoned for violations of the Sherman Act (U.S. v. Allegheny Bottling Co., 1988b). Here the court heard evidence of a conspiracy between the Mid-Atlantic Coca-Cola Bottling Company and the Allegheny (Pepsi-Cola) Bottling Company, initiated by the chairman of the board of directors, and the president and executive vice president of Allegheny, to engage in price fixing in Baltimore, Norfolk, and Richmond. Prior to the conspiracy, these bottling companies were engaged in intense competition. In 1982 both companies agreed to set identical, inflated prices on Coca-Cola and Pepsi-Cola products. Profits from the price-fixing were estimated at over $1 million.

In sentencing the Allegheny Bottling Company to three years imprisonment, simultaneously suspended, and a fine of $1 million, Judge Daumar stated that "the key to corporate imprisonment is this: imprisonment simply means restraint" (p. 860). Thus, corporate imprisonment, the judge reasoned, has an analogue in the tort of false imprisonment. Proof of false imprisonment does not require a showing of incarceration, but merely the express or implied use of force in the restraint of a person's liberty. This could be accomplished, according to Daumar, by placing the convicted corporation in the custody of the United States Marshal. Such custody could result in the seizure of physical assets or the creation of restrictions which would otherwise deprive the corporation of its liberty. Upon contacting the U.S. Marshal, Daumar reported that closure of a corporation's physical plant, limiting employee movement, or restricting sales were all available forms of imprisonment.

After the sentencing opinion was issued on September 8, 1988, the Antitrust Division of the U.S. Department of Justice decided that it could not defend the imprisonment sanction. The Division corresponded with Judge Daumar. It claimed that the sentence of imprisonment was unlawful and that the effect of having a marshal seize assets or limit operations "could adversely affect competition and further injure consumers" (*U.S. v. Allegheny Bottling Co.*, 1988b, p. 59,967). Judge Daumar responded that imprisonment of a corporation need not parallel individual imprisonment in every respect. Moreover, corporate imprisonment cannot be dismissed merely because it results in costs and adverse consequences. The court concluded that the sentence of corporate imprisonment "derives from the basic principle that, to the extent possible, the law treats all persons—whether natural or corporate—equally. Any other treatment would belie that basic principle and create a special class of persons which this court is unwilling to foster" (p. 59,986).

On January 11, 1989, the Fourth Circuit of the United States Court of Appeals vacated the District Court's sentence. It held that the sentence was a "nullity" because the District Court exceeded its statutory powers in its selection of sanction (*U.S. v. Harford*, 1989). The scope of the holding by the Court of Appeals is worth emphasizing. Its holding was based on the finding that the Sherman Antitrust Act contained no sanction of corporate imprisonment. Given the finding, and the constraint that there are statutory limitations on a court's power to select sanctions, the Court concluded that a sentence of corporate imprisonment was a "nullity." The *Harford* court's holding therefore should be construed narrowly: as prohibiting a sanction of corporate imprisonment for violation of the Sherman Antitrust Act and not as denying the possibility of corporate imprisonment. Accordingly, the Court's denial of the possibility of corporate imprisonment is dicta (p. 59,986). Hence the *Harford* court's holding should not be treated as a dismissal of the possibility or appropriateness of the sanction.

As stated earlier, we have not maintained that forms of sanctions must be identical. Rather, in order to ensure that comparable messages of wrongfulness and condemnation are expressed, comparable mixes of sanctions should be available. This may be assured by considering a corporate analogue to individual imprisonment in the form of a series of incapacitative interventions, some of which have already been delivered as a condition of probation (Gruner, 1988; Rush, 1986). Such interventions would have one objective: providing judges with an additional series of sanctions so that they may approximate the message of condemnation visited upon individual offenders.

Braithwaite and Geis (1982) note many strengths of incapacitative strategies in order to control corporate crime. In fact, they claim that incapacitation is a far more practical strategy for corporate-crime control than individual-crime control. Its strength lies in a corporation's dependence on maintaining legitimacy within a particular market or economic sector. And, as we will see below, incapacitative sanctions are plentiful, ranging from the most invasive (charter incapacitation) to the least invasive (transactional incapacitation).

Corporate Incapacitation through Probation Conditions

In enacting the SRA, Congress did little to differentiate between corporate and individual offenders. While we await the delivery to Congress of the final guidelines for organizations from the U.S. Sentencing Commission, existing provisions of the SRA must suffice. Section 3563 delineates mandatory as well as discretionary probation conditions. The former include fines, restitution, and community service. The latter consist of a collection of twenty additional conditions that place restrictions on a probationer's freedom, such as reporting to a probation officer, submitting to visitation, and remaining within a particular jurisdiction. Two discretionary conditions, Section 3563(b)(6) and (b)(20) are critically important for the purposes of corporate sanctions. These require that a defendant

> refrain, in the case of an individual, from engaging in a specified occupation, business, or profession bearing a reasonably direct relationship to the conduct constituting the offense, or engage in such a specified occupation, business, or profession only to a stated degree or under stated circumstances (18 U.S.C. sec. 3563[b][6]); satisfy such other conditions as the court may impose (U.S.C. sec. 3563 (b)(20).

Paragraph 6 is important because of its legislative history. When this paragraph was passed by the Senate (Ninety-fifth Congress) as Sec. 1437, it was cast in terms of individuals *and* organizations. Thus, courts were to have the leeway to sentence organizations to refrain from engaging in a particular occupation, business, or profession related to the conduct underlying the offense. What happened subsequently leaves the current law obscure. According to the Senate Report of the Committee on the Judiciary accompanying Sec. 1762:

> Because of business concerns that the listing of the conditions might encourage inappropriate use to put a legitimate enterprise out of business, that part of the provision has been modified to relate only to individual offenders. This deletion should not be construed to preclude the imposition of appropriate conditions designed to stop the continuation of a fraudulent business in the unusual case in which a business enterprise consistently operates outside the law. (S. Rep. No. 98-225, p. 97)

Thus, under paragraph 6 and the "catchall" provision of paragraph 20, sentencing judges may exercise their discretion in crafting incapacitative conditions, where necessary, to stop corporate offenders. Notably, the U.S. Sentencing Commission Proposed Guidelines also allow the possibility of judicial innovations in conditions. Under Sec. 8D1.3(b), the commission permits judges to "tailor" conditions so that they "(1) are reasonably related to the nature and circumstances of the offense, the history and characteristics of the defendant, and the purposes of sentencing; and (2) involve only such deprivations of liberty or property as are reasonably necessary to effect the purposes of sentencing."

Given the variety of circumstances presented to sentencing judges, a group of alternative incapacitative sanctions should be considered. This would provide a range of invasive conditions that could mirror, as much as possible, the range of terms of imprisonment for individuals. Six categories of incapacitative sanctions can be identified. The sanctions, imposed in the form of probation conditions, present a wide range of alternatives for a sentencing judge. They are

1. *Charter Incapacitation* (CI): In its least invasive form, CI may limit a corporation's charter for a specified term in order to control illegal business dealings. In its most invasive form, CI may require the termination of corporate existence, after a specified term of winding down, through the involuntary revocation of the offending corporation's charter.

2. *Operational Incapacitation* (OI): OI bars a corporation, by way of court order, from engaging in intrastate, interstate, or foreign commerce for a specified term.

3. *Registration/Certification Incapacitation* (RCI): RCI withdraws, for a specified term, that registration, licensure, or certification necessary to engage in business.

4. *Receivership Incapacitation* (RI): RI places the operation of a corporation under the supervision of a marshal.

5. *Transactional Incapacitation* (TI): TI bars a corporation from (a) engaging in a specific line of business, (b) engaging in business within a specified geographic area, or (c) engaging in business with a particular third party.

6. *Divestiture Incapacitation* (DI): DI requires the sale of that portion, division, or subsidiary of a corporation that has been identified as chronically offending.

Consider briefly each of these forms, with the exception of RI, which was discussed earlier. The most invasive incapacitative sanction available to state court judges is corporate dissolution, a descendant of the common law remedy of quo warranto (Note, 1927). An order of dissolution simply terminates a corporation's existence by demanding the forfeiture of the state-granted charter. Following widespread adoption of the Model Business Corporation Act (1969), virtually all states have provisions regarding voluntary and involuntary dissolution of corporate charters. The model provisions call for the involuntary dissolution in cases where the corporation (a) fails to file franchise taxes or annual reports, (b) procures its articles of incorporation through fraud, (c) continues to exceed or abuse the authority conferred upon it by law, or (d) fails to appoint and maintain a registered agent, or notify the secretary of state as to changes in such agent (section 94). Of obvious relevance here is (c), the involuntary dissolution proceeding brought against a corporation for exceeding or abusing its authority under law (Comment, 1968; Note, 1927).

CI is a variant of corporate dissolution but, contrary to suggestions of many commentators, does not really amount to a corporate death penalty (compare Braithwaite and Geis, 1982). Clearly, one of the most significant limitations of this sanction is the possibility that corporate "death" will be temporary, that is, the dissolved corporation will emerge in a sister jurisdiction. Moreover, our conceptualization of CI includes lesser forms whereby a corporate charter could be altered to ensure against the continuation of certain kinds of business activity (compare *State v. Abbott Maintenance Corp*, 1960). The effects from this lesser form approach those derived from Transactional Incapacitation (TI).

It is of some note that the Model Penal Code (section 6.04 [2][a][i–ii]) also allows for forfeiture of charter, upon a finding

> that the board of directors or a high managerial agent acting in behalf of the corporation has, in conducting the corporation's affairs, purposely engaged in a persistent course of criminal conduct and that for the prevention of future criminal conduct of the same character, the public interest requires the charter of the corporation to be forfeited and the corporation to be dissolved or the certificate to be revoked.

The proceedings of the American Law Institute clearly indicate that dissolution is seen as a penalty reserved for persistent misconduct, which is in fact the conscious objective of a high managerial agent or board of directors (ALI Proceedings, 1956, pp. 170–207). In commentary, the Institute justifies dissolution by making reference to the incapacitative consequences of long-term incarceration for habitual offenders. "As in the case of extended terms for individuals, the main justification for sanctions of extraordinary severity is their relation to public protection from the kind of criminal activity that has characterized the offender's conduct in the past" (Model Penal Code, 1985, section 6.04, comment [2]). Chronically offending corporations or corporations that exist solely to engage in crime appear likely candidates for this sanction. Of course, the Institute readily admits that given the severity of dissolution, it will be used sparingly.

OI bars a corporation from operating over a specified period of time. During this time the corporation is either shut down entirely or one particular division, office, or store is restrained from operating as a business. OI approximates the court-ordered injunction of a business operation. Courts are often called upon to enjoin ongoing criminal activity in corporations, where such activity constitutes a public nuisance. While the purpose of these injunctions is to inhibit ongoing criminal activity where irreparable harm may result, the effect is an incapacitation of business operations, for example, *Ritholz v. Arkansas State Board of Optometry* (practice of optometry); *Craven v. Fifth Ward Republican Club* (1958) (sale of alcohol); *Boykin v. Ball Investment Company* (1940) (loans). Unlike all forms of CI, OI is subject to fixed terms.

RCI allows courts to incapacitate a corporation by removing that certification, license, or registration necessary for the day-to-day operation of business. An example of RCI may be seen in *Toscony Provision Company, Inc. v. Block* (1982). In this case, a U.S. District Court upheld the U.S. secretary of agriculture's decision to withdraw a grant of federal meat inspection services to Toscony, because its president and major stockholder were "unfit" to conduct business as a result of their conviction for distributing adulterated sausage meat. Under federal law, Toscony Provision Company could not operate without these inspection services.

TI allows judges to restrain specific corporate activities, such as certain lines of business, business conducted within specified geographic areas, and business conducted with particular third parties. In *U.S. v. Nu-Triumph, Inc.* (1974), the U.S. Court of Appeals for the Ninth Circuit upheld an excellent approximation of TI, imposed as a condition of probation. Nu-Triumph, which had been convicted of mailing obscene material, was required to pay a fine of $5,000 and, by the terms of probation, not distribute pornographic material. The Court of Appeals reasoned that "the challenged condition of probation is not a general proscription of conduct on the part of the general public, but on the contrary, a proscription of specific future conduct on the part of the Corporation" (p. 595). TI sanctions should include only specific business transactions.

DI is modeled on divestiture, perhaps the most important and effective of all remedies for Sherman Act violations (see *California v. American Stores, Inc.*, 1990). DI gives judges the ability to sever that portion, division, or subsidiary of a corporation that has been identified as chronically offending. The sentencing judge will have discretion as to the distribution of the proceeds of the sale. Unlike the other incapacitative sanctions discussed above (with the exception of CI), DI allows for an exact and permanent incapacitation of one or more "components" of an offending corporation.

These six incapacitative sanctions provide a reasonable proxy for individual imprisonment. It has been argued that similar proposals for corporate "death," "imprisonment," and "incapacitation" are simply promoting economic penalties (Comment, 1985). True, these incapacitative sanctions exact costs, but not only financial costs. Each sanction expresses condemnation by empowering the government to seize control over an aspect of the corporate person, whether it is the charter, the day-to-day operations, the certification, or chronically offending subsidiaries. Beyond the economic costs, this conveys a message of wrongdoing that is made effective by various forms of deprivation (Morris, 1981).

Externalities

Concerns about negative externalities induced by corporate sanctions are legendary. Uncompensated costs imposed on third parties provide the most serious consideration against proposals for commensurate sanctions for organizations. We agree with Braithwaite and Geis (1982) that very little stands in the way of a greater acceptance of incapacitative sanctions for organizations. They claim that "all that is required is for legislatures, courts, and regulatory agencies to apply [incapacitative strategies] creatively, to overcome the conservatism that leaves them clinging to failed remedies carried over from traditional crimes" (Braithwaite and Geis, 1982, p. 308). But it is more than just conservatism that leads to exaggerated fears of judicial oversight, intervention, and overreaching. At stake, too, is the prospect of a variety of social costs associated with imposing corporate incapacitative sanctions.

We acknowledge the importance of determining the size of negative externalities produced by imposing incapacitative sanctions. The possibility of significant externalities should not be ignored. Still, the concern in part rests on two misconceptions about the prosecution of corporate offenders, both individual and organizational. One misconception relies on an unsound assumption about prevalent prosecutorial practice. Obviously, a focus on harm to innocent employees, shareholders, and other stakeholders must take into account the nature of those organizations actually prosecuted at both a state and a federal level. The image of federal prosecutors tackling one of the six hundred corporate giants studied by Clinard and Yeager (1980) is a distorted one. Table 1 presents selected characteristics of all organizational defendants sentenced in the calendar year of 1988. It suggests that nearly all corporations prosecuted by the federal government are privately held. Further, the median number of persons employed by these firms (39.5) indicates that most of the corporations prosecuted are of small to medium size. This is made more apparent by the low median net worth of the prosecuted organizations ($154,997). The data support the conclusion that the externalities typically attributed to invasive sanctions may be less significant than previously suspected.

A second misconception results from considering only the absolute size of the social costs of invasive organizational sanctions. In considering the absolute size of these costs alone, their magnitude may be overestimated. Externalities are more appropriately assessed by relative comparison. After all, all sanctions, whether imposed on individuals or corporations, induce negative externalities. The question is which sanction reduces the externalities associated with punishment more than other sanctions. Hence, given that sanctions are to be imposed on a corporation, the relative size of externalities is relevant when invasive organizational sanctions are imposed. An estimation is required of the size of externalities produced by imposing incapacitative sanctions as compared with

TABLE 1 · Characteristics of all organizational defendants sentenced in the calendar year of 1988

SAMPLE SIZE

N = 328

OWNERSHIP STRUCTURE (%)

Privately held	92.7
Publicly held	5.8
Nonprofit	.6
Unknown or not coded	.9

NUMBER OF OWNERS

Median	1.0
Mean	6.4

NUMBER OF EMPLOYEES

Median	39.5
Mean	212.3

ANNUAL REVENUES ($)

Median	3,185,065
Mean	76,461,766

NET WORTH (EQUITY) ($)

Median	154,997
Mean	12,309,782

Source: U.S. Sentencing Commission, *Organizations Convicted in Federal Criminal Courts, 1988*. Unpublished staff working document, November 15, 1990.

the size of externalities produced by imposing other types of sanctions. The estimation must take into account how reputational losses incurred by an offender can reduce the uncompensated cost of an offense.

We believe that such an estimation would not find the size of externalities always to be greater in the case of organizational offenders. This is because there exist market and nonmarket mechanisms, both at the individual and organizational level, that operate to internalize the social cost of crime. White-collar offenders generally are employed at the time of the commission of their offenses, well educated, and from the middle class (Wheeler, Weisburd, Waring, and Bode, 1988; Weisburd, Wheeler, Waring, and Bode, 1991). These offenders fear imprisonment for reasons relating to a loss of reputation (Clinard and Yeagar, 1980). Abstractly put, reputation represents an expected stream of profits from performing a given activity or selling a given product (compare Klein and Leffler, 1981). Because conviction either makes performance of an activity impossible or reduces demand for its performance, white-collar offenders suffer a loss in reputation. That loss is a cost to the offender. Included within the loss is part of the social cost of an offense. Incapacitative sanctions provide information to third parties about the quality of an offender's reputation. Such sanctions form a piece of a mechanism by which offenders internalize the social cost of their offenses.

A similar mechanism may operate in the case of organizations. Convicted corporations can suffer a loss in reputation. As a result, consumers and other corporations may pay less for the convicted corporation's products. Reduced prices realized is a cost to the convicted firm. A recent study found that reporting a criminal fraud diminishes the reported firm's market value in excess of one hundred times the loss incurred by victims of the fraud (Karpoff and Lott, 1991; compare Fisse, 1983a). The size of the diminution is far in excess of the expected legal sanction upon conviction, and plausibly includes the expected cost of fraud to the reported firm. Incapacitative sanctions provide information to third parties about the loss of reputation to a convicted firm. Given the information incapacitative sanctions provide, firms treat a loss in reputation as a cost. As in the case of the individual offender, such sanctions facilitate the internalization of social costs by the corporate offender's offense. Incapacitative sanctions therefore need not always induce more externalities than other types of sanction.

Conclusion

It is ironic that the Sentencing Reform Act was designed, at least in part, to address disparity in the sentencing of federal offenders.

Concerns were expressed over the disparity in sentence length and sentence type for similarly situated defendants (S. Rep. No. 98–225, p. 41). To add to the irony, the Senate Committee on the Judiciary expressed additional concern over the limited availability of sentencing options. In fact, the Senate report describing the SRA noted that "[c]urrent law is not particularly flexible in providing the sentencing judge with a range of options from which to fashion an appropriate sentence. The result is that a term of imprisonment may be imposed in some cases in which it would not be imposed if better alternatives were available" (S. Rep. No. 98–225, p. 50). We submit that the result is that a term of imprisonment may not be imposed for organizations even though it may be one of the better alternatives available. At stake is not only the equitable imposition of sanctions. Also important is the retention of harsh treatment as sanctions, not simply as prices attached to corporate misconduct.

REFERENCES

Alchian, A. A., and Demsetz, H. (1972). Production, information costs, and economic organization. *American Economic Review, 56,* 777–795.

Boykin v. Ball Investment Company (1940). 12 S.E. 574, 191 Ga. 382.

Bernard, T. (1984). The historical development of corporate criminal liability. *Criminology, 22,* 3–17.

Braithwaite, J., and Fisse, B. (1990). On the plausibility of corporate crime theory. In W. S. Laufer and F. Adler, eds. *Advances in criminological theory.* New Brunswick, N.J.: Transaction Books.

Braithwaite, J., and Geis, G. (1982). Theory and action for corporate crime control. *Crime and Delinquency, 28,* 304–314.

Brickey, K. F. (1984). *Corporate criminal liability.* Deerfield, Ill.: Callaghan & Co.

California v. American Stores, Inc. (1990). 495 U.S. 271, 1853, 110 S. Ct. 1853.

Clinard, M. B., and Yeager, P. C. (1980). *Corporate crime.* New York: Free Press.

Coffee, J. C. (1977). Beyond the shut-eyed sentry: Toward a theoretical view of corporate misconduct and an effective legal response. *Virginia Law Review, 63,* 1099–1278.

———. (1980). Making the punishment fit the corporation: The problem of finding the optimal corporate criminal sanction. *Northern Illinois University Law Review, 1,* 3–36.

Comment (1978). Criminal sanctions for corporate illegality. *Journal of Criminal Law & Criminology, 69,* 40–58.

——. (1979). Developments in the law, corporate crime: Regulating corporate behavior through criminal sanctions. *Harvard Law Review, 92,* 1227–1375.

——. (1985). Criminal sentences for corporations: Alternative fining mechanism. *California Law Review, 73,* 443–482.

——. (1990). Corporate criminal intent: Toward a better understanding of corporate misconduct. *California Law Review, 78,* 1287–1311.

——. (1990a). Criminal liability for corporations that kill. *Tulane Law Review, 64,* 919–948.

Craven v. Fifth Ward Republican Club (1958). 146 A.2d 400, 37 Del. Ch. 524.

Cressey, D. R. (1989). The poverty of theory in corporate crime research. In W. S. Laufer and F. Adler, eds. *Advances in criminological theory.* New Brunswick, N.J.: Transaction Books.

Cyert, R. M., and March, J. G. (1963). *A behavioral theory of the firm.* Englewood Cliffs, N.J.: Prentice-Hall.

Cyert, R. M., and Hedrick, C. L. (1972). Theory of the firm: Past, present and future: An interpretation. *Journal of Economic Literature, 10,* 398–412.

Darlington v. The Mayor (1865). 31 N.Y. 164.

DeGeorge, R. (1985). Corporations and morality. In H. Curtler, ed. *Shame, responsibility and the corporation.* New York: Haven Publications.

Donaldson, T. (1982). *Corporations and morality.* Englewood Cliffs, N.J.: Prentice-Hall.

Easterbrook, F. H. (1984). Two agency cost explanations of dividends. *American Economic Review, 68,* 650–658.

Elkins, J. R. (1976). Corporations and the criminal law: An uneasy alliance. *Kentucky Law Journal, 65,* 73–129.

Ex Parte Sohncke, 148 Cal. 262 (1912).

Fama, E. (1980). Agency problems and the theory of the firm. *Journal of Political Economy, 88,* 288–307.

Feinberg, J. (1965). The expressive function of punishment. *The Monist, 49,* 397–408.

——. (1985). *The moral limits of the criminal law: Harmless wrongdoing.* New York: Oxford University Press.

Fisse, B. (1983). Reconstructing corporate criminal law: Deterrence, retribution, fault, and sanctions. *University of Southern California Law Review, 56,* 1141–1246.

——. (1983a). *The impact of publicity on corporate offenders.* Buffalo: State University of New York Press.

French, P. (1979). The corporation as a moral person. *American Philosophical Quarterly, 3*, 207–215.

———. (1984). *Collective and corporate responsibility.* New York: Columbia University Press.

Gross, H. (1979). *A theory of criminal justice.* New York: Oxford University Press.

Gruner, R. (1988). To let the punishment fit the organization: Sanctioning corporate offenders through corporate probation. *American Journal of Criminal Law, 16*, 1–106.

Hart, H. M. (1958). The aims of the criminal law. *Law and Contemporary Problems, 23*, 1–24.

Held, V. (1986). Corporations, persons and responsibility. In H. Curtler, ed. *Shame, responsibility and the corporation.* New York: Haven Publications.

Hoffman, W. M. (1986). Developing the ethical corporation. *Bell Atlantic Quarterly, 3*, 1–10.

Jensen, M., and Meckling, W. (1976). Theory of the firm: Managerial behavior, agency costs and ownership structure. *Journal of Financial Economics, 3*, 305–360.

Karpoff, J., and Lott, J. (1990). The reputational penalty firms bear from committing criminal fraud. The Wharton School, University of Pennsylvania Working Paper, June 1990.

Klein, B., and Leffler, K. (1981). The role of market forces in assuring contractual performance. *Journal of Political Economy, 89*, 615–641.

Ladd, J. (1970). Morality and the ideal of rationality in formal organizations. *The Monist, 54*, 338–516.

———. (1986). Persons and responsibility: Ethical concepts and impertinent analyses. In H. Curtler, ed., *Shame, responsibility and the corporation.* New York: Haven Publications.

MacCormick, N. (1982). *Legal right in social democracy.* New York: Oxford University Press.

Manning, R. C. (1984) Corporate responsibility and corporate personhood. *Journal of Business Ethics, 3*, 77–84.

Melrose Distillers, Inc. v. U.S. (1959). 359 U.S. 271.

Model Business Corporation Act Annotated (1969). Chicago: American Bar Association and West Publishing Company.

Model Penal Code (1962). Proposed official draft. Philadelphia: American Law Institute.

Morris, H. (1981). A paternalistic theory of punishment. *American Philosophical Quarterly, 18*, 263–271.

Mueller, G. O. W. (1957). Mens rea and the corporation. *University of Pittsburgh Law Review, 19*, 21–51.

Note (1968): Corporate dissolution for illegal, oppressive or fraudulent acts: The Maryland solution. *Maryland Law Review, 28*, 360–371.

———. (1927): Quo Warranto: Forfeiture of franchise on account of crime. *Cornell Law Quarterly, 13*, 92–99.

Ozar, D. T. (1985). Do corporations have moral rights? *Journal of Business Ethics, 4*, 277–281.

Proceedings of the 33rd Annual Meeting of the American Law Institute (1956). Philadelphia: The American Law Institute.

Richberg, D. R. (1912). The imprisonment of the corporation. *Case and Comment, 18*, 527–529.

Ritholz v. Arkansas State Board of Optometry (1944). 177 S.W.2d 410, 206 Ark. 671.

Rush, F. L. (1986). Corporate probation: Invasive techniques for restructuring institutional behavior. *Suffolk University Law Review, 21*, 33–89.

Schlegel, K. (1990). *Just deserts for corporate criminals.* Boston: Northeastern University Press.

Senate Report No. 98-225, 98th Congress, 2d session (1984).

Sentencing Reform Act of 1984, Pub. L. No. 98-473, 98 Stat. 1987 (1984) (codified as amended at 18 U.S.C. §3551 *et seq.* [1990]).

State v. Central Lumber (1909). 24 S.D. 136, 155 N.W. 504.

State v. Abbott Maintenance Corporation (1961). 215 N.Y.S.2d 761, 175 N.E.2d 341.

Toscony Provision Company, Inc. v. Block (1982). 538 F.Supp. 318.

U.S. v. Allegheny Bottling Company (1988a). 1988–2 Trade Cases, pp. 68, 350.

———. (1988b). 1988–2 Trade Cases, pp. 59, 967.

U.S. v. Harford (1989). 1989–2 Trade Cases, pp. 68, 386.

U.S. v. Nu-Triumph, Inc. (1974). 500 F.2d 504.

United States Sentencing Commission (1990). Draft guidelines for the Sentencing of Corporations. Chapter 8. November 1990.

Von Hirsch, A. (1976). *Doing justice: The choice of punishments.* New York: Hill & Wang.

Walt, S., and Laufer, W. S. (1991). Why personhood doesn't matter: Corporate criminal liability and sanctions. *American Journal of Criminal Law, 18*, 263–287.

Weisburd, D., Wheeler, S., Waring, E., and Bode, N. (1991). *Crimes of the middle classes: White-collar offenders in the federal courts.* New Haven: Yale University Press.

Wheeler, S., Weisburd, D., Waring, E., and Bode, N. (1988). White collar crimes and criminals. *American Criminal Law Review, 25*, 331–357.

Winter, S. (1986). Competition, costs and the corporation. *Journal of Law and Economic Organization, 3*, 34–48.

Wolf, S. (1985). The legal and moral responsibility of organizations. In R. Pennock and J. Chapman eds. *Nomos XVII: Criminal Justice.* New York: New York University Press.

Zimmerman, M. (1988). *An essay on moral responsibility.* Totawa, N.J.: Rowman & Allanheld.

NOTE

We are grateful to Keith Muller for helpful comments on an earlier draft of this essay.

· 14 ·

Procedure Rules and Information Control

Gaining Leverage over White-Collar Crime

KENNETH MANN

In 1893 an American judge made the following observations about a civil case argued before him:

> While civil in form, all its other characteristics were those of a criminal case; its prosecutor was the government; its purpose was punishment; the defendant's conviction of a felony was essential to the plaintiff's recovery; the defendant's character and property were in jeopardy because the government sought to punish him in this suit; and the verdict and judgment here would be a bar to any criminal prosecution for the same offense. The case became a criminal case under the cloak of a civil suit. (*U.S. v. Shapleigh*, 1893)

This statement reflects a long-standing fundamental norm of Anglo-American legal process: legal sanctions historically have been divided into two categories, one labeled "criminal law," the other "civil law."[1] But it also hints at a parallel phenomenon: there are "mixed cases" in which legislatures have combined characteristics of the criminal and civil law in the same sanctions.

A frequent form of mixed sanctions is what I will call the "punitive civil sanction." A punitive civil sanction is imposed on behavior conventionally defined as a criminal offense (intentional behavior causing injury to a public interest), in the framework of typically civil procedures, and the sanction is a money payment that

· 332

is more than compensatory of the actual damage caused. In this sense punitive civil sanctions are hybrids, combining elements that are, on the one hand, typical of criminal law and, on the other, typical of civil law. The Federal False Claims Act includes an exemplary punitive civil sanction, providing a civil procedure for imposing a penalty of up to three times the damage caused, plus a fine of $10,000 for every false claim on the government. In a recent case, a medical prescriber was given a civil penalty of $130,000 for sixty-five small false claims amounting altogether to about $500.

The persistence of both the dominant model of sanctions (entailing an archetype dychotomy between civil and criminal) and mixed forms deviating from that model was a central issue in the work of Sutherland. In his treatise on white-collar crime, Sutherland argued for including certain kinds of civil cases in the criminal category because the underlying behavior and damage to society were essentially identical to those in criminal cases. In his survey of crimes of major businesses in the United States he counted sanctions by civil courts and administrative agencies, as well as criminal prosecutions. Criticism of this view focused on the "important differences" between criminal sanctions, particularly imprisonment, and stigma- and civil sanctions, which are largely monetary.

In this chapter I will discuss procedural aspects of the use of punitive civil sanctions in punishing and deterring what we have commonly come to think of as white-collar crime. From this perspective, the question of whether Sutherland was right in labeling corporations as well as managers and owners of corporations as criminals when they were subject to administrative and other civil sanctions is largely irrelevant. The question posed here is whether the civil, procedural framework is properly suited for discovering and bringing to the sanctioning forum evidence that is a necessary precondition for the meting out of sanctions. This question is important not only for those who are interested in the theory and practice of social control and the effectiveness of sanctions, but also for those who are interested in studying white-collar crime.[2]

The Relationship Between Procedure and Sanction

To grasp the relationship between procedure and sanction effectiveness, procedure must be defined independently of the nature of the behavior sanctioned and the nature of the remedy imposed at the end of the process. Procedure sets the rules of decision making that determine whether a sanction should be applied in a particular instance. The capacity of any system of law to mete out sanctions against wrongdoers depends, among other things, on its procedural characteristics. There are many variable features of procedure that effect sanctioning capacity, including, but not limited to, the nature of the party who mobilizes the authoritative institution (state or private party), the number of parties who can be joined together in one action (individuals or classes of individuals), the geographic spread of the authoritative institution's jurisdiction (broad or narrow), the permissible methods for subjecting parties to jurisdiction (that is, notice requirements), the means of reaching a decision on the merits (through negotiation and settlement or through judicial imposition of a decision), the period of limitations in which remedies can be sought, the finality and collateral effect of a decision to impose a remedy, the means available for obtaining access and presenting facts to the authoritative institutions (rules of investigation, discovery, and evidence), and the degree of certainty required in rendering a decision. I will focus on one dimension of procedure that is central for distinguishing civil and criminal sanctions: information rules.

Information Rules

Information rules are central to any sanctioning system because the decision to impose the sanction (except in a Kafkaesque society) depends on the presentation of facts that establish the occurrence of wrongdoing.[3] Some systems may provide for sanctions on the basis of minimal accusations only. Sanctioning systems in democratic countries generally require that a substantial amount of fact about the occurrence of prohibited behavior be provided to a decision maker before sanctions are meted out. Where facts are required, every system of legal sanctions must have rules about three critical information-related questions.[4]

First, the information rules must determine what methods of information access can be used to collect the facts. These rules define permissible means of investigation, such as when and where a search may be conducted, and they define the court's power to collect evidence, such as when a judge may compel witnesses to testify on penalty of prison. Criminal and civil process typically have different rules in respect to these questions. Criminal procedure has always been understood as allowing more intrusiveness into the individual and corporate domain, as well as the use of more power to compel testimony. These differences are best expressed in the police power of search and in-custody interrogation, and the prosecutor's power to subpoena witnesses before a grand jury.

Second, information rules must determine what sources or types of information are admissible in the decision-making process. Sanctioning systems may limit the sources of information that may be used in decision making. One system of sanctions may base its decisions on information provided by the subject of the sanction only. A different system may prohibit the use of information provided by the subject of the sanction, requiring reliance entirely on witnesses. The law of sanctions in the United States entails two different procedural contexts, in part because criminal procedure has traditionally been viewed as putting more limitations on the type of information that could be used in the decision-making process (expressed in evidentiary rules of admissibility) than in civil procedure. The self-incrimination privilege and the prohibition on character evidence are two examples of rules that were conventionally more restrictive in the criminal process than in the civil.

Third, information rules define what level of certainty is required as a prerequisite to imposition of sanctions. Variation in required certainty must be a central concern in any comparison of sanctioning systems. A sanctioning system may impose sanctions on the basis of facts that create a suspicion in the mind of a single person, or it may require that many members of a judicial body reach unanimous agreement that all exculpatory explanations of any probability are false. Criminal procedure has required more information than civil procedure, because it puts a higher value on certainty of decisions to impose sanctions than does civil procedure. This is expressed in the requirement of proof beyond a reasonable doubt . Civil procedure, requiring only a preponderance of evidence, allows a plaintiff to win a civil case while losing a criminal case based on the same evidence.

These three dimensions of information in sanctioning process— methods of access, type of admissible evidence, and degree of certainty—are shaped in different ways in civil and criminal law due to the varying weight of the public and state interest in applying criminal as compared to civil sanctions, and the varying interest in protecting the public from wrongful imposition of these sanctions. On the one hand, criminal conduct justifies greater intrusiveness in investigative procedures and heavier sanctions because of the greater injury to public interests caused by it. On the other hand, a fundamental principle of due process is the requirement of a positive correlation between the harshness of state-invoked restrictions on liberty (investigative instrusiveness, seriousness of sanction) and procedures aimed at protecting defendants from mistakes and overextension of state power. Information rules reflect this correlation by requiring special procedural protections for criminal-type investigative techniques, by restricting admissibility of evidence in criminal cases, and by requiring greater certainty in imposing criminal sanctions. Thus, the different procedural rules in the conventional forms of criminal and civil law reflect a distinctive attitude toward state power and due process (Goldstein, 1960, pp. 1180–1182).

Assuming the perspective of the party seeking to impose sanctions on wrongdoers, there are mixed information-related advantages in the two procedural settings based on a conventional definition given to their distinctive characteristics. The criminal law has had more leverage at the information-gathering stage, while the civil law has had more leverage at the decision-making stage at which information is assessed for relevancy and weight. Whether these differences give the criminal law or the civil law more leverage in sanctioning is difficult to assess. What can be said, however, is that changes in procedural rules over decades have substantially strengthened the information-related leverage of civil procedure (Ragland, 1932; Weinstein, Gleit, and Key, 1957; Millar, 1952; 8 Wigmore, sec. 1845). This has increased the value of civil procedure—from the perspective of the state or private party seeking imposition of a sanction—on the critical information-related aspects of sanctioning. When this development is combined with the increasing punitiveness of the civil remedy, the punitive civil sanction becomes increasingly effective as a tool for punishing and deterring white-collar crime.

The Role of Procedure in Expanding Use of Civil Penalties

Advantages of Criminal Procedure

The earliest differences between criminal and civil procedure were in the criminal law's use of extreme coercive methods against criminal defendants—"star chamber" practices—making its procedure fundamentally more powerful than that provided in civil proceedings. There was great dissatisfaction with these practices, spurring reforms that would eventually reduce the power of criminal investigation. During the sixteenth and seventeenth centuries, civil procedure in England involved the arrest and imprisonment of debtors upon issuance of summons in some types of civil proceedings. This was a highly coercive measure, similar to pretrial detention of criminal defendants, that could cause a defendant in a civil case to provide evidence against himself for the civil proceeding, just as pretrial detention did in criminal cases. Thus it may be that in the not-too-distant past, pretrial civil procedures were as coercive as investigative procedures in criminal cases.

In the later development of civil and criminal law there emerged clear differences between civil and criminal procedure. This is most clearly perceptible in the early period of the twentieth century, just prior to the far-reaching reforms that were to signify a fundamental change in the nature of civil discovery procedures in the United States.

It is quite well accepted that at the turn of the century civil procedure was cumbersome, formalistic, and often difficult to employ. In particular, the procedural devices for discovery of information from one's adversaries were scant and ineffective. With a few exceptions, parties in civil proceedings (including the government) were left to exhortation in order to persuade opposing parties and witnesses to cooperate before trial by handing over documents or by making pretrial statements on matters at issue. It was more likely that parties simply had to wait for trial to learn of their opponents' evidence. This was a procedural arrangement that made bringing a civil suit highly risky in respect to evidentiary questions.

Criminal procedure at this period was similar to civil procedure with respect to the parties' discovery rights after the filing of an indictment. The rule was, for the most part, that neither the defense nor the government had to provide discovery; and this meant that the government could not use discovery rules as means to further an investigation or prepare for trial. However, there were great differences between civil and criminal procedural rules with respect to information access at an earlier stage of a case, before filing. Criminal procedure provided for a wide array of prediscovery investigatory devices, while civil procedure had almost none.

The distinctive leverage of the criminal process for discovering information was, and continues to be, found in search and seizure and in grand jury and police interrogation. During the early part of this century, government investigators could use these criminal investigatory powers to search for evidence that might eventually be used in government civil enforcement suits, but the requirement of probable cause for search and seizure and for in-custody investigations meant that these information-gathering devices, if used properly, were available only in criminal cases. In criminal cases police could subject defendants to long periods of intensive questioning, drawing on a range of manipulative techniques, including what was known as the "third degree." Search and seizure as an investigatory tool in preparation for the bringing of a suit was largely in the hands of the police forces. The investigative grand jury operated at the beck and call of a prosecutor looking for evidence of criminal activity. Civil procedure had none of these investigatory devices for use against prospective defendants.[5]

Differences in leverage for getting access to information were important in establishing procedural superiority in the criminal process in obtaining statements, documents, and other kinds of potential evidence from parties and witnesses. Thus there is no question that at the early period in the history of American procedural rules, criminal procedure had a vast advantage over civil procedure in a focused investigation of a person or entity believed to have engaged in wrongful behavior. This would be a reason for choosing criminal law over civil law as legislatures considered how to increase law enforcement effectiveness. If criminal procedure and civil procedure were not greatly different in early British law, by the turn of twentieth century an important divergence in procedural rules had developed, making criminal procedure more effective at getting the information upon which imposition of a sanction was dependent.

Advantages in Civil Procedure

If the foregoing had been a complete picture of information-related characteristics of civil and criminal procedure, the informational advantage of criminal procedure would have been overwhelming. But other characteristics pushed the balance between civil and criminal in a diametrically opposed direction. These were (1) the different burden of persuasion on factual issues in criminal and civil cases, and (2) the perceived slowness and arbitrariness of the criminal process.

In criminal cases the moving party had to prove its case beyond reasonable doubt; as a general rule, in civil cases the moving party would win by delivering a mere preponderance of the evidence. This variation in evidentiary burden was central to the bifurcation between criminal and civil sanctioning. Simply put, more information would be needed in the criminal process than in the civil in order to impose sanctions. From this point of view, the civil process had a clear advantage over the criminal.

In addition to a lower evidentiary burden, the civil law was not subject to the bureaucratic vagaries of prosecutorial discretion and the difficulties inherent in persuading a grand jury to issue an indictment. Criminal procedure was definitely a more powerful tool if pushed to the extreme, but some thought that politically minded prosecutors and independent minded grand jurors often stymied needed criminal prosecutions. Criminal prosecutions were always dependent on the state bureaucracy, which could be difficult to move, whereas civil cases could be put in the hands of private parties. Private parties, on the other hand, were limited in financial resources, so the state retained an important advantage as the moving party in a case that might be expensive to litigate.

How can we compare the relative attractiveness of criminal and civil procedure, in respect to information rules, when an information advantage stemming from one facet of a procedural system may have been completely offset by information and other procedural disadvantages in another facet of the same procedural system? With greater scrutiny, we might be able to hypothesize a net advantage of one procedrual system over another on the combined questions of information access and sufficiency. If, for instance, civil procedures were completely devoid of information-gathering devices, this might make civil procedure so severely inferior to criminal procedure that the higher standard of proof in the criminal process would not matter.[6] The comparative advantage of criminal procedure would be even stronger if a plaintiff in a civil case would have to provide clear and convincing evidence, a standard of proof often said to approximate proof beyond a reasonable doubt. But any comparative conclusions would be highly suspect.

A more productive line of inquiry is found in assessing how

changes in civil and criminal procedure that came after the turn of the century provided civil procedure with substantially more information-related leverage than it had before. To state the conclusion before the facts, the reforms that occurred in civil and criminal procedure had the effect of strengthening the information access of the system of civil law, making civil procedure a better information-gathering tool than it had been. If the only advantage of civil procedure historically had been its lower burden of persuasion, it gained important information access resources through the procedural reform movements in the twentieth century, which made it more like criminal procedure. Though the criminal investigative ability would continue to be signficantly more powerful as a focused tool, the investigative arm of civil procedure became increasingly strong. This was a result of two important developments in the field of fact gathering in civil cases. One was the broad reform of the rules of civil procedure for discovery. The other was the growth in use and power of government agencies to compel disclosure of evidence in noncriminal investigations.

Convergence of Criminal and Civil Procedure

James and Hazard (1977) summarized the status of civil procedure in the nineteenth century with this critical note:

> What the nineteenth century reformers failed to see was that the old equity restrictions on discovery (which were a natural corollary of its original limited purpose) would hamstring its usefulness as a means for attaining the new and broader purposes which were beginning to be perceived. (P. 328)

The new and broader purposes emphasized the need for more and better remedies for injured parties, and greater access to facts about wrongdoing that caused injury to the public. Civil procedure was more comparable to a game of hide-and-seek, and thus inappropriate to the growing need for more effective sanctions on wrongful behavior.

Reforms in Pretrial Discovery

The major changes in American discovery were introduced with nationwide effect in the New York Code (Millar, 1952, p. 211). The important achievement of this code was to make oral deposition of parties a regular procedure (p. 206). The broadening of discovery in the States was adopted and expanded in the even more "liberal" federal rules of civil discovery. Millar reported in 1952 that the "new rules" of pretrial discovery in civil cases provided the taking by any party of the testimony of any person "by deposition upon oral examination or written interrogatories for the purpose of discovery or for use as evidence in the action or for both purposes" (p. 213). The power to obtain information in pretrial proceedings in civil cases was extended to any person with relevant knowledge, and to any relevant facts, not just facts that could be introduced in evidence. The U.S. Supreme Court, in *Hickman v. Taylor* (329 U.S. 495), emphasized the extent to which this represented a fundamental change in the principles for conducting civil litigation.

> Under prior federal practice . . . inquiry into the issues and the facts before trial was narrowly confined and was often cumbersome in method. [Under the new rules] civil trials in the federal courts no longer need be carried on in the dark. The way is now clear, consistent with recognized privileges, for the parties to obtain the fullest possible knowledge of the issues and facts before trial. (Pp. 500–501)

The advantages of discovery were thought to be several, including removing issues before trial, broadening the scope of available evidence, preventing fraud, and encouraging pretrial settlement. Each of these advantages was in fact a different facet of the increased access to information. As one commentator noted:

> Permitting the parties to use discovery devices tends to ensure that all evidence will be unearthed and that concealment of the relevant information and material will be minimized. Such full disclosure will tend both to prevent unfair surprise at trial and to reduce the number of judgments

which do not accurately reflect the actual state of the facts. (*Harvard Law Review*, p. 940)

This was also the view held by the Supreme Court. Even while limiting the new open discovery rule to protect work product, the Court proclaimed:

No longer can the time-honored cry of "fishing expedition" serve to preclude a party from inquiring into the facts underlying his opponent's case. Mutual knowledge of all the relevant facts gathered by both parties is essential to proper litigation. To that end, either party may compel the other to disgorge whatever facts he has in his possession. (329 U.S. p. 597)

There was a central assumption in these new rules that touches directly on the relationship between procedure and the aims of sanctioning systems: increased access to information under open rules of civil discovery facilitates fuller enforcement of rights. Emphasizing this change, James and Hazard (1977) wrote:

[Open discovery] makes possible the prosecution of actions (and sometimes the defense of actions) that would be impossible without discovery. With the wide-ranging discovery, it is possible to maintain an action or defense that is dependent on witnesses or documents known only to the opponent. (P. 229)

If open discovery brings into the adjudicative forum more facts about a case than restrictive discovery principles, more "wrongful behavior" will be discovered.[7] In this important sense, the opening up of civil discovery was one reason why the civil process became more attractive as a law enforcement setting than it had been in the past.[8]

Reforms in Government Civil Investigatory Powers

While the civil process was obtaining broad new information access power in the rules of discovery—applicable to both government and private parties, another change with a similar effect was limited to government investigatory powers in civil cases. Congress strengthened the bite of the process known as the civil investigative demand (CID), which provides an important indication of the expansion of government civil investigatory power (Perry and Simon, 1960; *Vanderbilt Law Review*, 1980). The use of the CID in antitrust investigations will serve as an example.

Though it was charged with law enforcement authority over antitrust violations, the civil division of the Department of Justice for many years had no authority to subpoena documents in antitrust cases. This meant that attorneys in the Department of Justice had to wait for the relevant administrative agency, the Federal Trade Commission, to take its own action. In 1961 lawmakers submitted a bill to Congress to change this situation, stating that "to enforce antitrust laws adequately on the civil side, the antitrust authorities must be able to make an adequate investigation to ascertain the facts" (House Report no. 1386, 1962). The House report criticized "ineffective" techniques for obtaining information necessary for civil enforcement. Those techniques had included (1) cooperation of the target of the investigation, which the report found unsatisfactory because "it leaves the public interest in the enforcement of the antitrust laws subject to the will of those who violate the laws"; (2) investigation through use of a grand jury subpoena, which the report found unsatisfactory because "it is an abuse of process to proceed by way of a grand jury investigation where there is no intention to bring a criminal suit"; and (3) the attorney general's statutory power to request that the FTC conduct an investigation, which the report also found unsatisfactory because "it is uncertain . . . whether the Commission has an obligation to make such investigation," and "because of the inability of the Department's attorneys to maintain control of such investigation."

As passed in 1962, the new bill gave the civil division of the Department of Justice authority to issue written, civil, investigative demands for documents, enforceable by district courts.[9] This significantly broadened the information-access powers of the Department of Justice in civil enforcement proceedings. In an important expansion of that power, the statute was later amended to allow the justice department to issue demands for information already obtained by a private litigant through civil discovery.[10]

The CID power in antitrust investigations served as a model for new powers in a broad range of enforcement areas. In 1986, for example, Congress passed an amendment to the False Claims Act giving the attorney general the power to compel production of information in all investigations of false claims on the government, using the antitrust CID as the model.[11] This greatly increased the scope of civil information collection powers held by the Department of Justice in the very large field of law enforcement, covering all false claims on government coffers.

Many federal administrative agencies had CID-type investigatory powers before the civil division of the Department of Justice obtained them.[12] Thus, when the scope of the authority of the attorney general to use CIDs was attacked in court litigation after the antitrust CID statute was enacted, the courts relied on the rationale behind administrative subpoena law to justify the expanded civil powers of the attorney general. Though the legal doctrine of administrative search could be used to justify the new CID power in the hands of the attorney general (Petition of Gold Bond Stamp Company, 221 F. pp. 391, 395–6, 8th Cir., 1963), it is important to indicate that civil administrative powers to compel production of evidence had been narrow during the early part of the century. Administrative agency access to information came only in the 1950s, marking the first inroad on the criminal law's distinctive investigative powers. In *Morton v. U.S.* (338 U.S. 632, 1950), a landmark case testing FTC authority to compel production of documents, the court reviewed the background of administrative investigative processes and said this:

> We must not disguise the fact that sometimes, especially early in the history of the federal administrative tribunal, the courts were persuaded to engraft judicial limitations upon the administrative process. The courts could not go fishing, and so it followed neither could anyone else. Administrative investigations fell before the colorful and nostalgic slogan "no fishing expeditions." It must not be forgotten that the administrative process and its agencies are relative newcomers in the field of law and that it has taken and will continue to take experience and trial and error to fit this process into our system of judicature. More recent views have been more tolerant of it than those which underlay many older decisions. (338, p. 646)

Two themes in this opinion summarize the development of civil powers for information access. First, real administrative investigative powers were new, compared to criminal powers. Only in the 1950s did administrative agencies become numerous enough and powerful enough to begin to offer an alternative to criminal investigation. Second, courts initially gave these new powers a narrow interpretation, restricting authority to compel production of information in civil investigative proceedings. Later this picture changed substantially. In *Morton v. U.S.*, the court set the new tone, providing an expansive interpretation of administrative powers:

> The only power that is involved here is the power to get information from those who best can give it and who are most interested in not doing so. Because judicial power is reluctant if not unable to summon evidence until it is shown to be relevant to issues in litigation, it does not follow that an administrative agency charged with seeing that the laws are enforced may not have and exercise powers of original inquiry. It has a power of inquisition, if one chooses to call it that, which is not derived from the judicial function. It is more analogous to the Grand Jury, which does not depend on a case or controversy for power to get evidence but can investigate merely on suspicion that the law is being violated, or even just because it wants assurance that it is not. When investigative and accusatory duties are delegated by statute to an administrative body, it, too may take steps to inform itself whether there is probable violation of the law. (338 p. 642)

The granting of broad investigatory powers to administrative agencies and to the civil divisions of state and federal enforcement agencies has to be seen as a fundamental shift in the information-related characteristics of civil law. If, prior to the reforms, moving parties in civil cases were essentially dependent solely on the trial process for discovery of facts, there was a great barrier to the use of the civil law sanctioning wrongful behavior. The civil process was simply not a good setting for even getting to first base, for without the facts describing the acts of the potential defendant, there was no way of moving the case to the stage of evidence assessment. The lower burden of proof in civil cases could not compensate for this weakness in civil process.

Procedural Rules and White-Collar Crime

In the United States during the 1950s and 1960s, the criminal process went through what came to be called a "due-process revolution." New procedural rules put up obstacles to police search and seizure and to in-custody interrogation and made more difficult government use of the grand jury to collect potential evidence. Information access in the criminal process was curtailed. Thus, the strengthening of information-access leverage in the civil law taken together with the weakening of information-access leverage in the criminal law has increased, relative to the past, the procedural effectiveness of the civil law in sanctioning wrongful behavior. While it had long been recognized that the lower evidentiary burden in civil process is an advantage for the party seeking to apply a sanction, the important interdependence of burden of persuasion and information access has not been clearly articulated. Put simply, the lower standard of proof could not be exploited unless sufficient information were available. Strong information access powers in the civil law only started to develop in the middle decades of this century—in administrative law, and in pretrial discovery rules. As this occurred, the lower evidentiary burden in the civil process began to have a strong effect on the choice between the criminal and civil law.

The convergence of procedural rules is an empirical phenomenon that stemmed first from the need to make information more available in civil proceedings, and probably had no connection to a concern for the relationship between civil and criminal law. But once the information access gap was narrowed, there was an independent reason to use civil sanctions: information access was good and the burden of proof was low. Thus, procedural reform was both a result and a cause of the expanding use of civil law in sanctioning wrongful behavior.

A major theme of this chapter is that information access rules effect directly the capacity of a sanctioning system to impose its remedies on wrongdoers. I have suggested that the change in information access rules during a long period of reform has at least in part been caused by the press for broader government sanctioning powers. At the same time, these very reforms have contributed directly to the expansion of the civil penalties because the civil procedural framework became more attractive. As courts permitted increasingly punitive sanctions in the civil process, the combination of punitiveness and information leverage has made civil penalties into a highly desirable legislative choice in expanding overall sanctioning powers of government. There were, thus, good reasons to expect an increasing use of civil penalties in sanctioning white-collar crime.

For those interested in studying white-collar crime, one of the major implications of these findings reaffirms the position originally taken by Sutherland: any representative study of offenders, offenses, victims, organizational features, causes, and other attributes of white-collar crime requires close attention to civil sanctions. On this background, the study of cases in the criminal process must necessarily be cautious in drawing conclusions about the "true" nature of white-collar offenses and offenders. Our view of these phenomena is necessarily limited to the information we have access to, and is thus dependent on the rules of sanctioning systems bearing on the power to investigate and discover information and to impose sanctions. Another way of putting it is that wrongdoers, whose purposes include keeping inculpatory information out of the hands of law enforcement agents, are limited in obtaining their objectives by legal structures that provide incentives or compel information disclosure. Researchers studying white-collar crime must take the varying accessibility of information into account in drawing conclusions about the nature of white-collar crime. In particular, more attention should be given to civil processes that bring into the open offenses that we want to study as part of the larger phenomenon of white-collar crime.

REFERENCES

Brazil, W. (1978). The adversary character of civil procedure: A critique and proposal for changes. *Vanderbilt Law Review, 31*, 1295.

Brennan, W. J. (1963). The criminal prosecution: Sporting event or quest for the truth? *Washington University Law Quarterly*, 292.

Damaska, M. (1972). Evidentiary barriers to conviction. *Pennsylvania Law Review, 121*, 506.

Fletcher, G. (1960). Pretrial discovery in state criminal cases. *Stanford Law Review, 12,* 293.

Goldstein, A. S. (1960). The state and the accused: Balance of advantage in criminal procedure. *Yale Law Journal, 69,* 1149.

Hall, J. (1943). Interrelations of crime and torts, Parts I & II. *Columbia Law Review, 43,* 753.

Harvard Law Review (1961). Developments in the law of discovery. *Harvard Law Review, 74,* 940.

Hickman v. Taylor, (1946). 329 U.S. 495

James F., and Hazard G. C. (1977). *Civil procedure.* Boston: Little, Brown.

Louisell, D. (1965). Criminal discovery and self-incrimination. *California Law Review, 53,* 89.

Mann, K. (1985). *Defending white-collar crime: A portrait of attorneys at work.* New Haven: Yale University Press.

Millar, R. W. (1952). *Civil procedure on the trial court in historical perspective.* New York: National Conference of Judicial Councils.

Mosteller, R. P. (1986). Discovery against the defense: Tilting the adversarial balance. *California Law Review, 74,* 1567.

Nakell, B. (1972). Criminal discovery for the defense and prosecution: The developing constitutional considerations. *North Carolina Law Review, 50,* 437.

Packer, H. L. (1968). *The limits of the criminal sanction.* Stanford, Calif.: Stanford University Press.

Perry, R. L., and Simon, W. (1960). The civil investigative demand: New fact finding powers for the antitrust division. *Michigan Law Review, 58,* 855.

Petition of Gold Bond Stamp Company (1963). 221 f. Supp. 391, 394.

Pettigrew, R. (1972). Information control as a power resource. *Sociology, 6,* 187.

Pfeffer, J., and Salanick, G. R. (1978). *The external control of organizations: A resource dependence perspective.* New York: Harper & Row.

Ragland, G., Jr. (1932). *Discovery before trial.* Deerfield, Ill.: Callaghan & Co.

Robinson, G. D., Gelhorn, J., and Bruff, H. H. (1986). *The administrative process.* (3rd ed.). St. Paul: West Publishing Co.

Traynor, R. (1964). Ground lost and found in criminal discovery. *New York University Law Review, 39,* 229.

U.S. v. Shapleigh, (1893). 54 F.R. 126, 134 (8th Cir.).

U.S. Code Congressional and Administrative News (1962). House Report No. 1386, Antitrust Civil Process Act 2567.

———. (1980). House Report 96–870, Antitrust Procedural Improvements Act of 1980. Ninety-sixth Congress, second session, 2716.

————. (1986). House Report 99–345. Ninety-ninth Congress, second session, 5266.

Van Kessel, G. (1977). Prosecution discovery and the privilege against self-incrimination accommodation for capitulation. *Hastings Constitutional Law Quarterly, 4*, 855.

Vanderbilt Law Review (1980). Note: The civil investigative demand, a constitutional analysis and model proposal. *Vanderbilt Law Review, 33*, 1451.

Weinstein, J., Gleit, E., and Kay, J. (1957). Procedures for obtaining information before trial. *Texas Law Review, 35*, 481.

Wigmore, 8, Evidence at Common Law, Sec. 1845.

Willmer, M. A. P. (1970). *Crime and information theory.* Edinburg: Edinburg University Press.

Wilsnack, R. W. (1980). Information control: A conceptual framework for sociological analysis. *Urban Life 8*, 467.

NOTES

1. For a classic analysis of differences between civil and criminal law, see Jerome Hall, "Interrelations of Crime and Torts, Parts I & II," *Columbia Law Review, 43*, 753, 967 (1943).

2. See H. L. Packer, *The Limits of the Criminal Sanction* (Stanford, Calif.: Stanford University Press, 1968). Procedures express societal values by determining how much certainty is required in the decision-making process and what part will be taken by values external to certainty, such as privacy and autonomy.

3. The idea that rules about information access and disclosure have a central role in procedure has not frequently been addressed. The major theoretical article is M. Damaska, "Evidentiary Barriers to Conviction," *Pennsylvania Law Review, 121*, 506, 522 (1972). He states, "the common law of evidence presents much more formidable obstacles to introducing incriminating evidence than does the civil law . . . the informational sources the common law prosecutor can use are less numerous than those of his continental colleagues" (p. 522).

4. In research on the pretrial litigation process in criminal cases, I have used the concept of information control as a central organizing theme for understanding defense and prosecution functions. See K. Mann, *Defending White-Collar Crime: A Portrait of Attorneys at Work* (New Haven: Yale University Press, 1985). See also, G. D. Robinson, E. Gellhorn, and H. H. Bruff, *The Administrative Process* (St. Paul: West Publishing Co., 1986). They state, "In one sense, at least, administrative agencies do not differ from other institutions; their effectiveness is determined by the information they have or can acquire. Any administrative action, whether formal or informal, is conditioned by the infor-

mation the agency obtains from its prior investigation" (p. 505). There is a more extensive literature on information access and control in related fields, the lessons of which have not been applied to law. See, for example, R. V. Pettigrew, "Information Control as a Power Resource," *Sociology, 6*, 187 (1972); J. Pfeffer, *The External Control of Organization* (New York: Harper & Row, 1978); M. A. P. Willmer, *Crime and Information Theory* (Edinburg: Edinburg University Press, 1970); R. W. Wilsnack, "Information Conrol: A Conceptual Framework for Sociological Analysis," *Urban Life, 8*, 467 (1980).

5. There is, however, an important caveat in this statement. Certain criminal procedural devices of investigation—in-custody interrogation and search and seizure—required probable cause as a precondition. These devices could not then be used as general surveillance methods. Eventually, civil procedure developed general surveillance devices, such as reporting requirements and the administrative inspection, neither of which required probable cause. Thus, the investigative strength of the in-custody interrogation and the search and seizure lay in a "focused" investigation, where probable cause already existed. This did not, however, apply to the grand jury interrogation, which could be activated without a prior evidentiary requirement, and provided a powerful investigative tool at the earliest period in a sanctioning process.

6. However, some administrative agencies received the important authority to immunize witnesses, breaking the back of the self-incrimination privilege as a barrier to information access.

7. Civil discovery has, of course, come under broad attack because of the high costs it imposes on litigants, giving advantage to richer over poorer parties. See W. Brazil, "The Adversary Character of Civil Procedure: A Critique and Proposal for Changes," *Vanderbilt Law Review, 31*, 1295.

8. In a much more recent period, discovery in criminal cases has become broader, moving away from the rule of strict limitation. For accounts of the restrictive past of criminal discovery and the slow erosion of barriers, see W. J. Brennan, "The Criminal Prosecution: Sporting Event or Quest for the Truth?" *Washington University Law Quarterly*, 279 (1963); G. Fletcher, "Pretrial Discovery in State Criminal Cases," *Stanford Law Review, 12*, 293 (1960); R. Traynor, "Ground Lost and Found in Criminal Discovery," *New York University Law Review, 39*, 229 (1964); D. Louisell, "Criminal Discovery and Self-Incrimination," *California Law Review, 53*, 89 (1965); B. Nakell, "Criminal Discovery for the Defense and Prosecution: The Developing Constitutional Considerations," *North Carolina Law Review, 50*, 437 (1972); G. Van Kessel, "Prosecution Discovery and the Privilege Against Self-Incrimination: Accommodation for Capitulation," *Hastings Constitutional Law Quarterly, 4*, 855 (1977); R. Mosteller, "Discovery Against the Defense: Tilting the Adversarial Balance," *California Law Review, 74*, 1567 (1986).

9. Pub.L. 87-664, 15 USC 1312. At the time of enactment, at least seventeen states had similar laws. See Petition of Gold Bond Stamp Company, 221 f. Supp. 391, 394 (1963).

10. Pub.L. 96-349 1980, 15 USC 1312. The House report said about this, "To preclude access to discovery materials already assembled and analyzed in another proceeding is wasteful, and in some cases, tantamount to denying access altogether. . . . More importantly, the expense of reassembling pre-existing materials and repeating the indexing and analyzing procedures can be very substantial, particularly in the case of large-scale antitrust investigation," House Report 96-870, Antitrust Procedural Improvements Act of 1980, *U.S. Code Congressional and Administrative News*, 1980, Ninety-sixth Congress, second session, 2716, 2719–2720. The report also recounted the government's successful attempt to obtain $400,000 from the GAF Corporation relating to its antitrust claim against Kodak. Eventually, the government received the documents and analysis made by GAF, giving it information that it probably could never have assembled on its on initiative.

11. Pub.L. 99–562, 31 USC 3733. The House report stated,"Civil attorneys themselves have no authority to compel production of documents or depositions prior to filling of suits. Currently, some cases are weeded out and not filed because information is missing—information that might have turned up through pre-suit investigation if the tools were available" House Report 99-345, *U.S. Code Congressional and Administrative News*, 1986, Ninety-ninth Congress, second session, 5266 and 5271.

12. Thus, earlier in the century the Federal Trade Commission had power to compel production of documents (see 15 USC 46, 49), as did the secretaries of agriculture, army, labor, and treasury, as well as other government agencies. See Petition of Gold Bond Stamp Company, 221 f. Supp., 391.

Returning to the Mainstream

Reflections on Past and Future White-Collar Crime Study

DAVID WEISBURD

KIP SCHLEGEL

White-collar crime has generally been relegated to the margins of the study of criminality. It has offered scholars a deviant case that defies traditional theories or stereotypes. But it has seldom played a role more important than that of ideological or theoretical gadfly, brought forth, often in simplistic terms, to debunk what seems certain about the origins or characteristics of "criminality." For sure, it is incorrect to see crime as a problem of the poor if it can be found in better neighborhoods and among those who live in situations of authority and privilege. Certainly, the harms of major stock or bank frauds, or environmental offenses, have more long-term impact than the petty offenses of most street criminals. While these challenges are much noted, they have not translated into substantial theoretical or empirical concern among criminologists about the problem of white-collar crime.

Indeed, the concept of white-collar crime itself has come under increasing attack. Much of this has been in the form of "soul searching" by those who want to more clearly define what the study of white-collar crime should encompass. Should we limit our concern to crimes of the upper socioeconomic classes, or to those that involve some occupational or organizational position for their commission? Should we focus on the offender or the offense, or should we see white-collar crime as the result of some special blend of interaction between them? Whatever direction the debate over definition in white-collar crime has taken, it has more often served to confuse those outside the small cadre of scholars concerned with white-collar crime than to put to rest the definitional confusions that have plagued this field of research since Sutherland first coined the term.

The attack from those who have traditionally limited their focus to more common forms of criminality has been aimed not at issues of definition, but rather at whether white-collar crime provides any useful purpose as a separate area of study. Travis Hirschi and Michael Gottfredson (1987) suggest that the concept of white-collar crime has served more to confuse debate over the origins of criminality than to clarify or develop such theory. We suspect that their position is one that is shared by many mainstream criminologists who have most often been silent about the problem of white-collar crime, and seldom allow it to muddy the waters of their insights or theories. Hirschi and Gottfredson's conclusion that the distinctions between white-collar and common crime are, for the most part, trivial is one that can provide comfort to a discipline that has drawn its primary portrait of criminality from street crimes.

In this concluding chapter, we want to focus our attention on these concerns. How should the boundaries of white-collar crime theory and research be defined? Is the concept of white-collar crime a useful one, and can it be brought from the margins of criminological study to its core? Finally, what are the areas of study that offer the most promise for future inquiry?

What Is White-Collar Crime?

The problem of definition is one that has plagued study of white-collar crime from the outset. As a number of other scholars have pointed out (Wheeler, 1983; see also Geis, chapter 1 in this volume; Coleman, chapter 2 in this volume), the confusion began with Sutherland, who failed to provide a precise statement of what, in fact, white-collar crime is. Sometimes he stressed crimes committed by an individual of high status, at other times crimes carried out in the course of one's occupation. In his most important empirical contribution to white-collar crime study, he focused on crimes committed by organizations or by individuals acting in organizational capacities (Sutherland, 1983). But whatever the definitional ambiguities of Sutherland's approach, it was very clear that his call was for concern with a body of criminal activity that had gone all but unnoticed in the traditional study of criminality.

In Sutherland's time, as today, the study of crime was primarily the study of common street crimes, the crimes of the poor and disadvantaged. In a series of important empirical inquiries, sociologists at the University of Chicago emphasized the link between social disorganization and poverty in certain inner-city areas and rates of criminal behavior (for example, see Thrasher, 1927; Shaw, 1929). Their work, which continues to have important impacts on American criminology (for example, see Reiss, 1986), served to focus attention exclusively on crimes of the lower classes. In drawing attention to the crimes of successful businessmen, Sutherland sought to broaden the scope of criminological inquiry, as well as to challenge its preoccupation with the relationship between poverty and crime.

In some sense then, Sutherland's attention to white-collar crime was not so much an attempt to define a distinct scientific category that was ready for rigorous empirical analysis, as it was an effort to provide a contrast—or at least a balance—to the preoccupations of criminologists of his day. Crimes committed by persons in comfortable circumstances, who lived in stable and secure neighborhoods, needed to be taken into account if criminologists were to develop general theories of criminal behavior. Sutherland's cause was to bring such crimes within the scope of criminological study. His level of success one can debate, but we have no doubt that Sutherland's focus on "persons of the upper socioeconomic class" (1983, p. 7) was a call to traditional criminology to broaden its focus beyond the crimes of the "lower socioeconomic class."

Looking at Sutherland's mission in this way, we are led to an understanding of white-collar crime that is inclusive rather than exclusive. In our introductory chapter we argued for abstraction rather than specification and narrowing. Like Gilbert Geis (see chapter 1), we do not think that definitions that seek to clearly limit the focus of white-collar crime study serve to make the concept more powerful. As our volume illustrates, white-collar crime has come to encompass a variety of behaviors—from crimes of organizations (for example, see Pontell and Calavita, chapter 8; Reichman, chapter 10; Simpson, chapter 12) to frauds (for example, Jesilow, Klempner, and Chiao, chapter 6; Levi, chapter 7) to crimes of the state (for example, Braithwaite, chapter 3; Kramer, chapter 9). It has also come to include a range of offenders much broader than the successful businessmen who were the focus of Sutherland's ground-breaking inquiries. Many of these behaviors and people would not fit squarely within Sutherland's original definition, but we think more harm than good would be done by excluding them.

While we are perhaps being elusive in avoiding a specific definition, our perspective may be better understood if we focus on one area where this approach would seem to most seriously threaten the early boundaries set for white-collar crime research and theory. From the outset, white-collar crime has been associated with those of high social status. For most scholars, significant economic and political influence lies at the core of what makes white-collar crime a useful and interesting area of inquiry (for example, see Geis, chapter 1; Braithwaite, chapter 3; Pontell and Calavita, chapter 8). Even while attempting to broaden the focus of white-collar crime research and theory, Gilbert Geis looks to "the abuse of power by persons who are situated in high places" (chapter 1). Is it useful to expand traditional conceptions to take into account crimes that are committed by those much lower down the social hierarchy? Or should the study of white-collar crime be limited to examination of those who hold positions of significant prestige and power?

As recent studies illustrate (for example, see Levi, 1987; Weisburd, Wheeler, Waring, and Bode, 1991), much of what has been assumed to be white-collar crime is committed by people in the middle rather than upper classes of our society. Many of the "fraudsters" who manipulate stocks or loan transactions are very far from elite status. Most of those who are prosecuted for crimes like bribery, tax fraud, or bank frauds are rather average in their social backgrounds and positions. As discussed in our introductory chapter, the predominance of the more common type of white-collar offender may be a function of the vagaries of prosecution rather than the realities of offending. Nonetheless, it is not a trivial fact that most of those prosecuted for so called white-collar crimes have little in common with the elite people who are most often alluded to when conjuring up images of the typical white-collar offender.

These criminals differ in status and position from more elite white-collar offenders, and their crimes are often as mundane as their social backgrounds. But it would be misleading to overstate the differences in their opportunities to commit costly and complex white-collar illegalities. One does not have to be a Fortune 500 corporate executive to develop a costly stock or land fraud. Such crimes are often committed in small firms or by those who hold relatively less powerful positions in larger ones. Antitrust violations involving millions of dollars are often committed by local businessmen or women. Frauds netting millions of dollars often involve middle-level bureaucrats in public and private agencies who have access to large sums of money through government aid programs.

The question is whether it is useful to begin with an understanding of white-collar crime that allows us to speak not only of the rich and powerful white-collar criminal who has traditionally fascinated scholars in this area, but also of those offenders much closer to the middle of our society who have recently become the subject of scholarly attention. A simple response to this question would note that narrowing the scope of white-collar crime research to offenses committed by the rich and powerful excludes the bulk of those people who are convicted for so-called white-collar crimes. Even if we assume, as have many scholars, that high-status white-collar criminals often escape detection and prosecution, it seems absurd to us to argue that most of those who are convicted for so-called white-collar crimes should escape systematic study.

Beyond this we believe that Sutherland's emphasis on elite status was in part a function of the different opportunity structure for white-collar criminality that existed in his day.[1] It was natural for Sutherland to focus on businessmen in lofty positions when examining the problem of white-collar crime, since relatively few Americans beyond these elite men had any opportunity for committing such illegalities. But changes in our society since Sutherland's day have placed the opportunity for white-collar crimes in the hands of a much broader class of Americans, most of whom were excluded from such activities in the past. In part it is the rapid growth of white-collar jobs in America in the last fifty years that has spawned such changes (Bell, 1973). But perhaps even more important are the dramatic differences in the way modern society functions. The advent of the computer, for example, gives large numbers of people access to the documents and transactions that are so much a part of white-collar illegalities. The growth of a welfare state has placed millions of dollars in the hands of people who would never have had any access to such sums in the past. The development of a credit economy has also expanded the opportunities for such crimes.

To limit study of white-collar crime to the most elite of offenders because that was the most useful approach in the late 1930s appears to us a recipe for making white-collar crime theory and research a very narrow and not very useful area of inquiry. We believe that it is in the general spirit of the enterprise Sutherland began to develop a very broad approach to the problem of white-collar crime, one that allows not just crimes of the middle socioeconomic class we have been discussing, but also the varied forms of offending that have been identified throughout this volume. In this we agree with James Coleman (chapter 2) that it is useful and natural to move beyond Sutherland's original conception in developing white-collar crime theory and research.

Is White-Collar Crime Different from Common Crime?

Having argued for a very broad definition of white-collar crime, we are faced with the difficult problem of drawing a clear boundary between white-collar and so-called common crimes, a difficulty that leads us to question whether it is really necessary to define a distinct area of inquiry as different from the study of criminality generally. Why do we need an area of study that we label white-collar crime? Why not, for example, see each of the varied offenses that have become attached to this label as a distinct category within the general problem of criminality? Such an approach would have the advantage of allowing examination of each specific offense, without the necessity of explaining its connection to the more general white-collar crime phenomenon.

It might be argued, in part, that white-collar crime has come to be viewed as a distinct empirical problem because it allows criminologists to be ideologically "correct." For some scholars the label "white-collar crime" has served more as a rhetorical device than a scientific category. Studying the bad deeds of the rich provides a defense against those who see the study of crime as a reactionary profession, misguidedly ignoring the "real crimes" of inequality and poverty in our society (see Taylor, Walton, and Young, 1973). Showing our concern with the rich and powerful criminals certainly provides an important balance to criminological study. But we suspect that there is a strong ideological component here, illustrated, for example, when social scientists (who take great care to protect the identities of street criminals) intentionally identify major white-collar offenders.[2]

Reflecting this sense that white-collar crime study has served more ideological than theoretical purposes, Travis Hirschi and Michael Gottfredson (1987) argue that there is little scientific reason to define a separate area of study labeled "white-collar crime." In an influential article published in *Criminology*, the journal of the American Society of Criminology, they contend that the differences between white-collar and common crime are mostly trivial, similar to differences between individual crime categories such as robbery or burglary. The isolation of so-called white-collar crimes from more traditional criminological theory has, in their view, served to confuse rather than develop our general understanding of the causes of criminality.

In some sense, Gottfredson and Hirschi's attack is not a challenge to the enterprise that Sutherland began, since his interest in white-collar crime can be traced in great part to his desire to develop a general theory of criminality. Sutherland's critique of traditional criminological concerns did not develop from a view that a special theory was needed to explain white-collar crime. Rather, he sought to show that existing explanations of crime, which focused on poverty and social disorganization, were inadequate because they could not explain why those who lived in established neighborhoods and were far from poverty also committed crimes (though of a different type). Sutherland wanted to weaken the dominant etiological theories of his day with the example of white-collar crime. At the same time, he believed that his own theory of differential association was equally powerful in explaining the deviant behavior of poor and rich offenders.

While time will tell whether Hirschi and Gottfredson's general theory of criminality will have greater success in developing an understanding of the crime problem than Sutherland's, we do not find any reason to discount the label "white-collar crime" merely because common etiological factors may influence white-collar and common criminals. When Sutherland first coined the term white-collar crime, he did so precisely because he wanted to develop a theory of criminality that would be generally applicable. When he examined white-collar crime he sought to widen the lens of criminological study, a mission we believe can still be served by the study of white-collar crime.

The utility of the white-collar crime label need not be seen as a function of etiological differences, but rather as developing from common attributes of white-collar offenses that are distinct from those ordinarily associated with criminality. For example, in virtually every white-collar crime there is the problem of organization and how organization intersects with individual motives, opportunities, and behaviors. While organization is of interest in the study of particular types of common crime, it must be a central concern for those who seek to understand the nature of white-collar criminality (see Vaughan, chapter 5). It would be impossible to provide the kind of insights Ronald Kramer (chapter 9) develops concerning the *Challenger* disaster without a clear understanding of the pressures exerted on NASA and the special organizational relationships between NASA and its private contractors. Similarly, Nancy Reichman's (chapter 10) observations concerning the development of regulatory policy cannot be disentangled from the business organizations that help to define what, in fact, constitutes their own lawbreaking. We believe that the centrality of organization is one characteristic that links different white-collar crimes to one another and sets them apart from what has become the mainstream concerns of criminological inquiry.

Victimization is a second area where white-collar crime scholars are faced with a very different set of problems than those who study other forms of crime. Victims are often unaware of their victimization. There is usually little direct contact between victims and perpetrators. And when there is, such interactions are not characterized by the violent confrontations that are a part of many street offenses, but by elements of misrepresentation and fraud. White-collar crime study forces us to think of different measures of victimization and different ways of studying how offenders and victims interact. For example, physical harm may occur in special cases of white-collar criminality (environmental and OSHA crimes are perhaps the most notable of these). Nonetheless, unlike street crimes, violence is not prevalent enough in white-collar offending to be seen as a general indicator of crime seriousness. Even in the case of economic harm, which is a central feature of most white-collar crimes, the differential spread of victimizations across persons and organizations makes it very difficult to think of the impact of such crimes in conventional terms (see Schlegel, 1990). This is, in great part, what is at the heart of Michael Levi's (chapter 7) discussion of the difficulties of assigning images of evil to economic white-collar offenders. This is, as well, one of the elements that link the broad range of white-collar crimes and set them apart from most other types of offenses.

The distinctions between sanctioning of white-collar and common crimes was one element that first brought Sutherland's attention to the offenses of high-status people. Sutherland was morally repulsed by the extent to which white-collar criminals avoided criminal sanctions and the ways in which they drew advantage in the criminal justice system's definitions and punishments of deviant conduct (see Goff, 1983). While the severity of sanctions for white-collar crime have changed much since Sutherland's day, white-collar criminality still presents a special set of problems for those who study enforcement and sanctioning.

Walt and Laufer (chapter 13) provide one illustration of the somewhat unique problem that white-collar crime presents. The centrality of organization in white-collar crime means that it is often possible to prosecute both organizations and individuals for the same crimes. Walt and Laufer are concerned that the most serious corporate sanctions do not approximate the severity of individual sanctions for similar crimes, an interesting twist on the disparity of sentencing issues ordinarily raised by researchers. We might add to this quandary the confusion that is raised when we have the choice of prosecuting individuals or organizations, or both. Can there be organizational deviance without individual deviance? To what extent can organizations be held blameworthy for the purposes of punishment, and how can deterrence best be achieved within the organizational environment? Such questions may apply to some common crimes, but they are essential to ask when speaking of the bulk of white-collar offenses.

Ken Mann's (chapter 14) study of the uses of civil prosecutions in white-collar crime points to one of the fundamental difficulties that has plagued white-collar crime research, and set it apart from most other studies of crime. A large number of those who violate laws relating to white-collar crime are prosecuted in the civil as opposed to criminal courts. This is, of course, one of the major reasons why Sutherland's empirical study of white-collar crime was concerned primarily with offenses that were not crimes as defined by law (see

Sutherland, 1983). But whether one calls such offenses "crimes" or not, the reality for those who study white-collar crime is that there is an entire governmental sanctioning system that stands behind the criminal sanctions that ordinarily define criminality. While an FBI record of criminal conduct may give a fairly good view of a criminal history of arrests for serious assault that were eventually dismissed, it would miss completely white-collar crime prosecutions that were successfully completed but led to civil rather than criminal penalties. Ken Mann's observation that the civil courts are now being used to bring punitive penalties makes this problem even more perplexing for those who study white-collar crime.

We have not tried to define clear boundaries for white-collar crime study. Indeed, our perspective, as indicated here and in our introduction, calls for a very broad approach to definition and research. At the same time, we do believe that the white-collar crime label is a useful one. As the examples above illustrate, it is not defined by the need for a particular source of explanation, but rather by a common set of problems that it raises.

Future Directions for White-Collar Crime Research and Theory

Having argued that white-collar crime is a useful area of inquiry, we want to return to the question of why it has failed to take a central place in criminological study. Part of the answer to this question is found simply in the fact that so much societal attention is brought to street crimes. White-collar crimes may be perceived as serious crimes by the public (Wolfgang, Figlio, Tracy, and Singer, 1985), but they are not the crimes that make us feel unsafe in our homes and neighborhoods. As a consequence, there has seldom been significant research monies available for the study of white-collar offenses.

But the lack of research support in this area provides only one answer. We believe that another lies among white-collar crime scholars themselves who have seldom sought to bring their research into the mainstream. The question we must begin to ask is how our understanding of white-collar crime alters or supports a more general understanding of crime and its control. In our view, it is time for white-collar crime research to inform more traditional studies of crime. This is an enterprise that Sutherland certainly would have supported, but one that has surprisingly eluded most of our efforts.

A good place to begin is with the areas that we have defined as distinguishing white-collar from other crimes: organization, victimization, and sanctioning. It is precisely in these areas, where white-collar crime presents a special set of problems, that we believe it can yield the most important insights for criminological study generally. Like Sutherland, we think that by widening the lens of the study of crime we can yield significant new insights.

Albert Reiss (1966) points out that there is an organizational matrix for most deviant conduct. Human behavior is intricately linked to organizations, and there can be no behavior without some social organization. Nevertheless, as we noted earlier, in white-collar crime the problem of organization most clearly manifests itself. We believe that this fact offers an opportunity for white-collar crime scholars to take a lead in developing and understanding the role of organization in crime. Some have already begun to do this, a path that is reflected in the work of Diane Vaughan (chapter 5). There is no reason why our insights into organization in white-collar crime should not play a role in developing organizational theory for the study of crime generally. Understanding white-collar crime is not enough. We must look at the centrality of organization in white-collar crime as an opportunity for explicating the role of organization in structuring and facilitating the myriad forms of criminal conduct.

While we make many assumptions about victimization in white-collar crime, we have few empirical studies from which to draw our conclusions. We have no real measure of the relationship between official and real offending. Though recent studies have shown that those convicted of white-collar crimes often have previous arrests (Weisburd, Chayet, and Waring, 1990; Benson and Moore, 1992), we have no basis on which to assess the reliability of such official records for identifying white-collar criminality. In contrast, studies of common crime have yielded fairly specific estimates of how official crime is related to actual offending. It is time to begin the very difficult task of focusing on rates of victimization in white-collar crime. Jesilow, Klempner, and Chiao (chapter 6) provide one example of how we might begin to carry out this enterprise. But we need a much broader approach that will allow us to speak in more specific terms about central criminological concerns. In the case of research on criminal careers, for example, we suspect that study of white-collar criminals can add a degree of complexity in terms of understanding the development of criminality over long periods of time that is mostly absent in conventional studies.

Finally, we are struck by the opportunities that white-collar crime study offers for the development of a broader understanding of the role of noncriminal governmental and nongovernmental social controls. The choice of civil sanctions in prosecution, the role of governmental and professional agencies in establishing compliance mechanisms, the attempts of corporations to "police themselves" (see Simpson, chapter 12) make the study of white-collar crime a fertile area in which to develop theories about the relationship between alternative social control mechanisms. In a time when our prisons are overflowing and the criminal justice system as a whole is overwhelmed, the insights of white-collar crime scholars can play an important role in developing alternative policing mechanisms and sanctioning systems.

White-collar crime presents an area of tremendous intellectual vitality and opportunity. But in addressing the problem of white-collar crime, scholars have more often fallen into ideological debate than they have into the development of clear and important theoretical and practical insight. We believe that our volume illustrates the many possibilities that are offered by white-collar crime scholarship and the tremendous strides that have been made in understanding white-collar crime in recent years. Nonetheless, the future lies in bringing our observations into the mainstream of criminological research and theory. This is where Sutherland began, and it must be where white-collar crime researchers return.

REFERENCES

Bell, D. (1973). *The coming of post-industrial society*. New York: Basic Books.

Benson, M., and Moore, E. (1992). Are white-collar and common offenders the same? A test of a recently proposed theory of crime. *Journal of Research in Crime and Delinquency*.

Benson, M., Cullen, F. T., and Maakestad, W. J. (1992). Community context and the prosecution of corporate crime. (This volume.)

Braithwaite, J. (1992). Poverty, power, and white-collar crime: Sutherland and the paradoxes of criminological theory. (This volume.)

Coleman, J. W. (1992). The theory of white-collar crime: From Sutherland to the 1990s. (This volume.)

Geis, G. (1992). White-collar crime: What Is It? (This volume.)

Goff, C. H. (1983). *Edwin H. Sutherland and white-collar crime.* Unpublished doctoral dissertation, University of California, Irvine.

Hirschi, T., and Gottfredson, M. (1987). Causes of white-collar crime. *Criminology, 25*(4), 949–974.

Jesilow, P., Kempner, E., and Chiao, V. (1992). Reporting consumer and major fraud: A survey of complainants. (This volume.)

Kramer, R. C. (1992). The space shuttle *Challenger* explosion: A case study of state-corporate crime. (This volume.)

Levi, M. (1987). *Regulating fraud: White-collar crime and the criminal process.* New York: Tavistock.

Mann, K. (1992). Procedure rules and information control: Gaining leverage in applying punitive civil sanctions to white-collar crime. (This volume.)

Pontell, H., and Calavita, K. (1992). Bilking bankers and bad debts: White-collar crime and the savings and loan crisis. (This volume.)

Reichman, N. (1992). Moving backstage: Uncovering the role of compliance practices in shaping regulatory policy. (This volume.)

Reiss, A. J., Jr. (1966). The study of deviant behavior: Where the action is. *Ohio Valley Sociologist, 26*, 808–823.

Reiss, A. J., Jr., and Tonry, M., eds. (1986). *Communities and crime.* Chicago: University of Chicago Press.

Schlegel, K. (1990). *Just deserts for corporate criminals.* Boston: Northeastern University Press.

Shaw, C. R. (1929). *Delinquency areas.* Chicago: University of Chicago Press.

Simpson, S. S. (1992). Corporate-crime deterrence and corporate-control policies: Views from the inside. (This volume.)

Sutherland, E. H. (1983). *White collar crime: The uncut version.* New Haven: Yale University Press.

Taylor, I., Walton, P., and Young, J. (1973). *The new criminology: For a social theory of deviance.* New York: Harper & Row.

Thrasher, F. (1927). *The gang.* Chicago: University of Chicago Press.

Vaughan, D. (1992). The macro-micro connection in white-collar crime theory. (This volume.)

Walt, S., and Laufer, W. S. (1992). Corporate criminal liability and the comparative mix of sanctions. (This volume.)

Weisburd, D., Chayet, E., and Waring, E. (1990). White-collar crime and criminal careers: Some preliminary findings. *Crime & Delinquency*, *36*(3), 342–355.

Weisburd, D., Wheeler, S., Waring, E., and Bode, N. (1991). *Crimes of the middle classes: White-collar offenders in the federal courts.* New Haven: Yale University Press.

Wheeler, S. (1983). White-collar crime: History of an idea. *Encyclopedia of crime*, 1652–1656. New York: Free Press.

―――. (1992). The problem of white-collar crime motivation. (This volume.)

Wolfgang, M. E., Figlio, R. M., Tracy, P. E., and Singer, S. I. (1985). *The national survey of crime severity.* Washington, D.C.: Government Printing Office.

NOTES

1. For a more in-depth discussion of these issues, see Weisburd et al., 1991, chapter 7.
2. We are indebted to Albert J. Reiss, Jr., for this insight provided at a panel on white-collar crime at the American Society of Criminology Meeting in 1986.

· C O N T R I B U T O R S ·

KIP SCHLEGEL is assistant professor of criminal justice at Indiana University in Bloomington. He received his Ph.D. from the School of Criminal Justice at Rutgers University. His research interests include the sentencing of organizational offenders, the organization and regulation of futures and securities markets, and the social organization of drug groups. He is the author of *Just Deserts for Corporate Criminals*, published by Northeastern University Press.

DAVID WEISBURD is Director of the Center for Crime Prevention Studies and associate professor in the School of Criminal Justice at Rutgers University. His interest in white-collar crime developed at Yale Law School where he worked with Stanton Wheeler in an LEAA supported white-collar crime research program. He has written a number of articles on white-collar crime and has published *Crimes of the Middle Classes: White-Collar Offenders in the Federal Courts* (Yale University Press) with Stanton Wheeler, Elin Waring, and Nancy Bode. His most recent work on white-collar crime (with Ellen Chayet and Elin Waring) develops from a National Institute of Justice funded examination of the effects of sanctions upon white-collar criminals.

GILBERT GEIS is professor emeritus of criminology, law, and society in the Program in Social Ecology, University of California,

Irvine. He is a former president of the American Sociological Society and recipient of that group's Edwin H. Sutherland Award. He has edited two editions of *White-Collar Crime* (the second with Robert Meier), and (with Ezra Stotland) a collection of original articles on the subject. The University of California Press this year issued *Prescription for Profit*, a study by Geis, Paul Jesilow, and Henry Pontell on Medicaid fraud by physicians.

JAMES WILLIAM COLEMAN is professor of sociology at the California Polytechnic State University, San Luis Obispo. He received his Ph.D. in sociology from the University of California, Santa Barbara in 1975. His works on white-collar crime have been published in such journals as the *American Journal of Sociology* and *Social Problems*, and he is the author of *The Criminal Elite: The Sociology of White Collar Crime*, which is currently in its second edition.

JOHN BRAITHWAITE is professor in the Research School of Social Sciences, Australian National University. He has written widely on the subject of white-collar crime. His most recent books are *Responsive Regulation: Transcending the Deregulation Debate* (with Ian Ayres) and *Not Just Deserts: A Republican Theory of Criminal Justice* (with Philip Pettit).

STANTON WHEELER is Ford Foundation Professor of Law and the Social Sciences at Yale Law School. He received his Ph.D. in sociology from the University of Washington. He has taught at Harvard University and the University of Washington, and he was a staff member of the Russell Sage Foundation and a fellow at the Center for Advanced Study in Behavioral Sciences. He is the author of numerous books, including *Crimes of the Middle Classes* with David Weisburd, Elin Waring, and Nancy Bode, and *Sitting in Judgment: The Sentencing of White-Collar Criminals* with Kenneth Mann and Austin Sarat.

DIANE VAUGHAN is associate professor of sociology, Boston College. Her interests are the sociology of organizations, deviance and social control, transitions, and qualitative methods. Currently, she is writing a historical ethnography explaining the *Challenger* launch decision and a book that develops the method of theory elaboration she discusses in this volume.

PAUL JESILOW is assistant professor in criminology, law, and society at the University of California, Irvine. He is the coauthor, with Harold Pepinsky, of *Myths That Cause Crime*, and he has written numerous articles on white-collar crime. He is coauthor, with Gilbert Geis and Henry Pontell, of the forthcoming book, *Prescription for Profit*.

ESTHER KLEMPNER received her B.A. in psychology from the University of California, Irvine. She is currently a law student at California Western School of Law.

VICTORIA CHIAO received her B.A. in social ecology from the University of California, Irvine. She is currently living in Taiwan.

MICHAEL LEVI is professor of criminology, School of Social and Administrative Studies at the University of Wales College of Cardiff. Professor Levi is a graduate of Oxford, Cambridge, and Southampton and came to Cardiff in 1975, becoming in 1991 the first professor of criminology in Wales. He is the author of two books on fraud—*The Phantom Capitalists* (Gower, 1981), a study of bankruptcy fraud, and *Regulating Fraud: White-Collar Crime and the Criminal Process* (Routledge, 1988)—and of a study of the decline of banking secrecy, *Customer Confidentiality, Money-Laundering, and Police-Bank Relationships* (Police Foundation, 1991).

HENRY PONTELL is professor of social ecology and social science at the University of California, Irvine. A sociologist and criminologist, he has written on such topics as white-collar crime, deviance and social control, criminal deterrence, and crime seriousness. He is investigator, with Kitty Calavita, on a two-year grant awarded by the National Institute of Justice of the U.S. Department of Justice to study fraud in the savings and loan industry.

KITTY CALAVITA is associate professor of social ecology at the University of California, Irvine. A sociologist of law and a criminologist, she has written on immigration and immigration policy, administrative law making, and white-collar crime.

RONALD C. KRAMER is professor of sociology at Western Michigan University and director of the Criminal Justice Program. He is also affiliated with the Western Michigan University Center for the Study of Ethics in Society and is chair of the WMU Peace and Global Futures Committee. His research specialty is corporate and government crime, and he has published articles on this topic in *Social Problems, Social Justice,* and *Humanity and Society.*

NANCY REICHMAN is associate professor of sociology at the University of Denver. Her current research examines how nonlegal professional networks define and implement regulatory law. She is working on a feminist critique of regulatory law and its implementation.

MICHAEL L. BENSON is associate professor and head of sociology at the University of Tennessee. He received his Ph.D. from the University of Illinois at Urbana-Champaign. His research on white-collar crime focuses primarily on formal and informal societal reactions to white-collar offenders and offenses. With Francis T. Cullen and William J. Maakestad, he currently is writing a monograph that will report the full results of their national study of local prosecutors and corporate crime.

FRANCIS T. CULLEN is professor of criminal justice and sociology at the University of Cincinnati. He is author of *Rethinking Crime and Deviance Theory* and coauthor of *Reaffirming Rehabilitation, Corporate Crime Under Attack, Criminological Theory,* and *Criminology.* He is the forthcoming president of the Academy of Criminal Justice Sciences and previously was editor of *Justice Quarterly* and the *Journal of Crime and Justice.* He received his Ph.D. from Columbia University.

WILLIAM J. MAAKESTAD, is professor of management at Western Illinois University. He has authored or coauthored numerous articles in the field of white-collar crime, including *Corporate Crime Under Attack: The Ford Pinto Case and Beyond* (Anderson, 1987). He also worked as a legal consultant on several leading cases during the past decade, including corporate homicide prosecutions of the Ford Motor Company and Film Recovery Systems. He currently serves on the board of directors of the nonprofit National Safe Workplace Institute in Chicago and the Corporate Criminal Liability Reporter in Beverly Hills.

SALLY SIMPSON is assistant professor in the Institute of Criminal Justice and Criminology at the University of Maryland. She received her B.S. from Oregon State University, M.A. from Washington State University, and Ph.D. in sociology from the University of Massachusetts, Amherst. She has written several articles about corporate crime that have appeared in *American Sociological Review*, *Social Forces*, and *Advances in Criminological Theory*. She currently is working on a book for the Free Press that examines corporate crime control.

STEVEN WALT is associate professor of law at the University of San Diego School of Law. He holds a J.D. from the Yale Law School and an M.A. and Ph.D. in philosophy from the University of Chicago. Prior to teaching at the University of San Diego School of Law, he taught at the California Institute of Technology and at the Wharton School, University of Pennsylvania. Steven Walt has published articles on commercial law and on topics in political philosophy and the philosophy of social science.

WILLIAM S. LAUFER is assistant professor of legal studies at the Wharton School, University of Pennsylvania. He holds a law degree from Northeastern University and a Ph.D. from the School of Criminal Justice at Rutgers University. He is current coeditor, with Freda Adler, of *Advances in Criminological Theory*.

KENNETH MANN is associate professor, faculty of law at Tel Aviv University in Tel Aviv, Israel. He holds a law degree from Boalt Hall, a M.A. from The Center for the Study of Law and Society at Berkeley, and a Ph.D. from Yale University. He is the author of *Defending White-Collar Crime: A Portrait of Attorneys at Work* (Yale University Press).

· INDEX ·

Please remember that this is a library book,
and that it belongs only temporarily to each
person who uses it. Be considerate. Do
not write in this, or any, library book.